The Story of Follies

The Story of Follies

Architectures of Eccentricity

Celia Fisher

REAKTION BOOKS

Published by
Reaktion Books Ltd
Unit 32, Waterside
44–48 Wharf Road
London N1 7UX, UK
www.reaktionbooks.co.uk

First published 2022

Printed and bound in India by Replika Press Pvt. Ltd.

A catalogue record for this book is available from the British Library

ISBN 978 1 78914 635 6

Contents

Preface 7

Introduction: A Taste of Follies 9

One **Seeking Out the Origins** 31

Two **Some Names to Conjure With** 59

Three **Telling a Story** 93

Four **Concepts of Freedom and Victory** 133

Five **Hunting and Husbandry** 173

Six **Waterside Follies and Grottos** 205

Seven **The Lure of the East** 247

Eight **From Ruins to Gothic and Picturesque** 285

Nine **Hermitages and Tree Houses** 317

Ten **Into the Future** 349

References 379

Further Reading 395

Acknowledgements 397

Photo Acknowledgements 399

Index 401

The Tower of Babel, Bedford Hours, British Library Add. MS 18850,
as seen through medieval eyes with all the details of its construction.

Preface

Some people, if asked whether unicorns exist, would simply say no, but others with more flexible minds might launch into a colourful homily ranging from narwhal horns to unicorn tapestries, and perhaps discuss the philosophy of existence itself. Follies certainly exist, but here the doubts are about definition. For instance, 'an exquisite little architectural experiment' would immediately raise the objection that not all follies are little, and, what is more, some are far from exquisite, even positively sinister, though the usual word is 'gothic'. Then there is a popular concept that follies were built for ornament and were by definition useless, but on investigation they reveal all sorts of functions from eye-catching boat houses to political statements. For academics it is considered wise to be specific in their definition, even designating follies as 'a Georgian phenomenon', but there were manifestations of the same building impulse before that, and long after. Besides, the fashion for follies extended throughout Europe and beyond, and did not originate in England, so to label them by an English dynasty would be inappropriate.

As every definition began to feel misleading, and every focus too limited, the prospect of exploring follies became ever more inviting, like a mystery to be solved. Guides and gazetteers have already been written, along with illustrated selections of the best follies and learned reviews (even controversies) concerning their individual histories and relationships. To all these works I owe a great debt, but a new framework seemed necessary to make fresh sense of this glorious, jumbled assortment of facts, names and places. So the chapter headings of this book evolved, to trace back the origins of garden pavilions and prospect towers, grottos and hermitages. While subsequent chapters uncover the whims and convictions that inspired landowners to create such buildings, and even whole landscapes of follies, it felt necessary in the earlier part of the book to pay tribute to (and sort out) the leading architects who gave such varied shapes to these human impulses. The name 'folly' applies to these buildings precisely because they embody that mixture of aspiration and fallibility which is so very human. There is a hint of biblical condemnation in the name – 'vanity of vanities; all is vanity' – but there is much pleasure and humour along the way. And, to an unexpected degree, follies echo the spirit of their age: they are not just marginal creations, or simply indicators of passing fashions, but immediate historical statements of their time.

While this whole book has become a continuous attempt to define follies by describing them, there is a more intractable problem: there are so many of them. This can only be a representative selection, an invitation to the feast. Or perhaps it is better to call it a quest, which leads us back to unicorns and the power of myth.

The Tower of Babel is such a myth. It was not the original folly, because it functioned as a temple, central to an early civilization and comprising huge terraces rising towards heaven. But, thanks to the interpretation inherited by our forebears, it became a powerful and enduring symbol, quite distinct from its reality. European artists have depicted it as a high tower laden with a moral message, and when follies were created they often invoked a similar ambiguous fascination, along with more than a hint of transgression. As Shakespeare's rude mechanicals in *A Midsummer Night's Dream* said when introducing their play, 'If we offend, it is with our goodwill.'

Introduction: A Taste of Follies

Defining follies is almost as tricky as defining art, and this book concentrates more on appreciating them – or rather a selection of them, because there are an astonishing number. The best follies are architectural gems and an element of surprise is key to their enjoyment. In addition many command fine settings and vistas, though some are artfully hidden from view until the final moment. Their name comes from the French word for madness (or the adjective in its feminine form), and during the eighteenth century in France *folie* was sometimes applied to delightful and extravagant buildings, although the usual word was *fabrique*. The fashion for building follies spread across the pleasure gardens of Europe, starting especially in Renaissance Italy and France, but the heyday of folly building was in the eighteenth century, and nowhere more so than in England. At that time those who created the individual buildings do not seem to have called them follies; they were instead given specific names of their own. Little temples that exemplified the classical style would be dedicated to Venus or another of the gods of ancient Rome, which aristocratic travellers encountered on the Grand Tour, opening up a world of literary allusion or innuendo. Towers and pavilions often declared a political affiliation or commemorated a victory in battle, and the eclectic architecture of follies reflected various fashions and contemporary preoccupations, fluctuating between classical and gothic, oriental and rustic.

Such follies were seldom purely ornamental, though that concept has also been used to define them. They were built to impress and entertain guests, even royal visitors, in diverse ways, including taking refreshment in a pleasant spot while sheltered from the vagaries of the weather, or climbing to a great height for a spectacular view. Others were linked to sporting pursuits like viewing the hunt or boating and fishing – and waterside follies also included bath houses and grottos that housed statues or shell and fossil collections. But in contrast to these sociable pastimes, follies could also be used as retreats from those busy households encumbered with many servants and relatives, and to mark this aspect they were secluded in sylvan settings in a rustic style, and sometimes thatched or ruinous and known as hermitages and tree houses. (Another possible origin of the word folly is a corruption of the French *feuillé* or 'leafy' – a word also adopted to describe a woodland setting.) Other follies were used to house animals, but built in a style so ornate that they qualify as eye-catchers and extravagances. Hints of the clandestine lurk in some, like the rabbit warren that disguised a secret Catholic chapel or the bath house mentioned in a divorce case as a place of scandalous trysts.

Follies are mostly associated with grand landscape gardens, forming part of a circular tour to coax walkers to further exploration and thrills of discovery. Many of these survive, well preserved and famous, still clinging to the narratives that inspired their creators and redolent of past glories. Others are more touching, restored from their ruins and facing a new age as holiday cottages and private dwellings; arguably these are loved by more people than ever. Yet other follies – pavilions of glass, metal and plastic, tree houses and architectural artworks – are still being created. So here in these pages is a selection and let's seize the chance

> To tell the beauty of my buildings fair . . .
> To tell my riches, and endowments rare . . .
> High towers, fair temples, goodly theatres,
> Strong walls, rich porches . . . sacred sepulchres,
> Sure gates, sweet gardens, stately galleries,
> Wrought with fair pillars and fine imageries . . .[1]

Folly architecture in England owed much to European fashions and to classical principles of ornament and proportion (of which more anon). A little building called the Chateau which sprang up in the Lincolnshire countryside in 1748 was a perfect example of a slightly outdated French style, miniaturized and certainly anglicized, because in taking it to their hearts the local people referred to it as the Shatoo. It stood picturesquely on its own small hill, looking towards Nottinghamshire across a loop in the river Trent.[2] Grassy pastures spread all around it and until the main house was built twenty years later the Chateau remained in solitary splendour on the manor of Gate Burton. The land had come through marriage into the estate of the Earl of Abingdon, who had little use for it and sold it cheaply to his land agent, Thomas Hutton. Hutton belonged to a family of Nottinghamshire yeoman farmers, an example of the aspirant middle classes because in two generations they became affluent lawyers in the nearby town of Gainsborough. Thomas's

The Chateau, Gate Barton, Lincolnshire, built in 1748, and so named to
emphasize its French style, though it became known locally as the Shatoo.

skill as a land agent caused the earl to call him 'my friend Tommy Hutton'
and to describe him as 'particularly endowed being both silver tongued and
lark heeled' – the latter quality signifying a good dancer and therefore gen-
tility. Another mark of a gentleman was building a folly, and to design his
chateau Hutton turned to John Platt, a skilled young architect whose upward
trajectory mirrored his own – from a family of masons, Platt proceeded to
a successful career, mostly among the stately homes of south Yorkshire. The
continental blend of architectural features that they achieved in the little
model chateau started with a rusticated base of cream-coloured limestone;
above this, the red brick walls were all beautifully framed with contrasting
pilasters and moulded architraves, again of creamy limestone, which was also
used to outline the handsome Georgian windows. The rectangular central
block projects forwards from the two flanking bays; these bays are smaller
and lower, so the proportions of the building are varied as well as harmonious. As a crowning mark of classicism and aspiration, a selection of urns
adorn the corners of the roofs.

At first Thomas Hutton used his chateau as a weekend retreat from
Gainsborough (his son later wrote, 'he could retire from the business of his
office from a Saturday evening until Monday morning'), and the design of

Bellmount Tower, Belton House, Lincolnshire, built in 1749,
and nicknamed Lord Brownlow's Britches on account of its commanding
archway topped by architectural features resembling a face.

the house allowed for some cramped servants' quarters beneath while the superior accommodation was on the floor above. Once Gate Burton Hall was completed in 1768 the Chateau became a summer house for picnics, a place for entertaining, which was the primary function of most follies. Succeeding generations of Huttons included military men (one was in the Charge of the Light Brigade), churchmen and fellows of Oxford colleges, as well as a scientist who was elected to the Royal Society and supported Charles Darwin's theories of evolution. When Gate Burton was sold in 1907 the Shatoo was described as a shooting box, suggesting that the Huttons had joined the hunting set and also illustrating how follies could morph as fashions required.

In about 1749, around the same time as the Chateau came into being, and a little to the south near Grantham, Sir John Brownlow, Viscount Tyrconnel, was building himself a folly at Belton House, which looked absurd enough to become known as 'Lord Brownlow's Britches', although officially it was

Bellmount Tower.[3] The nickname was due to the disproportionately tall, round-headed arch on which it stood, like legs. Inside the arch on either side, doors and spiral staircases led up to the single room above. To light the staircases, a vertical line of six small windows was curiously angled between the side walls and their supporting buttresses, which are stepped and then adorned with half-obelisks at the level of the upper room. This room has handsome Venetian windows and two small round windows above. To the imaginative gaze, this odd assortment of upper features can be assembled into ears, a mouth, a nose and eyes that look faintly surprised. The body (and face) of the tower is built of pale squared limestone edged with red brick quoins, and the buttresses are also brick, adding to the tower's assortment of decoration; since it is a folly all this is none the worse for being eccentric. Above the upper room the stairs led onto a flat roof with a turned wooden balustrade from which, it is said, seven counties could be seen (this seems to be a magic number attributed to most good views). But the immediate purpose of Lord Brownlow's tower lay nearer, because below it is the deer park and, like many another folly, the sporting element is important: from here the chase could be watched amid good company and refreshment. A fine prospect also lay along the tree-lined avenue towards Belton House, where there is a painting by John Harris ii, done around 1750, showing the whole estate, with the big house, the river, the formal gardens with parterres and pools, and that long vista rising up the hill to the Bellmount Tower. But evidently his lordship felt that something was not quite right about his eye-catcher, because Harris's painting shows that it originally had two side arches, which would have looked more Italianate; and there is a letter from Philip Yorke (Earl Hardwicke of Wimpole Hall) suggesting that 'Bellmount may well be clipped of its two wings, they are the most offending members, and I think should be cut off.' This advice was followed in the 1780s, after Lord Brownlow's time, but the tower always remained associated with him, just as the resulting straddled appearance recalled his breeches. His sister, whose husband Sir Richard Cust inherited Belton, referred to her brother's 'considerate attention to the poor, whose lives were by his compassion rescued from idleness'. Her remark suggests that the tower may have been built partly to relieve unemployment, a touch of philanthropy often associated with follies but seldom clearly recorded.

By contrast, a third, East Anglian, folly at Houghton Hall in Norfolk, home of Sir Robert Walpole, was not only perfectly proportioned but built for a purpose most unusual in a folly. It was called the Water House because it

Water House, Houghton Hall, Norfolk, built c. 1730 to act as a water tower,
but also employing Palladian principles to make it an architectural gem.

was designed to contain huge water tanks, and since it stands on high ground
this enabled the stored water to be piped to the upper floors of Houghton
Hall, which included a mighty wine cooler. Such a water supply was a surprising luxury at the time, but fitting for Sir Robert Walpole, 'scoundrel and
genius', who is widely considered to be the first British prime minister.[4] He
held office from 1721 until 1742, an unequalled length of time, during which
he amassed and spent a fortune, and it was characteristic that utilitarianism
should be masked with fine art. Houghton Hall is Palladian and so is the Water
House. Its frontage, first glimpsed through a gap in the trees, is theatrical.
A Doric balcony of grey columns and pilasters, topped by a classical pediment, rests on a rusticated base made graceful by three blind archways,
stuccoed and limewashed to reflect the light. This classical upper balcony calls
for an imperial wave, an operatic aria or a stealthy enactment of a murder,
should occasion arise. The loggia effect is replicated at the back, because the
Water House is perfectly symmetrical. On each side wall of the building is
a rounded doorway, with the same proportions as the blind archways, and a

Venetian-style window framed in grey stone to match the pillars. Houghton Hall was built in the 1720s, and the Water House existed by 1733 – verified because a drawing survives labelled 'the water house in the park designed by Henry Lord Herbert afterward Earl of Pembroke' (this helps to date it because the 'afterward' began in 1733 when he became an earl).[5] Why Lord Herbert should have turned his hand to Walpole's architecture may be explained by the resemblance of the Water House to the facade of Herbert's house in Whitehall, built in 1724 and designed by Colen Campbell. Robert Walpole presumably requested a sketch from Lord Herbert so that a local mason could reproduce features which had first been expertly created by Campbell, a leading architect of the neo-Palladian style. Eighteenth-century architects were happy to add follies to their portfolios, and many follies were directly copied from their designs or from pattern books.

Some follies, however, were uniquely odd, and none more so than 'Jack the Treacle Eater' at Barwick Park near Yeovil in Somerset, whose purpose has never been fathomed, except that it marks the eastern boundary of the old park.[6] It is a stepped archway piled up from rough stones, supporting a round tower with a doorway, then a cone and above all that a statue of Mercury poised on one toe, forever hastening forwards. Mercury (or Hermes to the Greeks) was the messenger of the gods, but also the guide who led dead souls to the underworld, a sinister figure who could trick or heal, whose hat and sandals were winged and whose caduceus or wand was twined with snakes. He became the patron of doctors and alchemists, travellers and thieves. In the past, statues of the gods were imbued with meaning culled from the classical stories that were part of every education. Statues of Venus, Mercury, Apollo and Pan were particular favourites, linked to garden temples and other follies. The Greeks and Romans used images of Hermes/Mercury as waymarkers and boundary signs, and in gardens they were fertility symbols, giving his Greek name to herms.[7]

Some of this was dimly known to those who nicknamed the folly Jack the Treacle Eater. Jack was said to be a messenger of the Messiters (who owned the property in the nineteenth century). Allegedly, he was able to run faster than any other between Somerset and London and lived in the tower feeding on treacle – 'treacle' in those days being the name given to any syrupy medicine or elixir (such as laudanum, which one could imagine Hermes administering). There are three more follies marking the other points of the compass at the boundaries of Barwick Park, which are less symbolic but equally peculiar. The Fish Tower to the north is a 15-metre (49 ft) column

Jack the Treacle Eater, Barwick Park, Yeovil, Somerset, *c. 1760*,
one of the most famously eccentric of follies, with a name to match.

of rubble with holes for light topped by a stone well-head, an iron cage and a fish weathervane, now lost. The Obelisk marking south, also of rubble, is thin and slanting. However, the Cone, although built of the same rough stone, is more beautiful; it stands to the west, 21 metres (69 ft) high and very slender, marked by diminishing rings of square holes and with a ball finial. Supporting the cone is a stone tripod consisting of three gothic arches, inside which one can gaze up into the hollow cone with its concentric rings of light. There are follies designed with arches and holes that served for cattle shelters and dovecotes, but this is not one of them. The date of these four follies has been as uncertain as their purpose, usually given as the 1820s when George Messiter allegedly devised them to provide employment when there was a depression in Yeovil's glove-making trade. This is a clear example of fabrication, because two portraits of John and Grace Newman, who owned Barwick Park before the Messiters, show that the follies existed in the mid-eighteenth century. Jack the Treacle Eater appears in the background of his portrait, the

Cone in hers. The portraits are by Thomas Beach and dated 1768, and they also prove that the arched base on which Mercury and his tower were mounted was smarter then, not tumbledown but with the stepped angles clearly defined and bearing finials. And this is another feature of follies: they sometimes appear in portraits of their original owners, like an expression of personality.

One of the few follies definitely built to relieve a famine situation is at Castletown in Ireland. Mrs Conolly, widow of the influential politician William 'Speaker' Conolly, the richest man in Ireland, ornamented her grounds with follies, the finest of which was known as Conolly's Folly and was built in 1739–40 during a frozen winter of famine when she provided food and employment. Her sister wrote in March 1740:

Thomas Beach, *John Newman*, 1768, showing Jack the Treacle Eater in the background.

> My sister is building an Obelix to answer a vista from the back
> of Castletown. It will cost her 3 or 4 hundred pounds at least and
> I believe more. I don't know how she can do so much and live
> as she does.[8]

To call it an obelisk was an understatement, though it is a very fine one nearly 50 metres (164 ft) high, because the glory of this folly resides in the multiple arches on which the obelisk is raised. The elaborate structure surrounds a large central archway supporting a pedimented cube which contains the highest of the arches (and two little decorative arches at the corners of the cube). This bears the obelisk soaring above. On either side are slightly smaller arches, one above the other, set back a little and framing the sky. Above them, square pillars echo the obelisk and are crowned with urns and eagles. Balancing the two corners of the edifice, set forward again, are short square towers containing arches and topped by cupolas and acorn finials. In all there are fourteen arches. This striking monument stands 3.2 kilometres (2 mi.) northwest of Castletown House on the highest point of land at the end of the main vista.

Eighteenth-century obelisks were an idea inherited from ancient Rome, rather than directly from Egypt, and were seen as a mark of imperial power. Standing alone, they could be grand but not at all unusual, but the one thus elevated at Castletown was so imperious that the memory of famine relief was quite subsumed when the Irish poet Michael Hartnett wrote 'A Visit to Castletown House'. Stepping out into the evening air, he imagined the black figures of Eviction and Droit de Seigneur dancing on the lawn and 'heard the crack of ligaments being torn, and smelled the clinging blood upon the stones'.

What of follies in literature, and above all Coleridge's evocative 'In Xanadu did Kubla Khan/ A stately pleasure dome decree'? The poet's image of China, no doubt filled with the chinoiserie of the age, may have been

Castletown Obelisk, Co. Kildare, erected in 1740 to provide employment during a time of famine.

freshly stimulated by Lord Macartney's notorious embassy to the Qianlong emperor (after which Macartney reported that the imperial gardens reminded him greatly of Stowe).[9] Coleridge's opium-clouded brain was even more stimulated by deep romantic chasms and the tumult of water rushing over dancing rocks – the same images that thrilled advocates of the Picturesque movement in landscape design. Any or all of the places that the poet visited, including Wookey Hole, Hafod in Wales and Culbone on the edge of Exmoor (where Baron King of Ockham was constructing follies at the time), may have been in his thoughts. Coleridge also left an indelible if hazy impression of a Chinese pavilion in 'Kubla Khan': 'The shadow of the dome of pleasure/ Floated midway on the waves.' It was a dome in air and there was a damsel with a dulcimer. That is all we know, but it is very memorable.

While Coleridge subscribed to the oriental and Romantic taste, many poets from Alexander Pope onwards sang the praises of landscape gardens where beautiful little buildings emerged from carefully planted vistas:

Consult the genius of the place in all . . .
Parts answ'ring parts, shall slide into a whole,
Spontaneous beauties all around advance,
Start, ev'n from difficulty, strike, from chance;
Nature shall join you; Time shall make it grow
A work to wonder at – perhaps a Stowe.[10]

These emotions were sedate (and even humorous considering that Stowe must have been a building site when Pope visited it) compared to the voluptuous outpourings inspired by the ruins of Rome, or the melancholy reflections inspired by the passage of time. However, follies were primarily intended for pleasurable associations, and George West, another poet who extolled the follies at Stowe, peopled the sham ruin with imaginary revellers, a theatrical aspect which garden statues were also intended to convey:

See, where the ruin lifts its mould'ring head!
Within, close-shelter'd from the peering day,
Satyrs and Fauns their wanton frolicks play.[11]

The love of ruins prompted not only a host of classical temples but a new appreciation of the medieval ruins of Britain, and should these be lacking in a gentleman's grounds a sham ruin might be erected. The melancholy and pleasurable shudders prompted by contemplating mortality, together with tales of haunting and perfidy, fed into gothic novels, which became immensely popular at this time. Jane Austen's *Northanger Abbey* showed a deep appreciation of the genre while seeming to mock it. The folly she mentioned specifically was Blaise Castle at Henbury, which commands a fine prospect near a gorge, overlooking Bristol and the river Avon. It was built in 1766 for Thomas Farr, a sugar merchant and slave trader, and it belongs to a tradition of building towers where shipping could be viewed by prosperous merchants. There was also a tradition of building triangular follies (ruinous or otherwise) which sometimes had religious or political symbolism, but practically speaking they were cheaper to build and more stable than any other kind of tower. Blaise Castle is triangular in having a circular core and three sturdy round turrets with crenellated parapets. There are hollow gothic windows, some with tracery, and quatrefoils and cruciform arrow slits. In *Northanger Abbey*, John Thorpe, who wanted to lure Catherine Morland into his carriage for a long outing from Bath, described it as 'the finest place in England, worth going 50 miles at any time to see', but slyly he (and Jane Austen) implied it was very old and very large with dozens of towers and galleries. Irony works well with follies.

Thomas Hardy has been associated with at least three folly towers in Dorset, heart of the lovingly described Wessex of his novels and poems. One is Clavell Tower overlooking Kimmeridge Bay, where he won the heart of the local coastguard's daughter Eliza Nicholls. For the frontispiece of his *Wessex Poems* Hardy used his own drawing of Clavell Tower, set against the sunset, with a couple walking towards it up a winding path. One can read a Hardyesque sadness into the scene because their affair ended in 1867 and she never married. The tower has been a landmark there on its clifftop since 1830, when it was built by the Rev. John Clavell, rector of the nearby parishes of Church Knowle, Steeple and East Lulworth. He inherited the estate of Smedmore from his brother in 1818 and seems to have built the tower to celebrate his seventieth birthday. The best contemporary description appeared in the *Dorset County Chronicle* on 21 July 1837, written from Weymouth:

> On the north side of our beautiful bay . . . the Observatory lately erected . . . a most conspicuous *coup d'oeil* from our Esplanade,

Clavell Tower, Dorset, built in 1830, prominently on the Dorset coastline, where it had to be rescued from erosion by the Landmark Trust.

reflecting the highest credit on Mr Vining [a prominent Weymouth architect] of Purbeck stone, the principal part dug on the manor of Smedmore, and of circular form . . . To celebrate completion the worthy founder entertained all mechanics and labourers to a dinner in the true and genuine style of old English hospitality.

Twice in the course of this eulogy the tower is called an observatory, and it would have been well suited for this purpose, with its spiral staircase up three floors to a flat roof, although there is no other evidence that the elderly rector was an astronomer. There is a possibility that other forms of observation were intended. This was notorious as a smugglers' stretch of coastline: the next bay to Kimmeridge was called Brandy Bay and certainly Clavell Tower became an important landmark from the sea. There was much local sympathy for 'the trade' – for example, coastal clergymen sometimes hid kegs in their churches. As for Hardy himself, his father had an old servant who was proud to have been a smuggler, and he would describe working in the fields by day and at night heaving great kegs, thumping against his back and chest,

Horton Tower, Dorset, possibly built as early as the 1720s to act as an observatory.

for many miles across the fields. Conspiracy theories aside, the tower is iconic, perched perilously near the edge of the crumbling sea cliff, from which it had to be rescued, dismantled and rebuilt.[12] It gazes over the sand and rocks of Kimmeridge Bay with wildflowers spread all around like an embroidered mantle. It is a circular tower with graceful, arched windows; a colonnade of columns surrounds the base, adding greatly to its style, especially now that the parapets pierced with quatrefoils have been restored above the colonnade and the roofline. Since, as the *Dorset County Chronicle* confirmed, it was built of local materials by local men, it was both unique and not entirely symmetrical (it may even have been hurriedly finished on account of the old rector's birthday), which adds to the quirkiness that gives a folly charm.

Another Dorset tower associated with Thomas Hardy is very different. Horton Tower is a dark and looming presence, wonderfully gothic, with a strong tradition (though no proof) that it was built as an observatory. This was, after all, a century of telescopes, when George III himself had an observatory built at Kew, and Captain Cook was dispatched to Tahiti in 1769 primarily to make astronomical calculations (after which he proceeded to 'discover' Australia). Horton Tower is claimed as the chief candidate to have inspired Hardy's novel *Two on a Tower*, where, against a backdrop of the stars themselves, Hardy set one of his tragic and illicit passions, in this case between a bishop's wife and a youthful astronomer. She was torn by guilt, he by his great dedication to science, culminating in the final scenes featuring his desire to observe the brief transit of Venus (which was also Captain Cook's objective on Tahiti). Horton is a grim triangular tower of reddish brick with six storeys of very narrow windows rising to a height of 43 metres (141 ft) and visible for miles around. Now all the floors are gone and it stands in a field of sheep, hollow and derelict, with tufts of grass growing in the cracks that add greatly to its atmosphere. The centre of the tower is hexagonal and supported by three round corner turrets, four storeys high and topped with ogee domes and finials; between the turrets are linking walls with classical pediments. The date of its building is unknown, though it was certainly built for a Humphrey Sturt, and is sometimes known as Sturt's Tower. The father with that name financed the rebuilding of Horton church in 1722; the son was MP for Dorset from 1745 until 1786 and known as an enthusiast for agricultural improvements – he thought nothing of eradicating a village for intensive cropping or to create an ornamental lake. This son was visited in 1762 by Edward Gibbon, who described 'an elegant turret 140 feet high . . . but such is the nature of the man that he keeps his place in no order . . . and makes a granary of his turret'.[13] However, in Taylor's map of Dorset dated 1765 it is called the Horton Observatory, and this, together with Gibbon's wording, implies that it was more likely to have been the elder Humphrey Sturt who built the tower – as an observatory and probably in the 1720s, when he was also endowing the church. In support of such a date, the design of the tower has even been attributed to Thomas Archer, one of Britain's leading Baroque architects, responsible for many churches and several grand follies in a curvaceous style, who, although his career was based in London, was working in Dorset in the 1720s.

Horton Tower does have a rival to be the inspiration behind Hardy's fictional observatory, where the lovers had their first dramatic encounter and subsequent trysts. Hardy himself said it was based on 'two real spots' in Dorset. The other is Charborough Tower, home of the Drax family and nearer to Wimborne and Hardy's home. In his novel Hardy covered his tracks well, and anyone reading the opening pages of *Two on a Tower* will know exactly how it feels to seek out a folly hidden away on private land. Hardy's imagined tower was 'built in the Tuscan order of classical architecture' (so, more like Clavell Tower) but otherwise gothic in atmosphere, surrounded by 'blue-black vegetation which the sun never pierced'.[14] However, as it rose above the trees it became 'a bright and cheerful thing flushed with the sunlight', which Horton Tower would never be – although Hardy did place his tower in the middle of a field, like Horton. While Horton Tower is stern baronial gothic, Charborough is more ecclesiastical gothic, with crocketed pinnacles, a fine traceried window and gargoyles of wild boar, hunting dogs and possibly panthers. It was built in 1790 and rebuilt after a lightning strike in 1839, somewhat over 30 metres (98 ft) high and octagonal. The two lower storeys have pinnacled buttresses, while gothic windows (mostly blank) adorn every facet of all five storeys, making it very ornate. Inside, the spiral steps are easy to climb, unlike most tower stairways, a feature which surprised Hardy enough for him to include it in his fictional description. But the setting of Charborough Tower is neither secluded nor wild: it has always been approached along a formal avenue lined by plinths and nowadays it is cushioned by rhododendrons.

Virginia Woolf also found a tower stirring her imagination enough to become the germ of a novel; in fact she was tempted to buy it. Laughton Tower in Sussex was near the country homes that she and her sister Vanessa Bell both owned, and in her diary for 20 September 1927 she wrote:

> When Vita [Vita Sackville-West, her lover] was here ten days ago we
> drove over to Laughton and I broke in and explored. It seemed that
> sunny morning so beautiful, so peaceful, so I came home boiling with
> the idea of buying it, and so fired L [Leonard Woolf, her husband]
> that he wrote to the farmer and we waited all on wires, edgy excited
> for an answer.

Then she revisited in a different mood, finding it 'unspeakably dreary, all patched and spoiled, and I noted the strength and vividness of feelings which suddenly break and foam away'. But a creative seed had been sown: 'One of these days I shall sketch here like a grand historical picture the outlines of all my friends . . . Vita should be Orlando.'[15] A year later *Orlando* appeared, her most joyous and colourful book, proceeding with varied scenarios from Tudor to modern times, like Laughton Tower. Admittedly the tower was not built as a folly, raising yet another query about definition – whether a building can turn into a folly. Laughton Tower belonged to the Pelhams continuously from the time Sir William Pelham built it in 1534 until Virginia Woolf saw it in 1927. Originally it was central to a moated manor house, raised above the surrounding marshes, which drained into the river Ouse and thence to the Channel. In the sixteenth century it was newly fashionable to build in brick and to use terracotta adornments (Layer Marney Tower in Essex is the most decorative example). Here the terracotta tiles carry the Pelham motif, a buckle captured from the French king at the battle of Poitiers. The tower would have been situated (like Sissinghurst Castle in Kent) at the centre of a complex of buildings, where it served as a lookout for shipping or hunting, or anything else that needed watching. In this case the Tudor Pelhams were responsible for defending the Sussex

Laughton Tower, West Sussex, built in 1534
as a Tudor watchtower and becoming a folly
when the buildings around it vanished.

coast against foreign raids. But the most prominent Pelhams came later, as eighteenth-century Whig politicians, prime ministers and folly builders; and, since they lived in far grander premises elsewhere, their Sussex tower took on the mantle of a folly.

To return to the imaginative source of architectural follies, the oldest and most influential tower in literature was the Tower of Babel, which was not a tower but a ziggurat and certainly not a folly. It nevertheless transformed into a high tower in European imaginations, which it proceeded to haunt as a symbol of foolhardy aspiration, but a fascinating one. The hills of Britain bristle with homegrown versions of this monument – good, bad and indifferent. There are cute little ones like Solomon's Temple near Buxton, not biblical but named after a local publican; or the Pepperbox near Salisbury, which became a shelter for highwaymen. Some are ugly but impressively high, like Farringdon and Sway Towers, both Victorian and both in Hampshire. The latter was built by Andrew Peterson, who returned from making his fortune in India determined to prove the superiority of concrete as a building material. It is said that he also intended to be given the funeral rites of a Parsi, left for his bones to be picked clean on the Towers of Silence, although there are no vultures in Hampshire. The dimensions of these two southerly towers are outshone by Wainhouse Tower in Halifax, which started as a factory chimney. In 1871 John Wainhouse, a mill owner, began to build it in order to pipe the smoke from his dyeworks away from the valley and up the chimney on the hill.[16] It stands above the tightly packed terraces of houses with a graveyard nearby and the Yorkshire Dales beyond. In 1874 Wainhouse sold the mill and the new owner refused the expense of finishing the tower for the purpose intended. So Wainhouse kept his tower and turned it into a folly with hundreds of steps and narrow window slits; he embellished the octagonal summit in fine Victorian style, so ornate that it has the look of Indian temple carvings. There are elaborate galleries with balustrades around the two viewing platforms, pillars, finials, cornices, buttresses and a corona dome much like an Indian stupa. Wainhouse claimed it was 'a general astronomical and physical observatory', which suggests the good folk of Yorkshire asked awkward questions about its purpose.

At 84 metres (276 ft) Wainhouse Tower may be of unparalleled height, but, for those who prefer an overall decorative scheme, Hadlow Tower near Tonbridge in Kent is ornate from base to tip, with all the details of Victorian Gothic Revival diminishing in layers like a cake and culminating in pinnacles and a lantern. It recalls the legendary gothic style of Fonthill Tower, built by

Racton Tower, West Sussex, built shortly before 1771 when Lord Halifax died, developed a reputation as a haunted folly.

William Beckford, which was first notorious because of the extravagance and sexual scandal that marred Beckford's reputation, and then after its collapse in 1822 assumed the aura of another Babel. Hadlow Tower has not collapsed, but it too has a seedy reputation of fleeing wives and sex parties. It is known as May's Tower, after its original owner, and continues to change hands in an ill-fated way. But it is not said to be haunted. That reputation belongs, above all, to Racton Tower in West Sussex, another triangular tower, built of brick and flints, with a five-storey central tower and three round towers at the corners. It is ruinous and threatening and reeks of atmosphere. Hollowness gapes through every opening, and its echoes and whispers might simply be the wind in the surrounding trees, but the sensation of being watched, touched and brushed against is more horrible than that. The tower attracts suicides

Waterloo Tower, Quex Park, Kent, inaugurated as a bell tower in 1819 and named as a triumphal tower commemorating the victory at Waterloo in 1815.

and the occult, but there is no specific ghost story associated with it. The second Earl of Halifax, who inherited nearby Stansted Park in 1766 and died in 1771, had it built during his brief tenure, when he was relandscaping the park. He was already the creator of several fine follies on his other estates and no doubt wanted a lordly viewfinder over the Downs and Chichester harbour (having in his time been president of the Board of Trade and First Lord of the Admiralty).[17]

Many towers were built as memorials, joining with obelisks, columns and statues in the patriotic cries of triumph which spread across the land. The earliest such association is Compton Pike in Warwickshire, an elongated pyramid with a ball finial linked to the Armada – possibly because the hilltop on which it stands carried a beacon for warnings and celebrations. The two later victories which prompted most tower-building were Culloden and Waterloo,[18] and of such structures the Waterloo Tower in Quex Park near Birchington in Kent is the most extraordinary. It was inaugurated in 1819 as a bell tower, with bells cast in the Whitechapel bell foundry and hung for change ringing. Large crowds gathered at its ceremonial opening in August 1819: 'The interest was considerably enhanced by its having no parallel – that of a gentleman erecting in his park a tower with a spire and placing therein a peel of 12 bells . . . and practising this manly art.'[19] The gentleman responsible was John Powell Powell, who so loved campanology that he later wrote a book (with an illustration of Waterloo Tower at the front) and a preface explaining this as 'an attempt to compose a whole peal of Stedman Triples which might be considered the most perfect by having the fewest number of bobs and singles'. Whether Powell's system worked is debatable, but the bells continue to peal forth and Stedman Triples are particularly associated with Waterloo Tower. This bell tower stands over 30 metres

(98 ft) tall, of smooth red brick, castellated and with lancet windows; the square central tower has four octagonal turrets four storeys high, one at each corner, and its crowning glory is a cast iron spire added in 1820: 'sprung from four quarter circle arches . . . a noble seamark being only one mile from that briny fluid'.[20] Not only is it significantly earlier than the Eiffel Tower (1887–9) or Blackpool Tower (1894), but its effect is light and graceful, since it is painted white. The 'quarter circle arches', which curve over to support the spire, are resting on each corner turret of the brick tower like an enchanted vision, weird and memorable. As a cast iron folly it was pioneering, and it was locally made – set between the girders of its supporting curves is a viewing platform, much like an iron cobweb and reached by a ladder, and here the name John Clark is inscribed. He was the estate carpenter, so presumably he carved the patterns from which the sections of the spire were cast. The casting was done by William Mackney, who was an iron founder in nearby Sandwich, to whom the Quex accounts record payments 'for iron castings for the ringing tower'. Another, unrecorded, local feat consisted of raising and assembling the sections of the spire. This was topped with a cross and a golden weathercock, and underneath it a second, smaller spire crowns the central tower, cleverly echoing both the curve and the spike, and this time bearing an urn.

Another more homely monument, not a tower but a fat white cone, commemorates the victory at Waterloo on Kerridge ridge, above the town of Bollington in Cheshire. It is a landmark visible for miles, beloved of walkers and local merrymakers (not to mention vandals, who are attracted to follies like wasps to jam). It is called White Nancy and has variously been considered as a sugar cone (reminiscent of the form in which solidified sugar used to arrive in households); as a beacon, because in 1810 the earlier beacon here was described as a 'small rotund of bricks'; or as an ordinance marker – because on maps the location used to be called Northern Nancy. It was erected in 1817 by the Gaskell family, who owned Ingersley Hall at the base of Kerridge Hill (and who some say had a daughter or a horse called Nancy).[21] They endowed its upkeep as a Waterloo monument with two shillings and sixpence. It acted as a shelter on the hilltop, with a circular stone table and seating running all around the inside wall, but now it is blocked up. It is at its most visible when painted white with a black ball finial. Whether it was like this from the start is uncertain, but its whiteness was recorded in 1856, when a eulogy for the departing vicar of Bollington described the local landscape and included the lines:

White Nancy, Cheshire, built in 1817 as a local landmark and, although generally plain white, sometimes adorned with commemorative symbols.

On the south, the hill Nancy, that all here do know
And its beacon at top is as white as new snow.

Mostly it is still white, but in the 1980s there was a spell of turning it into a painted Christmas pudding. In 2012 the queen's Diamond Jubilee was marked with a crown and the dates of her reign; then on the other side of the monument the Olympic rings were added, with a laurel wreath as the green Olympic ring, and to celebrate British triumphs a gold medal and the number 29. Since then there have been other transformations: in 2014 a red poppy for the hundredth anniversary of the start of the First World War; in 2015 a fine procession of black silhouettes in historic military uniforms to commemorate Waterloo again; and in 2017 a bee, as a symbol of solidarity with the people of Manchester after the bombing. Many follies are cherished, but this one has expressed community spirit at its most alive and vivid.

One

Seeking Out the Origins

The earliest English records of ornamental garden buildings, which were known as summer houses or banqueting houses, date from the fifteenth century. Henry v, victor of Agincourt, had 'a pretty banketyinge house of tymber' on a moated island called the Pleasance, half a mile from his Warwickshire castle at Kenilworth. Then silence falls until, at Hampton Court, Henry VIII created a mount with a spiral path 'like the turnings of cokel shells to come to the top without pain' and built a three-storey banqueting house overlooking the Thames on one side and his gardens and fountains on the other. The choice of location was seen to fit the suggestion of the Italian Renaissance architect Alberti that a pleasure building should be sited above the garden, to 'discover all the glories of the view'.[1]

The banquets for which such buildings were intended were not feasts of many courses, but a dessert of sugary concoctions accompanied by fruit, nuts and sweet wines, as dainty and tempting as the seventeenth-century still-lifes in which they appeared. The name derived from the French *banquette*, meaning bench, which emphasized the outdoor informality of the occasion, like a sumptuous picnic. On a practical level the removal of guests from the main dining area of a residence enabled the servants to prepare the hall for dancing or entertainments,[2] but using a banqueting house also became a pleasure in its own right. The great gardens of Elizabethan times all had them: those belonging to the royal palace of Nonsuch, the Cecils at Theobalds and Burghley, Robert Dudley at Kenilworth. At Holdenby in Northamptonshire, Christopher Hatton (whose grand London garden led to the naming of the capital's current jewellery quarter, Hatton Garden) remodelled his grounds to rise in a series of terraces, Italian style, and created a three-storey banqueting house large enough for a visitor to stay in, probably designed with the queen herself in mind. Likewise at Sissinghurst in Kent, Sir Richard Baker went into a frenzy of building ready for the queen's visit in 1573, and placed a banqueting house where she could walk across the garden to enjoy light

George Flegel (1566-1638), *Still-Life with Confectionary*, undated. A 17th-century banqueting still-life showing the kind of delicacies to be enjoyed in a banqueting house.

summer refreshments (though she would not have approved at all when it was later converted into the Priest's House).[3]

Other examples of Elizabethan banqueting houses survive. At Melford Hall in Suffolk there is a two-storey octagonal pavilion of mellow brick with eight pointed gables and a host of slender pinnacles, and at Montacute House in Somerset twin pavilions grace either end of the courtyard wall: little square buildings with ogee roofs, pinnacles and obelisks – the last, though small, being an architectural flourish signifying power. Robert Dudley, Earl of Leicester, Elizabeth's favourite, erected obelisks and pyramids throughout his gardens at Kenilworth when he entertained her there in 1575, and the other decorations, together with the performances he devised for her, were also laden with emblematic and classical allusions. Such themes continued to be a feature of folly gardens and buildings: 'Ornaments having some wittie device expressed with cunning workmanship, something obscure that when it is understood may the greater delight the beholder.'[4] This description of

Kenilworth during the year of Elizabeth's visit also featured the word 'terrace' for the first time, describing a walk 'of fresh fine grass, which also grows on the slope, raised high above the garden'. During the 1590s, Francis Bacon, in his principal London residence at Gray's Inn, created a terrace walk along his boundary that looked over open countryside. It was on this vantage point, in 1608, that he paid for 'a banqueting house capped with a griffon to be built upon the mount', followed in 1612 by another banqueting house next to a bowling alley. There were also 'sommer-houses well built of Roman architecture' at his ancestral residence at Gorhambury in Bedfordshire, and in his essay 'Of Gardens' Bacon advocated a terrace 'some thirty feet high . . . with some fine banqueting house'.[5]

The forgotten charms of those lost Tudor follies live on in full measure at Lyveden New Bield, which its creator Sir Thomas Tresham called 'my garden lodge', placing it on the highest eminence of his land where it commanded fine views across the Northamptonshire countryside as it rolled gently southwards towards the hunting grounds of Rockingham forest. To the east and west lay lucrative sheep pastures, which Tresham had ruthlessly enclosed, driving out the local tenants as was the way of Tudor gentry. In the valley to the north nestled the Old Bield, Tresham's manor house at Lyveden, with the

Lyveden New Bield, Northamptonshire, built c. 1595 with a wealth of religious symbolism but never completed after Tresham's death in 1605.

deer park beyond. The garden – and its terraces, canals and spiral mounts – stretches now, as it did then, up the slope between the Old Bield and the New, and it is a magical space. Sir Thomas Tresham was a man of learning. His library of over a thousand books included works by the Italian Renaissance architects Alberti, Palladio and Serlio, and alongside architecture Tresham's enthusiasms extended to the layout of his fashionable garden and its planting, but above all to his religion. Tresham became overtly Catholic in 1580, at a most uncomfortable time when plots to assassinate Elizabeth and place Mary Queen of Scots or Philip of Spain on the throne were regularly uncovered. Tresham himself sheltered the Jesuit priest Edmund Campion soon after he arrived from Europe that year with the express intention of galvanizing Catholic resistance in England. Subsequently Tresham paid many fines for refusing to attend Anglican services and spent years in prison (planning buildings and studying numerology). On the other hand, he seems to have been personally loyal to his suspicious monarch, and also remained on friendly terms with luminaries of the Tudor court. Christopher Hatton, at nearby Holdenby, supplied much of the stone for the New Bield from his quarries, and the Cecils at Burghley leased Tresham his deer park from their land.[6]

In 1605 Sir Thomas died and disaster struck the family: two months after Thomas's death his son Francis was implicated in the Gunpowder Plot and then beheaded (it was he who scuppered the plot by warning his cousin Lord Mounteagle not to attend Parliament). For this reason, Lyveden New Bield was never finished and never had a roof, though technically it is not a ruin but an unfinished building, still pristine in its details. It was begun in 1595, in the symmetrical form of a Greek cross, formed of five squares (a central square with an equal square on all four sides). This number symbolism of five dominates the measurements of the building: the bay windows on each projection of the cross start 5 feet (1.5 m) from the corner of the building and each has five faces, each 5 feet long. To Catholics this represented the five wounds inflicted when Christ was crucified, in both hands, both feet and his side. The carved frieze above the windows of the first floor has a repeat pattern of the seven instruments of Christ's passion (seven panels in all), including the crown of thorns, the nails, the dice with which lots were cast for his cloak and the purse of silver coins for which he was betrayed, all intricately clear. The upper frieze has Latin quotations, and the five-letter Jesus and Maria recur often. On each wing there are 81 letters in the inscriptions, and the same numerology exists in the total circumference of the building – 81 feet (24.7 m), interpreted as nine times nine, or multiples of three for the Trinity.

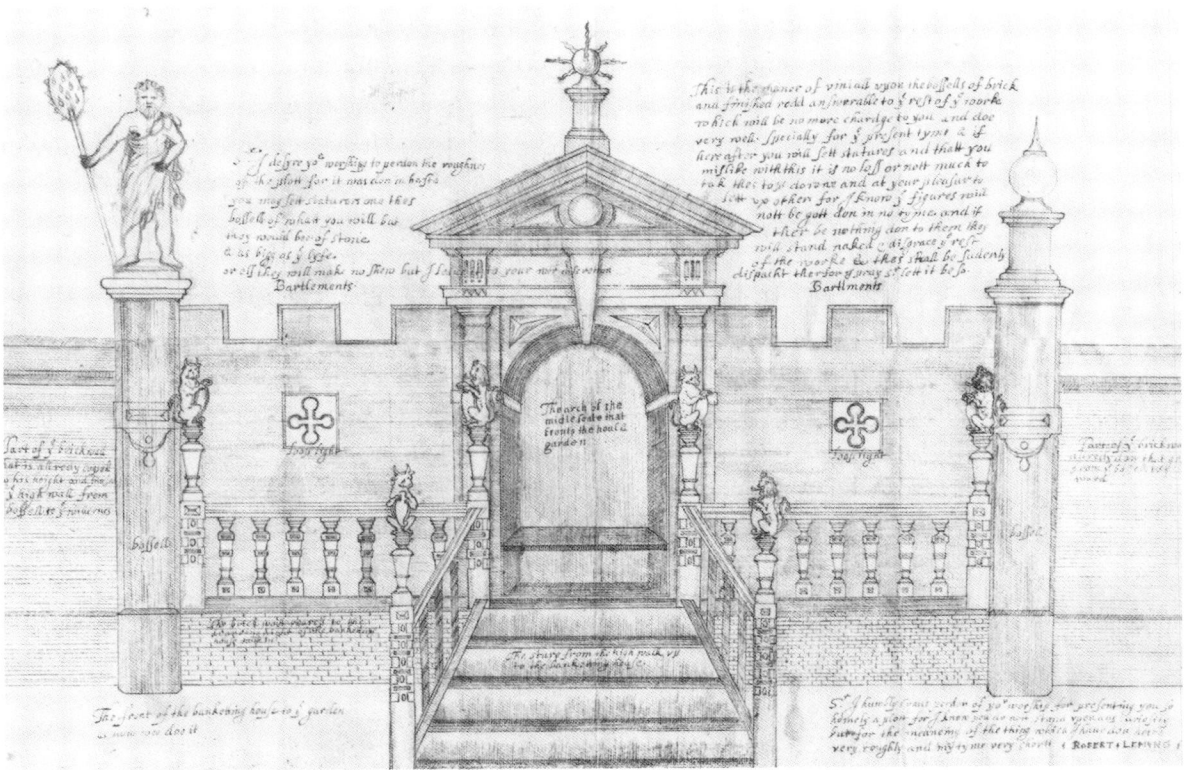

Robert Lyminge, *Design for a Banqueting House at Blickling*, c. 1620, never realized
but a fine example of the fantasies inspiring architects and their patrons.

But without any complicated counting or measuring it is an intricate and beautiful building, a handsome size for a banqueting house, with three floors – the raised basement, which contained the kitchen, stores and bread ovens; a great hall and parlour on the first floor; and possibly bedrooms above – all approached by a staircase in the south arm of the cross. Certainly, when not in prison, Sir Thomas entertained well. One year his household consumed over fifty cattle and two hundred sheep, but this does not seem quite like a banqueting house in the usual sense of the word. Some of these rooms may have been intended for a priest's secret dwelling or a Catholic chapel, or more innocently for Sir Thomas's retreat and study. It was never used, but it proves that from the start follies could mean more than their name implies, incorporating the owner's aspirations and quite often some form of dissent.

With the start of the Stuart dynasty, the elaborations beloved of the Elizabethans were adopted with enthusiasm. Robert Lyminge, architect of Hatfield in Hertfordshire and Blickling in Norfolk, favoured a rich mixture of pinnacles and parapets, Flemish gables, mullioned windows and arches. His design for a banqueting-house folly at Blickling survives, even though the folly itself doesn't, dated about 1620 and showing an arched and pedimented entrance topped with a spiky sun. There are crenellated walls reminiscent of a medieval fortress, with quatrefoil arrow slits, pretty carved balustrades and newel posts with heraldic beasts, and guarding the whole edifice a wild man wielding a club.[7] At court, fanciful masques were the favourite entertainment of James I's queen, Anne of Denmark, and later of Charles I and Henrietta Maria. Inigo Jones devised similarly elaborate sets for them, often featuring gardens and marvellous pavilions, which introduced perspective recession onto the English stage. A contemporary described such scenery as 'a prospect of curious arbours of various forms', but Inigo Jones's designs were far too architectural to be arbours formed of greenery.[8]

Two surviving examples of these tastes remain at Chipping Campden in Gloucestershire, where Baptist Hicks, first Viscount Campden, built a great mansion (burned down in the Civil War) and a fine garden descending in terraces, water features and parterres. At either end of the upper terrace was a banqueting house, the two facing each other, east and west. From both of them the garden below could be admired, and also accessed from the lower floors. The larger East Banqueting House also looked out from the back over the Coneygree, a field whose name indicates rabbit runs and therefore the fun of hunting forays – and beyond there was possibly a deer park. The elaborate roofs are the most individual and Jacobean features of both banqueting houses, with strapwork parapets, twisted barley-sugar chimneys and basket finials – all beautifully carved from Cotswold limestone. The workmanship was echoed in the internal plasterwork, some of which still survives in the West Banqueting House, together with a frieze of winged lions with men's heads. You could even imagine these decorations being replicated in the pastries served there for dessert (alongside meringues and 'marmalades' of jellied fruit), as described in the contemporary *Elinor Fettiplace's Receipt Book*.[9] The Jacobean love of curlicues, as manifested in the roofs, was offset by more classical facades patterned with arches – these were open loggias at first and were then filled in.

Baptist Hicks made his fortune in London's City, first as a mercer selling luxury fabrics and furbelows; he provided £3,000 worth of crimson velvets, damasks and satins for James I's coronation. He was also a moneylender, for which services he was even more valued at court, as was his brother Michael, secretary to Lord Burghley, who cultivated family friendships with people

East Banqueting House, Chipping Campden, Gloucestershire, built c. 1615 to face the West Banqueting House as they stood either end of the garden terrace of Old Campden House.

such as the Cecils and Francis Bacon. In 1628, a decade or so after the banqueting houses were built, Hicks was ennobled as Viscount Campden (the name still marks the sites of his various London properties), but he had no male heirs. The Cotswold estate went, through the marriage of his daughter Juliana, to the Noels of Exton in Rutland. His younger daughter Mary married Sir Charles Morrison, whose ancestral home at Cassiobury in Hertfordshire also had a notable garden, and their daughter Elizabeth Morrison married Arthur, Lord Capel of Hadham. With the last we have a splendid early example of the inclusion of follies in portraits, because their Hertfordshire garden at Hadham forms the background of the Capel family portrait painted by Cornelius Johnson around 1640 (just before their lives were ruined by the outbreak of the Civil War).[10] Beyond the radiating circular paths, which intersect the garden lawn to create trendsetting grass *plats*, is a raised terrace with a double staircase rising in the centre. A banqueting house (no doubt one of a pair) is visible at the end of the terrace, placed like those of Lord Campden to view the garden and the landscape beyond. Here too the upper floor would lead onto the terrace and the lower floor would be level with the park. By the date of the Capel portrait, under the influence of Inigo Jones and his oversized royal Banqueting House in Whitehall, the style adopted at

Hadham would have been more classical than at Chipping Campden, missing out on coils and pinnacles.

Records suggest that, from the start, banqueting houses were often positioned to enjoy spectator sports, either hunting or ball games. In the case of Swarkestone Pavilion in Derbyshire, it is intriguingly uncertain which of these it was intended for. In front is a walled area of grass known as the Cuttle, which has over time been described as a tilting ground, a bull ring or a deer enclosure. The main room of the pavilion – with its viewing windows and fireplace – is on the first floor, while below is an arched loggia at ground level supported on Tuscan columns and above is a battlemented roof terrace, all facing expectantly across the grass. On either side are sturdy three-storey

Detail of Cornelius Johnson, *Capel Family Portrait*, c. 1640, showing the formal garden and one of a pair of banqueting houses on the raised terrace beyond.

Swarkestone Pavilion, Derbyshire, built *c.* 1630 as a sporting
pavilion and to mark an advantageous marriage.

towers with mullioned windows and ogee roofs, making the proportions of
the whole building very pleasing. It has the look of a hunting lodge, and
has been known as Swarkestone Stand, but for such a purpose it would have
been surprisingly near the Hall, which it once faced across the Cuttle and
the formal gardens. It was built around 1630 when Sir John Harpur inherited the estate and married Catherine Howard, granddaughter of the Earl
of Suffolk and stepdaughter of William Cavendish, through whom she was
closely related to Bess of Hardwick and the Devonshire clan. The coats of
arms which demonstrated the linking of their families, a lion rampant and
little crosses, are side by side above the columns of the loggia, adding to the
romantic aura of the pavilion. The accounts for the year which recorded their
wedding expenditure also have an entry for the 'New Buildynge' – £111 12*s.* 4*d.*,
paid to Richard Shepperd, the mason. Later, a further payment was made
to Shepperd for 'boards for the Bowl Alley House', the only contemporary
clue to the purpose of the grass enclosure. At 50 × 60 metres (164 × 197 ft) it
was over-large for a bowling alley, but possibly extra space round the sides of
the Cuttle was intended for arbours and viewing areas.[11] Since Tudor times,
bowls had become increasingly popular (witness the importance Francis
Drake attached to the game that he was playing when the Armada was first
sighted). In 1541 legislation had been introduced to control the drinking
and gambling that bowling seemed to encourage in public places, but the

new law allowed anyone owning land worth over £100 a year 'to play bowls without penalty' within the precincts of their 'houses, gardens and orchards'. So the newly wed Harpurs were adorning their seat with a sporting and architectural status symbol, and the local populace may have been invited to join them there, subject to good behaviour.

Judging by the style, an important local architect, John Smythson, may have helped with or influenced the design of Swarkestone Pavilion. His magnum opus was Bolsover Castle, and his classical-Mannerist style favoured overall symmetry mitigated by large expanses of mullioned windows, ogee domes and arches. Smythson, with other leading architects, was mock-praised in a Ben Jonson masque performed before Charles I and Henrietta Maria at Bolsover: 'Well done my musical, arithmetical, geometrical gamesters . . . it is carried in number, weight and measure, as if the airs were all harmony and the figures a well-timed proportion.' Harmony reigned at Swarkestone until the Civil War when, in 1643, Sir John Harpur was defeated defending Swarkestone Bridge against a Parliamentary force, and then had to bide his time very quietly until the Restoration. This nearby bridge over the river Trent carried the main road south, and its final moment of glory came in 1745 when Bonnie Prince Charlie was forced to turn back there and began the long retreat to Scotland and Culloden. At the back of Swarkestone Pavilion there are the marks of two large holes, thought to have been used for firing through during one of these strategic moments of its past.

Nearby at Chatsworth House there is an archetypal hunting stand, the finest to survive from the reign of Elizabeth, dramatically situated high above the main house in order to view the hunt for miles around. It is a massive four-square, four-storey tower dating from 1582, sufficiently unadorned and purposeful for one to query its folly status, except that four frivolous little domes top its four corner turrets, which are encircled with countless mullioned windows. The tower at Sissinghurst, more beautiful with its mellow terracotta brickwork and graceful twin turrets, may also have been designed to view the hunt and may have been built slightly earlier, with Queen Elizabeth's visit of 1573 in mind. Hunting was a favourite pastime of hers (or viewing it as she grew older). In 1591 Lord Montequte at Cowdray prepared 'a delicate bower' for her

> under which were her Highnesse musicians placed, and a
> crossbowe by a nymph with sweet song delivered to her hands,
> to shoot the deer, about some thirty in number put into a paddock

. . . then rode her Grace to Cowdray to dinner, and about six of the
clock in the evening, from a turret, saw sixteen bucks pulled down
with greyhounds.[12]

An Elizabethan prospect tower with a different purpose watches over the
river Orwell in Suffolk as it flows between Ipswich and the sea at Harwich.
Thomas Gooding, a rich Ipswich merchant, bought the manor of Freston in
1553 and gained the right to bear arms (six red lion heads) in 1576. Like Baptist
Hicks he was a mercer, dealing in luxury fabrics, and from that he grew to
be a shipping magnate involved in the vital trade routes between England,
the Netherlands and the Baltic. Dendrochronology has dated selected timbers of the tower to the 1570s, which suggests the tower was built in time
for Queen Elizabeth's progress to Suffolk in 1579.[13] She arrived in Ipswich in
August and from there went down the river to Harwich (possibly with Sir
Thomas Gooding on board), surely noticing the unusual sight of a six-storey
tower looming on the bank and very likely enquiring after its owner. Freston
Tower is a handsome rectangular building of terracotta Tudor brickwork, patterned with blue-burnt bricks on the north and west sides, which are most
visible from the river. The windows, outlined in white, become larger with
each storey, and the three upper storeys have triangular pediments above
the windows – an unusual feature signifying a classical influence. The roof
has an arcaded parapet with slender pinnacles at each corner and a round,
crenellated turret for mounting even higher. As well as impressing everyone
for miles around, Gooding used his tower for entertaining, it being his version of a banqueting house. The finest room with the largest windows (and
probably tapestries, since he was a mercer) was at the top of the tower, with
long views allowing him to spot his own ships and many others passing to
and fro on the water below. The service rooms would have been at the base
of the tower, and it may once have been joined to another building on the
landward side. If so, it would have resembled the Clifton Tower at King's
Lynn which overlooks the Ouse, again with the principal rooms at the top
and abutting Clifton House. For such lookout towers, no place is more distinguished than Old Cadiz, where they commanded views of the port and
the ships returning laden from the Indies (or an armada in preparation).
Only one remains that might rank as a folly: La Bella Escondida (meaning
'the hidden beauty'), which was erected by a family of pearl fishers around
1730. It is octagonal, moulded with faux pilasters and columns and painted
as if with ceramic tiles.

In England, another tower with a kinship to Freston Tower is Luttrell's Tower overlooking Southampton Water, though it was built two hundred years later and with less worthy intent. Its owner, Temple Luttrell, came from a disreputable Irish family. His grandfather was a soldier of fortune and sometime Jacobite, who returned from France to England with 'a flattering tongue, some skill in war and more in intrigue'. He was shot in Dublin in 1717. Temple Luttrell's father, Simon Luttrell, was created first Earl of Carhampton in Co. Cork, and his mother was the daughter of a governor of Jamaica (from whom Temple Luttrell later inherited wealthy sugar plantations). Simon Luttrell was a quarrelsome and corrupt politician who espoused the grievances of the American colonies with eloquence but mixed motives. In 1774 Temple Luttrell himself became an MP and proved as violently outspoken and pro-American as his father, declaring that 'to force a tax upon your colonists, unrepresented and dissentient, is no better than a band of robbers.' Temple Luttrell was also very critical of naval conduct in the United States War of Independence and vehemently opposed the press-ganging and ill-treatment of sailors, about which he displayed a wide knowledge, probably derived from the smuggling fraternity.[14]

In 1780 Lord North's government finally succeeded in ejecting this gadfly from Parliament, and he retreated to his tower in Hampshire. Its existence was first mentioned on a print of nearby Calshot Castle by Paul Sandby, dated that same year of 1780: 'About a mile beyond Calshot the Hon Temple Luttrell has erected a very lofty tower which commands an extensive prospect, and affords a very fine object for the Isle of Wight.' The architect of the tower was Thomas Sandby, Paul's brother. His 'design for a Gothic Tower or Belvedere' survives, showing the three-storey square tower incorporating a round tower three storeys higher still. Both towers are battlemented in medieval style, but the overall elegance of the proportions, and especially the windows, are those of a Georgian building. Here, more obviously than at Freston, the highest window in the square tower is the finest, belonging to a room designed for entertaining in the grand manner, because by then Luttrell had royal connections. In 1771 his sister Anne (a merry widow) married the Duke of Cumberland, brother of George III (not to be confused with his uncle, the victor of Culloden). She was a beguiling creature with a colourful reputation: Horace Walpole described her 'lashes a yard long and

Freston Tower, Suffolk, c. 1570, built as an eye-catcher and with commanding views of trading ships on the river Orwell.

Luttrell's Tower, Hampshire, built *c.* 1780, overlooking the Solent
and its trade, and possibly used for smuggling.

as artful as Cleopatra', while a female contemporary called her 'vulgar, noisy, indelicate and intrepid . . . after being with her one ought to go home and wash out one's ears.' It was this undignified marriage of Anne Luttrell to the king's brother that precipitated the Royal Marriages Act of 1772. Reynolds and Gainsborough both captured her unusual, teasing beauty, and in the Royal Collection a group portrait, also by Gainsborough, shows her walking in Kew Gardens with her husband and behind them her sister Elizabeth (who was later ruined by gambling). The Duke of Cumberland was the Ranger of Windsor Great Park (as his uncle had been until his death in 1765), and he was the patron of Thomas Sandby, most of whose work was there. Since Temple Luttrell was great friends with his brother-in-law this would explain how Sandby came to design Luttrell's Tower.

In 1793, on a visit to France, Luttrell's quasi-royal status was recognized when he was arrested at Boulogne by revolutionaries who displayed him as 'a brother of the King of England' and imprisoned him until 1795. What was Luttrell doing in France at such a dangerous moment, and was it connected with his reason for building a tower overlooking the busy shipping of the Solent? As well as legitimate craft, the English Channel at night was infested with smugglers. Hundreds of items, from brandy to ribbons, were subject to excessive customs duties, and so-called Free Trade had too many sympathizers as well as profiteers. ('Watch the wall, my darling, while the Gentlemen go by!', as Rudyard Kipling put it.[15]) The spot where Luttrell chose to build the tower lay over a network of pre-existing tunnels, fifty years older than the tower, leading inland from the foreshore, and the cellars under the tower were enormous. Local legend insists that Luttrell's Tower was at the heart of smuggling in the whole New Forest area, and that the high round tower was used for signalling – for watching and guiding the arrival of ships full of contraband and warning them if Excise men were nearby, or giving the all-clear. Behind the 'captain', who organized the shipping from France, and the 'lander', who organized the distribution of goods inland, was a shadowy power who financed the whole operation – the goods, the ships, the men, and keeping the locals silent. This was said to be Luttrell himself, who was believed to have supplied brandy even to members of the royal family. His brother John Luttrell was Commissioner for the Excise and a local magistrate. His friend Robert Drummond, the king's banker, owned the surrounding Cadland estate. With contacts like this his cover would have been secure. Ostensibly Luttrell used his tower for hunting parties in the New Forest, or duck shooting in the marshes of Lepe. The tower and its telescope were open to visitors, as William Gilpin innocently confirmed in 1792: 'Luttrell's Tower was built as the station of a view . . . the whole area is constantly overspread with vessels of various kinds . . . not picturesque but amusing.'[16] Another visitor from the 1790s, J. Hassell, wrote in *A Tour of the Isle of Wight* that

> Luttrell's Folly is built close to the shore, the building is very
> whimsical but neat and agreeable . . . several subterraneous passages
> lead to a number of marquees . . . with beds and kitchens . . .
> another passage leads to a bathing house on the beach.

What a supreme example of hiding in plain view. At this date it was unusual for the tower to be known as Luttrell's Folly. In pre-Revolutionary France the word was increasingly used to describe extravagant little garden buildings, but in England these were known by individual names, which were seldom disparaging. Possibly Luttrell encouraged the name himself, to give the tower a frivolous aura which would hide its true purpose.

This usage of 'folly' was not entirely unknown. In the seventeenth century there had been the Folly on the Thames, a summer house for musical entertainment constructed on an immense barge moored off the Strand Embankment.[17] It was also known as the Royal Diversion because Charles II and later Queen Mary had enjoyed themselves there. It had the air of a folly

George Cruikshank, *The Folly on the Thames*; this print is dated 1842, but the pleasure boat appeared in the 17th century, and with it an early use of the word 'folly' for places of entertainment.

because of its roof platform with a balustrade and four corner turrets with seating, from which the view of the Thames was enchanting. Beneath was the music hall, with painted walls and ceilings and dancing at night. After its heyday it became a coffee house and then a place of ill repute but, long after it was chopped up for firewood, its memory was revived by William Harrison Ainsworth. In 1842 he published *The Miser's Daughter*, containing this evocative passage alongside a slightly grotesque illustration by George Cruikshank:

> As the party approached the aquatic hotel they perceived a number of persons of both sexes seated on the roof and in the little turret parlours, smoking, drinking and otherwise amusing themselves while lively strains proceeded from within. Several small craft were landing their passengers, and from one, a tilt boat, there issued a very pretty young woman though of rather bold appearance.

As well as eating, drinking and admiring the view, musical entertainment became another of the diversions associated with banqueting and summer houses. In Europe it was more usual than in England for delightful little Palladian buildings to be entirely dedicated to music; indeed, the young Palladio's own inspiration for garden pavilions (as distinct from villas and chapels) was probably to be found at Casa Cornaro in Padua, where in the 1520s a single-storey loggia was built for theatrical performances. It had five arched openings separated by Doric half-columns on pedestals, inspired by Roman ruins, which made it the first *all'antica* building in the Veneto. A few years later a second garden pavilion was built across the courtyard named the Odeo (meaning 'music building' in Greek) and intended for chamber music. This little gem was octagonal, with a rich interior of painted landscapes and grotesques.

One typically multipurpose English summer house did come to be called 'the Music Room'. Now it is in the centre of Lancaster, although originally it overlooked an extensive garden. It was built around 1730 by Oliver Marton, a prosperous London lawyer and friend of Edward Harley, Earl of Oxford and chief minister to Queen Anne. The Music Room was almost certainly not primarily for music: the nine Muses decorate the walls of the main first-floor room and the name is more likely to be a corruption of 'Muses Room'. This room is very ornate and features fine plasterwork, probably by an Italian *stuccadoro* working in England at the time.[18] The ground floor was originally an open loggia and in front there was a bowling green (marked on Mackreth's map of Lancaster dated 1778). So, like most follies, it served various purposes and musical entertainments could well have been one of them. Richard Bradley, an early advocate of less formal gardening, wrote in 1725 of serpentine paths wandering through groves of trees to summer houses, and he mentioned music as if it were a normal feature:

> It would be no small addition to the pleasure we propose if the
> bye-walks were so ordered . . . to be led to it by degrees, first hearing
> the music faintly, by turns losing and recovering it, till at last we
> come to enjoy its harmony complete.[19]

An earlier author on gardens, John Rea, writing in 1665 (when formal gardens were still 'in the form of a Cabinet with several boxes fit to receive and securely to keep Nature's choicest jewels'), hinted at music when he described summer houses 'serving for entertainments'; although his primary suggestion was more earthy and concerned the care of his beloved streaked tulips 'clothed in scarlet laced with gold'. For Rea the ideal garden should have a handsome octangular somer-house roofed everyway and finely painted with landskips and other conceits, furnished with seats about and a table in the middle, which serveth not only for delight and entertainment but for many other necessary purposes, as to put the roots of tulips and other flowers, as they are taken up upon papers.[20]

It was during the seventeenth century, when Rea was envisaging 'a handsome octangular somer-house', that the classical style superseded more ornate homegrown tendencies. The earliest surviving example is the Summer House at the Vyne in Hampshire, a perfectly proportioned little two-storey octagonal building, combining the circle and the square in a ground plan originally advocated by the classical Roman architect Vitruvius and espoused by Palladio, Inigo Jones and their followers. It is built of mellow red brick, the circle bears the dome and the square is cruciform, consisting of four symmetrical porches with arched doorways, each with a round-headed window above. Their framing brickwork and pilasters reach the height of the building, and above are pediments that break the roofline with triangles. The arched doors and windows are replicated in blind arches that decorate the four circular walls. This is a geometrical delight begging to be dated to the days of Inigo Jones himself, when the court of Charles I was watching masques and Van Dyck was painting their portraits. It has been assumed that John Webb, a former pupil of Inigo Jones, designed it around 1654, when he added a classical portico to the north front of the Vyne; but dendrochronology on the roof beams of the Summer House has dated them to 1632, confirming that it was built when the Sandys family owned the Vyne, before it was taken over in 1653 by the Parliamentarian Speaker Chaloner Chute (who added the portico). John Webb became an assistant to Inigo Jones in 1628, at the age of seventeen, so if he had a hand in building the Vyne Summer House, it would have been in the 1630s and he must have been using his master's design.[21] Similar summer houses can be seen in an old painting of Bedford House in Covent Garden, on a garden terrace adjoining the Piazza and

The Vyne Summer House, Hampshire, built c. 1632, an important early example of an English summer house in the classical style, possibly linked with Inigo Jones.

St Paul's churchyard. Since it was Isaac de Caus, an associate of Inigo Jones, who worked for the dukes of Bedford (and in other grand gardens of the time such as Wilton), it may be he who inspired the design for the innovative little summer house at the Vyne.

An admiration for classicism was not new. Correct proportions, rounded arches, pediments and obelisks had fascinated Elizabethans, as had statues and stories of gods and heroes, although they made their appearances with quirky vernacular interpretations. In 1550 the Duke of Northumberland had sent John Shute to Italy, 'there to confer with the doings of the skilful masters in architecture'. As a result, in 1563 Shute produced *The First and Chief Grounds of Architecture* for Northumberland's surviving son Robert Dudley, who at Kenilworth presided over a phantasmagoria of classical allusions (and a classically proportioned aviary). Thomas Tresham gathered all the architectural treatises in his library, and himself used numerical proportions with great skill, but to entirely different ends. In 1604 at James I's coronation, a triumphal arch was erected for his entry into London. It was decorated with the usual twists and curves and obelisks, but the overall proportions obeyed the rules of classical symmetry, and the great central arch was framed with Tuscan columns, so that Ben Jonson could boast of the 'general harmony so connected that no little part can be missing'.[22] The tide was turning. In 1624 Sir Henry Wotton, English ambassador to Venice, published an essay, *The Elements of Architecture*. Offering a lucid introduction to Roman and Renaissance precepts, *Elements* went into seven reprints during the following century. This, alongside the example set by Inigo Jones, and the first-hand experiences of aristocrats on the Grand Tour, gave ample incentive for classical architecture to become the dominant fashion. It was also becoming increasingly obvious to readers of authors such as Virgil and Pliny, who wrote lyrical descriptions of their country villas, that the very idea of a garden pavilion was classical.

Among the ancient models most frequently copied was the Temple of Vesta at Tivoli near Rome. It was in ruins, and confusingly no one knew whose temple it originally was. John Evelyn, visiting in 1654, called it the Temple of Sibylla Tiburtina and 'a round fabric still discovering some of its pristine beauty'.[23] Enough remained of its circular form and eighteen Corinthian columns for it to become the archetype of rotundas throughout Europe, added to which it stood so picturesquely above a steep gorge, with the river Anio foaming beneath, that prints and paintings proliferated and provided further inspiration. Among the great imitations were Nicholas Hawksmoor's Mausoleum at Castle Howard, Kent's Temple of Ancient Virtue at Stowe

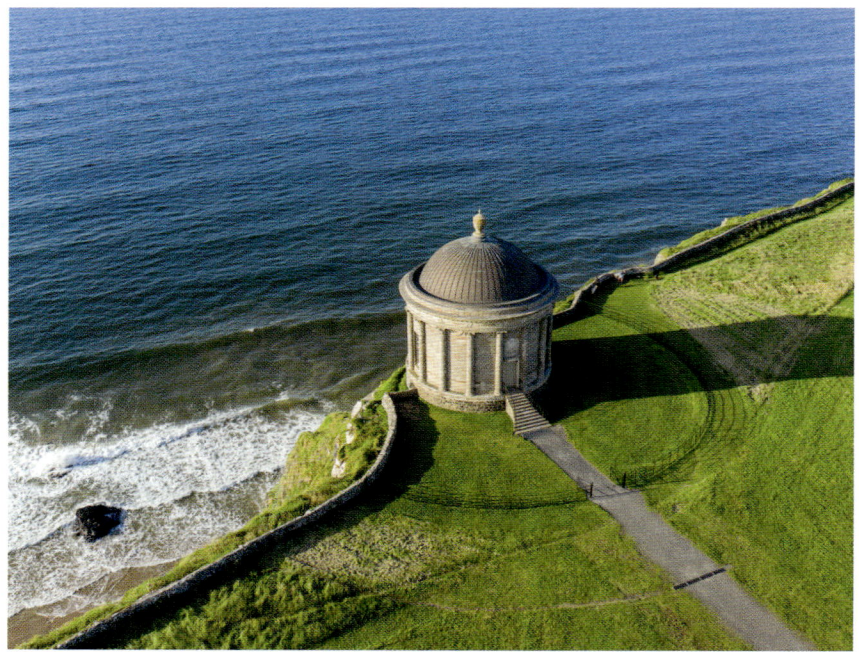

Mussenden Temple, Co. Derry, built in 1785, one of many follies inspired
by the Temple of Vesta at Tivoli. This, like the prototype, commands a superb view.

and Wyatt's Panorama Tower at Croome Park. But the example that best
echoed the Temple of Vesta's craggy waterside position was the Mussenden
Temple in Co. Derry. Built in 1785 for Frederick Hervey, Marquis of Bristol
and Bishop of Derry, it stood on a clifftop overlooking the Atlantic, with the
roar of the surf always present. In windy weather the bishop's servants were
said to almost crawl from the main house to wait on their master, and the
entablature had a Latin inscription from Lucretius (in Dryden's translation)
which read:

> Tis pleasant safely to behold from shore
> The rolling ship and hear the tempest roar.[24]

In true folly-building tradition the bishop not only enjoyed exciting views
(there are three windows overlooking the sea) but in the summer watched
sports taking place along the beach below. He instigated horse races between
Anglican and Presbyterian clergymen as well as even less dignified running
races – laughing heartily from his vantage point as the fatter clergy reached
the quicksands. He seems to have been kinder to Catholics, whom he allowed

to celebrate mass in the vaulted crypt beneath the Temple. The bishop, who was described as 'refined, well-travelled, an enthusiastic patron of the arts, with great wealth but little common sense', also used his folly as a library. A year or so before his death in 1803, a visitor described it as 'full of valuable but mouldering books, some on shelves and some piled in disorder upon the floor'. The bishop had certainly been to Tivoli (he was so well travelled that Bristol hotels all over Europe bear his name), and he was rumoured to have tried to buy the ruined temple itself from the innkeeper on whose land it stood. Instead he had a nice, weatherproof, circular folly, built in cut stone and rendered beautiful by the sixteen Corinthian columns that surround it, linked together by carved swags. The roof is a shallow dome, leaded and crowned with an urn.

The Pantheon in Rome was another archetype for circular, domed buildings, its distinguishing extra feature being the grand pedimented portico marking the entrance, supported on Corinthian columns. Columns were the most distinctive of all the classical features available for adoption into follies, and the three orders were inherited from ancient Greece but were to be seen on Roman sites all over Italy and elsewhere in Europe. The simplest was the unadorned Doric order, with the shortest shaft and the plainest capital (although the Tuscan order was an even plainer Italian variant). The second order was Ionic, with a slenderer column and voluted capitals, often described as rams' horns. Third and most ornate was the Corinthian column, with the slenderest shaft and a capital carved with acanthus leaves – and there was also a variant known as the Composite where the capital had both volutes and leaves.

On the strength of these classical orders follies were sometimes rather unimaginatively named Doric or Ionic Temples. However, in following a model like the Pantheon there was no obligation to follow the same order – that is, Corinthian – for the portico. The Pantheon was adapted to many settings, whether awe-inspiring like the Temple of Hercules at Stourhead (which does have Corinthian columns) or intimate like Garrick's Temple to Shakespeare beside the Thames at Hampton (which has Ionic columns). The story goes that David Garrick, to celebrate his success as actor, playwright and theatre manager, commissioned the leading sculptor Roubiliac to make a life-size statue of Shakespeare (with a face a little like Garrick's), and when it was finished in 1756 he had the temple built in his riverside garden to house it, surrounded by his collection of Shakespeare memorabilia. There was an embroidered leather glove, a signet ring engraved with ws and a dagger,

Johann Zoffany, *Garrick's Temple of Shakespeare*, 1762. The temple was
built beside the Thames in 1756, inspired by the Pantheon in Rome.

while William Hogarth designed a chair made from a mulberry tree that
grew in Shakespeare's garden in Stratford-upon-Avon. The last was noted
by Mrs Delany, after an 'excellent dinner', when the company retired to the
Temple to drink tea and admire 'a great chair with a large carved frame that
was Shakespeare's own chair with a medallion carved in the back'. Even if tea
had by this time replaced the original 'banquet' it was a very convivial place,
visited by everyone from Horace Walpole to Samuel Johnson and painted
by Johann Zoffany. Visitors were encouraged to write poems inspired by
Shakespeare and leave them at the base of the statue; sometimes Garrick had
these published, and such was the publicity generated that satirists including
Voltaire took up their pens. For his silver wedding in 1774 Garrick held a *fête
champêtre*, 'attended by a great number of nobility and gentry', and illuminated the temple and its garden with 6,000 candles. Each May Day Garrick
sat on Shakespeare's chair inside the Temple and distributed plum cake and
money to the poor children of Hampton. In quieter moments he sat in the
same chair to learn his lines or write letters. At other times there was fishing
– Zoffany's companion painting to one of Garrick standing on the Temple

steps with his wife Kitty shows a small group of friends taking tea on the temple lawn, one of them standing nearby with a rod, fishing in the Thames.[25]

When it came to rectangular classical follies, one of the chief models was the Temple of Fortuna Virilis in Rome, dating from the first century BC though replacing an earlier temple dedicated to Portunus, a guardian deity of livestock and crops. It remained unusually intact because of being consecrated as a church and was copied even in classical times, most notably in the Maison Carrée at Nîmes in France, which is larger than the original and has Corinthian columns. The pitched roof ends in stately pediments, extending at the front into an open portico supported on Ionic columns, four at the front and two more either side of the portico. Along the sides and rear of the building the pattern is continued by Ionic pilasters set into the walls – a Roman variant on Greek temples like the Parthenon, which is entirely surrounded by free-standing columns. The finest English replica of the Roman Temple of Fortuna Virilis is in Somerset, on the Halswell Estate at Goathurst, once a garden full of follies created by Sir Charles Kemeys-Tynte.[26] He started in the 1740s with a stepped pyramid and reached a climax with the Temple of Harmony, as his own Fortuna Virilis is called, in 1764. This temple now stands, restored and protected, in a grassy field near a stream, looking as peaceful and bucolic as its earlier namesakes (including Portunus) could have wished. Inside is a replica of a statue of Terpsichore, the Greek Muse of Dance and Poetry, who was an embodiment of the harmony which was thought, ideally, to order everything in the universe from the planets to man and nature.

The two most renowned examples of garden terraces complete with classical temples at either end are in Yorkshire, on the Duncombe estate.[27] The family fortune was made by Sir Charles Duncombe (1648–1711), a London goldsmith and banker who used his wealth to finance Charles II and James II and to acquire the land surrounding Helmsley and its castle. Duncombe Park was developed by his nephew and heir Thomas Duncombe, who from 1713 until 1718 created a curving, grassy terrace with spectacular views that included Helmsley Castle. In so doing, he anticipated the eighteenth-century appreciation of homegrown ruins and the fondness for eye-catchers. In pursuit of the classical mode he built paired follies at either end of his terrace: first an open rotunda with Ionic columns, circa 1718, possibly designed for him by Vanbrugh (who was then working on Castle Howard and who created the rotunda at Stowe in 1721); second, a round Doric Temple inspired by the Temple of Vesta at Tivoli (though the original had Corinthian columns). His son, also Thomas Duncombe, inherited in 1746 while still very

Ionic Temple, Rievaulx Terrace, Yorkshire, built in the 1750s and bringing the
rectangular form of the Roman Temple of Fortuna Virilis into a pastoral setting.

young and about to embark on the Grand Tour. On his return he was elected
to the prestigious Society of Dilettanti, married into the Howard family of
Castle Howard and became an MP. From 1749 to 1757 he created a second
great terrace, over a mile long, this time overlooking the ruins of Rievaulx
Abbey and therefore called Rievaulx Terrace. The temples he built at either
end were probably designed by Sir Thomas Robinson, a Yorkshire gentleman-
architect from the circle of Lord Burlington (and therefore Palladian) who
had also worked at Castle Howard. The first folly here was the circular Tuscan
Temple, again modelled on the Temple of Vesta at Tivoli and very similar to
his father's Doric Temple on Duncombe Terrace. It is not in fact plain enough
to be Tuscan (the simplest version of the classical orders), since it has a carved
entablature above the columns with rams' skulls and rosettes. The interior has
decorative plasterwork and a central octagonal table (dare one hope that it
was used to store tulip bulbs?). Finally on the Rievaulx Terrace came the rectangular Ionic Temple, completed late in the 1750s, in form like the Temple
of Fortuna Virilis, though without the pilastered walls, and probably also
designed by Thomas Robinson. Inside, scantily clad bodies enacted classical
myths across a frescoed ceiling. This was the banqueting house, with serving rooms in the basement, and by this date a banquet included everything
from roast meat to tea and coffee with sugar and cream.

Another garden terrace, created at Farnborough Hall, Warwickshire,
around 1750, also juxtaposed a rectangular and a round pavilion: the former an

Ionic temple, somewhat stunted at the rear, and the latter known as the Oval Pavilion, generally attributed to Sanderson Miller, which is very graceful. A circular loggia opening through four Tuscan columns supports an upper room with a domed ceiling and curved walls decorated with fine Rococo plasterwork. It is sometimes called the Prospect Tower, on account of the fine views it commands.[28] Meanwhile, a host of more or less accurate replica temples appeared across the folly gardens of England and Europe, borrowing whichever classical features best suited their creators, and often owing their appeal more to their setting than to any unusual charm or originality.

Oval Pavilion, Farnborough Hall, Warwickshire, c. 1750, a form of rotunda in the plain Tuscan style.

Occasionally a more exceptional inspiration came to the rescue. At Rousham William Kent, steeped as he was in Italian experiences, rethought the garden terrace as an amphitheatre. There were plenty of these among the classical ruins, and also arcades, but his primary source was the hillside of Praeneste (modern Palestrina) outside Rome, where the ruins of the Temple of Fortuna Primigenia rose in tiers of steps and arches, broken but very impressive. Renaissance architects often emulated their proportions, for instance in the arrangement on the sloping terrain of the Vatican Belvedere. The Praeneste temple became a favourite destination on the Grand Tour, not least for the cool breezes wafting across the hillside. In *The Spectator* Joseph Addison made sure to describe the 'fragments of this ancient temple' while quoting Virgil and Horace about its location.[29] William Kent's Praeneste was a very characteristic little English replica, created in the Oxfordshire countryside at Rousham in the late 1730s and reliant on the associations of its name. It is only one row of seven pedimented arches, not in ruins – just a single elegant line of curves and triangles in mellow Cotswold stone. Its vantage point on a terraced hillock, half shrouded in trees, viewed and viewing, demonstrated how architecture could best make play with the imagination.[30]

The Praeneste at Rousham, built 1738–40, one of William Kent's
masterpieces of theatrical scene-setting, which was enhanced by association
with its namesake, a hillside of terraced ruins outside Rome.

William Kent started his career as a painter – not a very good one – which
enabled him to see how landscape and buildings could be engineered to
produce the same jolt to the imagination as a great painting. This is what
Alexander Pope meant when he wrote, 'All the art of gardens must come
from the great landscape painter,' or Addison, 'A man might make a pretty
landskip of his own possessions.'[31] The very word 'landscape' came from the
Dutch *landschap*, meaning a painting of a rural scene – a genre which the
Dutch were the first to perfect during the seventeenth century. But the two
leading artists who added the classical dimension to landscape painting were
French. Nicolas Poussin (1594–1665) and Claude Lorrain (1604/5?–1682) were
contemporaries and to some extent friends. Both left France for Rome at an
early age, trained as artists and, once they were successful, returned to France
for a couple of years before retreating to the more congenial surroundings of
Rome for the rest of their lives. Both created some sublime works, placing
a classical event in the perfect setting. For instance, Poussin's two paintings
of *The Funeral of Phocion* show a landscape with a line of temples; and in his
Landscape with Orpheus and Eurydice Orpheus plays his lyre among the foreground trees while across the distant water he re-enacts his doomed attempt
to save Eurydice from the Underworld.[32] In this mode (as distinct from religious paintings) Claude was the more prolific of the two and a better colourist,
though no individual painting of Claude's is as stunning as Poussin could
sometimes be. Claude captured the tricks of light, atmosphere and infinite
recession, and after visiting the Bay of Naples he often used its coastline and

Canaletto, *Capriccio*, 1750s, typical artistic display of classical
edifices and ruins such as inspired the 18th-century folly builders.

the sunlight on the water for ancient scenes of arrival and departure. Above all, in terms of his influence on landscape gardening and the placement of classical follies, Claude knew how to balance trees and distant hills to frame the domes, pediments and columns of his buildings, and how to use sunlight and shadow to accentuate their geometry. Amid the poetic serenity of his templed landscapes, his small figures were not dwarfed but enacted their roles with heightened significance – at least for those who knew their classics.

The possibilities of evoking such scenes by building exquisite little follies in their own hills and valleys so excited the aristocratic landowners of Europe that replicas of classical temples proliferated. Simultaneously the walls inside their great houses were lined, if not with originals by Claude and Poussin, with imitations and *capriccios*. The latter was a genre which almost dispensed with landscapes and figures, because classical buildings jostled across the canvas in an effort to include every known variation of style. Even Canaletto produced some of these fantasies, when he realized during his decade in England (1746–*c.* 1756) how popular they were.

Andrea Palladio, Villa Rotonda, Vicenza. Begun in 1567, one of the most perfect
examples of the Palladian style that inspired generations of architects and patrons.

Two

Some Names to Conjure With

Architecture as an intellectual pursuit began with the rediscovery of *De architectura*, a ten-volume work by the Roman author Vitruvius, who lived in the first century BC during the time of Julius Caesar and Augustus. He was primarily a military engineer but he coined the three maxims of strength, utility and beauty to define the aims of architecture, while explaining in mathematical terms the configurations governing classical buildings. The manuscript of *De architectura* was discovered in the abbey library of St Gall by a Florentine humanist in 1414, and it remains the only surviving record of how the Romans created their stupendous and enduring works. Leon Battista Alberti reinterpreted it for Renaissance architects in *De re aedificatoria* circa 1450 – another ten volumes – although the best-known Renaissance illustration remains Leonardo's 'Vitruvian Man', which demonstrates with squares and circles how the proportions of men and buildings should correspond. The key word was *symmetria*, meaning not only symmetry in the English sense, but how every element should be governed by the same ratios as those of the whole, a model of consistency.

A hundred years later Andrea Palladio (1508–1580), a stonemason from Padua, arrived in Rome to measure and draw the most famous monuments. By 1556 he had provided the plans, sections and elevations to illustrate a new interpretation of Vitruvius written by his patron Daniele Barbero of Venice. In 1570, at the summit of his career, Palladio published *I quattro libri dell'architettura*; by then he was acclaimed for his Venetian churches, the palazzos of Vicenza and the countryside villas of the Veneto. The most perfect of all these, from the perspective of setting and *symmetria*, is La Rotonda, built in 1565/6 on a hillside outside Vicenza, and also known as Villa Almerico (or Villa Capra after its subsequent owner). Although as a folly it is on the large side and far from quirky, it was considered to be a summer house and fulfilled the criteria of being intended for parties and recreation. It was situated to frame beautiful views across the olive trees and meadows towards the river and the surrounding amphitheatre of hills – and it was an exquisite architectural novelty. La Rotonda references the Pantheon in Rome, except that, for total symmetry, each of its four facades has a portico, approached by steps. This square/cruciform plan of the building exists within an imaginary circle, its circumference touching the four corners and also the centre point of each projecting portico. Within is another circle, the central hall, supporting the dome. The proportions are mathematically precise, as laid down in the *Quattro libri* (with the smallest adjustments to the lie of the land, so clever that the eye sees only harmony).[1]

By the end of the seventeenth century another architectural heritage, linked to the numerology of classicism but absorbing ideas more ancient and arcane, influenced theories of building. For Freemasons the skills and secrets of the masons' trade could be traced to the pyramids of Egypt and the descriptions of Solomon's Temple, however cryptic, in the Old Testament. Among the initiation rites came the question 'Where was the first lodge?' and the reply 'In the porch of Solomon's Temple.' Masonic ritual included a symbolic enactment of the assassination of Hiram, the legendary architect of Solomon's Temple, by his three apprentices. Many existing symbols gained added significance – pyramids, obelisks, sphinxes, pillars, portals, planets, keystones, compasses and an all-seeing eye. More in tune with rationalism and the Enlightenment was the concept of God as the divine architect, ordering the universe mathematically and creating a natural harmony that man (it did tend to be man in those days) must ascertain and obey. Such idealism encouraged personal morality, in theory anyway, and could cement political allegiances. In England this was especially so among the Whigs, who considered themselves guardians of the constitution, upholding order, just government and ancient rights.

For architectural inspiration there was no need to turn away from Vitruvius and the Roman orders, but increasing knowledge of the eastern Mediterranean countries added new architectural models. As early as 1646 John Greaves, a mathematician and antiquary, wrote *Pyramidographia*, and as the Royal Society flourished (Christopher Wren was president 1681–3) it sponsored accounts of Palmyra, Baalbek, Leptis Magna, Persepolis, Ephesus and Athens. Among Wren's own *Architectural Writings*, Tract II praised the structures of Byzantium and acknowledged his debt to St Sophia: 'This eastern way of vaulting by hemispheres', while in Tract V he described Egypt, the Tower of Babel and Solomon's Temple and pointed out that the classical orders were also 'Phoenician, Hebrew and Assyrian and founded on the experience of all ages'. Wren's links with early Freemasonry are hazy; records suggest he belonged by 1691, although the movement in England was not organized under the Grand Lodge of London until 1717.[2]

THE ENGLISH BAROQUE

The first Baroque architect in England to create follies was Sir John Vanbrugh (1664–1726) and their defining characteristic was weightiness. Sir John Soane later called his style 'a bold and irregular fancy', and Abel Evans suggested his epitaph should be:

> Lie heavy on him earth for he
> Laid many heavy loads on thee.[3]

But there was nothing ponderous about Vanbrugh's character, except perhaps the 'colossal geniality' ascribed to him by Pope. He was a man of charm, wit and enterprise. His father was a Flemish cloth merchant and sugar trader (the family wealth came from Barbados), his mother was from the English gentry and his brothers were naval commanders. Vanbrugh started in the cloth trade, joining the East India Company at eighteen and being posted to Surat – his sketch survives of monuments in the English cemetery of Surat, where the shapes of the tombs ranged from pyramids and domes to miniature shrines in the Indian style, which proves his early fascination with architecture.[4] On his return from India in 1686 Vanbrugh joined the conspiracy to replace James II with the Protestant William of Orange, which led to him being arrested in France as a spy. He was imprisoned for five years, but while under house arrest in the Château de Vincennes he used the opportunity to learn the rudiments of French Baroque architecture.

On his return to England Vanbrugh spent the 1690s as a theatre manager (he designed and founded the Haymarket Theatre) and as a playwright (the character of Sir John Brute in *The Provok'd Wife* became one of David Garrick's favourite roles). Politically he moved among the leading Whigs who, having successfully helped William III to the throne, ruled the roost. Many of them were Freemasons. They had been, and probably still were, conspirators, and their social rendezvous was the Kit-Cat Club. Originally they met in a tavern near Temple Bar, where the Strand and Fleet Street meet, owned by Christopher ('Kit') Cat, who was famous for his 'Kit-Cat' mutton pies. These, and the toasts that members drank from special Kit-Cat glasses, gave the club its name and convivial reputation. Influential journalists like Joseph

Addison and Richard Steele, founders of *The Spectator*, mixed with publishers and playwrights such as Vanbrugh and William Congreve, alongside diplomats, MPs, dukes, earls and future prime ministers. Godfrey Kneller the court artist painted them, completing over forty Kit-Cat portraits between 1697 and 1721.[5] They championed Protestantism, Parliament and constitutional monarchy, with France as the particular enemy supporting autocracy and the exiled Jacobite cause. Horace Walpole (whose father Robert was a Kit-Cat member) remembered them as the patriots who saved England. At the Kit-Cat Club Vanbrugh met Lord Cobham, creator of Stowe, one of the first great folly gardens, for whom he designed the Rotunda (1721) and the Lake Pavilions. As Vanbrugh's reputation increased, he became involved in massive building projects at Blenheim and Castle Howard. He was also involved in the Commission for Building Fifty New Churches (enacted in 1711), when he proposed the creation of new burial grounds on the outskirts of overcrowded London, in an echo of his youthful experience in Surat.

The first folly Vanbrugh built was the Belvedere at Claremont in Surrey. He bought the estate for himself in 1709, but in 1714 sold it to his fellow Kit-Cat member Thomas Pelham-Holles, later Duke of Newcastle and prime minister. Pelham-Holles invited him to enlarge the house and to build the Belvedere Tower on the highest hillside, with views as far as the Thames – a project Vanbrugh may already have determined upon – which was completed in 1717. It has the substantial air of a hunting lodge, if not a fort, with a square central section of arched windows and four square, crenellated towers rising above each corner. The approach is a sweeping grass vista between tall evergreens, recalling Vanbrugh's theatrical penchant. Perhaps in an effort to lighten the effect, the Belvedere was originally whitewashed, as can be seen in the background of the last Kit-Cat portrait ever painted, in 1721, which is uniquely a double one, of Thomas Pelham-Holles with his brother-in-law Henry Clinton, Earl of Lincoln, about to raise a toast in their Kit-Cat glasses.[6] The Belvedere was in fact then known as the White Tower, and below it in the 1720s Charles Bridgeman created the grass amphitheatre at Claremont, and the lake, which William Kent embellished with a grotto and a small island folly. Meanwhile, Vanbrugh was building his last folly, in 1725, in the grounds of Grimsthorpe Castle in Lincolnshire. It is reminiscent of the Claremont Belvedere in being robust yet elegant, and it may have been a

John Vanbrugh, Claremont Tower, Surrey, *c.* 1717, designed
for himself but sold on with the estate to the Duke of Newcastle.

Sir Godfrey Kneller, Kit-Cat double portrait of Thomas Pelham-Holles,
Duke of Newcastle, and Henry Clinton, Earl of Lincoln, c. 1721, with
Vanbrugh's Claremont Tower, painted white, in the background.

hunting lodge since it looks over a field where deer still frolic. If so, it served
a dual purpose as a summer house. Again the central pavilion is tall and rectangular, with arched windows and flanked by taller crenellated towers. Like
many follies nowadays it is approached along an unmarked lane and rears up
suddenly beyond the trees.

Vanbrugh's closest architectural associate was Nicholas Hawksmoor
(c. 1661–1736), who outlived him by ten years and completed his work at
Castle Howard, notably the Mausoleum. Ironically no follies are fully credited to Hawksmoor and it is hard to assess how much Vanbrugh relied on his
ideas and technical skill. Certainly they formed a complementary partnership
because, coming from a yeoman family in Nottinghamshire, Hawksmoor
lacked the confident charm needed to win aristocratic and political patronage.
Sir Christopher Wren first recognized his 'early skill and genius', taking him
on as a clerk at eighteen. Master and pupil shared a fascination with ancient
architecture and, although there are no records to prove that Hawksmoor
became a Freemason before 1730, it is very likely that Wren introduced him

earlier. As well as being a brilliant mathematician, Hawksmoor was a keen antiquarian: filling his work with references to Greek and Roman monuments, introducing pyramids over gateways and into churchyards, inserting decorative, oversized keystones as a Masonic symbol, puzzling over arcane measurements like the East Gate of Solomon's Temple (as described in Ezekiel), and, in his 'Explanation of the Obelisk proposed for Blenheim', relating it to the sun, as Freemasons would.[7]

It is above all for his six London churches, built following the Commission of 1711, that Hawksmoor is remembered; and if ever a church spire could count as a folly it is St George's, Bloomsbury. Here Hawksmoor was inspired by the pyramids and statues on the Mausoleum of Halicarnassus, another tantalizingly little-known wonder of the ancient world. The spire of St George's is a stepped pyramid topped by the figure of George I dressed as a Roman emperor. At the four corners of its base the lion of England and the unicorn of Scotland confront one another. Heraldically they act as supports for the royal coat of arms, but Hawksmoor contorted them dramatically to suggest they were fighting for the crown, a reference to the popular rhyme and the Jacobite rebellion of 1715.[8] William Hogarth, a prominent Freemason and, like his friend Hawksmoor, something of an outcast from the elite, paid him the doubtful tribute of including his iconic spire in the background of his notorious print of *Gin Lane*.

Also in this group of English Baroque architects was Thomas Archer (1668/9–1743), who came from the Warwickshire gentry and was the son of an MP. He spent four years on the Grand Tour and fell heavily under the influence of Bernini and Borromini developing a style often regarded as foreign and over-elaborate. For this he was criticized by the Puritan tendency, as exemplified in John Evelyn's *Account of Architects and Architecture* (1707), which even described the Corinthian column as 'tricked up and adorned like the wanton sex'. However, Thomas Archer's

Nicholas Hawksmoor, spire of St George's Church, Bloomsbury, London, designed c. 1716 and consecrated 1730, showing architectural and political features more characteristic of a folly.

Thomas Archer, Cascade House, Chatsworth, *c.* 1703, very ornamentally designed but also concealing pipes, which spouted water down the walls and into the long cascade.

position and patronage were secure since he was given a court appointment for life by Queen Anne. He too joined the Commission for Building Fifty New Churches, and his most famous, St John's Smith Square, earned the name 'Queen Anne's footstool'. It has four corner towers and monumental broken pediments, allegedly because, when he asked Queen Anne how it should look, she kicked over her footstool (she suffered from gout) and said 'like that'.[9] Archer's other churches are St Paul's Deptford and St Philip's Birmingham, and his most stately folly is the Grand Pavilion at Wrest Park, but his loveliest is the Cascade House at Chatsworth. It deserves a more fairy-tale name, because it is everything a folly should be. It was built around 1703 for the first Duke of Devonshire, a leading Whig politician and member of the Kit-Cat Club, who had Chatsworth house and garden much improved. The original cascade was built in 1696 by a French hydraulics engineer and was fed by water from the hill above. Later the system was improved, notably by Joseph Paxton around 1840. Archer's Cascade House reigns above a long sheet of water, descending gently over a series of elegantly shallow steps, while immediately in front two fountains play. Its unique grace owes much to a little stepped dome topped by a lantern, at the base of which nymphs and a river god recline. The entrance wall curves round in a semicircle, framed with rusticated stones and embracing two massive carved dolphins on either side of the doorway. Inside, trick jets of water sprang from spouts in the floor which are still visible (though harmless now). The whole pavilion was discreetly fitted with pipes, enabling the dome itself to pour forth water, which cascaded down over the walls. It looks Italianate, even slightly oriental, and would not be out of place in a story from the *Thousand and One Nights*.[10]

As the Cascade House was materializing, James Gibbs (1682–1754), another Baroque architect, whose best-known building was to be St Martin in the Fields, was travelling through Europe to Rome, ready in turn to fall under the spell of Bernini and be trained by his successor Carlo Fontana. Gibbs was Scottish, a Catholic and a Tory, but very quietly so, and this discretion earned him both Whig and Tory patrons. For Lord Burlington at Chiswick House, he designed (in 1716) the first folly in the grounds – a domed and colonnaded temple, sometimes called the Pantheon – as a focus for the vista from the main house. For Lord Cobham at Stowe, he created the Boycott Pavilions (1729–34), set emphatically either side of the approach road, and originally with pyramidal roofs that were later replaced with domes. Gibbs's most sensational folly, the Gothic Temple at Stowe, came later, when Lord Cobham had turned his back on classicism.

All these, in their different ways, might deserve Horace Walpole's jibe 'Gibbs like Vanbrugh had no aversion to ponderosity,' but Gibbs was able to synthesize Baroque and Palladian elements gracefully, as best exemplified by

Donald Insall's sketch of James Gibbs's The Octagon, Orleans House,
Twickenham, 1716, a graceful blending of baroque and Palladian elements.

the Octagon at Orleans House in Twickenham. Its owner, James Johnston, had been a diplomat who helped to secure the succession of George I when Queen Anne died, having spent time advantageously in Germany at the Hanoverian court, making friends. In 1716 Johnston commissioned the Octagon for the garden of his Thames-side home, specifically for lavish entertaining (a banqueting house in the modern sense), with cellars, kitchens and an extra room for fruit. James Johnston elected to depart from the flat Palladian style of his main house, because he appreciated that Hanoverian taste was more Baroque. To create the required effect Johnston chose Gibbs, partly because he was a fellow Scot but mainly because he was able to balance Baroque flourish with Palladian restraint. The eight walls are of yellow brick, framed by pilasters of deeper terracotta, enhancing the angles of the octagon. The lower windows are tall and arched and outlined with white stone, as are the circular windows above, rendering the building both light and ornate. Inside all is Baroque, with swags and busts, putti and pediments, pilasters and gilding, surrounding enormous royal portraits. Here the Johnstons entertained – according to the neighbours 'a vast deal of company daily'; 'he frequently has Mr Walpole and the greatest courtiers with him'; and in 1724 George I 'was pleased to dine . . . in a pleasant room joining to the house, from whence is a prospect every way into the most delicious gardens'. Later, James Johnston also became a favourite of George II's wife Queen Caroline, who was 'much entertained with his humour and pleasantry'. In 1729 she dined in the Octagon with her children on dishes which included venison, chicken with peaches and capons with oysters. They may have washed this down with Johnston's own wine, described as 'most excellent'; 'his slopes for vines, of which he makes hogsheads each year, are very particular.'[11]

THE NEO-PALLADIANS

The rivals of the Baroque architects were the neo-Palladians – Colen Campbell, Henry Flitcroft and later William Kent – centred on the enigmatic and taciturn figure of Lord Burlington, 'the Architect Earl' (1694–1753). He was a prominent Whig and member of the Kit-Cat club, but perhaps only from expediency. He was also a renowned patron of the arts (initially music and opera), but behind his zeal for Italian culture and his visits to Europe there may have been a very well-kept secret. His Grand Tours of 1714 and 1719 took place when there was intense activity among Jacobites in Belgium, France and Italy who were hoping to restore the Stuart monarchy. On examination, his itineraries may be better construed as links between Jacobite and papal agents rather than as architectural visits; for instance, in 1719 when he was ostensibly touring the Palladian villas of the Veneto, the region was flooded and largely inaccessible.[12] Not that Burlington's enthusiasm for Palladian architecture was assumed; he carried his copy of the *Quattro libri* on his travels and brought back a fine collection of Palladio's designs and 'drawings after the antique'. He also amassed the works of Inigo Jones, which he published in 1727 and 1736, and his library became a centre for the architectural avant-garde. Perhaps his tastes should be seen as replacing the lost world of the early Stuart monarchs – the time when Inigo Jones was designer to the court, when masques and architectural scenery bore titles like 'the Golden Age', and when the religious observances were Catholic in all but name. Although Burlington's final European visit was to Paris in 1726, his name continued to appear on secret lists sent to the Pretender's court, in 1733 and 1743, encouraging another uprising. Perhaps his great friend Alexander Pope, an acknowledged Catholic and Tory, hinted at this secret affiliation in his *Epistle to Burlington* in 1731–2, using words not simply related to garden architecture:

Let not each beauty everywhere be spied
Where half the skill is decently to hide.
He gains all points who pleasingly confounds
Surprises, varies and conceals the Bounds.[13]

In 1715, when Burlington returned from Italy, his first major project was Burlington House in Piccadilly, where James Gibbs, as Burlington's initial architect, straddled the divide between his own Baroque style and Palladianism. In 1716 Gibbs was involved at Chiswick House, Lord Burlington's Thames-side retreat, designing the Pantheon and possibly also the antique portal, the two follies which ended two vistas of the so-called 'goose foot'. This celebrated arrangement, more fashionably designated in French as *patte d'oie*, consisted of three radiating avenues, forming triangles which were heavily infilled by clipped hedges. They have been interpreted as the basis for a garden of Masonic symbols. Burlington himself designed the third folly ending the third vista of the goose foot – the Bagnio or Cassina – 'The First Essay of his lordship's happy Invention Anno 1717' as Colen Campbell called it, no doubt having himself overseen the technicalities. It appeared in the background of Burlington's portrait, painted by Jonathan Richardson in 1717–19, and in several subsequent views of the grounds. Campbell described it in

Jonathan Richardson, *Lord Burlington*, 1717–19, showing the
Bagnio he designed at Chiswick House in the background.

1725 as 'a little villa where my lord often dines'. Behind it the brook that
flows through the garden towards the Thames was dug out to form a scenic
waterway and pools, thus giving the name Bagnio more meaning (unless it
signified ritual cleansing in a Masonic sense). It was a lovely little building,
pale and slender with its two storeys rising to a domed lantern, long arched
windows and four Palladian urns adorning the flat roof projections. Defined
by these three follies the goose foot looked very theatrical, indeed reminiscent
of Palladio's own Teatro Olimpico in Vicenza, or the areas in some Italian

gardens designed for outdoor performances. In Rigaud's view of 1734, the figures in the foreground and those approaching along the avenues do recall actors on a stage. But the only hint that the area was used for opera, or other dramatic and musical performances, came in a letter from Alexander Pope: 'His gardens are delightful, his music ravishing.'[14]

By 1717 the Scottish architect Colen Campbell (1676–1729) was gaining the upper hand at Burlington House and ousting his fellow Scot James Gibbs. He too had travelled in Italy – from 1695 to 1702 – and returned with a vitriolic dislike of the Baroque: 'affected and licentious works', 'capricious ornaments', an endeavour 'to debauch mankind with odd and chimerical beauties'. Campbell championed Palladian principles, as transmitted via Inigo Jones, and marketed them as a return to British independence from foreign excesses. His *Vitruvius Britannicus; or, The British Architect* was published in three volumes between 1715 and 1725, loyally dedicated to George I, with excellent engravings (including Burlington's Bagnio) and at a very propitious

time, when landowners were embellishing their estates with buildings large and small, many of them follies. At Hall Barn, near Beaconsfield in Buckinghamshire, Campbell was responsible for one of the earliest and loveliest rotundas dedicated to Venus, built circa 1725. Probably the link here was the patronage of John Aislabie, stepfather of the owner, for whom Campbell also worked at Studley Royal in Yorkshire. It was possibly Colen Campbell who submitted an initial plan for the villa known as Chiswick House, which he modelled closely on La Rotonda (this plan was subsequently used for Mereworth Castle in Kent). But Burlington was seeking to recreate a Roman villa 'in the taste of the ancients', and browsing through his library of plans he selected a tasteful amalgam of measurements, windows, octagons and adornments, with one dome and one portico, that became neither Roman nor Palladian but certainly British. Since it was

Colen Campbell, The Rotunda, Hall Barn, Buckinghamshire, *c.* 1725. One of the earliest follies dedicated to Venus and an exemplar of English Palladian style.

Peter Andreas Rysbrack, *The Ionic Temple, Obelisk and Amphitheatre at Chiswick House*, built c. 1726, painted 1729–30. The best and most scenically situated of Lord Burlington's classical follies.

not built as a residence but as an architectural experiment, it might count as a folly, intended to house an art collection on the upper floor and the library and cellars underneath. It was also a Masonic lodge – the colours and dimensions of the upper rooms, and the symbolic ceiling paintings by William Kent, all indicate this. Nor was this a secret, since a contemporary verse extolled Burlington thus:

Then in our songs be justice done
To those who have enriched the Art
From Jabal down to Burlington . . .
Let noble Masons health go round
Their praise in lofty lodge resound.[15]

The villa was completed in 1729 during a decade of much activity at Chiswick, Burlington having married the heiress Dorothy Savile in 1721 and increased his available funds. The most iconic of the smaller Chiswick follies, known as the Ionic Temple, was built at this time, around 1726, presumably designed by Burlington himself and perhaps with Colen Campbell. It is circular, along the lines of the Pantheon, with a portico of Ionic columns (another such portico appears painted on the ceiling of the Red Velvet Room inside Chiswick House). The Ionic Temple's beautiful setting, known as the orange tree garden, consists of a circular pool centring on an obelisk and surrounded by a miniature amphitheatre of three stepped rings of grass. Their pleasing geometry may have contained an element of Masonic numerology, but in horticultural terms these grassy circles were where orange trees were placed in their white tubs during the summer months, weaving their own circles round the obelisk. It was against this background that Lady Burlington elected to have her portrait painted by Arthur Devis.[16] She is a lady all in white – a silvery satin dress, a lacy bonnet and a posy of white flowers in her hands; to her left is the white Ionic Temple and the obelisk frames the portrait on her right, while behind her are the green curves of the amphitheatre. Beyond, to the rear of the Ionic Temple, flows the water of the enlarged brook, where a utilitarian back door encourages the thought that the Ionic temple may have doubled as a boat house.

The decade in which Burlington built his villa and Ionic temple also saw the end of his association with Colen Campbell and the rise of Henry Flitcroft (1697–1769) as favoured architect. His father was a gardener at Hampton Court and Henry himself was apprenticed as a carpenter. He came to work at Burlington House, where he was unremarked until he fell from some scaffolding and broke a leg. On a sympathy visit Burlington realized his skill as a draughtsman and employed him to help prepare the designs of Inigo Jones for publication (in 1727). This architectural sponsorship earned Flitcroft the nickname Burlington Harry, and by 1726 he had gained a place in the Office of Works, where he rose to be Comptroller of the King's Works in 1758. By 1736 Flitcroft was in Yorkshire, involved in the palatial architecture of Wentworth Woodhouse, and there in 1748 he designed Hoober Stand, the first and strangest of his Triangular Towers, which commemorated the victory of the Duke of Cumberland at Culloden. A little later, in the 1750s, Flitcroft joined the Duke of Cumberland, who was Ranger of Windsor Great Park, in his ambitious alterations to the existing landscape – Thomas and Paul Sandby were creating Virginia Water – and near it Flitcroft built the second of his idiosyncratic triangular towers, which was originally known as Scrubs Hill, then renamed Fort Belvedere and finally Cumberland Lodge. This gothic folly tower was another startling move away from classical forms, a looming, three-sided curiosity, redolent of moonlight and hauntings. Flitcroft repeated the triangular idea at Stourhead when he designed Alfred's Tower,

Alfred's Tower, Stourhead, Wiltshire, designed by Henry Flitcroft and built 1772.
One of Flitcroft's trademark triangular towers, patriotically dedicated
to the memory of King Alfred defeating the Danes.

and he inspired several imitations – from Broadway in Gloucestershire to Powderham and Haldon in Devon. But despite this, it is for his superbly situated classical follies at Stourhead that Flitcroft is most admired, as a consummate example of how to place temples in an English landscape of lake, trees and gently rolling lawns.[17]

William Kent (*c.* 1685–1748) was the most individualistic of all Burlington's protégés. They met in Rome in 1714 and travelled together in 1719, becoming firm friends – an endearing example of the social fluidity that art, architecture and gardening could achieve, because Kent's origins were in humble Yorkshire stock, his education was minimal and his first painting skills were practised on coach panels and inn signs. Enthusiasm won him patronage and was fuelled by his years travelling, working and imbibing all the aesthetic experiences that Italy could offer. It was a love affair, and for the rest of his life Kent peppered his speech with Italian phrases and was known as the 'Signior' or 'Kentino'. On his return to London with Burlington in 1719 he became his lodger and worked primarily as a painter of interiors (of Chiswick House, Kensington Palace and Rousham). In more architectural mode he also worked alongside Henry Flitcroft, preparing the Inigo Jones archive for publication. Only in the 1730s did his unique gifts emerge, when he became involved in loosening the straight lines that rendered the gardens at Chiswick old-fashioned. The work intensified after 1733 when Burlington went into open opposition to Walpole over the Excise Bill, abandoned any pretence of Whig allegiance and made Chiswick his main residence.[18] Kent's efforts centred on the Exedra lawn, the area between the villa and the goose foot, bounded by the slope down to the water and the Ionic Temple on one side and the ha-ha and deer houses on the other. This Kent peopled with statues and sphinxes, framed by yews and cedars (some of the first in England), all to such effect, so theatrical and yet naturalistic, that his transformative touch was in wide demand – from the royal gardens at Richmond, Kew and Carlton House to Claremont, Rousham, Stowe and Badminton (to name only some).

At Badminton in 1746 Kent designed his largest folly for the Duke of Beaufort, known as Worcester Lodge (the earldom of Worcester was an older title). It served several purposes, as many follies did. As a gatehouse it guarded the entrance like a fortress, with the more mystical addition of two pyramid roofs on the service wings either side, which like the sphinxes of ancient Egypt let none pass who were unworthy. The rusticated stone of the ground floor adds almost brutally to this impregnable air. Above, smooth-stoned and domed, with the Beaufort arms in the central pediment, rose the 'grand room where the Duke dined in summer', full of Palladian grace.

William Kent, Worcester Lodge, Badminton, 1746, the largest folly Kent built, which functioned as gatehouse, viewfinder, banqueting house and hunting lodge.

The arches and rectangles of the windows and niches are so beautifully balanced that no incongruity is felt between the upper and lower halves of the building. The gatehouse was therefore also a banqueting house, and not just a summer house since the finely moulded ceiling of the dining room depicts the four seasons, and winter parties were entertained after riding, hunting and shooting. The gatehouse commands the highest point of the Badminton estate, looking across miles of countryside and certainly used to view the Beaufort hunt. It also served as a dramatic eye-catcher, such being another speciality Kent had developed.[19]

In 1734 the Earl of Carlisle at Castle Howard received a letter from Sir Thomas Robinson:

> There is a new taste in gardening just arisen, which has been practised
> with so great success at the Prince's garden in town [Carlton House]
> that a general alteration of some of the most considerable gardens in
> the kingdom is begun, after Mr Kent's notion of gardening viz.,
> to lay them out and work without level or line.[20]

This was Kent's approach as a painter and theatre designer, able to bring particular perspective skills to landscape scenery. Kent also remembered the dramatic *mise en scène* characteristic of Italian gardens, but was able in a more practical way to open and frame naturalistic vistas – as Horace Walpole put it to 'remove and extend perspective by delusive comparison'. Kent's working practice is evident in his drawings, not plans but romantic sketches, by moonlight sometimes, creating the scene and setting follies and statues among hillocks, grottos, pools and trees. In his drawings little boats drift by, horse-drawn carriages speed along drives and at Chiswick he allowed his humour full rein with a naughty little dog that chases rabbits and pisses against walls, and once even Lord Burlington's leg.[21] Three more of Kent's lively drawings show Alexander Pope and his grotto, further along the Thames at Twickenham, where Kent created a weird little shell house that collapsed after ten years. The poet was a keen ally of Lord Burlington, though originally more of an outcast, being Catholic, impecunious and unwell, but able to compensate for all this with his brilliant mind and keen wit. Pope's poetic sense was a major influence on the impressionable Kent, to whom he no doubt quoted many a relevant passage from the classics, and from his beloved Milton's *Paradise Lost* – because it was Milton who first suggested that paradise was a 'steep wilderness', 'shade above shade, a woody theatre of stateliest view'. There

Arthur Devis, *The James Family*, 1751. In the background the family estate displays the types of landscape which William Kent and later Capability Brown created and adorned with follies.

the river of Eden, 'through the shaggy hill . . . with many a rill watered the garden'. 'So lovely seemed that landscape' that even Satan paused to wonder at it.[22] In 1711 Pope made friends with the equally Tory Jonathan Swift and formed the Scriblerus Club (that being their satirical *nom de plume*). But sometimes Pope crossed the political divide to write for the Whig journalists Joseph Addison and Richard Steele, contributing to their *Guardian* and *Spectator.* They shared a passionate belief in making gardens more naturalistic (or more like a landscape painting by Claude Lorrain), and as influential writers they shared the honours with Burlington and Kent for spearheading the eighteenth-century landscape garden movement.

The other heroes of the movement were the gardeners themselves. Charles Bridgeman (?1690–1738) was credited with introducing the ha-ha, although it had existed in France since the 1660s, the difference being that in England the ha-ha was a device to roll the garden vistas into the countryside, whereas in France the formal contrast was maintained. Bridgeman prepared many of the landscape gardens, including Richmond/Kew, Rousham, Stowe and Claremont, where Kent later softened the contours, adding fresh glades and curves, follies and statues. It seems their partnerships were complementary and Bridgeman retained his position as the horticultural expert. Horace Walpole in his *History of Modern Gardening* gave credit where it was due, saying that Bridgeman (who had also worked on the Walpole estate at Houghton in Norfolk) made 'the leading step of all that followed', before adding his more oft-quoted accolade that Kent 'leapt the fence and saw all nature was a garden'.[23] Another practical gardener who was influential in the movement's developing phase was Stephen Switzer (*c.* 1682–1745), nurseryman, seedsman and garden designer, who, as early as 1715, was advocating that 'all adjacent country be laid open to the view'. Unlike Bridgeman he published his ideas, in *Ichnographia rustica* (1718 and 1742), reviling topiary, formality and the Dutch style as 'crimping, diminutive and wretched'. Switzer wrote of Liberty and the 'unbounded felicities of distant prospects'; of the merit of preserving woodland in its natural state – he extolled Wray Wood at Castle Howard in a memorable passage; and he suggested that, if necessary, a dip should be dug in one place to create a hill in another. By the time he published the 1742 edition of *Ichnographia,* Switzer had lived to welcome the emergence of the *ferme ornée* as an expression of his ideas.[24]

CAPABILITY BROWN
AND HIS ARCHITECTURAL ASSOCIATES

Capability Brown (*c.* 1715–1783), whose given name, Lancelot, has been inevitably replaced by his apt nickname, started his career as a gardener – unlike Kent, who trained him at Stowe in those visionary aspects of gardening without which he would not have earned such fame. Within a year of his arrival at Stowe in 1741, Brown was appointed head gardener and housed in the Western Boycott Pavilion (designed by James Gibbs), which became his family home until he moved to London in 1751. At Stowe, which was already a famous folly garden, Brown created the Grecian Valley, a long glade of grass between trees, chiefly admirable because it was for this that he invented a tree-moving machine, which enabled mature specimens to be planted rather than saplings, a basic element of his success in summoning instant landscapes into being. The accusation of his rival William Chambers that 'whole woods have been swept away to make room for a little grass' was less than just, since Brown planted thousands of trees with the aid of these machines. He was also expert at hydraulics, undismayed by diverting, draining, extending or damming water as required. He could ride round unsatisfactory or old-fashioned grounds and within an hour identify its 'capabilities'. Brown certainly appreciated the role of follies in a landscape garden, but to what extent he designed any is uncertain, since he worked in partnership with many architects and craftsmen. In 1795, in a letter to Humphry Repton, William Mason gave this enigmatic assessment of Brown's role as an architect of follies: 'he who disposes the ground and arranges the plantations ought to fix the situation at least, if not determine the shape and size of the ornamental buildings.'[25]

Of all the properties (estimated at over 170) that were altered or transformed by Capability Brown's skills, Croome Park in Worcestershire is the apogee, 'a scene of rural beauty and grandeur rarely surpassed', rescued by Brown from what its owner the Earl of Coventry described as a morass. Starting in 1752, miles of drainage culverts were dug to create a new 'Croome river' and to raise the depressingly low level of the lake (to the end of his life Brown was still keeping an eye and making adjustments). In 1765, still on the watery theme, Brown created a scenic grotto above the lake from roughly cut stones and cave-like archways, where springs trickled down to make a suitable home for a nymph. In the 1780s shells, corals, fossils and semi-precious stones were added, and in 1804 Sabrina's statue arrived, reclining half-naked with an urn from which waters should flow. According to Geoffrey of Monmouth, she was the divinity of the river Severn, and Milton had evoked her thus:

Sabrina fair, listen where thou art sitting
Under the glassy, cool, translucent wave.[26]

The other folly at Croome Park that Brown is believed to have planned himself is the Rotunda, built around 1754, a simple but finely proportioned round building with a shallow dome. Its walls of tawny limestone are encircled by tall pedimented windows and a matching glazed door; inside is a richly stuccoed interior. In 1763 the six carved panels with swags designed by Robert Adam were added to the exterior above the windows, an excellent final touch. The Rotunda is the folly nearest to the house, approached through the shrubbery and past herms; set beautifully among cedars, it is a fitting introduction to the elegant classicism that prevails throughout the grounds; 'seated on its proud eminence', said the 1824 guidebook, 'its great charm is its fine prospect' – because like so many follies the Rotunda is a viewfinder, gazing across to the Malvern Hills.

The earl was a keen plantsman, a collector of new exotics (like cedars), and in Brown he had a designer who knew exactly how to plant evergreens to enhance follies, and how to alternate various trees in the landscape to

The Rotunda, Croome Park, Worcestershire, built *c.* 1754, possibly to Capability Brown's own design, as he was relandscaping the grounds, then embellished by Robert Adam in 1763.

emphasize their contrasting beauties. The greenhouse was where the earl nurtured plants newly arrived from around the world (including the first wintersweet, *Chimonanthus*, from China in 1766). A greenhouse can be a folly when it looks like a temple and in the one here, built by Robert Adam in 1760 when he first joined Brown at Croome, the plants were placed in the finest and largest classical temple on the estate, fronted by six Doric columns supporting first a carved frieze, then a pediment festooned with fruit and flowers. In winter large windows were placed between the columns to protect the plants (the window slots are still visible in the floor) and there was underfloor heating from a furnace in the bothy behind. The side windows of the temple were originally niches containing statues of Ceres and Flora as presiding deities (while elsewhere in the grounds Pan reigned over the shrubbery).

Robert Adam (1728–1792) was the most eminent in a whole family of successful architects. His father William Adam was Scotland's foremost architect and author of *Vitruvius Scoticus*. At Chatelherault, on the outskirts of Glasgow, William had created a fine folly in Palladian style for the Duke of Hamilton, which combined banqueting rooms with hunting stables.[27] William had three sons, all of whom he trained. John, the oldest, continued the family business in Scotland; Dumfries House is his best-known work. Robert and James went to seek their fortunes in London, and what gave

Robert Adam the edge was the Grand Tour he undertook from 1754 to 1758, seeking instruction and drawing inspiration from classical antiquity, but no longer through the eyes of Palladianism, which he dismissed as 'ponderous and disgustful'. Instead he sought an interpretation that was less static, and described this as *movement* in architecture, by which he meant diversity and contrast. This was very much in tune with Capability Brown's gardens – Robert even explained his theories as the 'same effect that hill and dale, foreground and distance, swelling and sinking, have in landscape'.[28] For the conclusion of his Grand Tour Robert journeyed as far as the Dalmatian coast (Croatia), being determined to view the ruins of Diocletian's Palace at Spalato (Split). He saw the ruins first from the sea – the long, arcaded facades rising against the mountains, the different orders of columns and rich friezes, the emperor's tomb – and he recorded them all in a monumental work of descriptions and engravings. Small wonder that on his return to practise in London (in partnership with his brother James) he worked mainly in a classical style, and subsequently his follies fitted ideally into Capability Brown's landscapes, as at Croome Park. Another fine example is Audley End in Essex. First, in 1771–2, he designed a Temple of Victory here along the lines of the Temple of Vesta at Tivoli, to celebrate the end of the Seven Years War (an inspiration provided by military victory, shared with a number of other follies). Ten years later he excelled himself with a unique tea house that served also as a bridge, a

Robert Adam, Tea House Bridge, Audley End, Essex, c. 1780, admired for its exquisite proportions and qualifying as a folly by combining a bridge with a tea house.

James Wyatt, Panorama Tower, Croome Park, Worcestershire, 1801–12, one of the finest follies inspired by the Temple of Vesta at Tivoli.

deceptively simple loggia on four Ionic columns, but so graceful with the river Cam reflecting and rippling beneath that his claim to create movement in architecture was entirely vindicated.

Other architects also worked for the Earl of Coventry at Croome Park, including Adam's great rival James Wyatt (1746–1813), who designed the Panorama Tower – possibly following a design by Robert Adam himself, who was dead by 1801 when the commission began. Years earlier Adam had accused Wyatt of plagiarism, to which Wyatt had replied that the Adam brothers had so corrupted public taste that no other manner was fashionable. He belied his own retort by earning celebrity as a master of the gothic style, adding towers, spires and battlements as required by advocates of the Picturesque. Thus he first appeared on the scene at Croome Park, in 1794, to create a distant eye-catcher on Broadway Hill, 15 miles from Croome on the Gloucestershire border. The story goes that, before agreeing to the project, the Countess of Coventry had a beacon lit on Broadway Hill to ensure that not only she, but all the neighbouring gentry for miles around, would be able to see it. She need not have doubted. Ever since, Broadway Tower has been everybody's best-known eye-catcher, and for those who climb, thirteen counties are said to be visible from it. Being Wyatt, he borrowed Flitcroft's idea of triangularity to make his tower more striking.

Since Wyatt had done the Grand Tour, six years of it from 1762 until 1768, he was also masterly in the classical style, but enough of a maverick to manipulate it to great effect. In 1772 his highly fashionable career took off with the opening of the Pantheon in Oxford Street, a great domed interior with two storeys of columned galleries and niches for statues, irresistible even to the most aristocratic shoppers. When it came to the Panorama Tower on the outskirts of Croome Park, he dramatized the Temple of Vesta prototype with internal archways, looking shadowy and theatrical inside the outer columns, while above a pretty balustrade circled the flat roof to create a viewing platform. An upper storey supports the dome, and inside it is the summer house/hunting lodge/viewfinder, built high above the grounds of Croome Park so as to admire the house, the Brownian landscape, the hunt and all across the surrounding countryside. The increasing spread of follies towards the outskirts of great estates, as exemplified at Croome, reflected the growing fashion for excursions on horseback or in coaches, not only for hunting but to enjoy the great outdoors for its own sake and for the varying scenery, to which Capability Brown had contributed in opening people's eyes. On the other hand, there was no intriguing narrative to be unravelled in a Lancelot Brown garden. Many found them formulaic, for example Mrs Delany: 'The garden is no more! A fine lawn, a serpentine river, wooded hills, gravel paths meandering through a shrubbery'; or Horace Walpole, with deceptive mildness: 'his representations of nature are so true to life that they risk passing unnoticed'; or William Chambers, his most virulent opponent, after Brown had relandscaped Kew Gardens: 'he turned to lawn what once was fairy land.'[29]

INDIVIDUALISM, ORIENTALISM, ECCENTRICS AND GOTHICS

Like James Wyatt, William Chambers (1723–1796) was capable of producing fine follies in the classical style. By way of architectural qualification, he spent from 1749 to 1755 in Rome, and his grandest project was Somerset House in the Strand. His classical follies included the Temple of Pan at Osterley in west London (along the lines of the Temple of Fortuna Virilis); the charming neo-Palladian Casino at Wilton House in Wiltshire; and the far more ambitious Casino at Marino near Dublin – so lavish in detail that Lord Charlemont had to sell land to pay for it. The building, which takes the form of a Greek cross, is raised on a pedestal with lions guarding the four corners. Twelve Doric columns outline the walls and support an ornate frieze, plus pediments, balustrades, statues, swags and two great urns acting as chimneys.[30]

But the expertise for which Chambers was most famous, admired and mocked in due measure was his knowledge of Chinese style. He was the son of a Scottish merchant resident in Stockholm, and as a supercargo he voyaged with the Swedish East India Company between 1742 and 1749, visiting India and China. Although, like all Europeans in China, he was confined to the Company factories of Canton, he absorbed all he could of Chinese culture, and his subsequent work fed into the great fascination with oriental style which already existed in Europe. Chambers launched his architectural

William Chambers, Chinese Pavilion at Amesbury Abbey, Wiltshire, 1772,
a rare example of the chinoiserie architecture for which he claimed expertise.

reputation with *Designs for Chinese Buildings* in 1757; followed in 1763 by *Plans, Elevations etc of the Gardens and Buildings at Kew*, based on his architectural work for the young George III, including the iconic Pagoda. In 1772 came his *Dissertation on Oriental Gardening*, in which he described the Chinese emphasis on nature's contrasts and 'beautiful irregularities'. Ironically this contributed to the French referring to landscape gardening as *jardins anglo-chinois*. Also in 1772 Chambers created another chinoiserie folly, at Amesbury in Wiltshire, more in the spirit of a Chinese garden pavilion than those at Kew. It evokes the sense that here a Chinese sage might read, write poetry, paint or fish. The owners of Amesbury Abbey, in whose grounds the folly still stands hidden, were the Duke of Queensbury and his duchess, Kitty, 'pretty, witty Kitty' as Pope called her, who dressed gorgeously and was not afraid to insult George II or lead demonstrations to Parliament. She was the patron of John Gay, who wrote *The Beggar's Opera* but then fell foul of the censors for mocking Robert Walpole and subsequently spent long periods at Amesbury, where there was once a grotto known as Gay's Cave. Chambers's Chinese Pavilion was built after Gay's time, over the remnants of an earlier effort, on a bridge over a tributary of the river Avon. The walls are of knapped flint, arranged in quasi-Chinese patterns, the unglazed windows are round, and the deep projecting eaves are reddish, with a Chinese key pattern. Steps lead up to a fretwork balustrade, which also serves for the bridge, and the undergrowth all around threatens to engulf this romantic spot, as it has in the past.

Designing follies for a living would suggest a degree of eccentricity and in one case it may have been a sign of frustrated genius. Thomas Wright (1711–1786), the son of a Durham carpenter, showed exceptional mathematical ability and was apprenticed to a clockmaker. From there he progressed to navigational instruments and London, then astronomy and, in 1750, a Theory of the Universe (distant galaxies) to which Immanuel Kant admitted he was indebted: 'in this great celestial creation . . . general doomsdays may be as frequent as birthdays are with us.'[31] Wright's love of astronomy never left him, and after he retired home to Durham in 1785 he built himself a small observatory tower in Westerton, round with buttresses and arrow slits, which might not be regarded as a folly but for his wizardly reputation. Wright lived at a time when experimental science and observation were occupations for the gentry, even royalty, and he was invited to read papers to the Royal Society, but he was not made a Fellow. Perhaps his origins were too humble; his 'awkward formality' was mentioned, and his oddity:

> His temper was gentle and affable and his mind was generous, but
> his studies . . . left him very little conversant with the ordinary duties
> of life. There was something flighty and eccentric in his notions,
> and a wildness of fancy followed even his ordinary projects.[32]

So Thomas Wright led a peripatetic life, serving aristocratic families in need of a tutor, happy to have access to their great libraries, fascinated by literature and theatre, embracing Freemasonry – and, as his design skills became apparent, designing follies. In 1755 and 1758 he published *Universal Architecture*, of which Book I offered six original designs for arbours and Book II six grottos. His favoured materials were tree trunks, preferably 'the roughest bark of oak variegated and compartmented with knots', or roughly hewn stones 'such as would serve for a Grotto of the Antique Ruin kind, supposed to have been the Abode of an Anchorite'.

Wright's longest association was with the dukes of Beaufort at Badminton, where he was both tutor and hermit and where he ennobled a number of farm buildings with castellated facades. Probably his finest follies were built for Lord Halifax, but it was on the estate of another fervent Freemason that his most intriguing folly was built. Sir Charles Kemeys-Tynte created a folly garden at Halswell in Somerset that has barely survived. Classic temples and

William Hogarth, *Sir Charles Kemeys-Tynte with the Bathstone Bridge at Halswell*,
c. 1753, showing the importance Sir Charles attached to the work of Thomas Wright.

idiosyncratic monuments hint at a Masonic sequence relating to initiation. There is a stepped pyramid on a Masonic cube setting the scene near the house; it covers a spring and there is an obliterated inscription. Another inscription found in the grounds reads: 'Passanger prepare for chaunge.' Thomas Wright's own involvement was with the bridge and grotto that formed dams on the lakes and cascades of Mill Wood. Here the initial inscription referred to Moses striking the rock and 'forth gushed the stream'. Wright's grotto has a series of three arches and niches, scenic but not arresting, while the Bathstone Bridge defies interpretation. Its attribution to Wright is authenticated by his surviving sketch, entitled 'Breakwater', and its significance is proved in a portrait by William Hogarth of Sir Charles Kemeys-Tynte (*c.* 1753) looking affluent and jovial, with the Bathstone Bridge in the background (this of all his follies being the one selected and immortalized in paint).[33] The Bridge, like the grotto, has three arches, a perfect number for Freemasons: two below, through which the water flows, and a larger one above, which forms a semicircular niche like an apse. The proportions of these three arches recall the ruins of the Baths of Diocletian in Rome, and the 'apse' has an accoustic echo like a miniature Roman amphitheatre. There are stone carvings of rockwork and shellwork on either side of the 'apse' that slope upwards towards the pediment above it, and at either end of the bridge herms were placed, although only one, which is female, remains. There was a reference to the herms in Sir Charles's diary for August 1756: 'very early in the wood with Lady Tynte to fix the homogenius', a name which would certainly suit such a curious and forbidding creature, emerging from its leafy sheath. This sheath consists of reeds, a decoration also to be found in the plasterwork of the main house. Nor was Hogarth the only great artist to record Wright's handiwork at Halswell, and in the process to add to its allure. In 1987 John Piper painted both the Grotto and the Bathstone Bridge in colours befitting enchantment.

John Piper, *The Grotto, Halswell*, 1987, showing the homunculus on the bridge in the glowing, atmospheric colours typical of Piper's architectural studies.

The fashion for follies in the gothic style was a mid-eighteenth-century phenomenon, but the seeds went back earlier. The influence and designs of Batty Langley (1696–1751) should not be ignored, though people tended to do so because he was another eccentric, and because the subsequent arbiter of all things gothic, Horace Walpole, dismissed all he did as 'clumsy efforts which those who know nothing of the matter mistake for imitations'.[34] Bartholomew (for which Batty is an abbreviation) started work alongside his father, who was a gardener in Twickenham, and rapidly grew to be a garden designer. He was a friendly and convincing self-publicist, a prolific writer and a Freemason. His first book, *Practical Geometry* (1726), followed Switzer's *Ichnographia rustica* (1718) in advocating naturalism, as expressed by meandering paths and trees that retained the shape God gave them, and above all replacing the symmetry of formal gardens with variety and surprise – hence the need for 'Ornamental Buildings of Delight'. In the 1730s Batty moved to London and set up as an architect, running a building school in Soho which taught both craftsmen and gentry how to improve parks and gardens; instruction included how to design geometric plans and elevations for temples, hermitages, caves, grottos, cascades and theatres – meaning that, although Batty's name is generally absent from garden records, his designs were influential at this period. He also wrote for the *Grub Street Journal*, advocating a return to native 'Saxon' architecture as opposed to the foreign styles of the Romans and Palladians. These ideas certainly took root, while his vigorous attacks on classical design won him enemies. Basically his efforts, being a Freemason, were directed at giving classically perfect proportions to buildings with a gothic character – hybrids in fact. In 1742 he published *Ancient Architecture*, in which this synthesis was the prevailing theme.

The most delightful example of Batty Langley's slightly questionable achievements is the Gothic Temple at Bramham Park in Yorkshire, built in 1750. The setting was perfect, being a great formal garden of radiating vistas between high hedges, canals and geometric pools, but inviting in the landscape with a ha-ha and leaving the woodland and contours of the garden to nature. The layout was created by Robert Benson (later Lord Bingley, MP for York and Chancellor of the Exchequer) after his return from the Grand Tour in 1697. Most of the follies (Doric and Ionic temples) were added after 1750 by his son-in-law and heir George Lane Fox, in order to create statements at the ends of vistas, but the Gothic Temple is from Plate 57 of Batty Langley's *Gothic Architecture*, which is in turn an adaptation of James Gibbs's classical/Baroque design for the Octagon at Orleans House (where Batty Langley

Gothic Temple, Bramham Park, Yorkshire, designed by Batty Langley and built by James Paine, *c.* 1750, an example of how gothic style was blended with classical proportions.

gardened as a youth). At Bramham Park the pilasters became buttresses for the Gothic Temple, the window arches became pointed and ogee gables with trefoils completed the transformation. Prettily situated on a stretch of lawn known as the bowling green, it may once have been a sporting pavilion as well as a summer house – in which case it links with another folly attributed to Batty Langley, the Bowling Green House built around 1740 at Wrest Park. The latter is not gothic but, as proof of Batty's versatility, it consists of a classical rectangle with Ionic columns, a balustraded roof and dainty wings with slanting roofs on either side.

All the neo-gothic architects had classic strings to their bows, just as classicists like Robert Adam could create a startlingly gothic fantasy like the Brizlee Tower, on the Alnwick estate in Northumberland. The actual builder of Bramham Gothic Temple was James Paine (1717–1789), an important architect in his own right, sponsored originally by Lord Burlington, honoured with a portrait by his friend Joshua Reynolds, and a builder mainly of stately homes and bridges. He created other follies at Bramham, including the square Ionic Temple (*c.* 1760) with a balustraded portico which was originally an orangery and banqueting house. So too, on a more magnificent scale, was Paine's Temple of Diana at Weston Park in Staffordshire, built for

Henry Bridgeman, later Earl of Bradford, who inherited in 1762 and employed Capability Brown to improve his parkland. In 1770 Paine's Temple of Diana became the centrepiece, an arcaded orangery superbly glazed between Ionic pilasters and backing onto a domed and winged pleasure pavilion. The other virgin goddess Minerva (Athene) already had a temple designed by James Paine (*c.* 1755) at Hardwicke Hall, Sedgefield, Co. Durham, where a cube surmounted by a domed octagon was rendered into a beautiful eye-catcher and viewfinder by twenty Ionic columns, creating a covered, square colonnade all around the building. Inside and out Minerva's wise and heroic attributes were recalled by busts and statues of supposedly appropriate Greeks and Romans.

Although he did not inaugurate the Gothic Revival, Sanderson Miller (1716–1780) is regarded as its greatest architectural exponent, master of castellated ruins that evoke the Middle Ages on distant hillsides. As the son of a rich wool merchant of Warwickshire he was sent to Oxford and, as well as developing his antiquarian interests and social bonhomie, he made important friends including the future Earl of Coventry of Croome Park. His gift for friendship remained wide-ranging, from the practical Lancelot Brown to those fierce critics of society Dean Swift and Horace Walpole. As an architect he remained a gentleman amateur whose designs were offered free, and therefore in the records the professionals got the payments and the credit. This was probably the case at Croome Park, where Capability Brown was credited with building the house itself, though almost certainly he oversaw work on a design that originated with Sanderson Miller, who first introduced Brown to the earl. However, the house at Croome is not gothic and, that being Miller's special attribute, credit went to him instead for the eye-catcher to Croome on Dunstall Green. There, three slender towers loom with blind windows and the remnants of battlements, joined by two elongated archways, also in a pleasingly ruinous state. However, this sham ruin was not built until 1784, by which time Sanderson Miller was dead, and Robert Adam wrote to the earl: 'I think it might be built to have a good effect at a distance and at no great expense as there does not require much delicacy in the workmanship' – which sounds very like a builder asked to work on another man's design.[35]

If Dunstall Castle could be regarded as Sanderson Miller's posthumous folly, his first was for his own home at Radway Grange, which he inherited in 1737; ten years later he built the folly Radway Tower, to mark the supposed spot where Charles I raised the standard at Edgehill (the first memorable but inconclusive battle of the English Civil War, in 1642). Radway is an octagonal tower with thin protruding battlements modelled on Guy's Tower at

Sanderson Miller, Dunstall Castle, Croome Park, Worcestershire, built in 1784 but attributed as posthumous since it is typical of his graceful sham castles which led the fashion.

Warwick Castle, though Miller drew romantic inspiration from other fine ruins in the area, at Kenilworth, Banbury and Oxford. Like many follies, Radway Tower became a centre for social gatherings. The inaugural dance was held in September 1750; guests entered the tower by a drawbridge and mounted to 'a fine octagon gothic room with four windows and some old painted glass', or they could proceed further upwards to view the Cotswolds, the Malvern Hills and the Welsh border.[36] Simultaneously Miller was working on Hagley Tower in Worcestershire, the most admired of his sham ruins, which connected him to some of the most politically active families of the time. From this came another commission in 1749, to build a ruined tower at Wimpole Hall in Cambridgeshire for Philip Yorke, the Lord Chancellor (and soon to be first Earl Hardwicke).[37] It was not built until 1772, for the second earl, and again Capability Brown acted as overseer, possibly because by that time Miller was succumbing to periodic bouts of insanity. It is far more eerie than his other ruins: four storeys with hollow staring windows and arrow slits, grey and defensive, and with broken walls stretched on either side. Even Lord Hardwicke's instructions sound bleak: 'As the back view will be immediately closed by the wood there is no regard to be had to it, nor to the left side, but only to the front and right side as you look from the house.' Most follies aroused more affectionate enthusiasm than that.

While Sanderson Miller's reputation caused more sham ruins to be attributed to him than he actually built, another confusion existed at that time, typical of many follies, when one architect was commissioned to finish or improve another's initial design; or a local mason might build a folly on the instructions of his patron armed with a pattern book. Architects burnished their reputations by issuing such pattern books, often entitled 'Plans, Elevations etc.' and, like the follies themselves, their numbers increased with the fashions. One of the most enchanting was William Wrighte's *Grotesque Architecture or Rural Amusement,* published in 1767 and reissued several times. It consisted of 'retreats and grottos – many of which may be executed with flints, irregular stones, rude branches and roots of trees'. They needed only a marrow-bone floor, a skull or an owl to complete their gothic authenticity. Some flaunted oriental attributes: minarets, crescent moons or fretwork. All types and conditions of follies and their builders appear in the following chapters.

Three

Telling a Story

The idea that as one walked around a garden a story would unfold began in sixteenth-century Italy. The narrative depended mainly on statues, while architectural forms like terraces, temples, niches and grottos made the setting theatrical. The representations of ancient gods and heroes recalled their exploits and transgressions – and their beauty. Such a garden, by offering different routes, contained an element of chance; while choosing the direction and puzzling over meanings could suggest a serious quest, or could be fun, it certainly involved deciphering a wealth of literary allusion. The most fruitful classical sources were Virgil's *Aeneid* and Ovid's *Metamorphoses*, added to which a popular contemporary author had set his adventures in a garden. In 1499 Francesco Colonna, a Venetian monk with a fine line in erotic innuendo, anonymously published *Hypnerotomachia Poliphili* (anglicized as *Poliphilus' Dream*), lavishly printed by Aldus Manutius with 168 woodcut illustrations – a collector's item. Poliphilus, restless from the miseries of rejection, dreams of reaching his beloved Polia (who under the guise of an elusive girl might be the meaning behind all things, which the name Polia suggests). His quest begins in a dark and labyrinthine wood and includes escaping from a dragon into a cave, struggling over and through the body of a colossus, hearing strange echoes, drinking from inspirational springs and choosing one of three portals. Once in the garden he joins Polia and encounters triumphal processions and architectural follies. There are mysterious inscriptions and antique remains. They take a boat to the island of Venus; Poliphilus mislays his love again and wakes up.[1]

Introducing the grotesque to emphasize the beautiful, and to arouse curiosity, was a feature of Italian Renaissance gardens. Leonardo da Vinci described his own sensations: 'And after having remained at the entry some time, two contrary emotions arose in me, fear and desire. Fear of the threatening dark grotto, desire to see whether there was any marvellous thing within it.'[2] He could be describing the gaping monster mouth at Villa Aldobrandini, or the colossal statue of Appennino at Pratolino, where a personification of the mountain range with a melancholy bearded head broods over the water (inside the rock-hewn giant was a network of grottos and fountains). The Boboli Gardens in Florence had a fountain of harpies, and among the water features at Villa d'Este in Tivoli were grotesque heads, transformations worthy of Ovid, and the goddess Diana with a multitude of breasts. Some have discerned hints of initiation rituals, coming through terror to understanding, and no garden comes closer to this possibility than Bomarzo.

BOMARZO: MONSTROUS FANTASIES

In the mid-sixteenth century Vicino Orsini, Duke of Bomarzo, turned his back on the symmetries and refinements normal in Italian gardens and used the woodland in the valley below his family castle to make his own extraordinary itinerary, naming it the *Sacro Bosco* or Sacred Grove. The area around Bomarzo has Etruscan remains, carved tombs and a stepped pyramid with sacrificial altars, making it already hallowed ground in an archaic sense that chimed with Orsini's humanism and scepticism. Originally Bomarzo was intended to be a Garden of Epicurus, where refinements of pleasure and art were the only reality, but Orsini was a *condottiere* in the papal army, often away making war, and in 1553 he was captured and held prisoner in Germany for three years, ending his military career. It was only after his return that he started adding *cosi stravaganti*, extravagant images hewn from the natural volcanic rock. Then in 1560 his wife Giulia Farnese (namesake of the infamous 'wife' of the Borgia Pope) died, leaving him heartbroken, so that a concept already formed was dedicated to her memory, adding a sense of doom and another layer of incongruity to the phantasmagoria. In 1578 a friend of Orsini, after reading a book on Arcadia, wrote wistfully: 'Reading the present volume I have found descriptions of hills and valleys which recall Bomarzo and gave me the greatest longing for it,' and the following year Orsini himself wrote: 'I can find relief only in my beloved forest, and I bless the money I have spent and continue to spend on this magical place.'[3] But if the site of Bomarzo is lovely in an Arcadian sense, it guards strange secrets and seems fragile and threatened by the monsters within.

Even the point of entrance to Bomarzo remains uncertain. At one gate are two sphinxes, which traditionally used riddles to bar the way against the unworthy, and the first plinth reads, 'You who enter this place, observe it piece by piece, and tell me afterwards whether so many marvels were created for deception or for art';[4] more enigmatic inscriptions proliferate

Casa Pendente and the Theatre, Bomarzo, Italy, c. 1510, a fantasy garden
that led the way in creating folly buildings with a dream-like narrative.

along the way. There is another doorway to the garden and a unique folly
building, the Casa Pendente, leaning at 30 degrees, not ruined but strangely
reminiscent of the Tower struck by lightning in the tarot pack. Tarot cards
were first recorded in the fourteenth century and became widespread in the
courts and taverns of Italy, though the Church denounced them as a ladder
to hell. Their 21 trumps (*trionfi* or 'triumphs' in Italian) were always viewed
as subversive, partly because they included death, a fool, a female pope, a
hanged man and the ill-fated tower. Sometimes the iconography of a tarot
card shifted, and the Tower either showed a man falling from its summit or,
in a Florentine version, morphed into the gates of paradise with Adam and
Eve being expelled. If Orsini was intrigued by tarot symbolism and included
it in his dreamscape, perhaps the imposing lines of oversized pine cones and
acorns, urns and vases, were reflections of the four suits, which originally

represented male and female objects. The black suits of the tarot pack were portrayed as swords and clubs sprouting leaves, the red suits were receptacles, chalices and platters, and originally the suits were hallows to summon the gods of fertility. There is another processional row at Bomarzo, formed by male and female herms, the fertility gods of Greek and Roman gardens, with carved baskets of fruit on their heads and leaves masking their genitals.

Next to the Casa Pendente is a more exquisite folly, a small mock amphitheatre – not designed for use but signalling the dramas ahead. Its semicircular stone backdrop is a retaining wall (with a line of giant urns above) and it has empty niches suggesting absent figures. The centre of the stage is a circle of mossy grass edged by shallow steps rising in concentric circles. These could represent the seating pattern of a classical theatre, except that the steps go downwards from the centre and not upwards. This makes them look more like a circular labyrinth, the kind that was used as a dancing floor, into the centre and out again. If a labyrinth was intended, one of Orsini's sources was Virgil's *Aeneid*, Book v, which described the funeral rites of Anchises, Aeneas' father, culminating in a circular dance by young Trojans on horseback which 'recreated the twists and turns of the Cretan labyrinth'. Book vi contains the great prototype of otherworld journeys, in which Aeneas saw the labyrinth carved on the gates of the underworld – 'the wandering track which might not be unravelled' – and after entering the underworld discovered the future of Rome from the ghost of his father, Anchises.

The tarot pack also contains a labyrinth, disguised as the Wheel of Fortune. In the popular woodcut tradition of the cards (rather than the courtly versions) the tarot wheel retains a clue to its labyrinthine origin, because monstrous animals cling to the wheel instead of people, their claws, hoofs, tails and general ugliness suggesting that, like devils in hell, they were descended from the creatures which haunted the journey of the soul in the legends of the ancient world – sphinxes, harpies, Cerberus – all of which are to be found at Bomarzo among the monstrous statues. The name of Orsini's garden, the *Sacro Bosco*, is also Virgilian, since Aeneas' descent to the underworld began in a sacred grove, where he had to pluck the golden bough as a talisman for his safe return. 'All the forest gives it protection, and it is enclosed by shadows in a valley of little light . . . if it is indeed you whom the Fates are calling it will come easily, if not, by no strength will you remove it.'[5] These were the words of Virgil's Sibyl, a wild prophetic creature whose shrine was in a cavern with 'a hundred openings through which the [S]ibyl's answer comes forth in rushing streams of sound'.

Hell's Mouth, Bomarzo, *c.* 1510, used as a banqueting
house and introducing humour to the scenario.

The third and most famous folly at Bomarzo has been called Hell's Mouth,
the gaping entrance to a head with fiercely staring eyes like a gorgon. It alludes
to the Sibyl's cavern because the acoustics allow any whisper from inside to be
clearly heard outside. Over the open mouth is inscribed *Ogni pensiero vola*,
'all thoughts fly', clearly a reference to the echo, but the words are poised
enigmatically between solemnity and humour, allowing several interpretations. It recalls the inscription over the gates of Dante's *Inferno* (which had a
gorgon's head above it), 'Abandon all hope you who enter,' and the Bomarzo
words could be taken to mean abandon thought (or reason) as you enter.[6]
Contrariwise this could be an invitation to be carefree and witty, because
inside the cavern is a table where those who entered could eat, drink and be
merry, after being 'eaten' by the monster's mouth. It may seem a dark and
dubious pleasure, but in the summer heat it would be cool and, as Leonardo
suggested, enticing.

The paths through the *Sacro Bosco* lead upwards past monsters and scenes of conflict: a giant in the act of tearing another in half; a dragon confronting two lions; a war elephant capturing a soldier in its trunk. All are possibly sublimating Orsini's experiences in war, or replicating visions of hell. And what is to be made of the gigantic tortoise, always proverbially slow, with the windswept figure of fame or victory on its back, or another gaping monster mouth, known as the Mask of Madness, with emblems of the Orsini on its head, a globe topped by a lantern?[7] As in a dream there is no apparent sequence among the monstrosities. An enormous stone nymph lies sleeping on the ground; an equally colossal and mossy Ceres sits serenely with an urn-like cornucopia on her head. Very near the steps to the summit Cerberus and Persephone face one another, here incongruously guarding the way to paradise, not hell. Persephone's legs form a seat, but everyone in Orsini's time knew that her seat in hell was a trap where one stuck fast. Up the steps the wood clears, opening into daylight and grass underfoot. At journey's end, the fourth folly is the classical Temple of Eternity, dedicated to Giulia Farnese. The proportions are Vitruvian, a rectangle with an octagonal dome. The unusual beauty is in the entrance: mounting the curving steps past 'Etruscan' carvings and entering the double-columned portico under the archway cut into the pediment. It is very calm and sophisticated after the rough-hewn statues, as if civilization had triumphed over psychosis. The narratives of other folly gardens never aspired to be as surreal as Bomarzo, or as hard to understand. It was too mysterious and ugly to be emulated. But, by providing the shock of the new, it proved that garden landscapes could be used, with statues, buildings and thought-provoking wit, to tell a story that felt both personal and universal.

CASTLE HOWARD: A TRIUMPHAL PROGRESS

The name of Castle Howard, the first and most monumental of England's folly gardens, hints at its baronial character but not its grand scale. It was created for the third Earl of Carlisle, a member of the Howard clan, who were all descended from the first Duke of Norfolk. They rose to power under the Tudors and two lost their heads; but the ancestor of the earls of Carlisle, Lord William Howard, married into the Dacre family of Yorkshire, inheriting their land and wealth including Henderskelfe Castle, the medieval fortress on whose site Castle Howard was built. The project was conceived at the Kit-Cat Club in 1699, when the youthful Charles Howard, wishing to take full advantage of his earldom and his almost limitless wealth, met the ebullient theatre impresario John Vanbrugh. Carlisle was surely right in thinking, at that moment in time, that no mere architect could have combined landscape and buildings so boldly and to such effect. The vision was Vanbrugh's, the faith was Carlisle's and a vital third element depended on Hawksmoor, whom Vanbrugh took into partnership both at Castle Howard and Blenheim. It is impossible now to disentangle the ideas of one from the other; they apparently worked perfectly together, starting with Castle Howard itself, a massive Baroque pile which presents a forceful aspect on the public south front and a more ornamental, even playful, aspect to the north, which faces over the garden and features Corinthian pilasters and statues of goddesses.

The 3-mile approach to Castle Howard takes full advantage of the undulations of the land to emphasize its grandeur, first dipping to pass through the Carrmire Gate, then rising along a steeply banked road towards the Pyramid Gate, where through its archway appears a view of the Obelisk reaching into the sky, compelling the road to swoop towards it. But this is not the order in which they were built. The Obelisk, symbol of power and probably Masonic, came first in 1714, inscribed with a tribute to England's hero the Duke of Marlborough and with this declaration from Carlisle himself:

If to perfection these plantations rise
If they agreeably my heirs surprise
This faithful pillar will their age declare
As long as time these characters will spare.

The Pyramid Gate and the inner wall came next, completed in 1719 and designed by Vanbrugh. The wall is massive, with eleven gothic bastions, all of them different: either square, round or hexagonal, all castellated and some with cruciform arrow slits. Each could be a folly in its own right, and in total these battlements would be worthy of a medieval fortified town in some dangerous borderland, proving that Vanbrugh could be as inspirationally gothic as he was Baroque. The gateway itself is in the latter style, a triumphal arch topped with a correspondingly huge pyramid and linked to the wall by long, classically proportioned pavilions (used as guesthouses for visiting gentry). The outer wall and the Carrmire Gate were completed in 1725 and designed by Hawksmoor. This gate is smaller and more decorative: a rusticated arch with a broken pediment, framed by six pyramids on brick piers, clustered three on either side, and joining a castellated wall that is lower and less forbidding than the inner wall.[8]

Having passed through these triumphal approaches, with their combinations of medieval English, Roman and Egyptian stone pageantry, the largest of all the pyramids stands away in the landscape, facing the front of the house. It is a monument to the founding father, Lord William Howard, built by Hawksmoor in 1728 to enshrine the ancestral bust; and as one mounts the Temple Terrace it haunts the view, especially if it is misty. This may in part be due to the mastery with which the lines between all the buildings of Castle Howard were geometrically surveyed and planned. Computer research has proved that the proportions are Vitruvian, and yet they fit the natural topography of the site.[9] If the concept behind this was Vanbrugh's the measurements must surely have been Hawksmoor's, and the Howard family appreciated it well enough; perhaps they quoted the Vitruvian precept to one another – 'beauty is that reasoned harmony of all the parts within the body' – or else relied for words on the poetic daughter of the house:

The Temple of the Four Winds, Castle Howard, Yorkshire, 1724–6, a fine example of the collaboration of Vanbrugh and Hawksmoor.

Buildings the proper points of view adorn
Of Grecian, Roman and Egyptian form . . .
Lead through the park, where lines of trees unite
And verdrous lawns the bounding deer delight.[10]

As an example of conservation, Wray Wood on the garden side of Temple Terrace was kept (after some debate) as a natural grove with pathways, and a Temple of Venus was planned by Hawksmoor though never executed. It would have been a rotunda, domed and supported by rusticated pillars 'suited to a rural and sylvan situation' and containing the goddess's statue, as in many another landscape garden.[11]

Temple Terrace forms the spine of the grounds, running between Wray Wood and the landscape with the ancestral pyramid of Lord William Howard. It slopes upwards away from the house towards the Temple of the Four Winds, and there is a processional line of tall gods and goddesses, straight and severe, until one reaches the *Borghese Gladiator*, dramatically thrusting forwards with his outstretched arm. Vanbrugh raised the Temple terrace to form a viewing promenade comparable to Duncombe and Rievaulx, but it also follows a natural rise in the ground and may contain vestiges of the medieval castle walls, especially where it bends to create Vanbrugh's desired effect of obscuring the Temple until it suddenly bursts into full view. The Temple of the Four Winds is the most prominently placed and famous folly at Castle Howard, built by Vanbrugh from 1724 to 1726 at the end of his life. Like many other follies it is both a belvedere commanding the highest views and a banqueting house with a cellar and kitchen beneath. It is modelled on Palladio's Villa Rotonda (a square, four porticos with Ionic pillars, a dome and a lantern) and shares its beautiful proportions, but while that seems to float above its olive groves, this stands dark and ponderous above the heavily wooded Yorkshire landscape. Even the frivolous urns adorning the roofs seem weighty, and the goddesses facing the winds are severe. Follies can be serious affairs, and this is in part a *memento mori* because now, in the landscape far beyond, the Mausoleum becomes visible.

Like other features of Castle Howard, the Mausoleum is a first, and Carlisle was rejecting a traditional Christian place of burial in favour of the ways of antiquity (Horace Walpole seemed to approve, saying it would tempt one to be buried alive). The Roman tombs along the Appian Way must have been the primary inspiration and, since the Mausoleum is round, the tomb of Cecilia Metella may have been the starting point. Vanbrugh must also have

described to Carlisle the days of his youth in Surat, where the English cemetery honoured the Christian dead with extravagant architectural monuments, although they were banished to the edge of the Indian town. The Howard Mausoleum, though planned, was not designed until after Vanbrugh's death in 1726, and only completed around 1740, when Hawksmoor too was dead. It is credited to Hawksmoor, who was always fascinated by the prototype mausoleum at Halicarnassus, the monumental tomb of the Persian general Mausolos which was described as having colonnades and a stepped pyramid. The Howard Mausoleum also has a colonnade, supporting a frieze and then a dome, but no pyramid, although it looks across the landscape towards Lord William's pyramid. Nearby a river flows under a bridge with three arches; it is an Arcadian spot very distant from the great house, a place of transition from one world to another.

ET IN ARCADIA EGO

The idea of Arcadia as a remote place, undisturbed, idyllic and inhabited only by shepherds, was Greek, and the concept of introducing a tomb into the scene appeared first in Virgil's *Eclogues*.[12] In 1622 the Italian artist Guercino did a painting of a storm-tossed wooded scene with two shepherds gazing in consternation at a large skull resting on a tomb, with an inscription reading 'ET IN ARCADIA EGO'. These are understood to be the words of Death, who was even present in Arcadia; but contemporaries tended to believe they were the words of the dead within the tomb, meaning 'I too lived in Arcadia.' The impact is similar. More famously, Poussin painted two versions of the scene, the first (dated 1627) is in Chatsworth and very Baroque; the shepherds are just discovering the half-concealed tomb and reading the inscription with curiosity, straining forward to see. The stormy skies and lowering tree trunks, the overgrown tomb and skull, confirm the threat they are under. The shepherds are engrossed, ignoring the scantily clad shepherdess behind them, who is raising the hem of her shift up her thigh, presumably arrested in her dance. Poussin's second version, painted in 1637 and now in the Louvre, is stately and classical. Even the landscape is calmer, retreating into distant trees and mountains. Three shepherds frame the tomb, solemnly considering the inscription, which one traces with his finger while another turns to the female as if for

The Mausoleum, Castle Howard, designed 1726, completed 1740, the last of the classical/Baroque follies envisaged by Vanbrugh and Hawksmoor, placed in a distant Elysium of its own.

enlightenment. She is standing in profile, very still and clothed in gold, and looks like a goddess rather than a shepherdess. She directs the emphasis back to the inscription with its appalling reminder, to which there is a reference in a number of folly gardens.

ROUSHAM: HAUNT OF THE GODS

William Kent enriched many an eighteenth-century garden with follies large or small, but at Rousham in Oxfordshire, which is considered his master-piece, it was his creation of a setting for them that was supremely important, summoning the classical gods to act their parts in a rural English scene. Kent's reputation was already well established through his work at Chiswick, Claremont, Kew and Stowe when, in 1737, he was invited to Rousham by James Dormer, a retired general from the epoch of Marlborough's victories and 'a curious gentleman well skilled in books', who wished to enhance his ancestral domain. Bridgeman had made a start on this awkward area, which slopes steeply down to a bend in the river Cherwell and is shaped much like a mutton chop. But follies and statues were needed to transform it, and in doing so Kent created an atmosphere more numinous than any other garden.

There are various possible approaches and ways through the garden. A handsome Palladian gateway on the road, with statues in niches, opens into a grassy area with large urns and a castellated gothic seat, commanding a view over the farmland on the other side of the river. This is a first taste of what Kent achieved in blending English and Italianate, gothic and classical, more harmoniously than ever before. For the classicists it seemed authentic enough, because the Roman authors themselves – Virgil in his *Georgics*, Pliny in his *Letters* – had described the rural idyll of their villa gardens looking out over the surrounding farms and vineyards. Indeed, it was Pliny who first advocated 'calling the countryside into the garden' as Kent did at Rousham. Here by the Palladian gate is the prelude to many viewpoints opened up and dramatized, from the terraces at the top of the sloping garden and from the riverbank below. In the fields beyond, Kent created eccentric follies which were christened with the new word 'eye-catchers'. The largest on the horizon was the Grand Triumphant Arch in Aston Field (related to a poem eulogizing General Dormer's victories in the European wars): rectangular in the centre like a Roman triumphal arch, with a smaller arch on either side – a pattern Kent was fond of; the whole supported, since it is only a screen, by medieval-style buttresses; and topped by a rustic curvature and a tiara of stubby pinnacles (was the unusual shape inspired by the gothic splendour of Milan Cathedral?). It stands above the cornfields and cow pastures looking ruinous, romantic and eccentric. Nearer to the river is the Temple of the Mill, disguising an old corn mill with a frontage framed by flying buttresses, then rising to stepped gables, pinnacles and a lantern – an example of how even cowsheds and pigsties might be transformed. As Pliny had said of his property in Tuscany, 'you would think it not a real but a painted landscape'; and to quote General Dormer's gardener John Macclary, 'the prettiest view in the whole world . . . the natural turnings of the hills to let that charming river downe to butify our gardens'.[13] Another way of approaching the garden, and this view, would be to mount the terrace beyond the bowling green and pause by the great pedestal with the statue of a *Lion Attacking a Horse*, a replica of the one in the Tivoli Gardens of the Villa d'Este, which looks over the Roman campagna. As well as recalling that other scene to everyone who had been on the Grand Tour, the cruel statue acted as a *memento mori*. Another statue, further along the terrace, was the equally famous *Dying Gladiator*, erected here in 1741 when General Dormer himself was dying, a repetition within the iconography of Rousham of the message 'Et in Arcadia ego'.[14]

William Kent, *The Vale of Venus, Rousham*, commissioned and designed in 1737, here imagined and brought to life in a drawing by Kent himself.

From here, descending the wooded slope, Arcadia is reached in the heart of the garden, called the Vale of Venus, where a stream runs down over Kent's rustic cascades into pools and rills. The first cascade, formed of one arch, bears the statue of Venus, a replica of the *Medici Venus*. She stands looking over to one side, maybe a little startled at being seen, moving her hands as if to protect her breasts and groin but succeeding only in gesturing towards them. As the goddess of beauty, fertility, gardens, love and lust she was all things to all men, classically pure in the sculpted lines of her body but also an object of desire. Around her, in the grassy amphitheatre opened up by Kent, attendant gods adopt characteristic poses. A satyr peeps, Pan leers over his pipes, Bacchus leans tipsily backwards, Ceres maintains her dignity and Mercury points the way up a dark path. Within their charmed circle Venus' stream splashes on through a pool and over a larger cascade of three arches. It is easy to imagine that at twilight, when none will see them, or when the moonlight touches their marble flesh, the statues come to life and the gods play their parts. Kent's past experience as a painter and designer of theatre sets is nowhere more in evidence. Behind them is a steep slope, which is the other side of that terrace of grim statues, built up by Kent and supported by a line of arches known as the Praeneste. This is another of his innovative

The Temple of Echo, Rousham, *c.* 1738–40, a small but atmospheric building standing in a secret glade near the statue of a male god, evoking if not representing Narcissus.

follies, although inspired by the Temple of Fortuna Primigenia rising up the hillside of Palestrina, overlooking the Roman campagna. It is a single arcade of seven pedimented arches, but its design also hints at ancient theatres, including the Colosseum, and again the imagination is stirred. Kent sketched this scene as if it had an audience, with the statues in the background, the cascades watered by high-spouting fountains and many contemporary figures promenading and pointing as they would have done in the pit of a theatre.[15] The enchanted walk continues along a winding path to a tiny temple dedicated to Echo, the mischievous nymph deprived of her voice by the angry goddess Juno, who then fell hopelessly in love with Narcissus as he gazed at his own reflection in a pool. Nearby there is a stature of a beautiful young man, modelled on Hadrian's beloved Antinous and called Apollo, but surely he was originally meant to be Narcissus. The little temple is suitable for a forlorn nymph, pale and classical; the interest is in the frieze running under the roofline, looking like an ancient language waiting to be deciphered, an echo of echoes.

FROM MYTHOLOGY TO TRANSGRESSION

The *Medici Venus*, copied at Rousham and in many another stately garden throughout Europe, was itself a Hellenistic copy (dating from the first century BC) of a Greek original, and was installed in the Vatican garden. In 1644 John Evelyn saw it and considered it 'without parallel', but by 1680 it was declared too indecent for a papal environment and ended up in the Tribune of the Uffizi in Florence, where Edward Gibbons described it as 'the most voluptuous sensation that my eye has ever experienced'. The first copy to arrive in England belonged to Thomas Howard, Earl of Arundel, where it joined the collection held in his Thames-side residence, and in 1618 Daniel Mytens painted his portrait, with his staff pointing at a suggestive angle towards her.[16] There was a variant, another *Medici Venus*, in Florence, in the *Grotta Grande* of the Boboli Gardens, dating from the 1580s. The marvellously encrusted grotto has three chambers, one painted like a trellised garden with vines, where Venus stands in a raised fountain as if emerging from her bathing pool, bending forwards, one hand supporting herself on a short column and one foot stepping provocatively upwards, while round the rim of the fountain four fauns are peering up at her. Beauty matches well with humour, and Homer had long since called her 'laughter-loving' Aphrodite. She is also associated with water: the *Medici Venus* has a dolphin beside her as a reminder that she sprang from the foam of the sea, while another favourite statue, the *Crouching Venus*, has her kneeling on one knee beside a pool, because her shrines were in watery grottos where she cleansed herself after orgies.

However, in England grottos often had a statue of a nymph instead of Venus, and the favoured situation for Venus was initially a rotunda, where she could be viewed from all sides and from afar, which corresponded to Pliny's description of her shrine on the island of Cnidus.[17] One of the first rotundas was designed by Colen Campbell at Hall Barn in Buckinghamshire circa 1725, standing at a high point from which walks radiated, with a dome supported on eight Ionic columns, very prettily decorated with a frieze of swags and horned skulls outside while inside cherubs danced around the base of the dome, trailing vines.[18] There was also a rotunda at Stowe, among the first of its many follies, built for Lord Cobham by John Vanbrugh in 1721, large and prominent with ten Ionic columns and the *Medici Venus* on a high pedestal. Ten years later, in 1731, another temple was built by William Kent, across Lord Cobham's enlarged lake, so that Venus gazed over the water towards a garden retreat dedicated to *Veneri hortensi* (so-called because Venus was also the goddess of gardens and fertility). The style is rustic Palladian, all arches, niches and pediments, and Kent used a tawny limestone that blends softly with the trees and reflects golden in the water when the sun touches it. The niches were embellished with busts of debauched emperors and temptresses; the ceiling was painted with a naked Venus and the walls with revels and satyrs; among the furnishings was a 'pleasuring sofa'.[19] Such temples naturally attracted satire, and in 1753 Francis Coventry published an article in *The World* describing the garden of Squire Mushroom, with 'a pompous, clumsy and gilded building said to be a temple and consecrated to Venus; for no other reason that I could learn, but because the squire riots here sometimes in vulgar love with a couple of the orange-wenches taken from the purlieus of the playhouse';[20] while Samuel Johnson, on seeing a *Medici Venus* beside a lake, suggested throwing her in the water to hide her nakedness and cool her lust. Rotundas, however, remained desirable. Hawksmoor planned one for Wray Wood at Castle Howard, for which he thought 'the Greek Venus gilt will do very well'; and when the palatial gardens of Europe emulated the landscape movement they outdid the earlier Venus rotundas in ornate splendour and settings, Worlitz being the prime example. In France the court artist Hubert Robert painted *The Bathing Pool* circa 1780 for the Château de Bagatelle, imagining a rusticated rotunda shadowed by trees, Venus glimmering within

The Temple of Venus, West Wycombe, 1748, the most overtly suggestive
of all the monuments dedicated to the classical goddess of love and lust.

and curving steps down to a pool where bathers frolicked.[21] Other options
were possible: at Chiswick Lord Burlington put his Venus high on a pillar,
and at Hagley Lord Lyttelton was one of the first to put Venus 'in a grotto
where the water runs'.

The most transgressive of the follies dedicated to Venus was built by
Sir Francis Dashwood at West Wycombe, Buckinghamshire, in 1748, on
a mound known either as Venus Parlour or *Mons Veneris*, with a dark oval
entrance constructed from knapped flints. The implication of the design was
put beyond doubt by John Wilkes, a member of Dashwood's Hellfire Club,
when he called it 'the same entrance by which we all came into the world'
(though it was also described in more Virgilian terms as 'otherworldly'). This
entrance is flanked by a retaining wall against the mound – made from flints
with small pyramids, possibly representing knees spread wide – and above,

in her Ionic rotunda, stood Venus.[22] West Wycombe is a garden of illusions, hidden meanings and jokes. Benjamin Franklin called it paradise but many believed it closer to hell, because Sir Francis Dashwood earned himself a terrible reputation. There were other statements of erotic intent among the garden buildings, starting with the two entrance lodges built in 1745: Kitty's Temple was named after an actress pursued by Dashwood and Daphne's Temple after a nymph pursued by Apollo. Both were built of flint like the entrance to Venus Mound, and Kitty's Lodge had a pyramid roof and stone balls at each corner bisected by a projecting square equator, a variation on a Masonic theme. Daphne's Temple matched this but was only a facade because at the back it became an open temple with Ionic columns, an introductory example of the curious mirror images and innuendos of West Wycombe. Facades of flint are the leitmotif, linking classical temples, arches and workers' cottages; one cottage has a mock ruin on one side, another a pediment, while St Crispin's Cottage (named after the local shoemaker) has a beautifully proportioned sham church tower. Even more gothic and far more notorious, the Hell Fire Caves were excavated in 1750–52 (relieving local unemployment and providing material to construct a new road to High Wycombe). This flint facade centres on a gloomy gothic entrance, like one side of a church tower, with a dark archway into the tunnel. The flanking screens of flint form a semicircle peaking in triangular gables, with hollow apertures like staring eyes. The tunnels within lead to a large banqueting chamber and to the altar of the inner temple. The gossip in the coffee houses and taverns told of black masses and orgies. In 1755 Dashwood acquired the nearby ruins of Medmenham Abbey and, since he enjoyed nothing more than dressing up, a group of friends calling themselves the monks of Medmenham scandalized the neighbourhood. When Dashwood and the Earl of Sandwich attended a service at the local church, Sandwich released a small monkey and the congregation fled, convinced it was a devil. This stream of bad publicity had begun twenty years earlier with another prank involving the Calves-Head Club, which on the anniversary of Charles I's execution drank toasts to Cromwell and to revolution and served a calf's head on a dish. In January 1734 there was a riot off Pall Mall when a calf's head was cast onto a bonfire; the papers were full of it, Hogarth made a print and Dashwood was implicated.[23]

In his strange world of reflecting images, Dashwood was also responsible for rebuilding a church, in 1763, on existing medieval foundations, high on the hill above his folly garden. He embellished the interior and added a tower topped with an enormous golden globe (in which inevitably he was believed to hold sacrilegious rituals). It formed a magnificent eye-catcher and belvedere and, whatever else he did up there, he could certainly view his grounds, where the trees and vistas were allegedly planted in the shape of a colossal naked woman. Also in 1763, Dashwood inherited the title Lord Despencer, and ordered a new coach with *Pro Magna Carta* in gothic lettering on the panels. Another motto was Do What Thou Wilt, and Dashwood blatantly espoused the cause of Liberty, at times mixing with the respectable Whig opposition, like Lord Cobham's set, but also with John Wilkes (a journalist, MP and thorn in the side of monarchy). At West Wycombe a Roman triumphal arch (made chiefly of flint) is inscribed *LIBERTATI AMICITIAEQUE SACRUM*, the same motto that graced Lord Cobham's Temple of Friendship at Stowe (both therefore dedicated to liberty and friendship). Built in 1761, it masks the stables and was often called 'cockpit arch' because it sheltered cockfighting, but it was dedicated to Apollo, whose statue stood in a niche. In the 1770s two new facades were added to the house itself and, being Dashwood, he dedicated them as temples to the ancient gods. The east front portico, guarded by sphinxes, became the Temple of Diana; the larger colonnade of the west front was the Temple of Bacchus (plus statue). This was inaugurated with a procession of bacchantes and satyrs wearing skins wreathed in garlands of leaves. Having finished a sacrifice, they proceeded noisily through the trees to a tent on the lake for more hymns and libations.

The lake with its bridges and cascades, around which Dashwood's follies revolve, is the centrepiece in a series of paintings he had made of his beautiful landscape garden. On the island in the lake he built the Temple of Music, the loveliest of his follies, reminiscent of the Temple of Vesta with its encircling columns (although apart from the bay at the front it is rectangular, not round). It looks appropriately serene for appreciating music; a painting from 1781 by Thomas Daniell shows parties ferrying across the lake in gondolas for a performance on a summer's evening, and on the hill beyond is the church with the golden globe. It serves to emphasize the civilized side of Dashwood's larger-than-life character.[24] His architect for the Temple of Music, as well as the classical portico temples by the house, and also the Grecian Temple of the Winds, was Nicholas Revett, who likewise corresponded to Dashwood's more civilized and scholarly interests. Revett spent years in Greece measuring and drawing classical buildings; in 1762 he published *Antiquities of Athens* and was instrumental with his co-author James Stuart in the Greek Revival architecture of the period. Dashwood himself had toured the classical sites more extensively and repeatedly than most, and pursued his adventures as

Temple of Music, West Wycombe, built in the 1770s and the finest
example of Dashwood's patronage of Greek Revival architecture.

far as Greece and the Middle East. As well as his convivial and disreputable clubbing, Dashwood was a member of the Royal Society, the Society of
Antiquaries and the Society of Dilettanti, which fostered classical appreciation
and sponsored expeditions such as Revett's to study the ruins of Greece. 'The
nominal qualification', Horace Walpole remarked, 'is having been to Italy.
The real one is being drunk.' The Divan Club was an offshoot, founded by
Dashwood, for those who had visited the Ottoman Empire and, true to his
penchant for dressing up, Dashwood had his last portrait painted in jewel-
encrusted oriental robes and a turban, raising a glass.

THE 'GENIUS OF THE PLACE'

Venus was not the only classical god associated with transgression and with
gardens. The horned god Pan, though often linked with the revels of Bacchus,
was more primitive than either and presided over the earliest Arcadian landscapes. Poussin paid him due homage in two great paintings dated 1636,

the *Triumph of Pan* and the *Revels of Bacchus*, where Pan appears as a herm, horned and garlanded with leaves, in one painting red-faced, in the other grinning as his goat-like follower grabs a dancing girl.[25] He could be dangerous. Pan is the Greek word for 'all', but panic and pandemonium arise from his capacity to instil terror and riot, and true to form garden statues generally endowed him not only with his summoning pipes but a deeply sinister expression. In Painswick, or Pan's Wyck, he was the presiding deity of the eighteenth-century Gloucestershire garden created by Squire Benjamin Hyett, and also of the village and surrounding countryside. In the garden of Painswick John Van Nost's compelling statue of Pan once watched over the pool where naked bathers revelled, and on the hill beyond the house, known as Coldbourne Grove, Hyett built Pan's Lodge as a pleasure house, a beautiful folly of mixed styles. The central entrance was a columned and pedimented portico supported by gothic wings with steep triangular gables, then two smaller castellated wings; underneath was the dark archway of a subterranean entrance that led to extensive cellars.

Pan's Lodge appears now only in a series of views, painted by Thomas Robins after the garden was created in 1744–8. They clearly record the original

Thomas Robins, *Pan's Lodge, Painswick*, 1748, showing the folly as it commanded the grounds of Painswick. Pan's statue stood by the pool in the centre.

spirit of what is now known as Painswick Rococo Garden, renovated and san-itized with pretty gothic pavilions and a carpet of snowdrops in early spring. Robins's paintings certainly have Rococo borders, one decorated with shells, another around Pan's Lodge with leafy branches where owls, a magpie, crow and cuckoo perch, and in the valley beneath the lodge Robins has included revellers dancing. Another black-framed view shows Painswick garden on its steep slope, formally laid out with its tiny pavilions, while Robins's third painting has Pan himself in his goatskins appearing among a group of local gentry and gesturing towards the extensive and Arcadian landscape, where Painswick Church lies in the distance. Robins's preliminary sketch of this scene was inscribed *Pan deus Arcadiae*, words from Virgil's *Eclogues*. It seems Squire Hyett linked his classical education with local folklore, because from Painswick Church, according to the vicar's journal of 1760, there was an annual Pan procession to Hyett's woods. The *Gentleman's Magazine* of 1787 confirmed it as disgraceful: 'drunkeness and every species of clamour, riot and disorder formerly filled the town on this occasion.' Now only a churchyard ceremony centring on the yew trees, with a clipping dance and a clipping hymn, is remembered – along with curious references to puppy-dog pie. One house in Painswick retains some fine plasterwork interiors, with puppy dogs and horned masks among the Rococo swags. Beyond that the trail goes cold.[26]

Painshill, the other eighteenth-century landscape that may once have been haunted by Pan, although there is no proof of this, is of another order. Certainly it is Arcadian, but the vagaries of ancient gods do not disturb the set pieces placed so harmoniously in the rise and fall of the land. This part of the Surrey Downs, near Cobham and bounded by the river Mole, was acquired in 1737–8 by Charles Hamilton, youngest son of the Earl of Abercorn, after two Grand Tours which enriched him with painterly inspiration and a collec-tion of sculptures. But he lacked funds, and from the start he was increasingly indebted to his friends the wealthy and corrupt Fox family, who were influ-ential Whig politicians. Finally, in 1773, he was forced to sell Painshill and retire to Bath, despite being greatly praised for his achievement in creating the perfect landscape garden.[27] He started with a blank canvas; indeed Horace Walpole acknowledged that 'he has really made a fine place out of a cursed hill.' It was poor heathland, where Hamilton first improved the soil accord-ing to the best precepts of eighteenth-century landlords, harrowing, planting turnips and feeding them to sheep who in return manured and aerated the soil. It was twenty years before he began a brisk programme of folly building. Instead he planted trees, and was at the forefront of the collector's mania that

Gothic Pavilion, Painshill, built in 1761 as an entry point,
and designed to set the scene across the landscape.

seized certain aristocrats (including Frederick, Prince of Wales[28]) for introducing new species; America was the most fruitful source but many also came from the Middle East and beyond. Hamilton's skill was in arranging these young trees and shrubs to create variety of colour, shape and density, so that his plantings were more botanically varied and more dramatic than others. Visitors in the 1750s (like the blue-stocking Elizabeth Montague, who wrote 'the art of hiding art is here in such sweet perfection') were referring entirely to the landscape as the follies were yet to come, although the lake had been created, raising water from the river Mole by a series of locks and waterwheels to form a beautiful source of reflected light in the valley as it curved to look larger than it was. Thus the scene was set for the follies to appear, like the great melodramatic actresses of the age, who chanted their words and struck their poses for maximum effect.

The first folly to greet the visitor was the Gothic Pavilion, also called the Gothic Temple, built in 1761, reached along a path through beech trees and up into the amphitheatre, where an oval lawn with statues was surrounded by shrubs and trees planted in tiers. At the far end stood the Gothic Pavilion, a light and graceful signature building, though basically a wooden frame covered in plaster. It has ten pointed arches with tracery, supported by slender buttresses rising to pinnacles, a castellated roofline and a fan-vaulted ceiling; all forming a composite of decorative gothic details possibly derived from Batty Langley (who may have worked for the Hamiltons, since he dedicated two of his books to Hamilton's brother, who became Earl of Abercorn in 1734). The pavilion certainly attracted the same criticism from Horace Walpole as Langley's writings had – 'an unmeaning edifice' – his tenuous argument being that gothic architecture should imitate a church, castle or mansion because no one in the Middle Ages built temples or garden pavilions. But Hamilton was creating picturesque scenes in the spirit of Pope's lines:

To wake the soul by tender strokes of art
To raise the genius and to mend the heart.[29]

The Mausoleum and Bacchus Temple, Painshill, built 1758–62, showing how the folly buildings both contrasted and complemented each other as they were juxtaposed in the landscape.

From the Pavilion, suddenly after the tree-lined approach, a bright vista opens out, swooping down the grassy slope to the lake, across to the opposite hill with the Turkish Tent and to the far boundary of the garden where the Gothic Tower was also built by 1761. This tall red-brick tower, square and castellated with a circular turret, is the usual eye-catcher and belvedere. Within the thick woods and bracken enclosing this extremity of the grounds no one could deny its gothic credentials, but the Tower also contained part of Hamilton's sculpture collection, it being another function of some follies to act as a personal museum. Within this reclusive atmosphere (which Walpole described as 'composed almost wholly of pines and firs, a few birch and such trees as assimilate with a savage and mountainous country') there was another folly, the Hermitage, built of rough wood, which fitted admirably into the scenery and attracted a degree of publicity about resident hermits. It was first mentioned in 1752, making it Hamilton's earliest folly by some years.

Hamilton's final folly, built in 1772 just before he was forced to sell Painshill, was also gothic: the Ruined Abbey consisted of a wall of tall pointed arches between broken towers. The novelty of the Abbey lay in its two dramatically contrasting facades. Approaching from the Gothic Pavilion it is gloomy – there is a steep bank heavy with conifers, where the ruined walls of the Abbey are dark brick and the windows like empty sockets. The other facade, which faces over the lake, is rendered like pale stone and very light, almost ethereal with its reflection floating in the water. Beside it, the slope of a nearby vineyard evokes the romance of southerly climes. Before he built the Ruined Abbey Hamilton had already joined the fashion for sham ruins with his first classical folly, built in the late 1750s, which was a Roman arch, generally named the Mausoleum. It was almost contemporary with the similar Ruined Arch built by William Chambers in the royal gardens at Kew – both had statues in niches with carved fragments lying around – but the arch at Kew provided pathways through and over it, whereas Hamilton's stood in a melancholy dip surrounded by yew trees and was more indicative than Chambers's arch of 'the debility, the disappointments and the dissolution of humanity; which fill the mind with melancholy and incline it to serious reflection'.[30] Around this ruin Hamilton added a sarcophagus, Roman altars and Latin inscriptions for good measure, and visitors found the dreary effect magnified by the rank grass and weeds allowed to grow all around and through cracks. This Mausoleum, out of all of Hamilton's follies, received the accolade of being included in the Wedgwood 'Frog Service', made for Catherine the Great of Russia and decorated with scenes from famous gardens (as well as the signature frog).

Hamilton's other classical folly was the Temple of Bacchus, built by 1762 in a completely different setting, aptly called the Elysian Plain because here the scene is pastoral and the grass smooth, 'dressed and clumped with flowering shrubs, sweet trees and flowers'. It is a rectangular temple (recently restored), with Doric columns in the porticos at either end and Doric pilasters along the sides. It is most closely comparable to the Maison Carrée at Nîmes, and therefore also resembles the Temple of Fortuna Virilis in Rome, or, because this was the early period of Greek Revival, the Temple of Bacchus at Baalbek. In England its near-contemporary was the Grecian Temple at Stowe, built in Capability Brown's Grecian valley circa 1749. At Painshill, the pediments of the front portico had a scene of Bacchic revels, and the niches by the entrance included statues of Apollo, Venus and Mercury, while inside was the statue of Bacchus himself, a little tipsy, which Hamilton bought in Rome for a real antique, although it was common practice in Italy to meld ancient fragments into new statues for the tourist trade. Around the inside walls were twelve busts of Roman emperors on decorative pedestals which, like the ceiling, were attributed to Robert Adam, whose designs for them survive. It is uncertain whether he designed the Temple itself, but it was certainly the most august of Hamilton's follies.

The Turkish Tent of 1759, like the Temple of Bacchus, has a pastoral setting often surrounded by sheep (not flowerbeds). It is framed but not enclosed by trees, since it is positioned to be viewed from the Gothic Pavilion across the lake, and to return back an even lovelier view of the Pavilion. It was one of the few eighteenth-century garden tents in England designed as a permanent structure with a brick core, draped in the Ottoman mode with blue and white canvas over a peaked dome, flaunting a golden crescent and an ornate blue cornice (all now fully restored). The other folly with an oriental flavour is the Grotto, the most fantastic creation at Painshill and again in a setting designed to enhance its particular atmosphere. It is on an island, approached by boat or over a bridge, which has been called the Chinese Bridge because of its fretwork railings. All over the little island, alongside the path to the grotto, are outcrops and arches of tufa and limestone, which prepare one for the mineral marvels to come and are also reminiscent of the Chinese love of weirdly shaped rocks, which they too place strategically in gardens – a curious fact which Hamilton may have had in mind, because it was known in Europe since the account and engravings of Nieuhof's expedition to China in the 1650s.[31] Painshill's balance of classical, gothic and oriental follies, including sham ruins and a tower, was typical of many eighteenth-century gardens, and

Hamilton was not the first to try it. In most, even Stowe, Kew and Stourhead, the mixture proved an uneasy one, even if individual follies were very fine. The impulse was surely an attempt to assimilate past traditions with the discoveries of new continents and cultures. What Hamilton achieved better than all others was precisely that reassuring illusion of fitting it all into an idealized English landscape.

A VIRGILIAN LANDSCAPE REALIZED

Stourhead in Wiltshire rivals Painshill in the beauty of its landscape. The river Stour was dammed to form a large lake in the 1740s, including various outlets needing bridges and with pleasingly curvaceous banks that concealed and revealed the way, but it was sufficiently circular to form a great natural amphitheatre amid the wooded hills. The pathway, though sometimes steep, was always raised significantly above the water's edge and formed a proper circuit, with excellent vantage points for views and glimpses of the follies that surround it, sometimes hidden, sometimes transforming a vista. It all began with the family wealth of the Hoares, founded by the goldsmith Richard Hoare, who in 1673 set up a banking business at the sign of the Golden Bottle in Cheapside (and strongly opposed the founding of the Bank of England in 1694). Richard sent his son Henry abroad for banking and cultural experience, and it was when Henry inherited the business in 1718 that he bought the manor of Stourton in Wiltshire and built himself a Palladian house, designed by Colen Campbell (simultaneously he greatly increased his wealth by selling his South Sea shares just before the bubble burst in 1721). His son, also Henry, who became known as the Magnificent, inherited in 1724 and it was he who created the landscape and its best follies. Like Painshill it was previously 'nothing more than naked hills and dreary valleys, which now are so beautifully adorned by art assisting nature with trees'. Henry knew the formula – 'the greens should be ranged together in masses as the shades are in painting' – and like Hamilton he planted beech, fir, cedars and exotics from as far away as China.[32]

The key painting that seems to have inspired Henry Hoare's garden iconography was Claude Lorrain's *Aeneas at Delos* (1672), where Aeneas appears

Following pages
Temple of Hercules, Stourhead, built 1753–5 and also known as the Pantheon, of which it was a replica, and containing a huge statue of Hercules.

(in a red cloak) seeking guidance from the priest of Apollo. Beyond them is a temple like the Pantheon, and a tower, and below is the harbour of Delos, though it was modelled like many of Claude's paintings on the Bay of Naples. The scene is from Book III of Virgil's *Aeneid*: 'To Delos now I sailed' – Apollo's island – where Aeneas entered his temple and prayed. The temple quaked and a voice prophesied the future of Rome ruling the earth. It was inspirational stuff, with appeal to the painterly and literary mind, and to the English impulse to expand and form an empire as the Romans had done. In Stourhead there were many esoteric references to Aeneas' journey, which would have served as intriguing clues for Hoare's classically educated friends. The way from the house to the garden passed a statue of Apollo and the first temple to be reached was also the first to be built, in 1744. Originally this was dedicated to Ceres, the mother goddess of fertility, and later to Flora, goddess of springtime and flowers (the functions of the two are complementary). The Temple of Flora is a modest Doric edifice set back among the trees, but with an arresting inscription on the architrave: *Procul, procul este profane* (away, you uninitiated). This was the cry of the Sibyl before she led Aeneas to the underworld, where again he was seeking to learn his future fate and how to achieve it. It was a perilous undertaking with dire warnings, including the famous 'I see Tiber streaming and foaming with blood.' More famous in Hoare's time was another quotation, *facilis descensus in Averno*, which Hoare quoted in a letter of 1765 as a joking reference to one of the steep, rocky paths at Stourhead. In its full form, the quote meant 'the descent to Avernus [the underworld] is not hard . . . but to retrace your steps and escape back . . . that is the challenge.' The building of follies owed much to the English sense of humour, so Hoare was ready with his joking allusion, but there was more to the quotations than that. Stourhead (like several other folly gardens) was created against a background of bereavement; over the years Henry Hoare lost both much-loved wives and all his sons. In 1712 Addison had written about the phenomenon of comfort: 'Delightful scenes whether in nature, painting or poetry, have a kindly influence on the body as well as the mind, and not only serve to clear and brighten the imagination, but are also able to disperse grief and melancholy.'[33]

To return to the route, there is more than one steep path at Stourhead, but the descent to Avernus is generally held to refer to the Grotto, created in 1748. It lies across the lake from the Temple of Flora (where there was an earlier little grotto just below the temple) and has a rocky opening framing an exquisite view over the water. Within this view Henry Hoare placed a great statue of Neptune, riding his sea chariot over the lake (possibly to quell a storm as in the *Aeneid*, Book I). Inside the second cavern of the grotto sat a similar bearded water god with his arm raised in greeting, known as the river Tiber. According to Horace Walpole there was once an inscription, *Haec domus est* (here is your home), as in the *Aeneid*, Book VIII, when Aeneas reached the banks of the Tiber, near the future site of Rome, and was greeted by Father Tiber with this prophesy. Then Aeneas followed Father Tiber's instructions and sought out allies among the Arcadians, arriving to find them sacrificing to Hercules, so that, when Rome was finally conquered, Aeneas erected his 'greatest altar' to him. The Temple of Hercules at Stourhead, built in 1753–5, is indeed the largest temple there, impressive when seen from viewpoints along the way and massive when the final bend in the path brings one underneath its great portico of Corinthian columns. The Temple is round and domed, modelled on the Pantheon in Rome (and also like the temple in Claude Lorrain's painting of *Aeneas at Delos*). Sometimes it is called the Pantheon, but it was certainly built for Hercules, whose statue by Peter Andreas Rysbrack dominated the interior. Hercules' labours made him a favourite hero of the eighteenth century, and he accrued extra legends – for instance, Hoare owned a moralistic painting of Hercules choosing between virtue and vice.

The third and final classical temple was the Temple of Apollo, ending the circuit with the deity whose statue began it. The way to the temple involves another steep path, which was perhaps the difficult ascent from Avernus to which Hoare alluded, since the temple was built in 1765, the date of his letter and quotation. As well as being the sun god, Apollo presided over the prophesies of the Sibyl, which was appropriate if Hoare had a spiritual journey in mind, inspired by the one Aeneas made. It is by far the most beautiful of the three temples, very like its namesake the Temple of the Sun, designed by William Chambers for Kew in 1761, and both were modelled on a recent discovery at Baalbek. It is a circular domed building surrounded by eight fluted Corinthian columns, rendered extraordinarily graceful by the roof-line curving inwards above each column and enhanced by the entablature of swags underneath.[34]

All three classical temples at Stourhead were designed by Henry Flitcroft, the protégé of Lord Burlington who rose to be Comptroller of the King's Works. They are his finest folly buildings in the classical style, but around 1762–3 Flitcroft began something quite different for Hoare: a red-brick gothic tower. Its three sides rose to 49 metres (160 ft) of sheer windowless height relieved by three circular turrets, one with ten tiny windows mounting upwards beside the stairs, which led to a wide panorama. Visiting in 1778, Defoe called it 'the most affecting simplicity and natural grandeur I ever remember to have seen in any single structure'.[35] It certainly outdid Hoare's friend and rival at Painshill, who built his gothic tower in 1761, and it was probably due to Hamilton's success in balancing classical, gothic and exotic styles that Hoare started to do likewise during the 1760s and '70s, thus compromising the integrity of the Aeneas story. The medieval church had always been part of the scenery, and the medieval Bristol Cross (which had been rejected by the citizens of Bristol as papist) arrived in 1764. A gothic cottage was built on the path between the Grotto and the Pantheon, and a hermitage above the Temple of Apollo. Further off in the thick woodland west of the lake a rustic convent with painted windows provided a goodly frisson for those who

Temple of Apollo, Stourhead, built 1765 to complete the circuit of classical temples and dedicated to the god of prophesy who had guided Aeneas' journey.

happened upon it in the gloom, and in the swampy meadows a fifteenth-century conduit called St Peter's Pump arrived from Bristol in 1768. There was a blue and white Turkish Tent, as at Painshill, and two chinoiserie follies, which were demolished by Henry's grandson and heir Sir Richard Colt Hoare in the 1790s, after he complained of 'nature overcrowded with buildings'. All these were fripperies compared with Flitcroft's magnificent (and final) triangular tower, which took ten years to build, begun while England was threatened on land and sea by the Seven Years War (1756–63) and completed in triumph in 1772. It was named King Alfred's Tower and said to mark the spot where he raised his standard to beat back the Danes (from the top of the tower it was claimed that all the old kingdom of Wessex was visible). The plaque on the tower is a hymn to nationalism and expresses the belief that defeating England's enemies in Europe, Asia, Africa and America brought 'peace and rest to the earth'. To King Alfred is credited 'the origin of juries, the creation of a naval force, the foundation of the monarchy and Liberty'. With the hindsight provided by these sentiments it is understandable that all Hoare's follies, including those relating to Aeneas' journey, have been interpreted as patriotic and imperialist statements.

IMPERIALISM MADE MANIFEST

There was victorious patriotism on a more personal level at Shugborough, the Staffordshire family seat of Thomas Anson, Earl of Lichfield, and his richer, more eminent younger brother, George, Admiral Anson, who was a latter-day Francis Drake. George's naval career began in his teens (while Marlborough led the field) and continued until his death in 1762 during the Seven Years War, by which time he was First Lord of the Admiralty. His best-remembered triumph was his circumnavigation aboard the *Centurion*, which started as a commission to attack Spanish vessels and settlements in the Pacific. In the Philippines he captured a Spanish treasure galleon crossing from Mexico. On board were well over a million pieces of eight and charts of the Pacific islands – islands which he proceeded to claim, including the Anson Archipelago. Greatly enriched by this piratical venture he reached home in 1744 and joined his brother in creating a folly garden. Appropriately, the first folly was the Chinese House, built in 1744 and based on a drawing 'from the skilful pencil' of Sir Percy Brett, Anson's First Lieutenant on the *Centurion*, which was done in Canton during the months they spent in harbour there. It was the first chinoiserie folly built by someone who had been to China.[36]

Chinese House, Shugborough, built 1744. It was the first chinoiserie folly
designed by a visitor to China – Admiral Anson, a commander of the fleet.

The exterior is disappointingly simple (and authentic): small and square with
fretwork windows, upflung eaves and a double *umbrello* emulating an oriental parasol atop. Originally it was more colourful, being painted blue and
white like Ming porcelain, and approached by a red Chinese Bridge. Inside
was far more ornate, with a Rococo chinoiserie ceiling of plasterwork monkeys (a style known as *singerie*) fishing with cormorants held on ribbons. On
the walls were scarlet panels interspersed with Chinese garden scenes painted
on glass, and all around was a fine porcelain collection, this being another of
the follies acting as a personal museum.

The second folly, dated 1750, is the Ruin sited between the house and
the river – not the ubiquitous sham edifice but an unusual compilation of
fragments from earlier buildings, including the Bishop's Palace at Lichfield,
piled in a charmingly haphazard manner affording glimpses of the grounds
through small archways and balustrades, with a philosopher perched aloft.
Originally the Ruin was far more extensive, with several slender and fantastical

arches and broken colonnades, as portrayed in a painting by Nicholas Dall in 1775. It is light-hearted and fascinating, though many from William Gilpin onwards have dismissed it for lack of authenticity! 'To give the stone its mouldering appearance . . . to make the widening chink run naturally through all the joints, to show how correspondent parts have once united . . . are great efforts of art.'[37] To what extent the enigmatic Thomas Wright was involved at Shugborough when the folly building was begun is unknown, but his name is most often linked, not with the Ruin, but with the Shepherd's Monument, built in the mid-1750s. The design of its arch is contemporary with, and resembles, one of Wright's *Six Original Designs for Arbours* of 1755. This is not an arbour, but is cunningly wrought in stone to surround a marble bas-relief based on Poussin's *Et in Arcadia Ego*, hence the name Shepherd's Monument. Here, adding to the puzzling words that the shepherds had to decipher, are the initials OUOSVAVV and underneath DM. No one has broken its code, though there have been various implausible suggestions.

After this there was a serious change of direction and the remaining folly buildings belonged to, in fact helped to inaugurate, the Greek Revival. As the shadowy presence of Thomas Wright receded from Shugborough, James 'Athenian' Stuart, co-author of the *Antiquities of Athens* (1762), appeared on the scene – the reason being that while the Admiral was travelling the world by sea, his brother Thomas, Lord Lichfield, had been exploring the classical

The Ruin, Shugborough, 1744, an early sham ruin
elegantly constructed from fragments of earlier ruins.

Triumphal Arch, Shugborough, 1762, a copy of Hadrian's Arch in Athens and part of the fashionable Greek Revival in architecture, also a memorial to Admiral Anson.

world. In 1732 he became a founder member of the Society of Dilettanti (the name has changed its meaning; then it signified a serious patron of learning). From this came the Ansons' link with James Stuart and his colleague Nicholas Revett, who had spent from 1748 until 1755 in Athens researching ancient Greek buildings under the auspices of the Society of Dilettanti. The first classical folly on the scene at Shugborough, in 1760, was the Doric Temple, with six fluted columns, based on the Temple of Hephaistos in Athens (Lord Lyttelton's at Hagley was two years earlier). This was followed by the far more unusual Triumphal Arch of 1762, James Stuart's copy of Hadrian's Arch in Athens. It rears up on a treeless hill, the highest point of the estate, and it is black with soot because a railway tunnel emerges nearby, though fortunately the effect of soot absorption on the stone has given the arch a marbled surface. The funereal look is appropriate because Admiral Anson died as the arch was completed, whereupon Lord Lichfield added the busts of his brother and sister-in-law, together with sarcophagi and urns, as his tribute to them. Contemporaries referred to triumphal arches set high up, with the view through them consisting purely of sky, as gateways to heaven; another example is the Triumphal Arch at Stowe.

The most unassuming Greek-style folly at Shugborough was the Temple of the Winds, a dainty little octagonal tower based on the Horologion of Andronikos in the Roman forum of Athens. The original was far more interesting, the first meteorological station in Europe, with sundials, a water clock and wind vane, and decorated with a frieze of large winged figures including bearded winds. The first copy was at West Wycombe (in 1759), decorated and screened with the flints that Francis Dashwood favoured but also lacking meteorological intent. Shugborough's Temple of the Winds dated from 1765 and was used by later generations as a gambling den and a dairy. Then, in 1771, as his final folly, Lord Lichfield commissioned the Lantern of Demosthenes, dedicated to the Greek orator, patriot and democrat, who was adopted as a suitable Whig hero.[38] The design of the Lantern in *Antiquities of Athens* showed a rotunda with Corinthian pilasters, said to be the earliest example of that most ornate of the classical orders. The Greek original, which dated from the first or second century BC, was a choragic monument, meaning a gigantic pedestal and rotunda on which to display a bronze tripod, which was the trophy for the winner of the drama festival of Dionysus, comparable to an Oscar. Anson topped his monument with an elaborately mounted Wedgwood bowl, long gone, but two impressive urns have now been placed one above the other, on a tripod more akin to James Stuart's original design. The curved roof tiles twist over the rotunda, so like the curls on an eighteenth-century wig that it was too much for Hogarth – even before Stuart and Revett's designs were published he was lampooning them in a print named 'The Five Orders of Periwigs'. All the stereotypes of classical beauty were reduced to preposterous hairstyles, which Hogarth described in terms of architraves, volutes and composites.

Hogarth may have struck a chord, even with those who built follies. Certainly, the urge to diversify away from classical temples was present during most of the century, hence the fashions for gothic and oriental styles. Painshill showed that balancing an eclectic variety of follies could be done amid perfect scenery, but few achieved this. Most folly gardens that were neither purely classical nor entirely gothic failed to achieve harmony, or to tell a story, although the individual follies could be fine, or at least fun. All over Europe, and especially in eighteenth-century France, they were assembled in much the same spirit as a cabinet of curiosities.

A CABINET OF CURIOSITIES

In France, after the Seven Years War ended in 1763, there was a surge of enthusiastic visits to English landscape gardens. The sweeping lawns and tree plantations were appreciated, although Walpole pointed out 'they can never have as beautiful landscapes as ours till they have as bad a climate.' Instead, French aristocrats were captivated by the variety of English follies and, being prone to philosophize, turned to the source of the Greek word 'eclectic'. The Eclectics were a group of ancient philosophers who on principle selected the best ideas from everywhere. It thus became a sign of Enlightenment to gather together architectural examples derived from all times and all places in one's park, just as earlier generations had collected odd samples of the world's marvels into *wunderkammern* or cabinets of curiosities. Walpole generally

Ruined Column, Désert de Retz, France, completed in 1782, sensational and almost
too palatial for a folly, set in a garden of mysteries and probably Masonic.

deplored the Parisian manner of achieving this, comparing the gardens he
visited to 'a tailor's paper pattern'. But, for its panache, the Désert de Retz
might have impressed even him.[39]

The Désert de Retz was a semi-derelict property near Chambourcy, west
of Paris, when François Racine, Baron de Monville, purchased it in 1774. The
approach lay through the royal forest of Marly, which was fitting because
désert meant an isolated and unpopulated place. The natural wilderness at
Retz was soon rendered thicker and leafier by Monville's enthusiastic planting
of exotic trees. But *désert* had a pleasingly ironic sense in fashionable circles,

signifying a retreat where one entertained – pursuing a multitude of interests both serious and sybaritic – and it also linked up with Rousseau's theories of untamed nature freeing the spirit. Monville's passions included music, sport, plants and actresses and he had a rare aptitude for scene-setting. It started with the original entrance from the forest, which went downwards through a grotto of jagged rocks, lit by two satyrs bearing torches, which felt very like a passage to another world. It may have hinted at Masonic initiation rituals, and the first monument along the winding path was a large Egyptian pyramid, one of the prime symbols associated with Freemasonry. But this pyramid covered an ice house, termed in French *une glacière en forme de pyramide*, conjuring the sense that nothing was as it seemed and the whole Désert could be enchanted and full of deceits. Of all the *fabriques* (there were at least seventeen, of which ten have been restored), the Broken Column was the most astounding. Monville called it his summer house but it was unlike any other, designed as the ruined column of a colossal imaginary temple, with a jagged roofline and great cracks opening in the walls. These walls are fluted, and in each recess three windows mount in a geometric sequence – rectangle, square, oval – belying any sense of classical imitation. However, the broken fluted column was a Masonic symbol and this may be a version of their mathematical calculations, or else an esoteric joke. From every angle the Broken Column looks weird as it looms between the trees, the smooth pale blocks from which it was constructed seeming ghostly, but if the exterior is daunting the interior is flooded with light. The oval reception rooms were lined with mirrors; the attics were lit through the cracks in the facade and light poured down the spiral staircase at the centre of the column, so that Monville's tender exotics were brought in from the greenhouses and flourished everywhere, even climbing up the bannisters. Was this a sly allusion to ruins where vegetation has taken over? In French it was called *La Colonne détruite*, and here the word 'destroyed' invoked a more immediate association with the Tower of Babel, a potent symbol at all times and certainly ironic in view of the impending revolution in France. Monville may also have envisaged the possibility of blowing up the Column himself, since alongside the highly decorated reception rooms he also had a laboratory there for his chemical experiments.

The paths from the Broken Column wound onwards through the trees to an open-air theatre – a raised dais of grass with an antique retaining wall and an urn – setting the scene a little like the mock-theatre at Bomarzo. Further along came two small temples almost engulfed in greenery, one dedicated to Pan with a rounded Doric portico, the other to Repose, of which only the columns remain; then the genuine gothic ruin of the medieval parish church of St Jacques de Retz, with one traceried window and covered in ivy. (There was a lawsuit in 1780, requiring Monville to pay his architect François Barbier, and the legal records suggest that Barbier designed the Temple of Repose and the greenhouses while Monville himself was responsible for the Temple of Pan and the Chinese House.) The Chinese House is gone, collapsing in 1967, but it was the first folly built at Désert de Retz, in 1777, and there Monville used to stay until the Broken Column was completed in 1782. It stood by a pool, as real Chinese pavilions often did, and from it a rivulet flowed into the main lake. It was surely the most exquisite, and possibly the most authentic-looking, of all the chinoiserie pavilions created in Europe. Its framework was of simulated bamboo, supporting panels and windows of intricate and many-patterned fretwork. The roof rose in three tiers with dainty chinoiserie tiles and gently upturned gables. From the record of old photographs no colour is discernible, but it must have glittered with red and gold. The other oriental folly, the Tartar Tent, has been restored to its former glory, though being designed to look like canvas it seems ephemeral. It is rectangular and roofed like a marquee, painted with fabric stripes and golden drapes that are raised in folds over the entrance. In 1785 the completed follies of the Désert de Retz were celebrated in 24 engravings included in *Cahiers des jardins anglo-chinois*, published in 1785.

Among these delights the Baron de Monville entertained painters, men of letters, actors, botanists, Freemasons and sportsmen. Despite their intellectual aspirations they seem not to have sensed the political abyss until too late. In 1792 Monville did succeed in selling the Désert de Retz to an Englishman, probably hoping to fund his escape from France. Rumour maintained he only just outwitted the revolutionary masses by pretending to be his own gardener. For a while he lived quietly at Neuilly with an actress, but during the Terror he was imprisoned in the Conciergerie. Unlike most of his friends he avoided the guillotine and was released on the death of Robespierre in 1794, but his health was ruined and he died in 1797. The gaiety and irony of the Désert never returned and eventually it was abandoned to ivy and brambles. In the spirit of Vicino Orsini, Monville had suggested that his *fabriques* were loaded with cryptic meanings, and also like Bomarzo a lively autobiographical element adds lustre to the buildings, so that, in his follies, enough of Monville's wit and ingenuity survives to puzzle and delight new generations of visitors.[40]

Four

Concepts of Freedom and Victory

Successful attempts to define follies are rare, but the doyen of folly enthusiasts Barbara Jones offered this: 'An ornament for a gentleman's garden and a mirror for his mind'.[1] No building was ever more so than the Triangular Lodge at Rushton, Northamptonshire, conceived by Sir Thomas Tresham while imprisoned in Ely for his Catholic faith, and built after his release in 1593 (the date on the wall of the folly). This means it was his first statement of Catholic emancipation, before his cruciform folly at Lyveden New Bield. Across its three walls, constructed in mellow stripes of cream and terracotta bricks, every detail is a hymn of praise to the Trinity expressed in triangles and trefoils. The three sides of the lodge are each 33 feet (10 m) wide, and there are three storeys and three windows to each level in each wall. The tiny basement windows have a triangle within a trefoil, the ground-floor windows enclose a cross within a trefoil and the first-floor windows contain patterns of triangles within a trefoil. The roof has three triangular gables on each of its three sides, which are outlined in stone flames, and above these the pinnacles and chimney are also three-sided and decorated with trefoils. Over the entrance to the lodge are the words *Tres testimonium dant*, or 'three bear witness'. In a letter Tresham related that, while in Ely prison he was reading a 'treatise of proof that there is a God and there was upon the wainscot table at that instant three loud knocks as if it had been with an iron hammer, to the great amazing of me and my two servants'.[2] It sounds obsessive, and so indeed was Tresham's faith, unlike that of many Elizabethans, who advisedly kept their beliefs to themselves. Consequently, from 1580 to his death in 1605 he was under constant surveillance, often imprisoned and heavily fined for his refusal to attend Anglican services. If Tresham felt that he was a martyr for religious freedom, he was forgetting that in countries under Catholic rule the persecution of dissidents was far more extreme.

The identification of himself with the religious symbolism of the number three lay also in the name Tresham, *tres* being the Latin for three and trefoils being a family device. The lodge is encrusted with heraldic shields and the

Tresham crest – a boar's head with a trefoil in its mouth – although family status was subsumed in the religious significance of the decorations – carved angels, doves, pelicans, lambs and candlesticks – and biblical inscriptions such as 'I have considered thy works Lord and been afraid' running around the walls. There are also several series of mysterious numbers, which may relate to the beginning and end of time, as calculated by Tresham. Elizabethans loved and admired devices and cryptic messages, and there was nothing too obvious on the exterior of the lodge that could be condemned as Catholic rather than Christian theology. High up there is lettering around the roof, which may be coded references to the wording of the Latin mass, and the chalice among the carved emblems, referencing the blood of Christ, could also be interpreted as a Catholic symbol. But perhaps to avoid the suspicion that it was in fact a forbidden chapel, the extravagant little building was always referred to in Tresham's accounts as the Warrener's Lodge or the Connegerie, and around it there are still traces of the embankments where rabbits were kept. Coney was the smart word for rabbit, derived from the Latin *cuniculus*, and the warrener was the estate servant responsible for their care and the processing of their meat, fur and bones. Ever since the introduction of rabbits into England in the thirteenth century they had proved a valuable commodity, walled in and guarded in artificial burrows characterized as 'pillow mounds' that were carefully drained and planted with small trees to stabilize them. Rabbit breeding was an excellent use of poor sandy soil, and at Rushton a large field south of the Lodge contained another warren, while estate accounts show that Tresham's rabbits were being sold by the hundreds in London. The interior of the Triangular Lodge conformed to the normal pattern for a warrener's lodge: one main room on each floor (hexagonal in this case) with the corners divided off to provide a stairway and storage recesses (triangular in this case). The upper room with a fireplace was the warrener's living space, while below the furs were processed, dried and stored. But perhaps the warrener at Rushton was a Catholic priest in disguise; all things seem possible in such a strangely wrought building. The interior is as bare as the exterior is intricate, but its atmosphere is numinous, calm and strangely lit through the patterned windows. If the worst parts of rabbit processing were confined to the basement, then the heart of the building may possibly have witnessed illicit Catholic masses. Rumour persists that a secret underground

Triangular Lodge, Rushton, dated 1593, a folly dedicated to the symbolism of the number three, built by Thomas Tresham, a fervent Catholic.

tunnel led from Rushton Hall straight to the Lodge, above which a tree-lined vista still exists, and later generations happily used the lodge as a summer house and eye-catcher.

Thomas Tresham's Triangular Lodge, and his Banqueting House at Lyveden New Bield, are unique among follies in their quasi-religious status and as sixteenth-century symbols of dissent. But if religious devotion seldom inspired follies, there were plenty which bore testament to political affiliations, either loyal to the government of the time, or in opposition, or in disgrace. At which point the designations Whig and Tory enter garden history. Both names emerged during the Civil War as derogatory terms. Whigs were Scottish cattle-drovers and rebellious non-conformists; Tories were Catholic Irish out-laws who fought a rearguard action against Cromwell's Parliamentarian army – both could of course be regarded as freedom fighters. After the Restoration of Charles II trouble brewed over the succession of his brother James, who was Catholic. Tories supported the legitimate Stuart heir despite his religion, while Whigs believed Protestantism and Parliament must be protected against a monarch who sought to override them. After three disastrous years James was deposed in favour of his Protestant nephew and son-in-law, William, Prince of Orange, ruler of the Netherlands, who became William III in 1688. The event was known as the Glorious Revolution, because it established the concept of constitutional monarchy more firmly, and the Whigs who had invited William to claim the throne dominated politics. For a while Dutch styles were all the fashion, from the royal palaces downwards, and two fine follies survive from the numbers created at that period.

The Tall Pavilion at Westbury Court in Gloucestershire floats above its own reflection in a long canal, just as a gem of Dutch architecture should.[3] As people living in a flat and watery land, the Dutch specialized in tall buildings – in towns they were crammed close together with their merchandise stored in the attics. At Westbury Court the height of the pavilion is emphasized by the thin columns of the downstairs loggia, the three elongated windows of the garden room, and the peaked roof topped with a lantern and a gilded ball – their combined height doubled by the reflection in the greenish water. The Tall Pavilion is the garden's focal point, and from inside its panelled first-floor room the layout of the formal gardens can be enjoyed to best advantage. From there a ladder mounts higher, to a little windowed room above the roof where, especially if armed with a telescope, the river Severn and its floodplain can be surveyed. The garden was also a perfect example of contemporary Dutch style, formality on a human scale, with a hedged parterre enclosing roundels and rectangles where flowers formed bright patterns; beyond were avenues of trees, clipped topiary, a quincunx and an orchard. Its immaculate green geometry was captured within a few years of its creation in Leonard Kip's birds-eye view, done around 1705–10. The property of Westbury on Severn had been inherited by Maynard Colchester, a pious Gloucestershire squire, in 1694, and the wealth of his wife Jane Clark, daughter of a London mercer, enabled them to create a water garden. They started with the long canal, fed by diverting the Westbury Brook, and added the Tall Pavilion between 1702 and 1704. It is uncertain who designed it, apart from an entry in Maynard Colchester's accounts for April 1702: 'paid Mr Pyke for paterne summerhouse'. A second formal canal at Westbury was probably created in the 1720s by Maynard's heir, and here there is a statue of Neptune from an earlier date, rather stumpy and bestriding a dolphin – Neptune may even have reached the garden

Tall Pavilion, Westbury Court, built 1702–4, when the Dutch style represented Protestant freedom and constitutional monarchy.

before the canals were built, because his presence signified a further tribute to William III, crossing the sea to champion Protestant liberties. Yet another link between England and the Netherlands was a love of tulips and, if this Tall Pavilion was not necessarily used for storing tulip bulbs, it is certainly reminiscent of a description in Alexandre Dumas' novel *The Black Tulip*, set earlier in the life of William of Orange, where the hero Cornelius van Baerle adds an extra storey to his garden building, 'with windows, set out with bulbs, bundles of labels, drawers with compartments and wire guards against mice . . . the interior of a tulip grower's with all the accessories'.[4]

In 1702, which was the year that William III died, Henry Grey, twelfth Earl of Kent, inherited Wrest Park in Bedfordshire. He had been a leading Whig politician in William's government, much admired the Netherlands and married into the Bentinck family, which had arrived with William from Holland (and shared his garden enthusiasms). The new garden at Wrest

Grand Pavilion, Wrest Park, 1711, Thomas Archer's Baroque creation, with a statue of William III representing the Glorious Revolution of 1688 in the foreground.

Park was therefore based on canals, avenues and topiary.[5] Its finest folly, the Grand Pavilion, was linked to William's memory by a large statue of the king crowned with a laurel wreath and looking arrestingly like a Roman emperor, aloof on a pedestal at the entrance. In front of him stretched the long canal and a large statue of Neptune brandishing his trident at the water's edge. The Grand Pavilion is in the Baroque style prevalent throughout Europe at this date – a fine example, heavy but gracious. The ground plan is a circle with alternating square and curving bays, and it is built of red brick and creamy stone with a high arched entrance and windows, and a tall lanterned dome. The architect was Vanbrugh's associate Thomas Archer, and it was inspired by his favourite Italian architect Borromini, specifically the church of S. Ivo alla Sapienza in Rome, which accounts for its size and ostentation. The interior is correspondingly ornate, painted in *trompe l'œil* shades of grey to represent stone pilasters, statues and niches, touched with gold. It was used as a banqueting house, with a kitchen in the basement approached by flights of stairs hidden in the bays. By the time the Pavilion was completed, in 1711, the Whigs had been ousted from power by Queen Anne's Tory government, under Robert Harley, Earl of Oxford. However, Earl Grey had been made Duke of Kent in 1710 for services rendered, and continued to plant his grounds in the Dutch/European manner, even though the fashion was changing in a different wave of patriotic feeling. Defoe pointed out, 'it is since the Revolution that our English gentlemen began so universally to acorn their gardens with evergreens'; Switzer condemned the 'mournful family of yews . . . a fashion brought over out of Holland by Dutch gardeners who used it to a fault'. But it was left to Horace Walpole to condemn Wrest utterly as 'very ugly in the old-fashioned manner with high hedges and canals, at the end of the principal one of which is a frightful temple by Mr Archer'.[6]

As Baroque architecture acquired the taint of absolutist rulers and enemy nations, especially the French, architects developed a range of varied styles to express their patrons' mindsets, many of them idiosyncratic. Thomas Archer himself, fresh from the Baroque certainties of Wrest Park (and also involved in Queen Anne's Commission for Building Fifty London Churches), is believed to have turned his hand to a most curious folly nearby in Bedfordshire. Queen Anne's Summer House is at Old Warden (once a Cistercian Abbey which gave its name to Warden pears), built on a sandy hillock known as the Warren because here too rabbits were once kept. From the 1690s the estate belonged to Samuel Ongley, who earned his wealth in the City, first cloth-trading and then rising to be a director of the East India Company and the South Sea Company. In 1712 he was knighted by Queen Anne, and the Summer House was almost certainly built to celebrate his elevation to the status of titled, landed gentry.[7] The folly is finely constructed of rubbed red bricks with rounded Queen Anne windows and doorway. It is square and very sturdy on account of the four round towers at the corners, like an upturned footstool. Hence the link with Thomas Archer, who designed St John's Smith Square, the London church nicknamed 'Queen Anne's footstool'. This was because the gout-afflicted monarch is reputed to have kicked her footstool towards Archer to express her opinion about the church's design. A further link with Archer lies in the one similarity between Queen Anne's Summer House and Wrest Pavilion, which was the design of both of their brick-vaulted basements, used by the servants as kitchens. Queen Anne's Summer House was well placed for those in need of refreshment, being at the axis of long walks through Olney's woodland.

Queen Anne's Summer House, Bedfordshire, *c.* 1712, architecturally linked
to Queen Anne's footstool, and historically linked to the South Sea Bubble.

At the time when the Summer House was built, Ongley was involved
in government financial strategy. In 1710 Robert Harley, Earl of Oxford and
Chief Lord of the Treasury, had formed a Tory government seeking to end
England's ruinous involvement in European wars and reduce the national
debt. The newly formed Bank of England had already tried running state lotteries on behalf of the government, but Harley turned to the racier-sounding
Sword Blade Bank, directed by John Blunt, and Ongley was the go-between.
From 1711 they ran successful lotteries, the second called the Two Million
Pound Adventure, thus creating a new appetite for financial speculation
which spread even to those of slender means (and familiarized the use of
paper money, credits and annuities). The South Sea Company was formed in
this venturesome atmosphere to exploit the previously unattainable riches of
South America. The war with Spain ended (temporarily) in 1713 and England
was granted the right to trade slaves from West Africa to key ports in Central
and South America (which also offered the more lucrative opportunity for
contraband trading). In return for their monopoly the South Sea Company
assumed millions of pounds of national debt. Queen Anne died in 1714,

Harley lost office and at some point Ongley ceased to be involved. He may well have sold his shares to great advantage when the market was high; however, his original partner John Blunt and the Sword Blade Bank remained embroiled. George I became a director of the South Sea Company and he, the Prince of Wales and the royal mistresses all bought stock, along with half the nation. John Aislabie, MP for Ripon (a man of fluid allegiances – first a Tory, then a Whig), was interested in the schemes from the start and, given his financial acumen, became Chancellor of the Exchequer in 1718. In 1719, with John Blunt, he arranged for the South Sea Company to take on the whole national debt by converting it into company shares. When Aislabie presented this to Parliament 'a profound silence ensued', but he forced the measure through (no one denied he was a skilled speaker). Much false propaganda and bribery was involved, in Parliament and the City, to foment the purchase of shares. Aislabie himself made a huge profit by selling off his shares when the market reached its height. The bubble burst in 1720; Aislabie was disgraced, imprisoned for 'most notorious, dangerous and infamous corruption' and barred from ever holding public office again. On his release from the Tower of London he retreated to his Yorkshire estates at Studley Royal, which he had inherited in 1693, to create a water garden graced with Palladian follies. It has been suggested that many aristocrats, financially embarrassed on account of the South Sea Bubble, abandoned major renovations to their stately homes and built follies instead.[8] It is ironic that a politician in such deep disgrace as John Aislabie should (in partnership with Colen Campbell) have helped to inspire the neo-Palladian fashion in England, linked as it was with classical purity and aspirations to moral integrity.

Studley Royal lies in the undulating valley of the river Skell, which Aislabie, with his head gardener William Fisher, diverted to form a series of ornamental lakes. The first was a large sheet of water at the garden entrance, where a stepped dam flanked by rusticated columns was set between two elegant, square fishing temples, each with the arches of a boat house underneath, built in 1727 and also known as the Cascade Houses. There are two sphinxes guarding the way, which leads along a canal lined by beech trees until the garden opens out into a wide amphitheatre of stepped grass terraces, where a Moon Pond and a Half Moon Pond are framed by the gently sloping green banks. Here is the Temple of Piety, renamed by Aislabie's son William in 1747, in an effort to redeem his father's reputation, because in John Aislabie's time it was the Temple of Hercules, no doubt referencing his labour in cleaning the Augean stables with floods of water. It is a Doric

Banqueting House, Studley Royal, *c.* 1728, designed by Colen Campbell to overlook the water garden, which was created by Aislabie after his disgrace in the South Sea Bubble.

temple, beautifully placed to gaze at its own reflection in the Moon Pond, where another Whig statue of Neptune wields his trident. There is no record that Colen Campbell designed this temple, but he was surely involved since he was working at Studley Royal around this date, 1728. The Temple of Piety, which is rectangular with six Doric columns supporting a pediment and a frieze, follows a Palladio drawing of its lost Roman namesake. This had been recorded in a sketch owned by Lord Burlington, with whom Colen Campbell had been working; and Campbell certainly designed the folly standing on the other side of the Moon Ponds, in a clearing which included a bowling green and more rolling embankments. It is by far the most original of the follies at Studley Royal, first intended as an orangery (although one cannot imagine plants thriving in the dim interior) and thereafter converted into the Banqueting House. The building looks amused, and at certain angles faintly surprised, which is fine for a folly. This must be due to the curves, like raised eyebrows, above the fanned glass in the two windows and the door. The facade is decorated with rusticated pilasters, with squiggly patterns in the stone known as vermiculation; there are three satyr masks above the fanlights and an ornamental balustrade around the roofline. To complete the illusion of a welcoming face there are two little alcoves, like ears, built into the side walls. This was not the end of Aislabie's classical follies; according to a print dated 1758 there was a rotunda further along the embankment, and higher up an octagonal temple, which his son William later altered with gothic pinnacles. The great showpiece, spreading out beyond the climb at the end of Aislabie's water garden, was Fountains Abbey, genuine medieval ruins to outshine those at Rievaulx, the envy of any eighteenth-century landscape garden, though not itself a folly.

The most extraordinary folly garden to emerge from political alienation was Stowe in Buckinghamshire, transformed successively over a thirty-year period by Richard Temple, Lord Cobham, a leading member of the Whig aristocracy and member of the Kit-Cat Club, who had been one of Marlborough's generals. He first experienced the alternative joys of gardening leave when the Tory government of Robert Harley dismissed him from the army in 1713. The following year, when George I came to the throne, his fortunes were again reversed, because the Whigs who supported the Hanoverian succession regained the ascendant; that is when Temple was created Lord Cobham. His finances were assured by his military ventures and by marriage to the heiress of a wealthy City brewer. During the following decade Charles Bridgeman began the long transformation of the grounds at Stowe into lawns, lakes and vistas, bounding them with an early version of the ha-ha and bastions reminiscent of those defensive forts which Cobham had attacked in Europe. Cobham's fellow Kit-Cat member John Vanbrugh designed a Venus Rotunda and a huge pyramid (now gone), and wrote in 1725 that Stowe was 'now so agreeable that I had much ado to leave it at all'. Another Kit-Cat member, the dramatist William Congreve, wrote in 1728:

> Say, COBHAM, what amuses thy Retreat?
> Or Stratagems of War, or Schemes of State?

Congreve was commemorated at Stowe with a little island monument in the lake, a pyramid topped by a monkey holding 'a mirror up to nature', as Congreve did in his comedies.[9]

The first dramatically political follies at Stowe were erected in the Elysian Fields, which had a certain authenticity because, according to the Greeks, dead heroes viewed their idyllic surroundings in the underworld with discontent when they considered the state of affairs above ground. William Kent was at work in the Elysian Fields in the early 1730s (when the Earl of Carlisle received Robinson's letter about the 'new taste in gardening just arisen . . . the celebrated gardens of Claremont, Chiswick and Stowe are now full of labourers'). At the upper level of the Elysian Fields, where the old mill stream flowed darkly among alders, chestnuts and evergreens, it was renamed the Styx. When it reached Kent's rocky grotto it formed a cascade, then drifted calmly through the lawns and dappled shade where Kent's three ill-assorted temples were built. This was the time of Lord Cobham's second loss of political favour. In 1733 he quarrelled with the Whig Prime Minister Robert Walpole, who had gained power in 1721 as the saviour of the nation's finances after the South Sea Bubble, but whose government appeared increasingly self-serving and corrupt. In 1733 Walpole's Excise Tax, imposing extra duties on trade, was widely seen as a sinister extension of government powers and damaging to the commercial interests of the City, which the Whigs were supposed to nurture. Lord Cobham spent the ensuing years in opposition, coaching his nephews the Grenvilles, Lytteltons and Pitts, known as Cobham's Cubs or the Boy Patriots, into a powerful political dynasty. In the Elysian Fields,[10] Cobham's Temple of Modern Virtue was built to resemble a classical building in ruins, and it enshrined a headless torso in contemporary clothes widely suspected to represent Robert Walpole (though a French visitor quite misinterpreted Cobham's meaning as a comment on parliamentary government: 'Reputations built solely on popular acclaim evaporate as easily'!). To contrast with this crumbling folly, and raised higher up the slope of the Elysian Fields, Kent designed the Temple of Ancient Virtue – circular, colonnaded and domed, based like many others on the Temple of Vesta at Tivoli, with Ionic columns and completed in 1737. Inside were the life-size statues of four ancient Greeks who embodied different virtues, which were explained in inscriptions: Homer (first of poets, herald of virtue); Socrates (wisest of men, innocent in a corrupt state); Lycurgus (just lawgiver of Sparta and defender of liberty); Epaminondas (a military leader who defended the liberty of Thebes).

Escaping this didactic atmosphere, across the stream there is a third and far more intriguing edifice, a Temple of British Worthies, where a row of eclectic busts in ruffs, helmets, caps and open-necked shirts stare out with varying degrees of gratification at being included. Their 'temple' of golden stone forms a gentle ellipse, with shallow steps leading up to a row of sixteen arched niches. The Italianate design was initially drawn up by William Kent for Lord Burlington's exedra at Chiswick House (where the figures proposed may also have had political implications that Lord Burlington decided were indiscreet). The monument has a central block topped by a stepped pyramid, where a statue of Mercury formerly pointed the way to paradise. Among the chosen busts Queen Elizabeth is the only woman – idealized defender of the faith – alongside her seafaring heroes Francis Drake and Walter Raleigh; Thomas

Temple of British Worthies, Stowe, *c.* 1735, William Kent's most overtly political folly, displaying busts of England's most patriotic leaders and impressive luminaries.

Gresham represents the growth of the City in her reign, and Shakespeare heads a cast of poets and thinkers including John Milton, Alexander Pope, Francis Bacon, John Locke, Inigo Jones and Isaac Newton. The overtly political choices are King Alfred, who founded the English constitution and guarded liberty; the Black Prince, who stood for Cobham's ally Frederick, Prince of Wales; William III, darling of the Whigs, the other worthy monarch; John Hampden, who first defended the rights of Parliament against Charles I; and John Barnard, merchant and MP for the City, a vigorous opponent of Walpole's policies. The Temple of British Worthies was much remarked by Cobham's contemporaries, who would also have noted how the chosen monarchs and men of action fought against France and/or Spain, as Cobham had himself and as Walpole refrained from doing.

One other monument in the Elysian Fields, although it arrived after Kent's time, testifies to a personal loss. The Grenville column, decorated oddly with protruding prows of ships, was erected in honour of Captain Thomas

Gothic Temple, Stowe, built for Lord Cobham by Gibbs in 1741, an extraordinary architectural departure for both, linking gothic style with Whig principles of freedom.

Grenville, one of Lord Cobham's nephews, who, since Cobham had no children, were like sons to him. In 1747 Thomas, commanding the *Defiance* in Lord Anson's fleet, was fatally wounded in action against the French off Cape Finisterre. Thomas had two brothers. Richard Grenville inherited Stowe after Lord Cobham died in 1749 and took the title Earl Temple. He was a Whig grandee, restlessly espousing principles of liberty, even supporting the radical journalist John Wilkes.[11] The second brother was George Grenville, who became Prime Minister briefly in 1763, introducing the Stamp Tax which precipitated the revolt of the American colonies. More illustrious by far was the husband of their sister Hester: William Pitt, Earl Chatham, one of the great eighteenth-century wartime prime ministers and father of the other. In their youth in the 1730s, this group of aspiring politicians was moulded for Whig opposition, holding the patronage of many MPs, and in 1742 they finally succeeded in causing Walpole's downfall. Their symbolic meeting place at Stowe was the Temple of Friendship, built on the southeast bastion of Bridgeman's ha-ha in 1739 and designed by James Gibbs. This marked Gibbs's return to Stowe after building the Boycott Pavilions ten years earlier beside the entrance drive, but his second group of follies had far more political implications. The Temple of Friendship (which is the only folly at Stowe with a basement kitchen and ample cellarage) celebrated the first visit to Stowe of Frederick, Prince of Wales, who led the opposition to his father's government. To organize these subversive activities Frederick employed another of Lord Cobham's politically important nephews, George Lyttelton, as his Chief Secretary.[12] The Temple of Friendship was ruined by a fire in 1840 but retains its sturdy arches and portico and, thanks also to its tawny limestone, it harmonizes with the follies built by William Kent, especially the Temple of Venus on the other bastion.

Despite all his political scene-setting, Lord Cobham continued to uphold the tenets of classicism in his garden buildings until a most dramatic departure, in 1741, when James Gibbs built his masterpiece, the Gothic Temple. Positioned like an outcast among the rough grass and crows of the Hawkwell Field, it is a superb and imposing manifestation of the spooky grandeur that 'gothick' came to imply. But in the mid-eighteenth century the word signified all that was most noble in the Anglo-Saxon heritage, as opposed to Roman imperial tyranny or the Baroque excesses of Europe's absolute monarchs. Gibbs drew inspiration for the Gothic Temple's traceried windows, battlements and turrets from medieval buildings in the perpendicular style, and he used reddish ironstone, which created an impression of brute force. It was intended to represent a bastion of integrity and its three-sided structure stood for the three Whig principles of Liberty, Enlightenment and Constitution – in proof of which Cobham's gothic folly was originally known as the Temple of Liberty, and it bore an inscription over the doorway: 'I thank the gods that I am not a Roman.' The sentiment was based on a reading of Tacitus, who described how the Germanic people, the Goths, held gatherings that were deemed to mark the origins of democracy. Inside the Temple, the golden mosaic ceiling was decorated with the shields of imaginary Saxon ancestors, and nearby stood statues of the Saxon/Norse gods who gave their names to the days of the week. As the temple was receiving its finishing touches Walpole finally lost power, and the way lay open for Cobham's Boy Patriots, led by Pitt, to gain the ascendant in Whig politics.

Lord Cobham's was not the first gothic folly, nor did Whigs have a monopoly of the glories of medieval history. In 1721 Lord Bathurst, a Tory bon viveur and friend of Pope and Swift, built Alfred's Hall in Cirencester

The North East View of **KING ALFRED'S HALL.**
Tradition says that a Treaty was signd here with Gormandus the Dane. It is certain that a Street and some remains of a Castle or Tower at Cirencester still bear his Name.

Thomas Robins, *Alfred's Hall, Cirencester Park*, print 1763, built in 1721 by the Tory Lord Bathurst, proving that gothic architecture and sham ruins were not a Whig monopoly.

Park, Gloucestershire, which was the earliest example of a mock gothic castle, banqueting house and sham ruin all in one, built on the site where Lord Bathurst believed King Alfred camped during his successful campaign against the Danes around Chippenham. Lord Bathurst's first effort was wooden and collapsed in 1727, just after Swift had visited, which was noted when Mrs Delany wrote to Swift in 1733 about its restoration: 'the day you left it, it fell to the ground, conscious of the honour it had received by entertaining so illustrious a guest, it burst with pride. It is now a venerable castle . . . with thicket overgrown grotesque and wild.'[13] This enlarged and strengthened version was extensive and included genuine medieval pieces taken from Bathurst's demolished Sapperton Manor. A print by Thomas Robins, dated 1763, of the northeast view, shows an enclosed area of low broken walls and traceried window frames to the right and a battlemented gatehouse on the left with round and square towers and lancet windows. Behind are the great trees of Oakley Wood and in the foreground Georgian visitors are relishing the atmosphere, but now Alfred's Hall has become a ruin of a ruin.

At the other extreme from this gothic pile is a very pretty gothic pavilion at Shotover Park, near Oxford.[14] This certainly belongs in the Whig gothic tradition, and may be its first manifestation, the unanswered question being just how early it was. Of the denizens of Shotover Park, James Tyrrell the father was a friend of John Locke, and to their contemporaries their writings on political philosophy were linked in importance as they debated 'the just extent of regal power' and 'the ancient constitution of English government'. Tyrrell was the author of *Bibliotheca politica*, which was full of these 'gothic' constitutional concepts, and although he did not have to flee the country, as Locke did during the reign of James II, the arrival of William III brought relief to both. Tyrrell began to redesign the park at Shotover in his later years, and a print of 1750 shows that its formal layout remained, with a rectangular lake and straight avenues of trees stretching between the house and the gothic pavilion, which face each other along the water (see overleaf). Did James Tyrrell senior plan, if not build, this gothic pavilion before his death in 1718, and did he enrol a leading architect, or was it his son, Col. James Tyrrell, who built it later? The son won military distinction in Marlborough's European wars, and in 1714 was appointed Groom of the Bedchamber to George I. From 1722 till his death in 1742 he was a consistently loyal Whig MP. In the 1730s he called in William Kent to render the grounds surrounding the formal lake more natural, and Kent built an octagonal folly. Did Kent also build, or perhaps restore, the gothic pavilion around 1734? It bears some resemblance to his other gothic work, like the eye-catchers at Rousham. Either way it is the earliest gothic pavilion built by an ardently Whig family, large and ecclesiastical, with three pointed archways leading into a cloistered interior, a round 'rose' window set in a triangular, battlemented gable, and the whole flanked by turrets, pinnacles and shallow niches. In the print dating to 1750, the gothic pinnacles (seen from behind) reach up high and proud above the treetops. It set a fine example of gothic style for the rest of the century, though in the course of time the political implications of gothic gave way to tales of mystery and imagination.

In Yorkshire, embittered family and political rivalry was expressed in colourful ways, including folly-building. It began in 1695 on the two Wentworth estates, when the Earl of Strafford died childless, leaving Wentworth Woodhouse, and his wealth, to a cousin through the female line. This cousin was Thomas Watson, who became Watson Wentworth. The

To the Honourable Augustus Schutz, Esq.

This Plate of Shotover House & Garden Is humbly inscribed by Geo. Bickham.

George Bingham, *Shotover Gothic Temple, Shotover House, Oxfordshire*, 1750, engraving. The temple, dating from the 1730s or earlier, faces the house across the water; its gothic pinnacles, a very early example, are clearly shown.

follies were built by his son, also Thomas, the first Marquis of Rockingham, followed by his son Charles, the second Lord Rockingham (owner of the stallion Whistlejacket). Both were leading Whigs in an area traditionally Tory, so that much wealth and lavish entertainment was expended on creating a local, and later national, base of loyal Whig MPs.[15] Their huge black follies at Wentworth Woodhouse are among the most characterful anywhere. Meanwhile their angry relative, Thomas Wentworth, who came from a clannish old branch of the family, royalist and Tory (whom Swift described as 'proud as hell'), bought the nearby Stainborough estate in 1708 and seized the moment of Tory ascendancy during Queen Anne's reign to get back the family title Earl of Strafford in 1711. He bought pictures in Italy, declaring: 'I hope to have a better collection than Mr Watson,' and by 1730 he had built his finest folly. He called it Stainborough Castle, thus preserving the old name of the estate and giving it a baronial air. It was among the first and largest sham castles of the eighteenth century, and its gatehouse had four round towers (now two), with an arched entrance and arched windows (unlikely but elegant). It was built among yew trees on the highest vantage point of the estate, which Strafford then renamed Wentworth Castle.

But alas for Strafford, and Wentworth Castle, because the scale of Wentworth Woodhouse was far more impressive. The Palladian mansion built between 1724 and 1749 was vast (twice the width of Buckingham Palace and alleged to have a thousand windows). To the north a suitably grand stable block was added by the second Marquis in the 1760s ('this lord loves nothing but horses,' sneered Horace Walpole after a visit in 1766), and this is where George Stubbs came in 1762 to paint Whistlejacket, the fabulous Arab stallion who won Rockingham 2,000 guineas in his most famous race at York in 1759. Horse and painting both became legendary, and in his time their owner was as well, not least for his gambling habit. One persistent rumour related to a race between five turkeys and five geese from Norwich to London. Another related to the Needle's Eye. This folly stands to the north of the house, on the direct line between the stables and the Pontefract gate, on what was once a beech-lined carriageway but is now a rough grassy track. The Needle's Eye is a beautifully tall pyramid, blackened by time and coal dust, built from massive blocks of stone. It is pierced by a high ogee arch straddling the original driveway, which gives the pyramid a soaring quality. On top is a great urn, seemingly in flames, which means that the pyramid lacks the final stone, known as the pyramidion. This 'unfinished' pyramid may be a Masonic sign, although in such cases an unfinished pyramid was usually topped by the

The Needle's Eye, Wentworth Woodhouse, date uncertain but before 1746: a most unusual triangular folly, forming a grand archway over the driveway and associated with a bet.

eye of providence. According to hearsay the second marquis built this folly because he had a bet that he could drive a coach and horses through the eye of a needle – but if he made such a bet it was because he already had the Needle's Eye in place. The first estate map to name it was made between 1734 and 1746, and therefore dated from the time of the first marquis. This was also the time when Bonnie Prince Charlie attempted to regain the throne for the Stuart dynasty. His march south from Scotland reached Derby in November 1745, and the dents of musket shots in the Needle's Eye may mark his passing.

Certain it is that Charles Watson Wentworth (then aged fifteen) joined the Duke of Cumberland as he marched north to stop the Scottish invasion (to his parents' horror and everyone else's acclaim). He fought at the Battle of Culloden in April 1746, where the Young Pretender and the Stuart cause were finally defeated. The second great folly at Wentworth Woodhouse commemorates the victory at Culloden, and an inscription declares that Thomas, Marquis of Rockingham, erected it in 1748 'in grateful respect to the preserver of our religion, laws and liberty King George II', who 'subdued a most unnatural rebellion'. However, it is not called the Culloden Tower, it is called Hoober Stand, because it stands on Hoober Hill, and the staircase within, leading to a balustrade around the lantern on its summit, shows that it was used as a belvedere. In its way this too is a pyramid, triangular with rounded corners and tapering upwards for about 30 metres (100 ft) of smoke-blackened stone. In contrast to the soaring quality of the earlier dark pyramid, this one looms and is strangely ugly, but with its own grandeur. The design is an optical trick, creating an architecturally sound building that appears to be falling down, the phenomenon being due to its triangular plan and tapering silhouette. Its source seems to have been Fischer von Erlach's *Entwurff einer historischen Architektur* (1721), an important compendium of ancient and Masonic architecture, which was published in English, as *Historical Architecture*, in 1730. In a letter to his son, the first Marquis of Rockingham named Flitcroft as the architect responsible for Hoober Stand, meaning that it was the first of his three remarkable triangular towers. The second was for the Duke of Cumberland at Virginia Water; the third was Alfred's Tower at Stourhead. Flitcroft had already worked at Wentworth Woodhouse a decade earlier, adding to the palatial house itself and probably building the Ionic Temple, a sturdy rotunda dating from circa 1735–6. It too is dramatically blackened by the coal mining that later enriched, and then ruined, Wentworth Woodhouse. It stands above the bastion walls which support the south terrace, created in emulation of those at Castle Howard.

The follies linked to the second Marquis of Rockingham are as remarkable as his father's, less of an eyeful but even more political. Admiral Keppel's monument is taller than Hoober Stand and also tapers dramatically upwards. The original design showed prows of ships projecting like the Grenville column at Stowe, but it ended as a plain column like Nelson's, with only its great height and attribution to make it interesting. Admiral Keppel became a national hero after his naval victories in the Seven Years War, but as trouble brewed in the American colonies Keppel, like Rockingham, was strongly opposed to fighting them. The Whig faction that coalesced round Rockingham, both when he was Prime Minister, from 1765 to 1766, and in opposition, sympathized with the American demands for the same treatment and representation as British people expected, and they understood that unfair taxation and terms of trade were counterproductive. In 1778 Admiral Keppel was court-martialled on spurious charges after an inconclusive battle with the French, and only in 1782, when Rockingham was again Prime Minister, was Keppel exonerated of 'malicious and unfounded' charges. The Keppel monument was therefore highly political, as was the Mausoleum built from 1785 to 1790, not to house the body of Lord Rockingham, who died in 1782 and was buried in York Minster, but as a monument to the liberal 'Rockingham' Whigs. Inside is a life-size statue of Rockingham himself surrounded by eight busts of like-minded politicians, including Edmund Burke, who had been Rockingham's secretary, and Charles James Fox, who continued his style of opposition (even finding merit in the French Revolution). If the Mausoleum had not been blackened by coal dust like the other follies at Wentworth Woodhouse, it might look too much like a wedding cake: it is three-tiered and based on a cube with four pedimented entrances, then arches enclosing a sarcophagus,

Culloden Tower, Richmond, Yorkshire, *c.* 1746, built to celebrate the victory of 1745 over the Stuart rebellion, possibly on the site of an earlier pele tower, which guarded the Scottish border.

and a rotunda above, all encircled with four diagonally placed obelisks (echoing Fischer von Erlach's sepulchral temple surrounded by columns). The Mausoleum was designed, as the stables had been, by James Carr of York and it most resembled the Roman tomb of the Julii at St Rémy in Provence, not much copied or even visited, but the cognoscenti would have known it and spotted it in the background of various *capriccios* and scene paintings.[16]

Victories and elections spawned other follies. Culloden was also celebrated with a tower at Richmond, Yorkshire, built soon after 1746 for John Yorke, Whig MP for York.[17] He had a relative who fought at Culloden and he represented many who had stood to lose all if the Stuarts had regained the throne. His sense of relief and gratitude was also reflected in the tower's alternative name, Cumberland Temple. The architect was Daniel Garrett, who was local but had trained with Lord Burlington and William Kent as their clerk of works. The tower is in the gothic style then being espoused by Whigs, but it shows decorative flourishes probably derived from contact with Kent. The tower is an octagon on a square base – possibly built on the site of one of the medieval pele towers that guarded the borders near Scotland. One flourish is the added staircase turret echoing the angles of the tower itself and capped with a leaded dome. Others are a decorative band of blind arches halfway up the brickwork of the tower, pointed windows and the stone parapet of the roof with diamond fretwork and pinnacles. Inside, the plasterwork of the rooms is gloriously ornate with everything from gothic tracery to satyrs' heads. Daniel Garrett was linked with other ornamental gothic follies in the area. In partnership with William Kent he supervised the construction of Aske Temple, near Richmond, designed circa 1745 for Sir Conyers D'Arcy, another Whig MP for York. Its fine edifice has many similar features: an octagonal tower with pointed windows, here flanked by two square towers, all crenellated and with the same band of blind arches halfway up the brickwork; and this fine frontage is lined up along an arcaded base ending in semicircular bows, with the same diamond-fretted parapets as Culloden Tower. As a banqueting house Aske Temple gained a dubious local reputation, which centred on the secret staircase at the back where, it was whispered, 'bawds' were smuggled in. Its gothic atmosphere is much enhanced by the dark surrounds of Crow Wood, but in front is a grassy slope which, on a map of 1761, was marked Coney-garth, meaning more rabbit warrens.

The most curious of Daniel Garrett's attributed follies is the Banqueting House, on the Gibside estate of George Bowes, near Newcastle, which was

Gibside Banqueting House, Gibside, Newcastle, built c. 1746,
a particularly flamboyant example of Whig gothic architecture.

probably finished by 1746.[18] This too is Whig gothic, built for a landowner enriched by coal deposits. Here, again, and more dominant because it is a smaller building, are the pointed gothic windows, the crenellations and quatrefoils as at Aske Temple and a bowed parapet, but in quite a different position. Here it is central, rising high above the roof and crested with three triangular gables, which give a flourish to the Banqueting House like a festive paper crown. The diamond fretwork patterns reappear, but here they are in the windowpanes and matching door. Inside the Banqueting House there is fine decorative plasterwork, which is in fact constructed from papier mâché, and it made a delightful destination for picnics at the end of long walks through all the surrounding woodland, gorges and lakes. It was built on the highest part of the park with a magnificent panorama, and nearby was the ultimate Whig statement, a Doric pillar 45 metres (150 ft) high surmounted by a colossal figure of British Liberty.

Follies also celebrated the next great period of conflict and victory, the Seven Years War. At Audley End in Essex, where Capability Brown relandscaped the grounds in the 1760s, Robert Adam formed a partnership with Brown, as he did elsewhere, and embellished them with follies. At the end of one vista stood a charming replica of the Temple of Vesta at Tivoli, with Ionic columns, named the Temple of Victory, which bore a triumphalist inscription to the 'Glorious and Unparalleled Success of the British Fleets and Armies . . . in Europe, Asia, Africa and America'. Also, from the victorious vantage point of the 1770s, King Alfred's Tower at Stourhead bore a similar inscription, which in gothic style also looked far back to ancestral battles against the Danes. Another triangular tower, named Severndroog Castle, was built as a memorial in the 1780s to commemorate one particular victory in India. Not the most famous battles like Robert Clive at Plassey or Eyre Coote at Wandiwash (Vandavasi), but an earlier skirmish in the lead-up to the war, when tensions between England and France, and between rival Indian rulers, were threatening trade and making it necessary (according to contemporary thinking) for the East India Company army to gain decisive control of the situation. The tower's extraordinary name is a corruption of Survarnadurg, on the Malabar coast, where a pirate stronghold attacked shipping. In 1755 Sir William James, commodore of the Bombay marine in the East India Company fleet, led a joint British and Indian expedition to destroy the fort. It was his finest hour and later, when he was Chairman of the East India Company, Sir Joshua Reynolds painted his portrait holding a plan of Survarnadurg fort.[19] After his death in 1783 his widow commissioned the tower in loving memory of her hero, on Shooters Hill in southeast London, just off the Old Dover Road and gazing over the City where so many made their fortunes from trade with India. The Tower is one of the finest triangular follies, strong yet elegant and supported by three hexagonal corner turrets, all crenellated. Its red brick walls are copiously provided with sophisticated arched windows, ensuring that its Georgian and gothic qualities are nicely balanced and yet maintaining an air of great eccentricity, as follies should.

Severndroog Castle, Shooters Hill, London, built in the 1780s
to commemorate a heroic naval victory in India.

Temple of Bellona, Kew Gardens, built in 1759 to celebrate the victory
at Minden, one of the turning points of the Seven Years War.

But who now imagines what the inscription tries to recall: 'achievement in the
East Indies . . . commanding marine forces in those seas . . . the conquest of
the Castle of Severndroog which fell to his superior valour and able conduct'.

It would be strange indeed if, in this era of victory temples, the royal family
had not also celebrated with buildings. The royal garden at Kew belonged
to the heir to the throne until 1760, when George III became king. He was
then able to unite Kew with the late George II's adjoining Richmond garden,
to make one large park stretching beside the Thames. Since they were originally two separate entities they have ever since been known as Kew Gardens.
In 1757 William Chambers was commissioned by Princess Augusta, mother
of George III, to create a programme of follies, starting in the Kew garden
and, since this coincided with the Seven Years War, a victory temple or two
became inevitable. One still survives, now called the Temple of Bellona after
the Roman goddess of war. In Rome, where the original Temple of Bellona
stood on the outskirts, the legions would sacrifice to victory as they marched
forth or returned victorious. The temple at Kew was built to celebrate the

Battle of Minden in 1759, which was a turning point of the Seven Years War on the European front, particularly dear to the Hanoverian kings of England, who cherished their German homeland. Minden is in Prussia and Frederick II (later known as the Great) was England's ally against France, Spain and Austria. This victory was hard-won by the combined armies of Prussia, with a contingent from Hanover led by Princess Augusta's brother, and the British forces led by the Marquis of Granby. It averted the very real threat to Hanover itself, and the marquis of became a national hero, with more pubs named after him than anyone else. The year 1759 was known as the *annus mirabilis*, when Wolfe's capture of Quebec secured Canada and lifting the French siege of Madras turned the tide in India. Walpole wrote 'our bells are worn threadbare with ringing for victories,' and the song 'Heart of Oak' was on everyone's lips. At Kew the Temple of Bellona was also called the Temple of Minden, although inside there are medallions commemorating other victories. It has been moved from an earlier position nearer the river and is now the first temple to be seen on entering the Victoria Gate at Kew, framed by trees on its mound, classically pale and well-proportioned with its Doric portico and dome, but mostly unremarked. There was a second domed Temple of Victory at Kew, which Queen Charlotte (George III's wife) nicknamed the 'mushroom temple'; also a rotunda dedicated to Pan and a Temple of the Sun, which was modelled on the recently discovered ruins of Constantine's basilica at Baalbek. All three are now gone, but there is a surviving Temple of Aeolus (a god of the winds), a little rotunda on an artificial mound that is pleasing for its location, especially when the daffodils are out.

Meanwhile, back at Stowe, a Temple of Concord and Victory had been built to outshine all others. The Grecian Valley at Stowe was the work of Capability Brown, who started his career there, and Lord Cobham graced it with his largest temple, during the final years of his life (1747–9), choosing the Grecian style because their civilization inaugurated a kind of democracy. It preceded the 'Greek Revival' of James Stuart and Nicholas Revett and no architect has been identified, nor any direct archetype, but it has a Greek air, standing magnificent and rectangular, surrounded on all sides by Ionic columns. Richard Grenville, Earl Temple, inherited Stowe when Lord Cobham died in 1749, and after the Seven Years War he proudly adorned the temple further. He was a founder member of the Society of Dilettanti, exceedingly rich, political and contentious. He derived great satisfaction from the progress of the Seven Years War, whose political direction involved many of his extended family – those Whigs who had grown up together under Cobham's aegis, especially his brother-in-law William Pitt, who was largely responsible for the successful war strategy. Richard Grenville himself and his brother George were also part of the government, though prone to fall out. The Grecian Temple was therefore renamed Concord and Victory, a massive stone relief was installed in the front pediment showing the four quarters bringing their various products to Britannia, and a statue of Liberty was placed on the apex above. Other statues adorned the corners of the temple roof, plus a Latin inscription from Valerius Maximus, translated into doggerel as:

> The times with such alarming Dangers fraught
> Left not a Hope for any factious thought.[20]

Thoughts were in fact always factious, and on the home front questions of liberty and taxation were never far away.

In Somerset Sir Charles Kemeys-Tynte, MP for thirty years from 1747 until 1777, exemplified the age. He inherited his baronetcy and Halswell Park in 1740 and greatly relished developing the surrounding park and woodland with what his estate steward called 'schemes', some of which were Masonic. His amiable portrait by Hogarth shows him seated with architectural tomes, an intelligent hound and one of his follies in the background.[21] Among these follies, his political statement was called Robin Hood's Hut. Sir Charles was an independent MP, not affiliated to either Whigs or Tories nor in the pocket of a leading political family, but voting on issues as he saw fit, so that when it came to getting himself re-elected to Parliament he needed money and to skilfully manoeuvre around the matters that concerned Somerset. One such was the cider tax. The election of 1768 was hotly contested by a demagogue, who circulated rousing songs against bullying landlords, and Sir Charles felt obliged to insert the following statement in the local newspaper:

> I spoke in the House of Commons against the cider tax. I voted against it. The one day I was absent I was afflicted with so severe a fit of the gout that I could not turn in my bed without assistance. I attended every meeting in the country and in London to concert proper measures against it, and I was carried to the house wrapped in flannels to vote for the repeal of that odious and detestable tax.[22]

Sir Charles was also involved in an outcry involving freedom of the press. John Wilkes, the disreputable associate of Francis Dashwood and MP

Robin Hood's Hut, Halswell, built in 1768 by the local Somerset landowner and MP as an eye-catcher, a statement of liberty and part of a parliamentary election campaign.

for Aylesbury, produced a paper called the *North Briton*. In 1763, issue no. 45 went beyond all normal bounds in deriding George III, and Wilkes was arrested for seditious libel. George Grenville, as prime minister, then issued a general warrant permitting the arrest of all those involved in publishing the *North Briton*, causing a storm of protests against such a restriction of citizens' liberty and freedom of expression. In due course general warrants were declared illegal, and John Wilkes continued his career as a champion of liberty, despite being excluded from Parliament. Around this time Robin Hood's Hut materialized in Halswell Park, and was completed by 1768, high up on the hill above Sir Charles Kemeys-Tynte's estate, where all could see and appreciate this fist raised to freedom.

It is a particularly extraordinary building because it was intended to combine the rustic elements of a hermitage, especially its thatched roof, with gothic features like its elegant ogee windows, all overshadowed by a swaggering canopy with hints of orientalism. This raised semicircular screen has been called the Umbrello, though it has more the look of Asian ceremonial tents, and beneath it the curving arches and slender columns resemble drapes pulled back against wooden poles, while the plasterwork inside the domed ceiling is formed into swags. The Umbrello certainly creates an eye-catcher, and from its hillside vantage point it looks as far as the Bristol Channel and

Wales. There is no apparent architectural link with Robin Hood, except in the mind of Sir Charles Kemeys-Tynte, who was appealing to memories of the folk hero of freedom for obvious reasons. Robin Hood lived on in the popular mind as a symbol of retribution against greed, corruption and unjust authority, protecting the oppressed, and usually winning. Everyone appreciated what he stood for, and by implication their local MP was upholding their rights too, specifically at that moment over the dreaded cider tax.

There is another raised fist linked to victory and elections across the water in Carmarthenshire. Paxton's Tower was built by Sir William Paxton, a Londoner who had made his fortune in India.[23] During the 1802 election he spent eyewatering sums (to win votes) on food, drink and ribbons, only to lose to the Tory candidate. However, in 1806 he won, and as MP he set his seal on the area, developing his own grounds at Middleton Hall and enriching the nearby town of Tenby, where he pioneered sea bathing. His tower is another eye-catcher, with a fine panoramic view and a banqueting house on the first floor. But above all it is a memorial 'to the invincible Viscount Nelson . . . the Empire everywhere maintained by him overseas . . . the death for his country which is the fullness of his glory'. The inscription is also in Welsh, and presumably they accepted these sentiments and appreciated having a triangular tower of their own, massive and complicated, with round corner turrets and a hexagonal central turret, all castellated, while below is an archway big enough to drive a horse and carriage through.

The concepts of freedom which came so naturally to aristocrats and gentry fighting rural elections came as a shock when the American colonies started to turn them back on their English governors. Paternalism had been acceptable during the first half of the century, but the Seven Years War created such debt that the English government, by increasing taxation and duties in their colonies, focused minds on the question of whether Americans should be taxed when they had no representatives in Parliament. George Grenville's Stamp Tax of 1765 caused the first outcry, which intensified over the following decade. Even so, new colonies were being optimistically planned. Sir Matthew Fetherstonhaugh of Uppark in West Sussex, who had large commercial interests in America, purchased Western Virginia from the Iroquois people, intending to found his own state. He had the backing of Benjamin Franklin although many settlers in Pennsylvania and Virginia disliked the scheme. It was to be called Vandalia as a compliment to Queen Charlotte, who was said to be descended from Vandals (a Germanic tribe like the Goths, associated at that time with early manifestations of democracy). In the circumstances the

The Library, Great Torrington, Devon, possibly a 17th-century banqueting house, converted to a library by the mid-18th century in which Denys Rolle planned his American colony.

new colony failed to materialize and the territory was absorbed into Virginia and Kentucky, but high on Harting Down stand the ruins of the Vandalian Tower, the folly built around 1770 to celebrate the new colony that never was. Now there are just some battered flint buttresses and archways with a haunted look, but once there was a ground-floor kitchen and above it a room for carousing. When Sir Matthew Fetherstonhaugh died in 1774 his heir, Sir Harry, a 'witless playboy', gained for the tower a reputation as another hellfire club. Here the youthful Emma Hart enchanted young gallants long before she became Emma Hamilton and then Nelson's mistress. Local memory did not forget her: it became known as Lady Hamilton's Tower, obviously an anachronism, or a haunting, because it was said that she gazed out from there, looking for Nelson's ship to come home.

The other folly linked to a failed American colony is in Devon. The so-called Library at Stevenstone near Great Torrington belonged to the Rolle family, who were extensive and influential local landowners. Denys Rolle was an eighteenth-century naturalist and educationalist, an idealist as well as an administrator. In Devon he acted as mayor, magistrate, MP and High Sheriff; in America he travelled widely, becoming well aware of its problems as well as its possibilities.[24] The exquisite little building in his grounds at Stevenstone was certainly in use as a library by the time Denys Rolle housed his books there and used it as his study retreat from the big house. But it has the original design of a banqueting house and sporting pavilion, with its open loggia below, where the three arches are balanced by the three large windows above; and the grass that still stretches beyond its steps would have suited a bowling green or other sporting arena. The Library's mellow red bricks, framed by contrasting tawny brickwork and Ionic pilasters, have the charm of late seventeenth-century architecture, as do the large carved faces on the three keystones of the loggia arches. All of which suggest an earlier date of construction, although no conclusive information is to be had from the records or the coat of arms. Within its walls, once Denys Rolle had adopted it for his Library, a colony in Florida was planned, during the twenty-year period when the territory was won from Spain in the Seven Years War, until it became an American state in 1783, after the War of Independence.[25] Denys Rolle's first settlers arrived in January 1767, bearing a letter of recommendation from the Earl of Shelburne, Prime Minister at the time, to James Grant, the first Governor of East Florida: 'I must recommend to you in a very particular manner so bold and useful a colonist as Denys Rolle Esq. It is his Majesty's gracious pleasure that you grant him every encouragement.' But Governor Grant was engaged in developing a plantation economy with slaves and was ruthlessly maintaining order, while Denys Rolle brought a shipment of free settlers intending to farm their own plots. Whether Rolle had succeeded in recruiting farmers is questionable, since a letter described them as 'sixty people consisting of shoe blacks, chimney sweepers, tinkers, sink boys, cinder wenches, whores and pickpockets'. From that time onwards conflicting and biased accounts described the antagonism of Grant and Rolle with their different visions. Three times Rolle crossed the Atlantic, bringing in total two hundred settlers (who mostly escaped to Charleston and St Augustin), before he too resorted to using slaves to farm his property. Rolle never gave up until Florida was given up, after which his slaves were settled in the Bahamas.

Meanwhile, the last British Governor of Virginia, John Murray, Earl of Dunmore, fled home in 1777 and built the most stunning folly of all time, in the form of a pineapple.[26] He didn't give up his colonial posting without a struggle. When the rebellious colonists of Virginia succeeded in expelling him he fought a rearguard action from his ships in the harbour, until smallpox decimated his crew of freed slaves and the colonists burnt the harbour down. General Washington was exasperated with his persistence: 'I do not think forcing his lordship on shipboard is sufficient. Nothing less than depriving him of life will secure peace in Virginia.' However, Dunmore did reach home, and in true Virginian style he celebrated with a pineapple. In America it was the custom for seafarers returning from a successful voyage to splice pineapples on their gateposts as a sign of open hospitality. In his Scottish estate at Dunmore, near Stirling, the earl did so on a grander scale, perhaps to hide his failure. The Pineapple presides over a large walled orchard, on a south-facing slope with an upper terrace. The central pavilion on which the pineapple rests has a keystone dated 1761. Along the terrace immediately

The Pineapple, Dunmore, Scotland. The pineapple was added shortly after 1777 when the last Governor of Virginia returned defeated from the rebelling colony.

either side are bothies for the gardeners, and the walls beyond once supported the glasshouses where presumably pineapples were grown. They were first recorded in Scotland in the 1730s. To ripen, pineapples need succession beds of carefully heated compost, and developing the plants and fruit in rotation took much skill. At Dunmore the garden walls are double, with a cavity between for hot air to be driven through flues from the central stove, and the chimney pots along the tops of the garden walls are disguised as urns. Such were the practicalities behind the ostentation of producing a pineapple at table, a symbol of wealth as well as hospitality throughout the eighteenth century – for which reason pineapples became widespread as decorative finials in stone. The Dunmore pineapple was also a finial, though on a grander scale than any other, added to the earlier pavilion with the dated keystone after the earl's return from Virginia in 1777. There is no record of the architect responsible; it seems he was a local mason because any leading society architect like William Chambers or Robert Adam would have publicized his achievement – which is amazing. The pineapple is over 16 metres (52 ft) high, beginning with an octagonal drum with seven tall ogee windows and a matching door to the terrace. The mouldings between and above the windows run upwards to make the central ribs of the stone leaves, which curve out well over a metre, convincingly prickly and seemingly unsupported. What is more, the stones forming the leaves are graded and slanted for drainage so that damaging water and frost cannot collect. Growing from this wonderfully foliate base the fruit looks even more realistic, constructed in eight elaborate courses and diminishing to a crown of smaller leaves, as carefully carved and prickly as those below. Ingenuity and elegance remain in perfect balance. By contrast, the summer house inside is quite simple, with a plain dome and stone floor. Those within look out through the spacious windows, either over the orchard or back towards the spot where Dunmore House once stood in the distance.

Many English landowners sympathized with the American colonies, and a few celebrated their independence with follies. At Greystoke in Cumbria the Duke of Norfolk, a coarse and opinionated Whig, turned his farm buildings into folly forts, some said mainly to annoy his neighbour Earl Lonsdale, a Tory loyalist, who was equally belligerent. One fort was named Bunkers Hill after an early engagement of the war in 1775, which was so inconclusive that it encouraged the Americans to persevere. The other was called Fort Putnam, after an American general who gave his name to a defensive garrison at West Point, New York. Both follies have castellated screen walls with gothic windows, but Fort Putnam is the more impressive of the two. It has mock bastions, the walls set with wide pointed arches framing tall gothic windows, and the approach has a unique piece of architectural screenwork – a blind arcade with round blocked windows supported by rounded pilasters ending in stone petal coronets. But the Duke of Norfolk did not have the final word. In 1781, when victory for the colonies was assured by the surrender of General Cornwallis, Sir Thomas Gascoigne, an MP with republican leanings, erected a Triumphal Arch at Darlington Park, near Leeds, inscribed on both sides 'Liberty in North America Triumphant'.

Ironically it was among their French allies that the American War of Independence caused most upheaval, leaving a burden of war debts and encouraging republican theories. The extravagance of the French court and aristocracy did nothing to alleviate either of these, and it was in pre-Revolutionary France that the word 'folly' gained currency to describe fanciful and useless little buildings, or a whole park filled with them. There was the Folie St James

Fort Putnam, Greystoke, Cumbria, built c. 1780 and named after an American general to show support for the American War of Independence.

at Neuilly, just outside Paris, built by an erstwhile treasurer of the navy, a typical *jardin anglo-chinois* with a great deal of rockwork to counteract the flat terrain and little chinoiserie pavilions, temples and bridges, of which the Scottish gardener to high society, Thomas Blaikie, remarked: 'this garden is without doubt an example of extravagance rather than taste.' It was the same designer, François-Joseph Bélanger, who created the Bagatelle Gardens in the Bois de Boulogne for the Comte d'Artois, brother of Louis XVI, who in 1777 made a bet with his sister-in-law Marie Antoinette to create a garden in two months. Here too oriental fancy flourished, although the contemplative side was supposedly represented by a hermitage and a philosopher's pavilion; but given the hurried timescale they were fragile baubles designed for partying. Thomas Blaikie was the gardener responsible for the care of this 'English' garden, which he regarded as a parody, and his diary entries vented his frustration with the French inability to balance their exotic buildings with planting a naturalistic landscape. Equally crowded and unnatural was Marie Antoinette's own folly garden at Versailles called Le Hameau, where she would play at country pleasures.[27]

The most spectacular of the Parisian parks was Folie Monceau, also created in the 1770s for a member of the royal family. Philippe d'Orléans, Duc de Chartres, was a cousin of Louis XVI, but he despised the king and loathed Marie Antoinette, firmly aligning himself with the reformists, and even the revolutionaries when the time came. For this he earned the name Philippe Égalité, but in 1793 during the Terror it did not save him from the guillotine. At Parc Monceau some of his finest follies survive: a rotunda like the Temple of Vesta at Tivoli, a large pyramid and two poetically broken columns (he was a Masonic Grand Master). Best of all is a very beautiful curving colonnade, with Corinthian columns, at the head of a formal lake, modelled on Hadrian's Villa at Tivoli and used as a *naumachia* for water entertainments. Parc Monceau was created for the Duc de Chartres by Louis Carrogis de Carmontelle, a theatrical as well as a garden designer, who believed in illusion. 'Let us', he wrote, 'introduce into our gardens the shifting scenes of the opera.' There is a painting by Carmontelle himself, dated 1779, in which he is handing the keys of Parc Monceau to the duke, with gardeners busy in the foreground.[28] The view of the garden is framed on the left by a ruined fantasy castle and on the right by the columns of a ruined rotunda encircling a statue of the *Medici Venus*. Between them is a bridge with an obelisk, and fading into the background are several follies including a windmill – it looks curiously enticing, but according to Walpole it was 'a confusion of ruins and temples

Louis de Carmontelle, *Parc Monceau, Paris*, painted in 1779 to show the massed follies created there in the 1770s, part of the conspicuous extravagance that led to the Revolution.

crowded one upon another'; and one suspects another of Walpole's witticisms, about artificial hillocks, also applied here: 'almost as high as and exactly in the shape of a tansy pudding'. Further delights included a gothic pavilion that served as a chemical laboratory; tartar tents made of striped canvas; a minaret, a pagoda and a grotto; an island in the lake with sheep grazing; and sometimes more exotic animals including a camel led about by servants in Arabic robes. It was said that the *fabriques* at Parc Monceau were best viewed by candlelight to heighten their magical quality. Darkness would certainly have helped to dispel the overcrowding inherent in gathering together 'all times and all places' in the capricious confusion that Carmontelle favoured.

Not all French folly gardens were purely for diversion. At Ermenonville, the Marquis de Girardin, a wealthy but enlightened aristocrat with a military past, sought to put into practice a philosophical landscape. Above all he admired Jean-Jacques Rousseau and sought to facilitate the simpler lifestyle Rousseau advocated as an antidote to the corruption that had overtaken

Temple of Philosophy, Ermenonville, France, built before 1775 by Girardin, an enlightened member of the aristocracy, a patron of Rousseau and advocate of good husbandry.

society. Girardin journeyed to England in 1763, when the Seven Years War was over, to investigate landscape gardening, and he especially admired William Shenstone's Leasowes, where bucolic scenery was linked to thought-provoking inscriptions and evocative artefacts. To live up to his beliefs Girardin created a model farm near the château. 'To change', he wrote, 'from a forced arrangement to one that is easy and natural will tend to an increase in agriculture, and a more humane regulation of the country for the subsistence of those whose labour supports those who instruct and defend society.'[29] Girardin also hired the leading garden designer Hubert Robert to advise on the layout of a series of picturesque areas. These included rural Dutch scenery with working windmills and watermills alongside straight canals; the moorland or wilderness (*désert* in French) of sandhills, pines and rocks where Rousseau's cabin stood; and also the romantically gothic Tour de la Belle Gabrielle.[30] The Arcadian woodland around the lake was adorned with classical statues and temples, including the Temple of Philosophy, with its six columns dedicated to Newton, Descartes, Voltaire, Rousseau, William Penn and Montesquieu. This was another rotunda based on the Temple of Vesta at Tivoli, not precisely ruinous, because it was intended as an unfinished building, on the grounds that philosophy must evolve – and blocks of stone lay around as if waiting to be added. To crown it all, Girardin's philosophical guest Rousseau died while staying at Ermenonville in 1778, and his tomb was built on an island in the lake, surrounded by poplars. Thus Rousseau's monument (though he is actually buried in Paris) rendered Ermenonville truly iconic.

A little later, Prince Franz von Anhalt-Dessau, in eastern Germany, who was also a disciple of Rousseau, turned his tiny principality in the valley of the Elbe into a *Gartenreich*, espousing all the best practices from crop rotation to religious tolerance. He founded schools, academies and craft centres and opened up communications based on canals. It was inspirational, and Goethe especially praised his example. At the centre of activity was the Prince's own park at Schloss Wörlitz, incorporating orchards and crops among the landscaped grounds and with boating lakes and follies.[31] There were classical temples, including a rotunda built in 1794 with a statue of the *Medici Venus*, which was unusual only in the beauty of its situation, set above the lake at the conjunction of charming tree-lined vistas. There was a monument to Rousseau here too, a great urn surrounded, like the tomb at Ermenonville, by poplars. To honour the natural world there were rustic follies made from stumps and rough-hewn stone. In the gothic tradition Prince Franz created a fairy-tale pavilion, looking just like a large gingerbread house lavishly patterned with icing sugar. But the folly entirely unique to Wörlitz was a miniature volcano, inspired by the Prince's own youthful visit to Vesuvius, and his interest in William Hamilton's researches into volcanology. It was situated at the water's edge like an uninspiring grotto, made of piled rocks with a few rough archways; but a cone rose up inside which concealed a furnace in its depths. From this a fiery eruption could be enacted, to the delight and edification of all observers. Thus the ideal ruler sought to educate and liberate his populace by entertainment as well as instruction.

Five

Hunting and Husbandry

Hunting lodges and towers may well have been the earliest of follies, built to offer refreshment and shelter or for viewing the hunt, their style of architecture becoming more exuberant than necessary because they were places of pleasure and entertainment, and because they afforded a special opportunity to impress. The hunt was a ruling passion for centuries; medieval kings appropriated to themselves vast swathes of royal forest and allowed favoured aristocrats to enclose their own hunting parks. Sons of the gentry were distinguished for their skills in the hunting field, rather than literacy, and medieval hunting tapestries show how magnificently the spectators dressed for hunting parties. In Tudor maps there were hundreds of hunting grounds designated by ring fences, with one symbol for trees and another for a lodge, and during the eighteenth century more estates than ever had the word 'park' after their names.[1] Society artists like John Wootton and George Stubbs both went to study the old masters in Rome, but found their most congenial employment back home depicting hunting scenes, dogs and horses. In the novel *Tom Jones*, Henry Fielding made Squire Weston into a parody of the country gentleman, who thought of nothing but 'the field, the stable or the dog kennel', but even the prime minister Robert Walpole retreated to his Norfolk estate at Houghton whenever possible, to relax by outwitting a fox rather than his political opponents. In London, it was said, a letter from his huntsman or gamekeeper took precedence over a political dispatch, and he too had his portrait painted by John Wootton on the hunting field.[2]

The surviving folly which best embodies this sweep of history through the hunting centuries is King John's Hunting Lodge at Odiham in Hampshire. The link with King John is likely to be real. He was one of the energetic Plantagenet monarchs forever on the move around his kingdom, and there are echoes of his hunting lodges from Lacock in Melksham Forest (Wiltshire)

King John's Hunting Lodge, Odiham, Hampshire. The ornate facade was added *c.* 1740 but the basic hunting lodge is older and may well have been founded in the time of King John.

to Geddington in Rockingham Forest (Northamptonshire), and as far as Windermere in the Lake District. Odiham Castle was John's main stronghold between London and Winchester and from there his hunting lodge was a short ride into the forest, where ancient oaks and woodland still signal the approaches. Nearby, Dogmersfield Park had been granted for hunting purposes to the Bishop of Bath and Wells early in the twelfth century. By the eighteenth century it belonged to the St John family, relatives of Henry St John, Viscount Bolingbroke, a leading Tory politician under Queen Anne. He was exiled for his support of the Old Pretender at the time of the Hanoverian succession and declared a traitor after the Jacobite rebellion of 1715, but allowed to return in 1725. As a writer and political thinker he was a friend of Swift and Pope, and himself author of *The Patriot King*, which (seeing the Whigs remained in the ascendant) opposed party politics and factions in favour of governments of all the talents. It was during this time, when the St John family was much concerned with politics, that Bolingbroke's cousin Paulet St John turned the walks of Dogmersfield Park into a Rococo garden, including a white gothic belvedere tower: at the end of the longest vista stood the old hunting lodge.[3] The core of the building remained, but it was around 1740 that the Jacobean Revival facade was added. The height of the building was almost doubled by the three rounded and then pointed gables, topped with urns, which gave it a fantastical grace. Three blind windows look out from the gables and the forest is all around, adding to the aura of mystery. But the brickwork is warmly mellow and the real windows of the lodge are cosily latticed, so like all enchanted buildings it seems welcoming. The Jacobean style, with its hint of old Dutch, was the strongest architectural statement in all England in favour of the 'King over the Water' and a restoration of the Stuart monarchy. The Hunting Lodge became separated from Dogmersfield Park when the Basingstoke Canal was built later in the century, leaving it in quiet isolation to brood over the fishing rights of Winks Water. There is a payment in the Dogmersfield accounts of 1790 for '£300 for pulling down ornamental buildings in the park'.[4] Luckily this one survived.

The same Paulet St John was responsible for a second hunting folly, further west towards Winchester on Farley Down. The highest point is called Farley Mount, and there stands a white pyramid 9 metres (30 ft) high. It has three blank pointed arches but the fourth is open, allowing one to enter, shelter and read the dedication to a heroic horse that, in September 1733, 'leaped into a chalk pit twenty five feet deep a-foxhunting, with his master on his back'. Horse and rider emerged alive, and the horse was renamed Beware

Park Lodge, Sherborne, Gloucestershire, first described in 1634 and linked in style to Inigo Jones.

Chalk Pit, under which auspicious title he was entered a year later for the Hunters Plate on Worthy Down and won. As the case of Beware Chalk Pit demonstrates, hunting and racing became twinned sports, but before horse racing gained popularity after the Restoration, it was deer coursing that provided the favourite spectator sport. There were deer courses a mile long at Hampton Court and Windsor, with a stand for observers by the finishing line – Lodge Park at Sherborne in Gloucestershire has a rare surviving example. Here, alongside the straight mile of track, there are formal hedges where the traps and pens once stood from which the deer and greyhounds were released; and in a document also preserved at Lodge Park are the rules of deer coursing, stating that two dogs chased one deer. The enthusiast responsible for recording the rules was known as Crump Dutton (because he had a hunchback); he was a Parliamentarian and friend of Oliver Cromwell, who, when he was Lord Protector, granted Dutton the right to stock Sherborne Park with deer from Wychwood Forest. But the exquisite grandstand seems to date from before the Civil War, being very much in the style of Inigo Jones, and it would have served for a banqueting house as well as a racing stand. The upper and lower rooms both run the length of the building, lined with viewing windows, and the three protruding arches of the ground-floor loggia support a balustraded balcony. The roofline is also decorated with a balustrade, meaning that enthusiastic spectators could also mount up there, to view the coursing from the flat roof. Immediately below the roof run five broken pediments, adding an air of excited anticipation to the classical proportions of the facade. A hundred years later, Lord Burlington was so sure it was a perfect example of Inigo Jones design that he had Flitcroft draw it for his collection. The first contemporary description came in 1634, written by a Lt Hammond:

> a stately rich compacted building not unlike the Banqueting House in Whitehall . . . to entertain his worthy friends seeing the kingly sport in that rare paddock a mile in length and walled on either side . . . there are pens and places where the deer are kept and turned out for the course.[5]

Deer pens, being utilitarian, would seldom count as follies, but some were built as eye-catchers in the form of fortifications. At Sudbury, on the Derbyshire/Staffordshire border, the deer house has long castellated walls with blind arches and four castellated corner towers with arrow slits, which

The Deer Pen, Bishop Auckland, Co. Durham, 1760, a gothic eye-catcher belonging to a long tradition of hunting bishops.

rear up in fierce red brick above the wheat fields, while a latter-day 'Tudor' gatehouse, by adding to the architectural confusion, ensures its folly status. Similarly, the deer pen at Bishop Auckland in Co. Durham has architectural pretentions – a gothic rectangular fort of grey stone, with one square pinnacled tower which gives it a more ecclesiastical air, as befits the folly of a bishop; added to which its walls are arcaded like cloisters, which transform the castellations, arrow slits and quatrefoils into historical romance. Also in Co. Durham, at Coatham Mundeville, the Hallgarth Deer House, though it is on a more modest scale and built of rough stone, was still intended as an eye-catcher, with its castellations, round corner turrets, cruciform arrow slits and an attractive stepped gable. At Yorkshire Sculpture Park, near Wakefield, there is an unadorned eighteenth-century deer shelter, with no such fortifications or pretentions, built into the slope of the hillside. However, in the twentieth century it was rendered very special indeed, with the installation of a skylight by the American artist James Turrell. It enables one to sit as sheltered and quiet as the deer once were and to gaze up with great concentration at a patch of sky and clouds, framed to become art.

Stables and kennels, like deer pens, were utilitarian unless some freak of fancy or fortification turned them into follies and even beautiful eye-catchers. The finest example of all these, dating from around 1732, was William Adam's great Palladian screen at Chatelherault, high above the parkland and comprising stables, kennels and a hunting lodge. Building began in 1732 and in *Vitruvius Scoticus* William Adam referred to it as the Dogg Kennell (see overleaf). There was more to it than that: a long undulating brick screen joined four pavilions in Palladian order and style, with arched windows and doorways and pedimented roofs. One end was indeed for the hunting dogs and stables, with rooms for the staff. At the other end the Duke of Hamilton had his hunting lodge and summer house, and originally these banqueting rooms were distinguished by fine plasterwork interiors and fireplaces. Immediately in front was a bowling green, while beyond lay all the parkland, where the hunt and horse racing could be viewed from the folly's windows. A mile away along a sweeping, tree-lined avenue stood the ducal residence. From there William Adam's dog kennel was a splendid eye-catcher extending on the horizon. In 1776 William Gilpin visited and commented with admiration: 'two winding rivers the Clyde and Avon flow thro. the park with clumps of fine oaks and many new plantations . . . it is superior in richness and picturesque beauty to anything in Scotland.'[6] In the 1770s William Adam's son Robert Adam was commissioned to create a home farm on the grand scale in the Culzean estate

The 'Dogg Kennell', Chatelherault, near Glasgow, 1732–44, built by William Adam for the Duke of Hamilton as stables, kennels and a hunting pavilion, and certainly an eye-catcher.

on the coast of Ayrshire, for the Earl of Cassilis. Here stables as well as cowhouses, barns and pigsties were arranged around a stately courtyard, linked together by sandstone towers and turreted archways, the buildings themselves roofed with a flourish of stepped gables crowned with crosses. The gothic style was also favoured at Berkeley in Gloucestershire, home of the oldest hunt in England, founded on rights granted by William the Conqueror. The building is an eye-catcher for Berkeley Castle, distinguished by the contrast between the pale stone of the facade and the black stone used to outline and pattern its curves, angles and crenellations. At Nunwick in Northumberland and Muncaster in Cumbria, the fortified appearance of the stables and kennels evokes memories of defences erected against reivers raiding over the borders.

But the sturdiest fortifications of all are at Milton Park in Northamptonshire, protecting a pack of hounds established in the reign of Richard II, when the abbot of Peterborough was given the right to hunt in the surrounding royal forest. Most other hunting packs have been bred from them. Sir William Chambers, who created several garden buildings on the Milton estate in the 1770s, has been credited with designing the stables, which would be a mark of his versatility.[7] The high pointed doorway in the central wall, with exaggerated arrow slits either side, gives the kennels some resemblance to a medieval gatehouse, but the lack of symmetry is diverting. On the right is a sturdy round tower topped with a conical roof and the hunt weathervane. The left flanking tower is twice as tall and castellated, with two very fat buttresses supporting it. One casement window in this higher tower, together with the constant baying of hounds in the background, could be the scene set for an Arthurian romance.

There were other forms of hunting, based on smaller game like rabbits, hares and pheasants, which were preserved in warrens. The warrener's lodge became a common enough feature in the landscape to provide Shakespeare

Warren House, Kimbolton, Cambridgeshire, built as a dwelling for the keeper of the estate rabbits and embellished as an eye-catcher by 1763.

with a simile: 'as melancholy as a lodge in a warren'.[8] Such a remote warren house, where the gamekeeper lived and carried out his trade, was not normally a folly, and nowhere else came anywhere near the scale of the Triangular Lodge at Rushton; but at least one humble, timber-framed warrener's lodge had a facade added, in order to enhance a rural vista from the great house. This was at Kimbolton Castle in Cambridgeshire, inherited by the fourth Duke of Manchester in 1762, where he continued his predecessor's landscaping improvements and tree planting. An estate map of 1763 shows the Warren House in its embellished form, bordered by the 'warren spinney' and with two pillow mounds where the rabbits had their burrows. The facade of the Warren House, with its mildly classical dimensions of pediment and arch, seems to have been constructed from material salvaged from alterations to Kimbolton Castle, since there are intriguing and misleading mason's marks in the stonework. To add to the confusion, there is an unsigned drawing entitled 'Options for a Lodge or Folly', which seems to toy with adding either Dutch gables or gothic crenellations to the lodge, and which has been ascribed either to Vanbrugh, who was a fellow Kit-Cat with the first Duke of Manchester, whom he advised about work on Kimbolton Castle, or Robert Adam, who in 1764 designed a new gatehouse for the fourth Duke. The facade of the Warren House received neither of the embellishments suggested in the drawing; it is Palladian, but humbly so, as suits its character, and it serves well to focus a point of interest on a rather bleak area that had always been known as the heath. Well into the nineteenth century a gamekeeper still lived there, and wrote his memoirs, while the passing hunt added moments of excitement. The *Illustrated London News* for 29 June 1889 showed the Prince of Wales on a shoot at Kimbolton with the Warren House in the background.

A Victorian hunt painting at Althorp, featuring John, fifth Earl Spencer, on horseback with his hounds, has in the background a hunting lodge now known as the Falconry. It was the home of the present Earl Spencer before he inherited the title and Althorp itself, and later became a refuge for his sister Diana after her divorce from the Prince of Wales. It is a delightful building dating from 1611, when it had the alternative name of the Hawking Tower and was said to have been built in great haste for a royal visit, which would make the architecture genuinely Jacobean (not Jacobean Revival like King John's Hunting Lodge). To the fanciful the little obelisks on every gable give it an affinity with birds of prey – whether beaks, talons or feathers – since they suggest sharpness and flight. It is built in three bays, with a central cross wing forming a gabled porch the same height as the lodge. The first floor

John Charlton (1849-1917), *Countess Spencer on the Hunter 'Goldfinch'*
and John Poyntz, 5th Earl Spencer, on 'Misrule', with the Pytchley Hunt.

originally had open loggias for viewing the sport from all sides, though these
have subsequently been blocked in and replaced by real or blind windows.
Large stonework coats of arms are built into the gables, increasing the air of
great age and ancestry, and the deer park lies adjacent as it always did.

The passion for hunting had for centuries kept landowners committed to
the countryside, seeing it not just as a source of revenue but of pleasure, and
simultaneously instilling in aristocratic minds the importance of maintenance.
By the eighteenth century these sporting proclivities became increasingly
linked with economic and intellectual developments, which contributed
to the success of the landscape movement and the characteristic buildings
that went with it. For instance, ever since the Civil War a critical shortage of
timber made tree planting and management more vital. John Evelyn led the
campaign, publishing *Sylva; or, A Discourse of Forest Trees* in 1664, and lectur-
ing earnestly on the subject to the newly founded Royal Society. The initial
response saw great hunting landowners like the Duke of Beaufort planting
long avenues of trees, radiating out from their formal gardens across the countryside, as illustrated in the views of Kip and his contemporaries. Charles II

led the way, planting 6,000 trees at Greenwich in 1664. Ironically, a series of great storms soon after the Restoration, and at the turn of the century, devastated tree plantations and uprooted whole avenues, making Evelyn's message more painfully apparent, while also opening the way for the more naturalistic planting of the eighteenth century.[9]

Initially the fashion for planting trees and wildernesses was not especially English. In France the royal gardener Le Nôtre established the fashion, and from Holland William of Orange, who much preferred country life, popularized the Dutch word *rust*, as in 'rustic', among English court circles. It was during the eighteenth century that the prospect of bringing the countryside and even livestock right into gardens became more peculiarly English. The mindset was reflected in poetic quotes from Milton's *Paradise Lost* and Andrew Marvell's 'Upon Appleton House'; and Alexander Pope trumped them with a humorous adaptation of the rural poetry of ancient Rome, misquoting Horace, Virgil and Pliny on the pleasures of their country villas:

> Content with little I can piddle here
> On broccoli and mutton round the year . . .
> 'Tis true no turbots dignify my boards
> But gudgeons, flounders, what my Thames affords . . .
> To Hounslow Heath I point, and Banstead Down
> Thence comes your mutton but these chicks my own.[10]

In 1709 Lord Shaftesbury reflected the shift in aristocratic thinking: 'the passion is growing in me for things of a natural kind, even the rude rocks and broken falls of water will be the more engaging, with a magnificence beyond the formal mockery of princely gardens.'[11] And Addison, with his influential articles in *The Spectator*, made practical suggestions about linking game parks and farmland with the garden surrounding the house, giving the example of Greenwich: 'the prettiest landskip I ever saw . . . the green shadows of trees waving to and fro in the wind and herds of deer among them'.[12] At first deer were still regarded as the most ornamental animals for inclusion – at Chiswick Lord Burlington had two deer houses, a ha-ha and a deer paddock immediately to the right of his landscaping projects. But sheep and cattle were far more profitable than deer; besides, there were far more of them and, with the improvements in breeding livestock, hefty farm animals became status symbols. As Pope put it,

J. B. Wood, *Rams at Stowe Park*, 1831, showing the Rotunda and recalling
earlier attempts to reconcile grand folly gardens with livestock.

> Ample lawns are not ashamed to feed
> The milky heifer and deserving steed.[13]

The way Kent opened the gardens at Rousham to bring in views of the surrounding farmland was much remarked, although the gardener John Macclary,
ignoring Kent's eye-catchers, made his priorities clear: 'nothing sure can please
the eye like our short view, there is a fine meadow cut off from the garden
only by the river Cherwell, whereon is all sorts of cattle feeding, which looks
the same as if they was feeding in the garden.'[14] Even the royal gardens at
Richmond, and later Kew, had livestock and deer enlivening the prospects.

In view of these precedents, it is surprising that two relatively humble
estates were credited with setting a new mid-century fashion for the *ferme*

ornée; perhaps it was a question of emphasis. The more genuine of the two was Wooburn Farm, Philip Southcote's estate near Chertsey in Surrey, developed from 1734, of which Southcote himself wrote in a most unassuming way: 'All my design at first was to have a garden in the middle high ground and a walk all round my farm, for convenience as well as pleasure, to see what was doing in the grounds and have access where I was wanted.'[15] His raised circuit walk, 'with flowerbeds and hedged with jasmine, honeysuckle and roses', was crucial to making the most of the farming scene within, and also to 'borrowing' good surrounding views from the landscape beyond. Luckily Wooburn, in the words of Richard Dodsley, 'joins to the Earl of Portmore just beyond it . . . offering many prospects . . . enlivening every path with pieces of perspective'. Other descriptions were more specific about the farmland, pasture and cornfields, the bleating of sheep and clucking of hens. There was a poultry house in the form of a temple from which one walked alongside the canal towards the Thames, and also a waterside gothic octagon, said to be designed by Lord Burlington. Luke Sullivan's *View of Wooburn* (1759) shows the house, the lake with rustic arches (one of them a grotto) and sheep in the background, and in the foreground three cows, a maid milking and a lad leaning on a stick and watching her. As one observer wrote of Southcote's *ferme ornée*, 'the sight of his ground is apt to lead me to a pleasing smile and a delicious sort of feeling at the heart.'

The second famous *ferme ornée* was The Leasowes, in Shropshire, where William Shenstone took up residence in a family farmstead in 1743 and always called it 'my little farm', though there were few references to farming in his correspondence. He too built a circuit walk to enclose his garden and simultaneously encompass the views all around, which he framed with clever planting (or removing) of trees. One view included the sham ruin at nearby Hagley, where his rich neighbour George Lyttelton encouraged and praised his efforts – as did many influential visitors including Thomas Jefferson, who was inspired to create Monticello, and Rousseau, who took his ideas to France. Shenstone was a man of charm and learning, whose whimsicality evidently held a special appeal. He was a poor poet with a melancholy streak and prone to ditties: 'plant the sterile plain, with fruitful gardens and rich fields of grain'. However, some of his phrases resonate – 'my hills are white-over with sheep'[16] – and he did create the term 'landscape gardener'.

Shenstone's gardening practice was better expressed when he wrote straightforwardly about 'planting hollies, pyracanthus and other berry-bearing greens to attract those blackbirds'. Both inside the garden, and looking out beyond the artfully wooded circuit walks, there were seats for contemplation with inscriptions to distil the mood; there were twelve quotations from Virgil alone. He built and rebuilt hermitages, root houses and other rustic pavilions, some of which collapsed or needed improved design; their aim was to create atmosphere and promote poetic melancholy. In Virgil's Grove there were winding walks beside streams and cascades, urns and obelisks. There was a ruinous gothic wall costing just £10 to screen a tenant's house, but the most substantial folly was the Ruined Priory, near the entrance to the Priory Walk and Priory Pool. It was a little round tower with a narrow doorway, arrow slits and a quatrefoil, and Shenstone painted a watercolour of it looking very rustic among its encroaching trees, with a friar or hermit or very possibly himself in the foreground.[17]

Part of the appeal of The Leasowes may have been its creative quality of a work in progress or, as Shenstone put it, 'to involve the mind in the exploration of the garden'. Some of his friends had hilarious fun. When George Lyttelton brought James Thomson, author of *The Seasons*, to admire The Leasowes they joked about Shenstone's care for Nature, to 'caress her, love her, kiss her, and then descend into the valley', after which they proceeded to point out the 'bubbies and nipples of Nature and the fringe of Upmore Wood' before collapsing with laughter.[18] Dr Johnson, not being part of a merry group, more solemnly mocked how Shenstone 'began to entangle his walks and wind his waters with such fancy as made his little domain the envy of the great'. But a more sympathetic observer, writing in 1762 when Shenstone died (aged only 48), said: 'the garden was by this time completely grown and finished, the marks of art were covered with moss, nothing now remained but to enjoy the beauties of the place, when the poor poet died.' Alas, the farm was bought by a button maker from Birmingham, who cut down the gloomier walks and 'made vistas upon the stables and hogsties'.[19]

Obviously the relationship between livestock and gardens remained fraught, and all sorts of artful waterways, ha-has, fencing and bastions were necessary. Old Lord Cobham allowed no sheep to graze at Stowe, but Lord Temple quickly established a flock, which annoyed the dowager very much, as Anne Temple (her niece) wrote in 1750; 'I went to my Lady Cobham yesterday and she began in a violent manner about the sheep being put into the garden, and she told Mr [Capability] Brown she had cried all night and never slept a wink about it.'[20] On the other hand, Horace Walpole set up some rustic fencing in the gardens of Strawberry Hill and in the meadows by the Thames imported 'Turkish sheep with four horns and cows all studied

Edward Haytley, *The Brockman Family and Friends at Beachborough Manor*, 1744–6,
a most harmonious representation of a landowning family with their follies and livestock.

in their colours for becoming the view'.[21] Where trendsetters went, so others followed. The most engaging picture of cows, sheep and a temple alongside ladies in silk dresses is Edward Haytley's *The Brockman Family and Friends at Beachborough Manor* (1744–6). The park at Beachborough Manor lay between Folkestone and Hythe in Kent, overlooking the sea. In the picture James Brockman is centre foreground pointing towards the sketch his niece is making of the rotunda, which stands on an artificial mound. Between is the irregular but formal pool where other ladies are fishing. The surrounding park, a rolling natural amphitheatre, is full of livestock. A contemporary letter described Squire Brockman's dilemma: 'He wants some better name than that of pond . . . for he fears it is too small to call a Serpentine River, your father proposes he should call it ye Temple Pool or Sacred Pool.'[22]

What the French mostly lacked with their *fermes ornées* (which after all was their own terminology) was a strong sense of economic purpose and good governance to offset the follies and extravagance. The most sincere effort was Moulin-Joli at Colombes, west of Paris, where a dilapidated estate was discovered on a sketching trip along the Seine in 1754 and converted, in the spirit of Rousseau and with the help of the leading designer Hubert Robert, into a working ornamental farm, with inscriptions and views across the river to a castle and a church (though Walpole commented sarcastically that every nettle, thistle and bramble was in place).[23] At Chantilly there were thatched cottages representing a mill, a stable, a dairy and so on, all with richly decorated interiors. Possibly at Ermenonville, under the auspices of Rousseau himself, though lacking his concept of simplicity, Girardin achieved a successful agricultural community before the Revolution disrupted it. Carmontelle, the creator of Parc Monceau, which included agrarian buildings and animals, frankly dismissed the English style as lacking imagination. The conviction remains that Marie Antoinette was typical in seeking only her own amusement when she withdrew from the palace at Versailles, crossing the formal gardens Le Nôtre had created, to frolic at Le Hameau. This too was the work of Hubert Robert, created between 1778 and 1782 at improbable expense and forming a delightful contrast to court formality. Winding through the meadows, a stream with a mill wheel fed a small irregular lake. Here the queen's house with its verandas and balconies looked over the water towards a barn that was really a ballroom, plus a windmill, a dovecot, a dairy, a fishing house and a tower. On an island in the lake stood a little circular Temple of Love with a statue of Eros. Trees grew up to shelter this retreat, blind man's buff was said to be the game of choice and the pamphleteers of Paris described the queen's exploits, inventing what they did not know.[24]

Meanwhile George III, though less dangerously unpopular, earned the mocking nickname Farmer George and was eagerly developing livestock breeds, including merino sheep, among the temples at Kew. One folly there, the Ruined Arch, was linked to the farming activities inside and outside the royal gardens. It was designed by William Chambers to support a drovers' track going over the top for cattle, sheep and farm carts coming to and from the Kew Road. The Ruined Arch, which stood over the main pathway from one end of Kew Gardens to the other, was built in the Roman style and bore a marked resemblance to the Mausoleum at Painshill, which may have inspired it. Both had statues, inscriptions and fragments, in the niches of the arch and scattered artistically around. The Ruined Arch was built in 1759, and engravings in Chambers's publication on the buildings at Kew show it from both aspects; in one the now vanished Temple of Victory can be glimpsed through the archway. The bricks Chambers used were the regulation size, recently stipulated by Act of Parliament in an attempt to standardize building materials, which caused Walpole to comment, rather unfairly, that 'a solecism may be committed even in architecture'.[25]

Of all the improving landlords of eighteenth-century England, with their various interests in land drainage, crop rotation and livestock breeding, Thomas Coke, Earl of Leicester, was outstanding. He was a man of parts; as a fashionable youth on the Grand Tour he was portrayed by Pompeo Batoni next to the Vatican statue of *Sleeping Ariadne* (so often replicated as the nymph, or even a sleeping Venus herself, in grottos); and after twenty years' widowhood he remarried at seventy and fathered five more children. He was a Whig MP for Norfolk, strongly in favour of American independence and politically associated with Charles James Fox. In 1776 he inherited Holkham Hall in Norfolk, and by 1816 he had raised the yield of the estate from £2,200 a year to £20,000, setting an example to his peers and encouraging all who sought advice. Holkham Hall is on the grand scale, not much given to follies except for an obelisk and triumphal arch marking the entrance drive. But then, in 1845, the Leicester Monument was erected in his honour. It rivals Nelson's column, or rather it could be described as its rural counterpart: set in the greenery of a deer park, the Monument features 40 metres (130 ft) of fluted column, Corinthian-style, except that where the ornamental capital normally has foliage there are horned cattle. The column is topped with a lantern, like a choragic monument, except the Greeks would not have added a sheaf of wheat. Around the vast square pedestal of the column there are four angle extensions (like Nelson's column), but instead of lions these support a wheeled agricultural implement, a cow, several sheep and a plough, each with its own inscription, including 'breeding in all its branches'. Between these meaningful and yet utterly idiosyncratic statues there are friezes on the sides of the pedestal, showing groups pursuing agricultural matters from digging to committee meetings.[26]

Farm buildings can be counted as follies on the rare occasions when the landowner placed them in a prominent position and ornamented them sufficiently. Here too William Kent led the way at Rousham, not only with the two eye-catchers in the fields beyond the Cherwell, but also by giving a cattle shed within the grounds a gothic facade. The spirit of ornamental farming is captured in a painting at Kenwood House, where three long-horned cows

J. C. Ibbetson, *Kenwood Dairy with Long-Horned Cattle*, 1797, watercolour. The dairy was built 1794–6, when Repton relandscaped Kenwood Park. Dairies provided fashionable diversions for aristocratic ladies, and three cows represented the ideal picturesque number.

stand decoratively in front of three charmingly thatched buildings, which constituted the Kenwood Dairy on the edge of Hampstead Heath. In the 1790s Humphry Repton redesigned the grounds of Kenwood for the second Earl Mansfield and in 1794 the architect George Saunders created the ornamental dairy for the earl's wife, Louisa. It was both fashionable and functional. Lady Louisa could entertain friends in the small octagonal tea room or play at milkmaids in the cool, high-ceilinged dairy room with its marble floors and shelving. There was a central 'font' for cold water and, according to the original inventory, thirty black marble milk pans and basins. To ensure that the milk was properly processed into cream, butter and cheese, the milkmaid lived in the adjoining cottage and, if my lady and her friends wished to participate, the milkmaid was there to supervise. The spiral of smoke rising from the chimney marked the necessary process of 'scalding' or sterilizing the equipment, and it also fitted the strictures of Humphry Repton, who deplored most follies and (in his Red Book for Blaise Castle, 1795–6) suggested placing a simple cottage in the main view from the house, rather than a grander eye-catcher – 'the smoke from the chimney will spread a thin veil along the glen and produce that kind of vapoury repose which painters often attempt to describe.'[27]

By 1803 Repton was writing with gratification: 'A gothic dairy is now as common an appendage to a place as were formerly the hermitage, the grotto or the Chinese pavilion.' Perhaps he was especially thinking of Cobham Hall in Kent, where during the 1790s he remodelled the park for John Bligh, fourth Earl of Darnley. New garden terraces decked with flowers were set around the great Elizabethan house, and the chief eye-catcher, marking the boundary with the park, was the ornamental dairy. 'The House', Repton wrote, 'is no longer a huge pile standing naked in a vast grazing ground, the animals which enliven the landscape are not admitted as an annoyance, while the views of the park are improved by the rich foreground.' The architect of the dairy was James Wyatt, who was working on the interior of the house while Repton was improving the grounds. At its centre Cobham Dairy took the form of a tiny brick chapel with a bell tower – perhaps the bell was used to summon the cows for milking, or the ladies to take tea or the servants to serve it. The 'chapel' is enclosed by four corner pavilions with pyramidal roofs, joined round three of the four sides by little arcades consisting of three arches each, like miniature cloisters. The exterior has an Italianate simplicity and charm, while inside it is far more gothic, with vaulted ceilings, foliate ceiling bosses, corbels with plasterwork oak leaves, and niches with pointed arches. The windows are latticed with areas of stained glass which cast coloured shadows on the dairy walls. The central dairy area is high and cool as a dairy must be, while the surrounding spaces offered accommodation for the dairy maid and facilities for the other processes like 'scalding' (for this the bell tower concealed a chimney). The dairy was certainly functional, and nearby was a small rustic cow house, not the main cow barn of the estate but with room for a few, possibly ornamental, milch cows. All of which indicates that Cobham Dairy represented the latest fashionable diversion, for ladies at least. In 1791 Lord Darnley had married Elizabeth Brownlow, who spent the following decade producing at least seven children. Her dairy was an easy walk from the Hall, where she and her children could play at making butter and cheese, or her friends could join her for tea and admire her collection of china.

As early as 1769, Josiah Wedgwood had both created and captured the market by producing creamware for dairies, which he artfully named queen's ware – every sort of dish, bowl, pail and container – and tiles, including a popular border pattern of trailing ivy leaves, green and cool and dainty. The dairy at Ham House in Surrey is not a folly, simply an outhouse, but the interior is delightful, with white cow's legs supporting the marble worktop, Wedgwood creamware and the ivy-leaf tiles patterning the wall above. To add to the penchant for dairies, milk became increasingly acceptable as a drink, the elite suddenly appreciating its health-giving properties – might one even imagine Lord Darnley taking his cronies the Prince Regent and the exiled Duke of Orleans to Cobham dairy for a drink? – and when great ladies were actively encouraged to nurse their own babies, milk became the in thing. Sometimes existing buildings were converted into dairies. At Gunnersbury Park in west London, which between 1761 and 1786 was the rural residence of Princess Amelia (daughter of George II and aunt of George III), there is a Doric Temple beside a round pool. It has variously been attributed to William Kent late in his career, or to William Chambers circa 1760 while he was also working at Kew. During Princess Amelia's tenure this temple became known as the Dairy and it was described after her death, in 1786, as containing 'a cream room set with galley-tiles and marble side-boards, a churning room, china room, kitchen and two chambers'.[28] (Shugborough was another example where an existing classical temple was converted for dairy purposes.) Again in west London, in the 1780s, John Soane turned his hand to designing a dairy in the elegant form of an ancient temple, as part of an ornamental farm in Fulham, owned by Lady Craven (where Fulham FC's football ground now bears her name). At Hamels in Hertfordshire, Soane went to the other extreme with a rustic dairy design, using tree trunks as columns and peeling bark for the finishing touches.[29]

When the dramatic terrain at Belvoir, on the Rutland/Lincolnshire border, sprouted an equally dramatic medieval castle in the early years of the nineteenth century, James Wyatt, who was responsible for the castle, also created a very pretty dairy at the base of the great wooded cliff on which the castle stood. It was neither classical nor gothic, but in a pleasingly rural style of its own. Wyatt's inspiration for both castle and dairy was the Duchess of Rutland, a lady of many enthusiasms including agriculture and architecture, or, as one contemporary put it, 'a woman of genius and talent mixed up with a great deal of vanity and folly'. Dating to circa 1810, Belvoir Dairy is built of ironstone, rendered and colour-washed. In the twentieth century it became a cottage and fiercely pink, but in the past it was a more subtle ochre colour. In basic design it was not unlike the row of three little cottage buildings at Kenwood, although at Belvoir they are linked by a three-bay open loggia, running in front of the higher central building. This is octagonal, with a roof much like a spread parasol and quatrefoil windows on all eight

Thomas Alloum, *Belvoir Castle from the Dairy*, 1836, print, showing the scenic castle created by James Wyatt, and how his dairy below became a fashionable spot for picnics.

facades of the upper section. This would have been the working dairy, tall and cool. The two rectangular side pavilions have elongated gothic windows in the picturesque mode; one room was probably for the dairy maid, the other for the duchess to entertain.[30]

The jewel in the crown as far as dairies were concerned was created for the fifth Duke of Bedford at Woburn Abbey. It was built in chinoiserie style by Henry Holland circa 1789, following the fashion set by William Chambers and using representations of Chinese garden pavilions, possibly those to be found on painted glass. The dairy is approached by a long, covered arcade supported on red wooden pillars at the edge of a carp pool, where the reflection of the dairy floats poetically, like many a real Chinese pavilion. Fronting the dairy, at the base of the red pillars, and above them along its roofline, run Chinese fretwork balustrades, painted white. The dairy roof is tilted upwards at the eaves and above it is an octagonal lantern with fretwork windows. Inside is cool and marbled, but still in full chinoiserie style with 'bamboo' trellis work supporting the working surfaces, which were equipped with Chinese porcelain. The light filters through the latticed windows, and Chinese motifs with flowers, birds and butterflies are painted all around. The sixth Duke of Bedford's head gardener takes us there:

The Chinese dairy is of octagonal form, and contains a great variety of valuable old china. The floor and slabs are of different varieties of marble, the windows are all beautifully painted with Chinese figures and various fancy birds; these as well as the portico, which surrounds three sides of the dairy and lantern, are also painted in the Chinese style and the whole forms a very interesting feature in the pleasure ground. A small piece of water comes close to the base of the portico, supplies the dairy, and gives a highly picturesque effect to this part of the grounds. The banks, by the margins of the water, are planted with acubus, rhododendrons, azaleas, china roses, hydrangeas and other species that are native to China, in order that they may correspond with the Chinese style of the building.[31]

Not content with the finest of dairies at Woburn, Georgiana, the second wife of the sixth Duke of Bedford, also had a dairy in the rural style at their country retreat at Endsleigh in Devon, overlooking the river Tamar. The estate was designed by Jeffry Wyatt circa 1816 in a style reminiscent of the *ferme ornée* but without classical pretensions. Even the main dwelling was a large

Chinese Dairy, Woburn, c. 1789, a chinoiserie building unique not only in being an ornamental dairy but in being approached by a long red gallery beside water and a garden of suitably exotic flowers.

The Laiterie of Méréville, now in Parc de Jeurre, France, c. 1770, part of the French fashion for aristocratic milkmaids, led by Marie Antoinette, now only a lovely facade.

'cottage', and the grounds contained Swiss Cottage, Pond Cottage, a shell grotto and the dairy, set on its own little hillside in Dairy Dell. It was octagonal and thatched, with a thatched porch, and the inside was lined with white tiles edged with the Wedgwood green ivy borders. There were rustic cowsheds nearby, and here the duchess played at milkmaids with her daughters.

Ornamental dairies could be high-status buildings in France too. La Laiterie de la Reine was built at Rambouillet by Louis XVI to reconcile Marie Antoinette to leaving her beloved Hameau at Versailles when occasion demanded. Without a dairy to amuse her she found the medieval fortress at Rambouillet, stuck in the middle of royal hunting forests, insupportable. So Hubert Robert was called in and, as well as the cool marbled dairy, in a room beyond he created a grotto-like scene with elegant rocks, water and a statue of the water nymph Amalthea (looking very like Venus but identifiable by her symbolic goat). On the outside the dairy is almost austere, a classical cube with an arched entrance. Rambouillet is now a residence of the French president, and the dairy still survives, long outliving the monarchy.[32] Survival was of course a fraught matter in France during the years that followed the Revolution. The loveliest of dairies was at Méréville, in the picturesque folly garden near Paris, created by the Marquis de Laborde and Hubert Robert – who also painted a picture of Méréville in fairy-tale mode, its monuments apparently inaccessible above a river cascading through a rocky chasm.[33] The marquis, a rich financier, perished in the Revolution, and the four follies that remained in his derelict estate were removed to Parc de Jeurre, south of Paris. Here the dairy stands beside a lake, flanked by a large willow and backed by many other trees, while around the lake, like props in a long-forgotten drama, are empty pedestals leaning at angles, and statues, columns, urns and a sphinx. Now the dairy is only a facade, but it is classically perfect, a rectangle with a semicircular domed portico supported by six Ionic columns. The little dome has fish-scale shingles and above it the roofline forms a broken pediment, ornamented with downward crenellations and a decorative carved frieze. Whether it was ever used to churn butter seems immaterial.

As for ornamental cattle shelters, the most attractive in England is in Exton Park in Rutland, home of the earls of Gainsborough for centuries, and originally a deer park with great hunting connections – because this is Cottesmore country, one of the premier hunts in England. In the eighteenth century the park was remodelled to conform more closely to landscape fashions. The lakes were created in the first part of the century, but the follies were built by the sixth earl, Henry Noel, who inherited from his brother in 1759. The finest folly is called Fort Henry in his honour, and the cattle shelter shares the

Cattle shelter, Exton Park, Rutland, *c.* 1770, built as an eye-catcher for the old Exton Hall, to watch as the cattle came to feed and doves to roost.

Castle Barn, Badminton, *c.* 1750, the largest of Thomas Wright's follies
built as eye-catchers in the Duke of Beaufort's extensive farmland.

same gothic charm. Around a central octagon of two storeys is a projecting loggia with a pedimented entrance and a line of pointed arches either side. Beneath this loggia are the cattle troughs, and since it runs around the four southerly sides of the folly, which face Exton Hall, it was certainly intended as an eye-catcher. Not only could one watch the cows coming to feed but also doves coming to roost, because the upper octagon with its eight pinnacles and finialled roof is a dovecot – the pigeon holes run in a line directly under the roof. In fact dovecots were becoming less of a feature by this time, owing to the damage birds do to crops. As agriculture and livestock breeding grew in importance pigeons, like other game, became a less essential part of the winter diet. There are few other eighteenth-century dovecots which qualify as follies, except in Ireland, at Castletown near Dublin, built by the widow of William 'Speaker' Conolly, and at nearby Rathfarnham owned by Major Hall. Both were built as gigantic cones of stone and brick, like the sacrificial temples of some forgotten primitive religion. Tapering upwards, and marked with projecting circles for the doves to land, there are irregular openings not quite like a watchtower or defensive fort, and certainly not like any other dovecot. Each of these evocative buildings is paired with a barn, the Wonderful Barn at Castletown and Hall Barn, alias the Bottle Tower, at Rathfarnham. These too are cones, or rather tapering drums, with an external spiral staircase winding to the roof, even more sinister in appearance, partly because the staircase wall and the circular rooftop are decorated with castellations. But they were indeed barns; corn in years of plenty was to be stored (perhaps that explains the air of fortification) by being carried to the top and poured through a hole in the roof. The design may correctly be considered exotic because it was supposedly based on Indian rice stores.[34]

To return to cattle sheds (without leaving the theme of fortification), at Badminton in Gloucestershire, Thomas Wright spent the years 1748–56 as the resident tutor, architect and hermit, serving his greatest patron, the Duke of Beaufort. This was after Wright's initial attempt at a career among the astronomical elite was sidelined. He designed many castellated rustic follies at Badminton, including Castle Barn. It is magnificent, for a barn, and outshines most sham castles built as eye-catchers. Between two massive, castellated square towers – with blind windows, arrow slits and arched upper openings – there runs a long screen wall converging on the massive central barn, which has an ogee entrance big enough for haycarts, but now blocked. Two strong round turrets either side of this central entrance support a stepped gable adorned with a quatrefoil. Guarded within this folly fortress were cowsheds, barns and dovecots (in the square towers), and it can all be seen looming a mile away across the fields from Badminton House. More of Thomas Wright's castellated farm buildings, including stables and pigsties, also lay across the farmland of the estate, but more discreetly.[35] Scotland boasts an

The Coo Palace, Knockbrex, Borgue, Scotland, 1901–11, combining cattle sheds and a dairy in medievalist style with fine Arts and Crafts embellishments.

equally eccentric farm fortification called the Coo Palace, at Borgue on the coast of Dumfries, built between 1901 and 1911 by James Brown, who made his fortune as owner of a department store in Manchester and created himself a fanciful Scottish estate at Knockbrex. At the centre of his Coo Palace is the square Corseyard Tower, intended as a water tower but looking both defensive and decorative, with an additional round turret and very ornate battlements. Around the Corseyard Tower spread the barns, cattle shed and dairy, all apparently for just a dozen cows, which locals reckoned must be tethered with chains of silver. The outer walls are buttressed, and have arrow slits like Maltese crosses, arched windows, gables of all sorts and plenty of stone balls. The walls have mosaic patterns of pebbles, slate and stone, and the pantiled roofs are edged with intricate semicircular patterns, seemingly cut from sections of terracotta pipe. This beautifully unusual building was falling into picturesque and dangerous decay, but has been rescued.[36]

Worth only a passing mention, after the tour de force at Borgue, are the farmyard follies of Vauxhall Farm at Tong in Shropshire, built by George Durant – a hen house and pigsty both in the form of pyramids. But The Pigsty, overlooking Robin Hood's Bay in north Yorkshire, outdoes them all for eccentricity.[37] It is a temple of mixed influences with a touch of the music hall about it. Built into the steep slope of the hillside, the front portico is raised high on a supporting base of cut stone, giving it a light-catching prominence. The six wooden columns that support the pedimented roof are Ionic – the ramshorn effect of the capitals picked out in two shades of terracotta paint – but the proportions of the pillars themselves are more sturdily Doric. Above them is a fluted frieze, also painted, while the pediment has a circular disc at the centre and an anthemion at its peak. So far, so Greek, but to an expert eye the proportions of the portico itself and of the windows are more Etruscan, and the little windows at the back of the sty taper inwards more like a folly in the Egyptian style. All this architectural fusion is explained by the fancy of Squire John Warren Barry of Fyling Hall, who was responsible for The Pigsty. He was a keen traveller in Mediterranean lands and focused his enthusiasms on writing *Studies in Corsica*, published in 1893 and now a rare collector's item. Here the Squire made clear his delight in ancient Corsican culture, part Etruscan and part Greek, and there is a particular description of the road out of Ajaccio, running along the coast high above the sea, where a line of mausolea all faced across the bay, their style 'a rudimentary form of the Greek temple or a classicalised variety of the common barn'.[38] Elsewhere, Squire Barry again voiced his admiration for individuality and those builders

The Pigsty above Robin Hood's Bay, Yorkshire, completed c. 1890, to accommodate two pigs in a temple inspired by the architecture of the ancient Mediterranean world.

who 'follow a design of their own sweet will, taking a model either from the distant past or else from a foreign country, or else composing a mixture of their own'. Since Fyling Hall was already built, it made sense to concentrate his architectural whims on a pigsty, but it took two years to complete (probably around 1890) because he dithered between one style and another. The lucky inhabitants were two large white pigs, only two, and one assumes they were lucky, although it remains a mystery how they got in and out, unless there was once a ramp to take them into the field below, or perhaps they were confined to the small area behind the sty. The Pigsty was built at a time when pigs were fashionable. In 1871 Edward Lear had written 'The Owl and the Pussy-Cat' to include a clerical pig with a ring in the end of his nose, and the *Baby's Opera* of 1877, with the song 'There was a lady loved a swine', was illustrated by Walter Crane – and he too imagined a pedimented pigsty. By the 1890s Beatrix Potter had weighed in with *Pigling Bland* and *Little Pig Robinson*. But it is uncertain how long Squire Barry's temple remained a pigsty; at some point it became a hen house instead.

Hen or poultry houses joined dairies as fashionable playgrounds for high-class ladies during the nineteenth century. Queen Victoria had a palatial poultry farm at Frogmore in Windsor Great Park, where under tall chimneys, turrets and carved gables lived all types of fowl from swans to tufted ducks and hens, facing over their own lawns and an ornamental pond with

The Poultry House, Leighton Hall, Welshpool, 1861,
a fine Arts and Crafts building offering every luxury to poultry.

a fountain (visible now only in old prints). One superlative example of the genre remains at Leighton Hall near Welshpool in north Wales, built in 1861 (nearly two decades after Queen Victoria's and along similar lines) by John Naylor, a wealthy Liverpool banker, as a present for his daughter Georgina. It was designed by the Liverpool architect W. H. Gee, who was also responsible for Leighton Hall and the church. The style is very picturesque Tudor/gothic tending towards Arts and Crafts, with creamy brickwork framed in deep red timber beams under steeply pitched slate roofs. The central range with its exaggerated triangular gable has two storeys plus an attic; the upper windows are tall and narrow, the lower ones wide and narrow. It is flanked by single-storey inner wings and somewhat lower outer wings. Each has a doorway and a steeply peaked porch, echoing the high pointed gables of the central range. The wooden fascias of the gables and porches are all carved with Arts and Crafts curves and painted bull's-blood red like the other timbers – and the red central doorway has hinges to die for. This hen house is a wide and overwhelming folly, and it housed all manner of poultry including turkeys, geese and ducks, as well as hens of both farmyard and ornamental breeds. The different types were carefully segregated in their own areas with nesting boxes of appropriate size. There was a scratching yard where they were let out in turn; a pond for the water fowl; a storm shed for bad weather; and the whole grassy area around the poultry house had rustic fencing of the same red as the beams, except at the front of the enclosure where there is a reed bed. All was supervised by a poultry keeper, who lived in the nearby *cottage orné* – not as fabulous as the birds' residence, but attractively double-fronted, gabled and with tall barley-sugar chimneys.

There were also aviaries built in highly ornamental styles – for example, Humphry Repton's at Brighton was based on the Indian temples in paintings by Thomas and William Daniell. At Waddeston Manor in Buckinghamshire, home of the Rothschilds, the aviary has a Moorish air. At Woburn the aviary tended towards classical; and at Kew William Chambers created an aviary around a pool with a Chinese pavilion. But it could be argued that these were all primarily decorated bird cages, where function dictated form, rather than follies, where delightful and unnecessary architecture superseded mere function. Such distinctions may be borderline, but the Bird House at Knole in Sevenoaks, Kent, is weird enough to actually cast its function in doubt. It was built in 1761 at the time of the second Duke of Dorset, who lived up to the eccentric streak handed down through generations of Sackvilles. He was operatic in his musical tastes, with a penchant for dressing up and entertaining singers and poets (his own poetry was very poor). It is uncertain at what point his garden folly was used as a summer house, and for whom it became a bird house, except in the case of Lord Amherst. William Pitt Amherst was famous long before he arrived at Knole. In 1816 he led an unsuccessful embassy to the Qing Emperor of China in an attempt to open up trade, and from 1823 until 1828 he was Governor General of India. On their travels he, or rather his botanical wife Sarah, Lady Amherst, had various species of flora and fauna named after her, including the Amherst pheasant. It is closely related to the golden pheasant of China, but more silvery, and was introduced to the Amherst's Bedfordshire estate, where it naturalized. When Lady Amherst died her husband, aged 66, was consoled by the widow of his stepson, who was a Sackville. And from 1839 until his death in 1857 Lord Amherst lived at Knole. Certainly, one can imagine some of the Amherst pheasants came with him, along with other rare birds. Possibly they joined an existing household of exotic birds, doves and poultry. Vita Sackville-West confirmed the traditional family name of the folly, long after the Bird House had become simply a gamekeeper's cottage: 'That queer little sham gothic house called the Bird House always frightened me as a child because I thought it looked like a witch's house in Hansel and Gretel, tucked away in its hollow with its pointed gables.'[39] This cosily sinister appearance easily gives the Bird House folly status. Here too the slate roof is steeply pitched, with attic windows peeping out and three high chimneys encased in tapering pyramids of slates. The windows and door are pointed in gothic style, and beyond the Bird House there are sham ruins, said to have been assembled from the remains of the Archbishop of Canterbury's palace at nearby Otford.

It was not only rare birds that were afforded extravagant housing; menageries also featured. The second Earl of Halifax, another important patron of Thomas Wright, paid him three times during the 1750s for work at Horton House in Northamptonshire. The most remarkable outcome was the classical frontage for the zoo, which doubled as a banqueting house and eye-catcher, but was always known as Horton Menagerie. Palladio would have approved of this latter-day representation of perfect classical proportions adapted to a long, low-slung building recalling some of his country villas. The windows and doorways are enhanced by rusticated stone with vermiculate patterning, not in the usual Italianate style but 'long six-inch curls carved on keystones and sills, and flatter curls on the voussoirs and frames, as though the owner's great wigs had been stuck to the stones and petrified there'.[40] The large central pavilion, which was the banqueting house (with elaborate plasterwork decorating the interior), has a projecting semicircular bay with arched windows and a domed roof, and behind it the main roof is pedimented. Either side are wings with half-pediment, lean-to roofs. Screen walls, with arched windows matching the bay, join this central pavilion to the smaller corner pavilions; and these are replicated by two more, forming the back corners of the menagerie enclosure. Horace Walpole visited in 1763 and described this enclosure as 'a little wood prettily disposed with many basons of goldfish', by which he meant circular pools, four of which survive. More excitingly, Walpole went on to list 'several curious birds and beasts . . . racoons that breed there much . . . two hogs from Havannah with navels in their backs . . . doves from Guadeloupe with blue heads and a milk white streak crossing their cheeks'; also two eagles, two young tigers and a bear.[41]

There was another menagerie nearby at Castle Ashby, built for Spencer Compton, the eighth Earl of Northampton, in the 1760s. This was when

Capability Brown remodelled the grounds to include a dairy fronted like a temple and the menagerie – for which Robert Adam probably contributed the design, because the site of the menagerie and its ground plan appear on Adam's map of the site, even though no design drawing survives. It is a lyrical building centred on a projecting dome that rests on a semicircle of three Doric columns, while the curved rear wall of the portico forms an attractive elliptical space. Either side are two bays with handsome arched, recessed windows. A dragon on the dome and two recumbent lions above the bays are the only creatures still to adorn the menagerie, which on the final sale of its contents consisted mainly of birds.

The amusement derived from creating elaborate buildings to house animals and birds is reflected in their proliferation in pattern books, and more must have remained as passing fancies than ever existed in reality. When Timothy Lightoler produced the *Gentleman's and Farmer's Architect* in 1762, he probably hoped that every landowning household would pore over it, for diversion at least. There were 25 copperplate engravings suggesting ways to gothicize cow houses, stables, plant nurseries and even haystacks. Some were in the manner of a cloistered monastery; others sported gothic castellations and turrets. The overall aim was summed up in his 'Design for a sheep cote to be built on a hill which seen from a genteel house forms an agreeable object'. Even leading architects weren't scornful of offering the public fantastic patterns. Thomas Wright, already secure in his success at Badminton and elsewhere, published *Universal Architecture* in 1758, including an Aviary in Book I among his various arbours. It was made from gnarled oak trunks, bark and moss, 'the roof thatched, of a Roman pitch with a Palladian projection . . . the more fantastical and robust the better'. Later, the young John Soane, while still apprenticed to Henry Holland and therefore in the orbit of Capability Brown, sought out clients by designing animal houses. In 1778 he published a pattern book ('six shillings sewed') which included a dairy in the 'Moresque style', with characteristically lovely proportions of arched windows and urns. At the centre of the roof was a low dome fronted by a cow, and at either end tall obelisks topped with crescent moons. Linking animals with Islamic architecture was not original to Soane. In 1767 Samuel Wyatt designed a deer enclosure for Kedleston in Derbyshire with three minarets and eleven domes, but it was not built. In 1797 John Plaw rounded off the century with *Ferme Ornée; or, Rural Improvements Calculated for Landscape and Picturesque Effects*, offering more suggestions on how to use tree trunks and thatch to best advantage, how to add grotesquery with animal skulls or, alternatively, how to create a monastic effect with rough-hewn archways and a water trough designed in the form of a sarcophagus.

The spirit lives on in the Sheep Barn, also known as Colin's Barn, hidden away near the village of Chedglow on the border of Wiltshire and Gloucestershire, near Tetbury.[42] In 1986 Colin Stokes bought a field and started building a shelter for his sheep, using flat Cotswold stones that lay nearby and a dry-stone walling technique. As the sheepfold grew into an array of cairns he used cement to secure the foundations and the walls, which still stand firm although it was abandoned in 2000 when the Council and a slate quarry threatened Stokes's tranquillity beyond endurance. His sheep flock was named Braydon after the local stream, and was bred by Stokes himself from a ram of Celtic stock crossed with fleecier ewes, resulting in fine wool which he could spin, dye and weave. For these activities the building grew larger and included an upper room, where Stokes could sleep during the lambing season, and lofts for storing hay and fleeces. He even added a little pantiled 'concert hall' with stained-glass windows – this being another of his skills, manifested in roundels containing badgers, birds and sunsets. On the floors are some handsome Victorian tiles, glazed in brown and cream, and the decorative plasterwork includes garlands of wild arum flowers. Spiral staircases lead upstairs, where light falls in strange patterns from odd little window slits, and there are fine glimpses of the Cotswold countryside. Most extraordinary of all is the overall appearance of this modern folly, standing in its remote meadow overhung by trees. It consists mainly of rustic cones, large and small, with niches for doves (or owls) and small peering windows. The largest cone of the Sheep Barn is monumental; the smaller ones poke out like the turrets on a tumbledown fairy castle. It certainly has the air of a folklore dwelling, and those who contrive to find it evoke Tolkein, hobbits and *The Lord of the Rings*.

Six

Waterside Follies and Grottos

'In the midst of all the place was a fair pond whose shaking crystal was a perfect mirror . . . so that it gave show of two gardens, one indeed, the other in shadows' – the words of Sir Philip Sidney describing Arcadia.[1] For generations the pleasures of messing about on, in or beside the water took various forms, and could be much enhanced by a folly intended to fulfil these purposes. Fishing was an age-old occupation, but as a pastime it received fresh impetus when Izaak Walton wrote *The Compleat Angler* in 1653, so popular that it was reissued several times and much extended by the final edition, of 1676. It is an anthology that celebrates the technicalities and joys of fishing, incorporating previous treatises, songs, poems and anecdotes, and framed as a conversation between Piscator (the angler), a game hunter and a falconer. Walton's best-known quote refers to bait: whether frog or worm, 'use him as though you loved him, harm him as little as possible that he may live the longer.' But true to the book's subtitle, *The Contemplative Man's Recreation*, he also quoted earlier enthusiasts: 'angling was an employment for his idle time which was then not idly spent.'[2] Walton came from Staffordshire, but his living had been gained as a London linen draper, and through marriage, the Church and his literary abilities he won friendships with famous men, including John Donne, George Herbert and Richard Hooker, whose biographies he wrote. As his own fame grew there were also landowners, including bishops, who offered him hospitality and fishing rights, and enabled him to spend the last forty years of his life (he died aged ninety in 1683) fishing and writing. Among these benefactors was Charles Cotton, who built the most delightful Fishing Lodge, in 1674, on the banks of the river Dove, which flowed past his estate at Beresford Hall in Staffordshire. Here he and Walton would while away many happy hours fishing together, and it was Cotton who contributed the important section on fly fishing, which was an innovation in the 1676 edition of *The Compleat Angler*. The Fishing Lodge was built of tawny stone with a steeply pyramidal slate roof, and it had sufficient ornamentation to give it humorous pretensions to be a temple of fishing,

The Fishing Pavilion, Syon Park, Middlesex, rebuilt 1802 for the Duchess of Northumberland on the site of an older Thames boathouse.

and therefore a folly. The arched doorway is framed by Doric pilasters, with an entablature and the crest *Piscatoribus sacrum*. Inside the one room, with its large fireplace, comfort could be had in chilly weather, and servants from the Hall would bring lunch and liquid refreshments as required. There were originally paintings 'of persons fishing and the figures of trout and grayling well portrayed'.[3]

As if to prove Walton's direct influence on fishing pavilions, they started to spring up along the Thames, and the earliest painted view, by Jacob Knyff, dates from the 1670s.[4] It shows Corney House on the Chiswick riverside (between where Corney Reach is today and St Nicholas's Church). A pretty little stone room is perched, overhanging the river, built into the river wall of the garden with a projecting square bay allowing fishing from its windows. The roof is a jaunty ogee pyramid flaunting a weathervane. A little further upstream, on the Richmond riverside, a similarly placed pavilion still sits on a river wall (although the water is now further off than it was); and not quite opposite, at Syon Park, there is a grander affair, at the southern tip of the Duke of Northumberland's west London estate. This marks the historic spot where Lady Jane Grey was once launched by boat on her fateful bid to become queen; but in 1802 the old boat house was built over with a pink pavilion, a gift for the duchess. The centre is circular, a lofty domed room, the wide pink rim of the roof supported on four Ionic columns with three tall, arched windows between. These open onto a narrow, curving balcony over the river, and since it was named the Fishing Lodge, presumably the balcony served that purpose.[5] Viewed from the opposite bank, the pink reflection in the water doubles the pleasure the pavilion offers to passers-by.

Upstream again, at Bray in Berkshire, is Monkey Island, the name being a corruption of Monks Eyot, because monks from Merton Abbey settled nearby and held the fishing rights. After the Great Fire of London the eyots in the Thames were raised up beyond flood level when barges, carrying building stone from the Berkshire quarries, used the return journey to offload unwanted rubble from the fire onto the eyots, which made them suitable for building. At some point an octagonal fishing lodge appeared on Monkey Island, seemingly constructed from massive blocks of cut stone, which is in fact wood. In 1723 the young third Duke of Marlborough fell in love with this perfect fishing spot and bought it. The original fishing pavilion with its octagonal dome has a rustic Palladian air, complete with a pedimented porch, but rendered unusual by semicircular upper windows and balls on each angle around the rim of the dome. Inside, eccentricity was given full reign with decorations by the French artist Andien de Clermont, in a Rococo European style known as *singerie*, where monkeys disport themselves in quasi-human fashion. Here the monkeys net fish, harpoon a dolphin, carry a basket full of eels and shoot a kingfisher. In the centre of the ceiling they sail out to sea in a shell drawn by a dolphin, catching the wind in a swirling pink scarf. All this was completed by 1738 and the duke built a second pavilion balancing the first, with similar 'stonework' but square with high rectangular windows, a pyramidal roof and a two-storey porch. This interior was decorated with shells, plasterwork dolphins and mermaids. The duke died in 1758 and in the fullness of time Monkey Island became a riverside inn, visited by celebrities as diverse as Edward VII and Edward Elgar.[6]

Further upstream is Temple Island, another eyot, always associated with Henley-on-Thames because it is the starting point for the Regatta, although the folly there was built as an eye-catcher for Fawley Court at Remenham (with its situation enhanced by a small arboretum chosen for autumn colour). This folly was a Fishing Lodge, designed by James Wyatt in 1771 as one large room (ornamented inside 'in a very expensive manner in the Etruscan style') with a three-windowed bay. Then it was topped with a rotunda of Tuscan columns

William Daniell, *Chinese Fishing Pavilion, Virginia Water*, c. 1829, watercolour.
This pavilion was built in 1758 in Windsor Great Park for the Duke of Cumberland,
in the fashionable chinoiserie style.

supporting a shallow dome, thus transforming it into a folly. It remains very scenic though somewhat tarted up, and a nymph has been placed in the *tempietto*.

The most spectacular of fishing pavilions was built for royalty on an island of Virginia Water – the artificial lake created around 1750 for the Duke of Cumberland, victor of Culloden, who was ranger of Windsor Great Park and who employed his veteran troops on the project. Here a chinoiserie pavilion was built in 1758, possibly in consultation with Admiral Anson, who was a friend of the duke. The Chinese Fishing Pavilion consisted of three interconnected octagons; all three roofs were topped with an *umbrello* and the walls were decorated with trellis patterns. The island was named China Island. In 1766 Mrs Philip Lybbe Powys described it: 'the outside is white tiles set in red lead [she meant the roof] decorated with bells and Chinese ornaments, you approach by a Chinese bridge.'[7] Near the pavilion an even finer piece of chinoiserie, the Mandarin Yacht, was moored, surely inspired by accounts of the one on the lake of the Summer Palace in Beijing. The Duke of Cumberland was an enthusiastic collector of boats and altogether four incongruous vessels were assembled on Virginia Water in his time. In 1749 the largest, which became the Mandarin Yacht, began as a 12-metre hulk, which was dragged overland from the Thames and, over four years, was transformed by carving, painting, japanning and gilding. Along the hull a dragon appeared, with barbed tail towards the stern and long barbed tongue to the prow. On the deck, with its fretted balustrades, lanterns and banners, was an exquisite cabin with latticed windows and Chinese gables curving deliciously up around a striped roof, which was adorned with an *umbrello* and a grasshopper finial. It was a folly in the tradition of the old London pleasure barge on the Thames; nor was China Island used primarily for fishing, until Cumberland's great-nephew George IV recreated a miniature Brighton Pavilion there and devoted so much of his later years to the quieter pleasures of angling that he was lampooned as King Fisher. George IV's first renovations to the Chinese Fishing Pavilion, in 1825, were by Sir Jeffrey Wyatville (born Wyatt, nephew to James Wyatt, but ennobled thus for his work at Windsor Castle). In 1827 more extravagances were added by Frederick Crace (responsible for much of the interior of Brighton Pavilion), especially three soaring chinoiserie roofs with fish-scale tiles and dragons with bells in their mouths. A roofed fishing

J. Haynes, *The Mandarin Yacht*, 1753, print. The boat was refurbished in Chinese style 1749–53. The triangular Belvedere by Flitcroft appears in the background overlooking Virginia Water.

balcony was added with more bells along its gables, so that by 1828 over £1,500 had been spent.[8] After a visit in 1826 Lady Holland described it as 'in the Chinese taste, full of gilt dragons for ornaments, rather too expensive *on dit*, considering Windsor, Buckingham Palace, York House and the state of the country'.[9] In the evenings a band played on the Mandarin Yacht, and there were no fewer than eight canvas tents in the Turkish style, with crescent moons atop their poles, dotted about the gardens of the island for *al fresco* suppers. In 1860, by which time the Fishing Pavilion was falling into disrepair, Prince Albert commissioned more renovations, but nothing came of this last hurrah, and all that now remains to inform us of these fascinating royal fripperies are prints and paintings, including a hazy watercolour by Turner, all as confusing as they are evocative.

At Alresford in Essex, hidden away in a steeply wooded area known as 'The Quarters', is another Chinese fishing pavilion, also called The Quarters. This one was painted by Constable, a pleasing juxtaposition to his old rival Turner's work, but this fishing pavilion is on a far humbler scale. It was built in 1722, according to a builder's mark on the roof, by Richard Woods for Colonel Rebow, on the shore of its own little lake, where water birds disturb its reflections. The proportions are restrained and delicate, and for that reason more akin to real Chinese waterside pavilions. The roofline slides down over the eaves and veranda, grey, smooth and without furbelows. Constable's painting shows the veranda jutting out over the water to provide a fishing platform, although now the water's edge is several feet away. Inside, the octagonal room has disguised cupboards for fishing tackle cutting off its corners. In 1816 General Isaac Rebow, son-in-law and heir of the Colonel, commissioned Constable to paint a pair of little views specifically to provide him with funds to finally marry his fiancée Maria Bicknell. He wrote to her in August 1816,

> I am to paint two small landscapes for the General; one in the park
> of the house and a beautiful piece of water; and another a wood with
> a little fishing house where the young lady (who is the heroine of all
> these scenes) goes occasionally to angle.

How romantic.[10] A bridge leads to the opposite bank (where Constable painted), and through its rudimentary fretwork the pavilion can be viewed from the side, through a circle of wood like a Chinese moon gate.

Not far away and still in Constable country, at Stoke by Nayland, all that remains of Tendring Hall is a Fishing Temple, this time built along the

John Constable, *The Quarters behind Arlesford Hall*, 1816, depicting the chinoiserie fishing pavilion, a local commission about which the artist wrote to his fiancée, Maria Bicknell.

lines of Palladio's Venetian churches. Here is a square central block with a canted bay and a tall window recessed in an arch, a slate roof with a pediment that projects well over the windows, and lower wings either side with sloping lean-to roofs. The proportions are smoothly classical and enhanced by the temple's position at the head of a long rectangular canal, spring-fed, that once held trout. An estate map of 1723 shows the canal already in existence, but no building. Tendring Hall itself was rebuilt by Sir John Soane between 1784 and 1786, and it is easy to see why the Fishing Temple has also been attributed to him, but there is no record to confirm this. The estate was bought in 1750 by Admiral Sir William Rowley, who had distinguished himself in 1744 at the Battle of Toulon and was appointed Admiral of the Mediterranean Fleet, where he kept the French and Spanish at bay. In 1762 he succeeded Admiral Anson as Admiral of the Fleet. It would be satisfying to think that this more interesting member of the family enjoyed the Fishing Temple, but he died in 1768, and it was probably built for his son Sir Joshua, for whom Soane rebuilt Tendring Hall.[11]

Kedleston Fishing Pavilion, Derbyshire, 1770, one
of Robert Adam's finest follies, with many Italianate features,
including the Venetian window overlooking the water.

No group of follies would be complete without a castellated version and at Netherby on the Scottish borders there is a fortified salmon coop, consisting of two sturdy castle towers with traceried windows (where the salmon keeper lived) and between them a screen wall with arrow slits and an arched doorway. Netherby was where Walter Scott's 'young Lochinvar' snatched away his bride: 'He swam the Eske river where ford there was none;/ But ere he alighted at Netherby gate,/ The bride had consented . . .' It seemed he was too late – she was being married to another and the wedding feast was on, but he defied the assembled guests, danced with the bride towards the door and swung her onto his waiting horse, 'So light to the saddle before her he sprung!' They rode away. But the fish were guarded more carefully. Probably their Netherby stronghold was built in the 1750s, forming part of a dam across the river Eske, trapping the salmon. There were several Scottish raids by 'disorderly men' who resented the quantity of salmon being stopped, but they were 'repelled by Netherby tenants with all the spirit of ancient times'.[12]

At Kedleston in Derbyshire, seat of Nathaniel Curzon, later Lord Scarsdale (from 1758 to 1804), there is a Fishing Temple that has it all. It was the work of Robert Adam, who in 1758 wrote to his brother James that he had

> got the entire management of his [Curzon's] grounds put into my
> hands with full powers as to Temples, Bridges, Seats and Cascades . . .
> you may guess the play of Genius and Scope for invention. A noble
> piece of water, a man resolved to spare no expense, with £10,000
> a year, good tempered and having taste himself for the arts and
> a little for game.[13]

In 1770, once Bridgeman's more formal landscaping of the river Derwent had been transformed into an irregular lake with an island and bridge, Adam positioned his Fishing Temple to be visible obliquely from the house, and endowed it with as many elements of *stile antico* as could hang harmoniously together. Viewed across the water, it is tripartite; the two-storey block is taller in the centre, to hold a banqueting room above and a bath house below, contained in an arch. On either side of the bath house are two more arches, which are boat houses. These three arches float, bridge-like, over the water while at the roofline above them three equal pediments balance one another. But all is focused on the central Venetian window, surely one of the finest outside Venice, with a recessed arch fanning over the window, Ionic pilasters and every detail of moulding and balustrading just right. This lovely window is not ideal for serious angling, though the less committed might sit on stools (recorded in an inventory of 1804) relishing the situation in comfort. For those of the company who emulated Isaak Walton, the banks and boats would have been used for fishing, and the Fishing Room with its large fireplace would be used as a retreat from chilly weather, as well as for picnics and tea parties. On the land side the entrance is modelled on a triumphal arch, decorated with pilasters, swags and medallions, and over the door is an apsidal recess with spoke-like carvings. Inside the Fishing Room the plasterwork is typically Adam, and the theme is marine, with waves, sea shells, sea horses, nymphs – and Venus, whose statue is in a recess picking a thorn from her foot. There are hooks for fishing tackle, and paintings of fish around the walls. These are by the society artist Arthur Devis (who himself loved angling if the number of his portraits depicting the gentry fishing is anything to go by). But still-lifes of fish are rare in British art, and here Devis has devised background landscapes and lovingly portrayed mackerel on a Dorset shore; salmon and shad in a scene of the Wye estuary; turbot and black lobster beside the Thames estuary; pike, tench and chub among river rushes; and carp, crayfish and eel near a water mill and bridge.[14]

On either side of this highly themed room, a curving flight of stone steps descends to the bath house, where an underground spring emerges gurgling from the hillside into a stone basin in the floor, and thence into the lake. The Kedleston springs contain sulphurous waters, which were highly esteemed for their health-giving properties, and as well as this facility for himself and his guests, Lord Scarsdale developed a small spa at a nearby inn. After an invigorating cold plunge, the Fishing Room with its fire would again provide most welcome warmth and refreshment. The classically educated elite of the eighteenth century knew all about Roman baths; and the medicinal properties of certain springs were being increasingly sampled – Tunbridge

Wells, Bath and Harrogate were all being exploited as resorts by the end of the seventeenth century, and London had Sadlers Wells. In 1679 the Turkish merchants in the East End built a bath in the style of an Ottoman hammam in Bath Street near Old Street, which was followed by Kings Bagnio in Covent Garden – a circular bath with an arcade and cupola. In the *London Gazette* of 1693 John Valentine advertised his readiness to build 'any bagnio or hummums after the best manner for persons of quality'; and in the same decade John Flyte published a treatise on cold baths 'efficacious to invigorate the spirits, digestion, circulation, and especially for sufferers from gout, asthma and ladies recovering from labour'. As a finishing touch he suggested 'the immersion ought to be sudden and not gradual, to prevent a Horror.'[15] In 1707, a Dr Olivers wrote that such baths were best taken infrequently and as the focal point of a social occasion, with a grotto or pavilion in the park to make it an outing. The gentry seem to have become convinced of all this and many cold baths appeared on country estates. In a letter to Sanderson Miller of 1745, Lord Dacre summed up the prevailing attitude: 'The cold bath has restored me to good spirits and the Blue Devils are quite gone away, not I suppose relishing the cold water.' Such baths were not always housed in follies, but where a natural spring rose in a gentleman's grounds, and especially one with sulphurous properties, a temple might be built to adorn as well as utilize the site. Or, as at Kedleston, to combine it with other outdoor sports; and, like Robert Adam there, Sanderson Miller was another leading society architect involved in designing a bath house.

Walton Hall near Stratford-upon-Avon was the property of Sir Charles Mordaunt, who belonged to the neighbouring circle of architectural connoisseurs – George Lyttelton at Hagley, William Shenstone at The Leasowes and Sanderson Miller himself. In October 1749, Miller noted in his diary that he was 'settling accounts with Hitchcox about Sir Charles's bath etc'. This was Will Hitchcox, Miller's stonemason, who had recently completed Radway Tower for him. So the elegant little classical Bath House at Walton was designed by the leading exponent of gothic style, yet another example of eighteenth-century eclecticism. The rectangular base which contains the plunge bath is of gigantic stones from the local hillside, rather in the manner that the ancients enclosed their sacred springs. Above this craggy, cave-like base, where the spring water chuckles into the freezing cold bath, the little octagonal withdrawing room with its fireplace looks down through elegant Georgian windows. To set the scene in the wooded hillside, yew trees were planted beside the Bath House – Virgil and Livy had both recommended

Walton Bath House, Wellesbourne near Stratford-upon-Avon, 1749. The design
of the exterior is linked to Sanderson Miller and the interior shellwork to Mrs Delany.

this for Roman country villas – and already at Rousham an open octagonal
pool had been shadowed by yew trees. From Seneca had come another recommendation: that baths should have good views – an element in the placement
of many other types of folly. Inside the octagon room of Walton Bath House,
shell work and stalactites adorn the upper walls. Excitingly, these are the work
of Mrs Delany, best known for her delicately cut paper flowers, but her shell
work was another, and earlier, skill, one which she shared with her sister
Anne Dewes, who lived nearby at Wellesbourne Hall; hence the connection with Sir Charles Mordaunt. Dr and Mrs Delany knew Sir Charles well
from holidays spent at Wellesbourne, and it was possibly during a recorded
meeting with Sanderson Miller in 1753 that the sisters undertook to create
the eight festoons of decorative shells around the walls of the Bath House
octagon room. Mrs Delany collected the shells. There were scallops, mussels and razor shells from the seashores of Ireland, where she and Dr Delany
lived; others came from the West Indies, which she, like many other grotto
builders, commissioned sea captains to procure – including conches, clams
and tritons. In 1754 Mrs Delany wrote to her sister Anne, 'I have not yet got
shells enough for the festoons, but I will send barrels of shells to Sir Charles

Mordaunt.' Mrs Delany was also in correspondence with Mr Moor, Sanderson Miller's plasterer, about his 'icicles', which, like lines of little, well-ordered stalactites, adorn the ceiling above the shell festoons. The walls and ceiling were to be painted marine blue, that in-between colour which to many is green, a favourite choice of Mrs Delany's. The Bath House at Walton was used and fondly remembered for generations. A cousin wrote home from Naples imagining 'ye bathroom, and I am an invisible guest at ye tea table'. Later, Edward VII as Prince of Wales became involved in a notorious trial when Harriet Moncreiffe, the flirtatious wife of the tenth Baronet Walton, was accused of adulterous liaisons in the Bath House.

Capability Brown (departing like Sanderson Miller from his usual metier) is credited with the Bath House at Corsham Court in Wiltshire, a lovely example of gothic style created around 1761–3, when he was employed to transform the house and grounds – where it seems that stones and window tracery from the ruins of Chippenham Abbey may have been used, both in the Bath House and especially for the crinkle-crankle wall, or sham ruin, that runs nearby. Corsham Bath House has classical proportions disguised by gothic embellishments; it is a two-storey cube with an open loggia leading into the rectangular sunken bath, which has a moulded rim and steps down. At the back of the loggia are two narrow arched openings, very like

Burghley Bath House, Stamford, Lincolnshire, c. 1760. The Jacobean Revival style harmonizes with the architecture of Burghley House and is surprisingly attributed to Capability Brown.

an ecclesiastical building might have for the stairs to the monks' cells. The left archway opens onto a curving stair to the upper 'changing room' and on the right is a passage to the walled garden behind the Bath House. Over this back exit the Bradford Porch was added when a fifteenth-century manor house at Bradford-on-Avon was demolished in 1938. At the front, the Bath House loggia is triple-arched and its fluted columns are moulded with delicate pendant cusping, giving the building a Mediterranean lightness among its gothic features, which include stained-glass windows, canopied niches and a roof with ogee pediments and crocketed finials. Although the loggia leaves the bath open to the grounds, the Bath House is tucked away privately and hidden by yew trees, so not an eye-catcher. At much the same time Capability Brown was working at Burghley House in Stamford, where beside the lake he set a Bath House in yet another unusual style, Jacobean Revival, which is exquisite except that it has lost its bath. Again it is a simple cube, this time one storey and with three symmetrical arches, fan-vaulted, which may once have been open. The roofline is worthy of the Elizabethan extravagances of Burghley House itself, only more fanciful on this smaller scale – triangles, circles, crosses, diamonds, soaring finials and obelisks, curlicues, eyeholes and angulations, all singing out in stone. Here too yew trees sweep up against the pale stone of the building, enhancing it with their darkness.[16]

Princess Amelia, daughter of George II, lived at Gunnersbury Park, west London, from 1761 to 1786 and at some point built herself a Bath House in a secluded corner of the grounds, using dark pinkish-red brick dated to the second half of the eighteenth century, but including an earlier wall as the spine of the building. On one side was the deep cold bath, entered by a pair of symmetrically curved stairs, the surrounding walls decorated with shells, glass and mineral fragments. On the other side was a 'dressing room' that was large enough for Princess Amelia's close friends to join her there, probably to take tea. Outside the Bath House was a little rocky grotto with quartz crystals, alabaster fragments, an ammonite, cement stalactites and possibly ferns. Piped water cascaded over the grotto into the bath. The exterior of the Bath House was rendered gothic with buttresses and pinnacles. But it is uncertain how much was added in the nineteenth century, when it belonged to the Rothschilds; for instance, pieces of tile with a 'Japanese' pattern fashionable in the 1870s have been found in the grotto area, and memories from the 1860s of the 'outdoor swimming bath' include not only the coldness of the water but a lovely blue colour from the tiles lining the bath. Also the attached 'summer house' then had walls painted with pictures of African forests.[17]

At Wrest Park there is a truly rustic Bath House, tucked away privately in the grounds near a pool and cascade fed from an arm of the main canal. It was designed around 1769–71 by Edward Stevens, but very possibly inspired by the designs of Thomas Wright, since it is in fact a significant feat of engineering. It consists of two chambers side by side, constructed very ruggedly as if by a drystone walling method, but with skill since it has not collapsed, and is no more ruinous than it was constructed to seem. The changing room is octagonal with a conical thatched roof, the interior walls are smooth, the floor is cobbled with an inlaid pattern of deer bones (very Thomas Wright) and there are arched niches in the walls. The bathing room seems really ruinous, like a miniature relic of a Roman bath, with gaping archways and three irregular holes in the domed roof. But inside is the perfect and inviting circle of the sunken bath, with neat steps down and a circular spout in the form of a lion's head – sudden sophistication belying the apparent crudity of the exterior. The Bath House was constructed not during the earlier Baroque phase at Wrest Park but according to the later dictates of picturesque fashion, for Jemima, Marchioness Grey, daughter and heir of Earl Grey.

At Portmeirion in north Wales is a Bath House rescued by Sir Clough Williams-Ellis from Arnos Castle near Bristol, struggling to maintain its former dignity amid the bright jumble of theme-park buildings. It was built around 1760 for William Reeve, a wealthy Bristol copper smelter and Quaker. This Bath House had an oriental delicacy which is most pronounced in the domes of the square pavilions at either end. Between them curves an arcade of slender columns with foliate capitals, and above these are friezes and balustrades which combine oriental with gothic motifs. The Bath House had several pretty little rooms and a fine room for the bath itself with ogival arches, a sunken bath and Rococo plasterwork of waves, shells and dolphins. But overall the present fate of this particular bath house proves how greatly the spirit of a folly depends on preserving its original setting.

Despite the surge in popularity of bath houses, most gentry folk preferred messing about in boats rather than in the water itself. In general, of course, their boat houses were purely functional, but with exceptions, including the rare addition to Kettlethorpe Boathouse near Wakefield, where a medieval facade was rescued and installed in 1847. It came from the Old Bridge Chapel in Wakefield, which was a chantry built on the bridge itself in 1460, originally known as St Mary on the Bridge, a lovely example of medieval gothic at its most flamboyant. When the chapel was restored by Gilbert Scott, the facade was discarded and re-erected by the lakeside at Kettlethorpe Hall in

Newmillerdam, above the arch of an existing boat house, and supported by a room built on behind it. Pevsner described it as 'the most precious of all boathouses' – it could boast five narrow ogival arches with moulded triangular canopies and matching buttresses – and the upper storey, being already ruinous, was allowed to become picturesquely covered in ivy; but now the boat house has been demolished, and its charms are preserved only in old postcards, because it was a popular sight. In some instances boat houses were rendered ornamental by serving several purposes, as at Kedleston, and also at Enville in Staffordshire, where Lord Stamford topped his boat house with a gothic room for entertaining (possibly designed by his friend and neighbour Sanderson Miller circa 1769). The latter had a 'curious sliding window adorned with painted glass in whimsical groups of grotesque figures',[18] so that guests entering from the landward side found themselves facing over the water once the window was opened, enabling them to fish or view enactments on the lake.

The old chapel removed in 1843 & re-erected in the grounds of Kettlethorpe Hall nr Wakefield.

Boat House, Kettlethorpe Hall, Newmillerdam. The medieval facade was installed when the chantry chapel on the bridge at Wakefield, Yorkshire, was demolished.

The boat house at Enville exists now only in prints, from which it is apparent that one of its purposes was for watching curious boats performing pageants. This spectator sport may have been initiated by Frederick, Prince of Wales, for whom William Kent designed a state barge in 1732, rowed by 21 oarsmen and used for all sorts of visits and regattas. Subsequently many of Kent's drawings of landscapes and follies show imaginary vessels on lakes; and at Stowe, in 1733, Jacques Rigaud's print 'View from the Head of the Lake' depicts a fanciful boating party (with the rotunda in the background).

Following pages
Gibraltar Fort, Larch Hill, Co. Kildare, Ireland, built *c.* 1780 to stage mock water battles, and to mark the siege of Gibraltar, a prolonged resistance ending in 1783.

Very possibly Kent also designed the galley shown in Rigaud's print; it has a cabin towards the stern supported by caryatids, with urns along the roof and a pennant, and it is powered by oarsmen and a swirling sail. Around it, three smaller boats can be seen enacting some drama, and there are more boats in the distance. At Wrest Park several extravagant pleasure boats were recorded. In 1750 Elizabeth Anson, wife of the Admiral, wrote to her sister-in-law Marchioness Grey at Wrest Park, to say that the Admiral advised a galley would suit the canal best, 'as it has masts etc and is at the same time the most capable of decoration and ornament'. In 1766 a chinoiserie rowing boat was added to the little fleet, with a swan decorating one end and a tiger the other. On certain occasions, with the whole parish for audience, the family would assemble: 'Colours and streamers flew, music played, we embarked under the shade of the acacias and had a most prosperous voyage.'

In other places the action was more warlike. At West Wycombe Sir Francis Dashwood (whose family fortunes originated in seaborne trade with Turkey and India) kept several boats for mock battles, and in William Hannan's *View of the Lake at West Wycombe Park*, dated 1750, two of Sir Francis's boats appear, and a gaudy tent. In 1754 he erected 'a battery of guns in the form of a fort, to make a sham fight between it and the little fleet'. Unfortunately, the captain of one of the vessels was injured, and so put an end to the battle. At Newstead Abbey the fifth Lord Byron (father of the poet), who had a naval career before inheriting the title and whose brother John circumnavigated with Admiral Anson, was passionate about re-enacting seagoing exploits. In 1749 he expanded the lake, built a castellated fort at the water's edge, a folly castle on the hill above, and between them a battery of four guns. Then he press-ganged his gardeners and gamekeepers to be soldiers and sailors for the day. There was also Lord Bute, who, after being demoted from prime minister in 1766, retreated to his estate at Luton Hoo and had 'the model of a first-rate man of war to adorn the extensive canal now making'.

As a surviving symbol of these naval enactments, there is a fine fort-like folly on the lake at Larchill Garden, Kilcock, near Dublin. Built on an island in the lake (beside an enormous yew tree), it has five round towers between battlemented walls with lines of circular holes for gun placements. Its walls form a traditional pentagon – an ancient sign of power which inspired many European forts – and this one is a miniature replica of the fortress guarding the Rock of Gibraltar. That is the name of Larchill fort – Gibraltar – and it was built around 1780 at the time of the great siege of Gibraltar when, during the American War of Independence, the Spanish, and later the French, seized the opportunity to attack British possessions. The Governor of Gibraltar was General Elliot, who had built several extra garrisons during 1778 in anticipation of a blockade, which began in June 1779. Conditions in Gibraltar reached close to starvation, but relief convoys of small, fast sailing ships succeeded in running the blockade with exemplary daring, to the delight of all patriots reading their newspapers at home. Several enemy attacks ended in failure, including the Grand Assault of September 1782, and the siege was finally lifted in February 1783. General Eliot became a great hero and big triumphalist paintings appeared, plus cartoons of the French forces. Better by far, if one had boats and a lake, to restage such events rather than mere imaginary encounters.

Admittedly there is no record to confirm whether the siege of Gibraltar also inspired Henry Noel, sixth Earl of Gainsborough, when he built Fort Henry by the lake at Exton Park in Rutland. It certainly appeared during the same period, between 1786 and 1789, and it was used to stage mock battles on the lake, using miniature men of war crewed by his servants and tenants; and Fort Henry itself has the sleek lines of a battleship, albeit with gothic features. It was built on the site of an earlier boat house, which formed the base at the waterline. Above this the lower storey has a row of ogival windows

Fort Henry, Exton Park, Rutland, built *c.* 1786–9 in ornamental gothic style,
above an existing boat house, in order to view mock battles on the water.

Naumachia, Parc Monceau, Paris, built in the 1770s as a replica of the *naumachia* in Hadrian's Villa, outside Rome, a survival of an original arena for water fêtes.

looking over the water, and the building then stretches on either side into long low walls, which are both terraces and viewing platforms. The upper storey of Fort Henry consists of a large central room and smaller peaked pavilions at either side, all with decorative parapets and finely wrought obelisks and pinnacles gracing their rooflines. The retaining walls echo these crenellations, creating an elongated, graceful outline and making this one of the most exquisite examples of late eighteenth-century gothic. The reflections in the water enhance the effect, and at night, with lights shining through the windows, the magic intensifies. Indeed viewing Fort Henry from the opposite bank of the lake, framed by dark conifers, is as satisfying as entering its finely moulded gothic interior.[19]

In Europe the staging of mock battles and pageants on water had existed in Roman times, and these events continued to be known as *naumachia* when such festivities were revived from the Renaissance onwards. The finest watery arena remaining from the classical world was at Hadrian's Villa, and this was replicated at Parc Monceau in the 1770s, where it is one of the remaining follies. The introduction of water fêtes to the French court was credited to Catherine de Medici, wife of Henri II and, after his death, regent for her sons. For instance, there was the water pageant at Fontainebleau in 1564, which greeted her daughter Elizabeth, queen of Spain, with a dazzling array of vessels covered in carpets and brocades; and in 1573 the newly created Tuileries

Gardens witnessed a great pageant set against Bernard Palissey's new grotto, with half-clad nymphs, muses and Greek gods disporting on the rocks, where they appeared and disappeared in clouds of spray.[20] Such dramas reached the English court in the modified form of Inigo Jones's masques, which were indoor events although their scenery recalled outdoor theatres. Statues of the gods were an integral part of outdoor staging, whether in a garden amphitheatre or as fountains in a lake. They created the illusion that 'during the course of the play one can see the statues move.' Music heightened the effect, and was all the more unearthly if it was hydraulic, resonating from the pipes of a water organ, as it did at the Villa d'Este in Rome, the most famous such experiment, where statues of Apollo with his lute and Orpheus with his lyre added to the sense of music from another realm. Louis XIV introduced such devices to his court with renewed enthusiasm, not least because, at the impressionable age of 22, he had watched an amazing *naumachia* at Vaux-le-Vicomte, the palace of his chief minister Nicolas Fouquet, who soon after was disgraced for embezzlement.

Grotto of Apollo, Versailles. The rocky scene with statues was created for Louis XIV in the 1680s and moved to its present site in the 1780s by Louis XVI.

The chief scene of Louis xiv's self-aggrandizement was of course Versailles, where Le Nôtre transformed the gardens into a homage to Apollo, and therefore to Louis himself as Sun King. The major fountain showed the god driving his sun chariot towards the sky at dawn, and in the pavilion named the Palace of Thetis – Apollo's resting place at night – the statues represented the god at sunset, surrounded by attendant nymphs and his sun-horses being groomed. The Palace of Thetis was the initial setting for the king's outdoor plays, until in 1684 it was demolished to enlarge the palace itself. By then Le Nôtre had created the series of *bosquets* leading off from the Allée Royale, and within these groves he built elaborate theatrical settings amid cascades, pools and fountains. In the Théâtre d'Eau (created 1671–4), the auditorium was surrounded by tiers of turf benches, and to the rear of the stage three *allées* lined by soaring jets of water radiated through the trees, like a goose foot, or Palladio's Teatro Olimpico in Vicenza. The *bosquet* named the Salle de Bal was also an amphitheatre with fountains playing in the background; and in the Bosquet des Bains d'Apollon, the statues of Apollo with his nymphs and horses were relocated from the Palace of Thetis. Over them were placed three golden pavilions, like canopies of honour; the performance area was in front, and around them fountains jetted into a pool. In these *bosquets* operas, dances, pageants and the plays of Molière were staged. Just before the Revolution, Louis xvi, in his attempts to loosen the formality of Le Nôtre's Versailles, commissioned Hubert Robert to design an enormous rockwork grotto in the English Picturesque style, and it is there, amid the cascades, that Apollo still reigns in renewed splendour among his nymphs and horses.

It was a point of honour for other European courts to emulate Versailles. One of the most remarkable water theatres was the Temple of Night at Schönau in Austria, created from 1796 to 1800 by Baron Peter von Braun, director of court theatricals in Vienna. It was approached through a twisting rocky grotto, but the Temple itself was above ground, surrounded by a Corinthian colonnade with a dome above, representing the sky at night. A statue of Night, in a chariot drawn by winged horses, was illuminated by alabaster lamps, and an organ powered by water through a pinned cylinder played the music of Salieri, Mozart and Haydn. But for the staging of theatricals none achieved Louis xiv's absurd splendour except when Ludwig ii of Bavaria, known as Ludwig the Mad, with a passion for Wagner, created the Grotto of Venus at Linderhof Palace in the foothills of the Bavarian Alps, circa 1873. The stage was deep within the caverns of the grotto and best approached by boat, to where a waterfall fed the Lake of Venus in front of the stage. The grotto was lit by an early form of electric arc lighting that changed colour. Stalactites and garlands hung from the roof, and there was a throne of shells and a table of coral. A golden skiff curved like a shell, with a fat cupid at the prow, bobbed on the Lake of Venus and here Ludwig listened to *Tannhäuser* or the 'Ride of the Valkyries'.

Presumably for reasons of climate, dramatic entertainments seem to have been rare in English grottos, though there may have been unrecorded concerts. Horace Walpole's accounts of two evenings spent in Kent's rocky little grotto at Stowe provide explanation enough. In 1764 Princess Amelia visited, and in her honour,

> at 10 the gardens were illuminated with above a thousand lights, and the water before the grotto was covered with floating lights. At the further end of the canal, on the ship which was curiously figured with lights was a place for the music, which performed all supper time.

But in July 1770 Walpole wrote to George Montagu with less enthusiasm:

> on Wednesday a small Vauxhall was acted for us at the grotto in the Elysian Fields, which was illuminated with lamps as were the thicket and two little barks on the lake. The evening was more than cool, and the destined spot anything but dry. There were not half lamps enough and no music but an ancient militia man who played cruelly on the squeaking tabor or pipe. As our procession descended the vast flight of steps into the garden, in which was assembled a crowd of people from Buckingham and the neighbouring villages, I could not help laughing as I surveyed our troop which, instead of tripping lightly to such an Arcadian entertainment, were hobbling down by the balustrades, wrapped in cloaks and great coats for fear of catching cold.[21]

GROTTOS

Like the *naumachia* and other dramatic festivities, grottos themselves have a classical history. Caves with a natural spring (or tidal water) became places of ancient worship associated with a female goddess of fertility. The myths of Venus and Artemis bear traces of these watery origins, but many springs were named after a local nymph of the same ilk, and so the ideas spread through Europe (in Britain they entered Arthurian legend), just as the fashion

Giovanni Piranesi, *The Grotto of Egeria*, c. 1766, print. The grotto sanctuary dated
from ancient Rome but was adorned with increasing artifice, as depicted.

for grottos later spread. In Homer's *Odyssey* there is a perfect description of
a natural grotto:

> At the head of the harbour there is an olive tree with spreading leaves,
> and nearby is a cave that is shaded and pleasant and sacred to the
> nymphs of the wellsprings, and there is water forever flowing. It has
> two entrances, one where people may enter . . . but the other is the
> way of the immortals and no one may enter by that way.[22]

The word 'grotto' came from the Italian *grotta*, a cave, which in turn
(through centuries of mispronunciation) derived from the Greek *krypte*,
meaning a hidden thing. The natural gloom of caves, and in some cases hydro-
carbon gases, intensified the illusion and enabled the shamans, priests and
priestesses to become oracular. The Romans inherited the nymphs and their
shrines, sometimes naming the the former sibyls, as at Nemi near Naples,
and sometimes naming the grottos *nymphaea*. In Rome the Grotto of Egeria
became part of the foundation legend. Egeria was a water nymph and the

divine consort of Numa, an early king of Rome, to whom she taught the rituals and laws. When Numa died, Egeria dissolved in tears and thus became a sacred spring, which Vestal Virgins were set to guard. In due course the natural cave was reinforced with arches, decorated with marble, porphyry and mosaics, and the water captured in pools. In one of his *Satires* (*c.* AD 100) Juvenal regretted this: 'Nymph of the Spring! More honour'd hadst thou been,/ If, free from art, . . .'. But the process continued, and by the time Egeria's Grotto was a part of the Grand Tour and depicted by Piranesi, it was a magnificent ruin with statues, still mysterious but artificial, and another inspiration to folly builders.[23]

The first Renaissance grottos were often inside palatial houses, rather than separate garden constructs, but the design elements were there.[24] The Italian archetype was the Grotta Grande in the Boboli Gardens of Florence, a series of dripping, stuccoed chambers, full of statues and stalactites, culminating in the frescoed garden of Venus where she emerges from her fountain/ bath/spring under the lascivious gaze of fauns. A more numinous aspect was explored by Francesco Colonna in *Polyphilus' Dream*, where the grotto opened the path to initiation and shared the haunting qualities exemplified in the Bomarzo Gardens, where there were many more springs and cascades in the sixteenth century to create the atmosphere associated with grottos. In France the strangest sixteenth-century grotto was created by Bernard Palissy in the Tuileries Gardens: 'All manner of water-loving ferns and mosses grew on strangely shaped rocks and there were countless reptiles, making movements in imitation of nature.'[25] All are now gone, but Palissy was basically a potter and enameller, and his great platters survive to suggest how realistically his snakes and toads moved through the fronds, as water splashed over them on the grotto walls. Another feature of Renaissance grottos were the *trucchi d'acqua*, trick jets of water activated when an unsuspecting person walked by, and perhaps more acceptable as a joke in hot countries. John Evelyn certainly found it so, during his visit to Italy in 1645: 'The gardens delicious and full of fountains, in a grove sits Pan feeding his flock, the water making melodious sound through his pipe', followed by a walk 'at the sides whereof gushes out of imperceptible pipes, couched underneath, slender pissings of water'.[26]

At Wideville near Paris a lovely little building dating from 1635 to 1640 represents an early form of the grotto as shell house and garden folly. The exterior is rusticated, with a steep roof of grey slates that could only be French, fronted by a decorative pediment with a nymph and a river god reclining either side. The doorway and windows, with their gilded foliar curlicues of ironwork, belie the rustic effect of the walls, and a similar contrast exists between the clipped formal evergreens along the approach to the folly and the steep, wild wood behind it. The grotto faces the Château as an eye-catcher. Inside is Rococo in every sense of the word, all surfaces patterned with pebbles and shining with shells – silvery mother of pearl, pink interiors of conches, dark mussels and amethyst. There are masks made of shells, reminiscent of Arcimboldo's fantasy heads, with white coral beards and pointed whelks for noses. The grotto was built for Claude de Bullion, Finance Minister of Louis XIII, and there his guests would assemble at 'the hour of the nymphs' while water trickled musically in the alcoves. Subsequently the Château de Wideville was the residence of Louis XIV's mistress Mme de la Vallière.[27]

There was an English version of such a grotto at Wilton House in Wiltshire, designed in the 1630s by Isaac de Caus for the fourth Earl of Pembroke, patron of Van Dyck. (Salomon de Caus and Inigo Jones collaborated on Wilton House and Isaac de Caus was responsible for the garden.) Isaac was a Huguenot, well versed in French and Italian style and a hydraulics expert, who laid out the great parterre and fountains to be the best of their kind in seventeenth-century England. The facade of his grotto, supported on four pilasters topped with busts, is ornately carved stonework, as is the pediment above with its foliate swirls, rosettes and faces, giving an overall effect that is sturdy, grey and a little rigid (where Wideville is tawny and golden). Now the facade is all that remains of the grotto, having been rescued and re-erected in woodland in 1834 and called the Old Schoolhouse. There were two pavilions at Wilton, both illustrated by Colen Campbell in *Vitruvius Britannicus* and linked to Inigo Jones: the larger one (now altogether vanished) had three arched entrances and faced towards the house, and since Campbell called it the 'Loggio in the Bowling Green', there must have been a designated area of grass behind it. The smaller grotto, whose ornate facade remains, was to the west of Wilton House, in an Italianate garden of its own. Originally the main room had a central water feature and moisture showering down the walls from pipes in the domed ceiling, while statues of tritons 'wept water on the beholders'. On either side were two smaller rooms; from one came birdsong including 'nightingerills' which lured the visitor over the threshold, activating trick water jets, but most intriguing of all is a description by John Aubrey: 'Mr de Caus had here a contrivance by turning a cock to shew three rainbows, the secret of which he did keep to himself . . . so upon his death it was lost. The grotto and pipes did cost ten thousand pounds.'[28]

John Evelyn had a grotto where he retreated and sometimes 'sulked when displeased'. It was not ambitious like Wilton, but a family concern, because the ancestral home at Wotton in Surrey belonged to his older brother George, until it became John Evelyn's in later life. In the 1640s, together with their cousin George, who was a military engineer, the Evelyns remodelled the gardens in European style, drawing water for ornamental purposes from the river which also powered their water mills.[29] John Evelyn travelled abroad during the worst of the Civil War and work was completed in the 1650s when he returned. The grotto, or rather *nymphaeum* since it was not rocky but did contain a nymph, was built into the wall of the garden terrace, facing the house as an eye-catcher and taking the form of a small temple portico with four Doric columns and a classical frieze above. Inside were three niches, and the central one is still occupied by a statue of Artemis (as the nymph) and a marble basin representing her pool. Outside is a real circular pool which may once have sported a fountain.

As with all other follies, the eighteenth century was the time when English grottos came into their own. The most iconic was Alexander Pope's, created underneath his villa by the Thames at Twickenham, where he went to live in 1719 and by 1725 had completed four cavernous chambers by extending the cellars. A road divided the villa from his riverside garden, and in 1720 Pope obtained permission to make a tunnel under it to join his two properties, incidentally uncovering the spring that made his excavations more truly a grotto; as he wrote to Edward Blount in 1725, 'it falls in a perpetual rill that echoes through the cavern.' Dr Johnson later commented: 'he extracted an ornament from an inconvenience and vanity produced a grotto where necessity forced a passage.'[30] The chambers of the grotto were arched and columned, then decorated with shells, flints and mirrors. In the largest central chamber Pope would sit to summon his poetic muses (nymphs and muses were interchangeable for writers) and there he was depicted in two sketches by his friend William Kent. But Kent's third and best drawing shows the entrance to the grotto that faced Pope's villa.[31] In front is the Shell Temple designed for Pope by Kent and completed in 1725, 'entirely composed of shells and consisting wholly of a cupola supported on rustic columns', which certainly added to the external effect of the grotto. The cupola of the Shell Temple was octagonal and rested on eight spindly columns which curved outwards at the base. In his sketch, which is all that remains of this curiosity, Kent added some scene-setting flourishes (which were characteristic of his sketches) including himself and Pope admiring the scene with Pope's dog Bounce; naked nymphs,

William Kent, *Pope's Grotto and Shell House*, drawing, 1725, showing Kent himself
with Pope and the dog Bounce, admiring the folly with the grotto entrance behind.

possibly meant as statues, disporting themselves; and a sacrificial altar and
tripod. But the little glimpse through the grotto to the river and a boat is
the most important detail, a reminder that the steep slope of the ground
enabled scenic river views within the grotto too. As Pope wrote in 'On His
Grotto at Twickenham':

> Thou who shalt stop where Thames' translucent wave
> Shines a broad mirror through the shadowy cave;
> Where ling'ring drops from min'ral roofs distil,
> And pointed crystal break the sparkling rill . . .

Reflections are a magical element of grottos, most easily appreciated in
the bright, sunny climates of their origins. A simple archway of rock over a
pool, with a green view beyond, reflects the sunlight on the water with rippling lights and shadows which move across the walls and then vanish with
the sun – a reminder of why grottos became sacred in ancient times.[32] Pope
contrived such effects in his grotto, using the river and mirrors – there were
three at the back of the central chamber – placed to reflect each other and
cast light over the minerals and glass on the walls, 'as to seem two arches
opening to the river each side, as there is one real in the middle'. Pope, and

no doubt his many visitors, took delight in watching boats passing on the river – 'the view of the river with sails passing suddenly and vanishing as through a perspective glass' – and when the door of the grotto was shut a circular lens acted as a camera obscura, 'the boats forming a moving picture in their visible radiations'.[33]

In the 1740s Pope's enthusiasm for his grotto entered a second phase, a serious collector's mania for additional stalactites, stones and minerals, which was inspired by a visit to Hotwells Spa in Bristol. In return for their subsequent offerings Pope's friends received gifts of poetry and pineapples. Sir Hans Sloane sent two slabs from the Giant's Causeway in Northern Ireland, and among many other donors were Frederick, Prince of Wales, Ralph Allen of Prior Park in Bath, and William Borlase, a supplier from Cornwall.[34] Their sources ranged across Europe to Egypt and across the Atlantic to the Caribbean and even Brazil. Pope and his grotto became legendary, but a reverse movement started even in his lifetime, as Robert Dodsley remarked in the ditty that he added to the grotto guidebook which he published for Pope:

> Then some small gem, or moss, or shining ore
> Departing, each shall pilfer, in fond hope
> To please their friends, on every distant shore
> Boasting a relic from the cave of Pope.

Among the remains in the dank and partially restored chambers of Pope's grotto are ammonites, amethyst, glass slag, faience ceramics, Bristol diamond and fossilized wood. A statue of St James of Compostela presides, with a scallop shell in his pilgrim's hat, and (according to contemporary sketches) in the side chamber to the north Pope once had a cold plunge bath, which he called the Bagnio.

As part of Pope's circle, William Kent knew his grotto well, but those he created in other gardens followed a different formula of rough-hewn archways, as at Claremont, and were sometimes cascades rather than grottos, as at Rousham and Chiswick. Kent's only grotto known to have been decorated was at Stowe, where it too formed part of a cascade, at the top of the Elysian Fields. Either side were two little pavilions very like the Shell Temple he made for Pope, 'the one ornamented with shells, as the other is with pebbles and broken flints'. An engraving shows the one on the right with twisted columns supporting its domed roof. The other had Ionic columns. A visitor of 1738 described the Shell Temples 'covered with the shells of large tortoises

The Grotto, Stourhead, created *c.* 1748 by Henry Flitcroft, complete with the sleeping nymph in her cave-like sanctuary, with trickling water and a superb view over the lake.

intermixed with small ones', and inside the dome the shells depicted human faces.[35] The grotto itself, like John Evelyn's, was a little temple rather than a cave, though the facade was rusticated and opened through one simple archway. The grotto's nymph was a replica of the *Crouching Venus*, and the interior was 'furnished with a great number of looking glasses in the walls and ceiling, all in artificial frames of plasterwork set with shells and broken flints'. In 1780 the grotto was 'modernized' in the Picturesque style; earth was banked up to render it more cave-like, tunnels led to it on either side and evergreens were planted. The facade was reinforced with 'the roughest stones' and the inside walls covered with fresh encrustations.

The grotto created at Stourhead from 1748, under Flitcroft's supervision, continued the tradition of the *nymphaeum*. In this case the nymph was based on the statue of *Sleeping Ariadne* in the Vatican, and Alexander Pope (who had hoped to acquire his own nymph) donated to Henry Hoare the pseudo-Virgilian translation he had made in anticipation. It is inscribed around the pool, where the waters of the Stour cascade gently under her reclining form:

Nymph of the grot these sacred springs I keep
And to the murmur of these waters sleep
Ah spare my slumbers gently tread the cave
And drink in silence or in silence lave.

Her cavern is atmospherically solemn and grey, with a pebble floor, flint walls and stone dome, but it opens onto a limpid view across the lake, a green lightness contrasting wonderfully with the gloom inside and highlighting the serene pallor of the nymph (who according to any chosen legend is waiting to be woken by a god, hero or prince). In the even darker second chamber is the challenging figure of the River God, frowning, bearded and arm raised. Beneath him an urn channels another spring of the river Stour into the lake. For those following the story of Aeneas' journey to Rome he is also regarded as the river Tiber, while for some he represents Hades, god of the Underworld, who held Persephone (another nymph) captive for half the year in the land of the dead. If the grotto is part of the Aeneas narrative, the steep uneven passageways leading to it may be what Henry Hoare jokingly referred to, in a letter of 1765, as the descent to Avernus. But the Latin inscription over the arched entrance calmly reiterates that this grotto is the abode of nymphs.[36] Capability Brown, who knew Stourhead, created a *nymphaeum* at Croome Park in 1765 with the same *aquae dulces* (sacred springs) inscription, and the beautiful white statue leaning on an urn of water is Sabrina, a nymph of the river Severn. Brown, being an expert in hydraulics, would have ensured that spring water once flowed from her urn into the lake, and an iron hook above her indicated that at night she was illuminated by lamplight. Her grotto is a curving screen of limestone blocks and tufa, creating an impression of a cave entrance, over which the nymph presides from outside. In the 1780s it was embellished with shells and minerals to conform to the dominant fashion for geological grottos.

The elite grotto builders of the mid-eighteenth century were Joseph and Josiah Lane, father and son, stonemasons of Tisbury in Wiltshire. Joseph came to prominence working for Alderman Beckford at Fonthill, on whose estate he lived. The Beckford fortune was founded on Jamaican sugar plantations and slavery, and the Alderman, a rough diamond, was prominent in the City both financially and politically. Alongside the creation of a new Palladian house at Fonthill, it seems that the Alderman set Lane to work on a grotto soon after buying the estate in 1745. Circumstantial evidence of his early interest includes Beckford supplying Lord Shaftesbury with Jamaican sea shells for a grotto in 1749; and in 1801 Richard Warner, author of *Excursions from Bath*, wrote that Lane 'exhibited the earliest specimens of his talents in the construction of a grotto at Fonthill'.[37] Little remains, except a muddy cavern overlooking the lake in the manner of Stourhead but ruinous, and in another cave there are the broken remains of statues known as 'the sleepers',

The Grotto, Painshill, Surrey, begun c. 1762 by Josiah Lane; one of his finest creations, with glittering crystalline walls, shell displays and archways over the lake.

which haunted the youthful imagination of the Alderman's son William, left fatherless at the age of nine. Charles Hamilton was related to the Beckfords, through his cousin the Alderman's wife, and no doubt this was how he learnt of Joseph Lane, who began around 1762 to create the grotto at Painshill, an Aladdin's cave now restored to glory.

The Painshill grotto is on an island in the lake, approached either by bridge or boat, and Hamilton the master scene-setter ensured that the island itself was suitably rocky with arches and outcrops of tufa which have a curious bumpy allure.[38] The grotto itself starts as a long crystalline tunnel, treading a pathway of crushed shells to the central chamber. This opens out with a luminous array of crystals – quartz, spar and Derbyshire bluejohn. The stalactites are made from pendant wooden lathes plastered with chips and flakes of calcite, fluorite and gypsum (the successful render for attaching them was a Masonic secret of Josiah Lane's). Through rocky apertures the chamber opens onto the water of the lake, and during the day the reflections shimmer over the crystals with a shifting, silvery glow that is finest towards evening, as the grotto faces west. In small alcoves there are pools and arrangements of coral and giant clams from the South Seas – but the scene is best evoked by a contemporary:

> it consists of several vaults resting on pillars, and is on the inside ornamented with spars and stalactites, baldachins and chandeliers of all possible forms and shapes hanging from the vaults. From the floor, which is encompassed with a running stream, one sees branchy corals growing up. In diverse niches water trickles down like a gentle rain from the strainers concealed in the vaults, and all this water cascades into the lake, from which the sunbeams are reflected through the spars and crystallisations.[39]

The Lanes (and there may have been several members of the extended family involved as well as Joseph and Josiah) were extremely busy in the 1760s. At Oatlands in Surrey, for Henry Clinton, ninth Earl of Lincoln, they were probably grottifying an earlier construction which was more conventionally architectural. There were three downstairs rooms to transform into 'chambers', including a gaming room reminiscent of West Wycombe's caves, and a bath chamber with a deep sunken pool of icy spring water where the *Medici Venus* presided; and above was an upper chamber which caught the sun and was possibly for the ladies. The Lanes transformed these with tufa and their trademark stalactites on wood, which here had sharp little teeth of felspar. Here too were enchanting views over the lake and reflections off the water. It became a playground of royalty in 1790 when the Duke of York (son of George III, brother of the Prince Regent) purchased Oatlands. A great Waterloo supper held there in 1815 is on record, but all is now gone. What does remain – unique in its original state – is the grotto at Ascot Place in Berkshire, started a little after Painshill. From the house a fine pile of rocks and a cave mouth are visible across the lake, and the approaches wind through rock, tufa and cascades to a Great Chamber. This is supported by a huge flinty arch stretching right across a pool surrounded by a pebble-patterned floor. Light comes through many apertures in the walls and vaults, from which the Lane-style stalactites hang, almost threatening in their felspar spikiness, the effect heightened by zigzag patterns and glittering with crystal fragments. The grotto becomes labyrinthine, winding past a series of antechambers, some overlooking the lake, some unusually adorned with dark clumps of minerals set against the silvery crystals (there are no shells). The caverns were lit with lanterns and witch-balls of coloured glass; now electricity is used, but the privacy of this intact treasure is carefully guarded.

As the century progressed Josiah Lane took over from his father and was responsible for more grottos back in Wiltshire. For Lord Arundell at Wardour Castle he built a tunnel of brick, and used tufa and stone to create an atmospheric gothic entrance of pointed, mossy stonework, enhanced by the surrounding yew trees. At Bowood House for the Marquis of Lansdowne, a friend of Charles Hamilton, Joseph Lane created an impressive cascade beside the grotto entrance, which crashes down over three tiers of mossy rocks:

> The dashing and roar of the waters, jumbled confusion of the rock, the wildness and seclusion of the place, and the various subterranean passages under the head of the river conspire to render a scene strikingly pleasing to everyone of taste; but more peculiarly so to the painter and admirer of the picturesque.

The entrance to the grotto is suitably dark and ivy-clad and from within the tunnel there are views over the lake, as green but not as classically pure as Stourhead, after which the rest of the labyrinth has collapsed and, apart from some embedded ammonites, little decoration remains.[40]

Meanwhile in Bristol, Thomas Goldney created another type of grotto, more in the spirit of Pope's second collecting phase, which was a massive

Goldney Grotto, Bristol, begun in the 1730s and adorned
with a wide-ranging collection of shells and minerals.

showcase for fossils and shells. Also, like Pope's grotto, it was genuinely underground, which most grottos were not. It probably all started in 1708 when Thomas Goldney (grandfather of the grotto builder), a Bristol merchant banker and slave trader, funded a voyage round the world in two frigates, the *Duke* and *Duchess*, 'to establish trade with the South Seas'. He profited handsomely, and in another successful venture he backed Abraham Darby of Coalbrookdale, who perfected the technique of using coke to smelt iron ore. A smattering of shells from the Indo-Pacific regions, the glazed Coalbrookdale tiles on the floors and the beam engine that pumped water all bring the spirit of the founding father into the grotto. The Goldney Grotto was begun in the 1730s, too early to be influenced by Pope's collecting phase, and it is possible that the inspiration came from the Netherlands, which Goldney's father visited in 1725: he wrote of a grotto in Utrecht with 'antik varieties of fancy all of shells', including 'a woman very fine made in shells and out of her nipples run streams of water'.[41] Another possible inspiration was *The Arabian Nights*, first translated and published in England early in the eighteenth century, in which Aladdin, Sinbad and Ali Baba all discovered bejewelled caves. There is the usual river god with water pouring from his urn into a cascade and pool, causing the sound of water to echo through the tunnels (but no nymph). The columns are encrusted with Bristol diamonds, the stalactites are made from Bath Stone; other crystals include quartz, chalcedony, agate, jasper and amethyst, all sparkling amid iron minerals and pyrites. Most of these are local, because for seven years Goldney employed men to collect from the Avon Gorge, and the fossils too are local – ammonites known as Keynsham snake stones, together with fossilized oysters and scallops. The shells are far from local, though of all the different species there are 53 British. Of the rest, 68 come from the Caribbean, 38 from the Pacific and 9 from West Africa. Classified biologically rather than regionally, there are many thousand molluscs, gastropods and bivalves; among the exotics are queen conch, giant clams, sea urchins, fan mussels and cowries; also reef corals and brain corals. In 1756 Mrs Delany visited Goldney and wrote to her sister: 'it is not much more than half finished . . . very boldly adorned with everything the

Goodwood House Grotto, West Sussex, begun *c.* 1730 as a garden room with a fine Georgian interior, the best example of shellwork done as a hobby by aristocratic ladies.

earth and sea can produce . . . all in her highest perfection . . . the pillars set with spars as if with jewels.' Maybe Mrs Delany sensed the grotto was intended as a display of the banker's wealth; she regretted that the loveliest shells would deteriorate and would have lasted better in a cabinet. She also described Goldney as 'a great humourist and a niggard', although he gave her 'some pretty coral'.

Mrs Delany was an expert amateur in shellwork, and her first recorded effort was in Ireland in 1732 (after her first husband died and before marrying Dr Delany in 1743). She was staying with the Bishop of Killala's family and each day, as she wrote to her sister, they 'walked up to a little grotto on a hill to adorn it with shells. The Bishop has a large collection of very fine ones. Phil [another female guest] and I are the engineers, the men fetch and carry for us and think themselves highly honoured.' The home she later shared with Dr Delany was at Delville near Dublin, and there she decorated both a chapel and a grotto with shells (all that remains of the latter is a distant sketch). In her second widowhood, after 1765, she renewed her close friendship with the Duchess of Portland, another blue-stocking and ardent collector of items of zoological and botanical interest, which she housed at Bulstrode in Buckinghamshire, nicknaming it the Hive. During the 1770s Mrs Delany and the Duchess decorated a cave-like little grotto at Bulstrode with shell patterns seemingly dominated by snails – though Walpole called it 'a cave in fine taste' – but here too all that survives is a sketch, dated 1781.[42] A shell grotto does remain in Ireland, at Curraghmore, Co. Waterford, to represent the work of a talented lady amateur, the Countess of Tyrone. It is a cruciform stone building, freezingly cold but not dark, being lit by circular skylights as well as windows at each arm of the cross. A white marble statue of the countess stands in the centre like a rather matronly nymph, holding a conch in one hand and a scroll in the other announcing that the shell work was done in 261 days. The floor is intricately patterned with pebbles and the walls and ceilings are encrusted with shells in clever and complex arrangements.[43]

A good proportion of the shell houses that proliferated around Britain testified to the skills of lady amateurs, from A la Ronde near Exeter, with the upper shell gallery made by the Parminter ladies, to Goodwood House Grotto in West Sussex, where the Duchess of Richmond and her daughters made the most intricately lovely shell patterns, inside a garden pavilion 4 metres square. The internal proportions of Goodwood Shell House are mainstream Georgian, with window alcoves and niches in the walls and no attempts to evoke the mythical or picturesque – no rocks, stalactites or lumps of mineral;

no trickling water or nymph. Just shells laid all over, very geometrically in panels, then along the dados, and following the curves of the alcoves and the vaults of the ceiling. The careful symmetry highlights the aesthetic effect of all that variety of shells, the rectangular outlines formed of white whelks and scallops, with the backs of the shells pointed outwards to create a subtle rippling effect. There are backgrounds created from tiny black molluscs to dramatize the colours in the designs; diamonds and spirals; abstracted sunbursts and floral motifs; swags, urns and arabesques.[44] It is possible that Caroline, one of these skilful Goodwood daughters, retained her love of shellwork and was part of the mystery behind Margate Grotto. In 1744 she eloped with Henry Fox, later Lord Holland, creating a *cause célèbre* at the time. He was a prominent Whig politician who had remained loyal to Walpole and continued to hold office until 1765 when, as Paymaster General, he was finally accused of embezzlement and retired.[45] Part of the Fox fortune had been deployed to help Charles Hamilton create Painshill, and when Henry and Caroline retreated to Kingsgate, their estate on the Kent coast, they settled down to enjoy their own follies, which were described scathingly by the poet Thomas Gray in 1766:

> Here mouldering fanes and battlements arise
> Turrets and arches nodding to their fall.

There was no grotto at Kingsgate, but at nearby Margate there is a very fine tunnel grotto whose undocumented origins are a source of much speculation, including imagined links to ancient religions. Far more plausible is the suggestion that the tunnel was included, legally or otherwise, in the Holland estate, and that theirs was the only local fortune vast enough to encompass such a project.[46]

The passageways of Margate Grotto, easily high enough to walk through, are carved from the chalk and supported by archways; the bricks used for vaulting are definitely eighteenth-century. At either end of the main serpentine passage are chambers, one round and one rectangular. At the entrance to the grotto, the passage curves either side of the round chamber or rotunda, and joins again at the dome. This has a skylight high above, which sends daylight glistening down the mother-of-pearl circles of oyster shells which line the dome. From here the winding passage leads over 20 metres (65 ft) to the rectangular chamber, which has an altar, and here the shell patterns have a planetary theme, with suns, moons and stars. The construction is wondrous

Margate Grotto, Kent, probably c. 1800, an ambitious project with an undisclosed origin and mysterious planetary symbolism in the shellwork decoration.

and the decoration is breathtaking, since it took millions of shells. Most are local – mussels, cockles, whelks, limpets, scallops and oysters. However, the backgrounds to the designs are made from flat winkles, placed aperture outwards, in immeasurable quantities, and these were rare on the Kent coast, although common further west beyond Southampton. Most of the exotic shells are from the Caribbean. This alone would rule out theories relating to the ancient world, although these received a mild boost when the adhesive was found to be fish oil and crushed shells, a method used in Roman times, but also of course since. The elaborate mosaic patterns of the shells do relate to a style Caroline Fox, Lady Holland, would have remembered from her youthful shellwork at Goodwood; and they also relate to the shell house which her sister Emilia, Duchess of Leinster, created at Carton, her Irish home in Co. Kildare. The patterns are symmetrical, with rectangular panels outlined in matched shells, or curving outlines following the arches and vaults. The backgrounds are made with the dark little flat winkles. The floral, geometric and arabesque motifs are cruder than Goodwood – one would hardly consider Lady Holland working in a tunnel herself – but she may have sketched designs, including vases of flowering plants and other interlacing foliar swirls. The grotto was probably finished long after her lifetime (she and her husband both died in 1774), and a generally accepted date is circa 1800, the time when Kingsgate belonged to her son Charles James Fox. A local memory, derived from the Bowles family, told of two brothers who were involved in the shellwork, who emigrated to America around 1812 and blocked the tunnel before they left.[47] The tunnels were rediscovered in 1835, and Margate later became a fashionable Victorian venue, even graced with paintings by Turner, at which point the grotto also became a tourist attraction and decades of gaslight coated the shells like treacle. When some shells were cleaned their colour was gone, so the grotto retains an aura of Victorian mahogany.

In 1769 the actor-manager David Garrick wrote a complimentary poem, 'Upon a Certain Grotto near Hampton'. He knew Pope's grotto well, and had even copied the idea of a tunnel under the road to reach his own riverside garden and his Temple of Shakespeare. It was possibly to Garrick that Dr Johnson expressed his oft-quoted verdict on grottos: 'a pretty cool summer habitation for a toad'. But Garrick's poem was about the grotto at Hampton Court House, designed by Thomas Wright for Lord Halifax, or rather for his mistress, a beautiful singer he had met at Marylebone Gardens:

A Grotto this, by Mortal Hand?
Oh no we tread in Fairy Land,
'Tis raised by Mab's enchanted wand

Grotto, Hampton Court House, Surrey, dated to the 1760s, the work of Thomas Wright with a rustic exterior and shellwork inside.

So rare so elegant so bright
It dazzles while it charms the sight.[48]

Already in the 1750s Lord Halifax had employed Thomas Wright in his Northamptonshire estate at Horton, and Hampton Court House belonged to Lord Halifax in his role as Ranger of Bushey Park. The rustic Grotto was set in the garden that Wright also designed, beside a heart-shaped lake, exemplifying the grotto designs published in his *Universal Architecture*. The exterior is heaped up stones, flints and slag in a circular edifice, with an arched entrance and two side wings, suggesting that a bath house and sitting room were also intended. Inside this fashionably derelict exterior is an exquisite little room, the walls covered with a fine collection of exotic shells, especially conches. A nymph glittering with glass shards and set in a niche dominates the wall facing the door. Presumably she is Venus since she is rising from a sea shell. Above is a blue ceiling set with yellow stars, an expression of Wright's love of astronomy and emphasizing Venus' celestial aspect as the planet or evening star.

Thomas Wright's namesake William Wrighte published *Grotesque Architecture, or Rural Amusement* in 1767 with even more eccentric suggestions about grottos, including 'a Rural Grotto of rough rude stone to be set in a morass near some water'; a Chinese Grotto 'to be placed at the head of a grand canal with a bath and a Chinese temple attached'; a Modern Grotto with a bath and tufa and shell ceiling; and the Gothic Grotto with a grand total of six rooms, all lined with shells. The burlesque ditty on the title page included the lines:

Or pebbles, shells or calcin'd matter mix
The frozen isicles resembled form,
Or sea-green weed your grotto must adorn.

Fragments of glass and mirror also belonged in the tradition, but until recently no one thought of using whole bottles to create a rustic grotto. Now one has been created at Westonbury Water Garden in Pembridge, Herefordshire – the folly garden designed by Richard Pim at the turn of the century. He was first inspired by the old mill stream of Westonbury, flowing past weeping willows, yellow water irises and boats, because Pim was a hydrogeologist. He honed his engineering skills on irrigation projects in the Sahara – 'when you're in the desert you tend to fantasise about bubbling brooks,' he explained – and on retirement he unleashed his energies at home. First Pim

Bottle Grotto, Westonbury Water Garden, Herefordshire, created *c.* 2000 onwards
as a modern example of grotto creation, using bottles to reflect a kaleidoscope of light.

rescued the old iron water wheel that had served the corn mill, and to set it back in action he built a stone tower; then he installed a bucket chain fed by the water wheel, to carry the water up inside the tower to a tank. When full this releases the water noisily through the gargoyles, which are set around the top of the tower, and it spouts downwards from their mouths in streams as satisfying as a fountain and more startling. The multicoloured Bottle Grotto is just as original. The frame is a low concrete dome, like a hot cross bun, filled in with hundreds of wine bottles – blue, clear and all shades of green from brownish to yellowish. The light shining onto the glass circles on the outside of the dome is attractive, and inside, where the necks of the bottles look like a new type of encrustation on the walls of a grotto, the effect is kaleidoscopic and magical.[49]

Seven

The Lure of the East

In Xanadu did Kubla Khan
A stately pleasure-dome decree:
Where Alph, the sacred river, ran
Through caverns measureless to man
Down to a sunless sea.
Samuel Taylor Coleridge, 'Kubla Khan'

Around 1690 John Vanderbank, a Flemish tapestry weaver with a workshop in Soho, was appointed Chief Arras Maker of the Great Wardrobe, and commissioned by Queen Mary to provide tapestries 'designed in the Indian manner' for her China Room in Kensington Palace. She was an avid collector of Chinese blue-and-white porcelain and these tapestries were to provide a suitably oriental background. Until 1717 Vanderbank continued to weave quantities of such enchanting scenes for stately homes,[1] happily mixing Mughal princes seated on carpets with Ottoman musicians on horseback, Chinese in palanquins and junks, and people climbing palm trees – all set among a wondrous array of exotic plants and birds, pavilions and pagodas. The tapestries expressed the European view of the Orient at the start of the eighteenth century, a confused fascination gleaned from various accounts and pictorial sources. Another example was the word *sharawadgi* (variously spelt), which had been introduced by William Temple, English Ambassador to The Hague, to describe how Chinese gardens were not based on symmetry, like the formal gardens of Europe, but followed the variations of the landscape, creating naturalistic settings alongside water, hills and woods, 'contriving figures where the beauty shall be great and strike the eye but without any order that shall be easily observed . . . where it hits the eye at first sight they say the *sharawadgi* is fine.' Temple astutely pointed out: 'this style is to be seen in textiles, screens and porcelains . . . a beauty without order.' The word was adopted by the early advocates of landscape gardening and has now been

John Vanderbank, detail from a tapestry, c. 1690, showing a
decorative 17th-century take on oriental pavilions and tents.

traced to Japan, where in a southern dialect *sorowagi* signified asymmetry. In
1712 Addison in *The Spectator* suggested that, on this principle, whole estates
might be turned into gardens, 'by some little additions of art'; and the following year Sam Molyneux advocated 'the beautiful scaravagie of noble grown
trees in a wild wood'. Both Temple and Addison contrived to link naturalism with other forms of liberty and implied that artifice was associated with
tyranny. Pope, Kent and Horace Walpole all followed suit, until *sharawadgi*
became emblematic of freedom, Walpole adding follies into the scenario: 'the
dispersed buildings . . . give a whimsical air of novelty that is very pleasing.'[2]

Nothing could be more pleasing or whimsical than an oriental folly
and, as depicted in the Vanderbank tapestry, one eminently practical type of
garden pavilion was based on a tent – known in Europe as Turkish, Tartar
or Ottoman. Such terms were accurate enough though limited, since these
structures derived from the nomadic peoples of Central Asia, entering China
as Mongols, India as Mughals and Turkey as Ottomans. Europeans first
encountered them as war tents, but their decorative aspect was familiar by
the eighteenth century, since they were used throughout the Islamic world as
garden pavilions, beautified with textiles, tassels and carpets. In Europe the
prevailing mode was stripy, and paintings testify to their existence as summer
structures at West Wycombe and Audley End; the naturalist Gilbert White had

The Turkish Tent, Painshill, 1759, the archetypal blue and white structure, which was considered to have an oriental air and inspired many copies.

one at Selborne; and in 1776 Mrs Philip Lybbe Powys described the Turkish Tent at Stourhead as 'very pretty . . . it is painted blue and white in mosaic.'[3] At Stourhead, Henry Hoare had been inspired by Charles Hamilton's Turkish Tent at Painshill (now restored), which also sported blue and white canvas and was intended as a year-round structure to afford enchanting prospects. Erected in 1759, it had a brick floor and the core was a brick drum; the drapes were canvas (now fibreglass since canvas deteriorated too fast) and the roof was leaded on a timber frame, topped with a crescent moon on a gilded stem.

There was a more permanent and possibly earlier Turkish Tent in the grounds of Wotton Underwood, a folly garden in Buckinghamshire, where Capability Brown worked as a young gardener in the 1740s, during the time when he was also working at Stowe – the Grenville family of Wotton Underwood being closely related to Lord Cobham. In the 1740s the lake at Wotton Underwood was already extensive, but lacked interest: 'if the water at Wotton were all exposed, a walk of near two miles along the banks would be a tedious length, from the want of those changes of scene, which now supply through the whole extent a succession of perpetual variety.'[4] This variety was due partly to skilful landscaping, but mainly to a series of follies around the lake and on the island, everything from a Doric temple to a grotto, but none unique except the Turkish Tent. It was probably constructed

Turkish Tent, Wooton Underwood, Buckinghamshire, an early example, built in the 1740s, when the young Capability Brown was extending and landscaping the lake where it stands.

alongside the others in the 1750s, although sadly unrecorded. It is a dainty little building, six-sided and painted white, looking over the lake from its open veranda, which is ornamentally carved. Along the gables is an upcurving line of 'ivory tusks'. The roof is copper and slightly concave like the roof of a tent, and topped with a golden crescent.

Far better known, even now that it is long gone, was the Turkish Pavilion in Vauxhall Pleasure Gardens, painted by Canaletto in 1751 and built ten years earlier in 1741–2. It was situated in the central grove of the gardens beside the Grand Walk and next to the Orchestra Pavilion. Listening to music in the open air, while promenading or dining, was one of the main enjoyments of Vauxhall. There were concerts newly composed by Handel, romantic and patriotic songs and tunes for dancing. The novelist Henry Fielding voiced his delight through his heroine Amelia: 'I could not have imagined anything like this in the world . . . the delicious sweetness of the place, the enchanting charms of the music and the satisfaction which appears on everyone's countenance carried my soul almost to heaven.'[5] This fairyland was the creation of Jonathan Tyers, who redeveloped the former gardens in the 1730s, opening with a grand *ridotto* in 1732, attended by Frederick, Prince of Wales (he was the royal patron, in whose Duchy of Cornwall estate Vauxhall was included). The prince became a frequent visitor, adding to the celebrity attraction which brought boatloads of aristocrats and ordinary folk over the river as evening fell. Frederick and his friends had their own dining area, but for most *al fresco* diners there was a long arcade of supper boxes in Chinese/gothic style, in which William Hogarth and Francis Hayman contributed scene-setting paintings as backgrounds. The Turkish Pavilion was highly favoured as the central dining area, and reminded some contemporaries of *The Arabian Nights*; in fact Henry Fielding considered it 'far beyond the imaginings of the East', which might be true.[5] The bulbous curving roof was painted blue and gold, supported on twelve slender golden columns and low blue railings, and the merry-makers inside could see and be seen. Fielding recorded another moment of pure magic when, every evening, over a thousand oil lamps were illuminated almost simultaneously in the Grove:

'all in a moment every object was made visible . . . and my ears and eyes were captivated at once.' For those seeking amorous adventures after supper there were the 'dark walks' where nightingales sang. In due course 'nightingales of Vauxhall' became a euphemism for prostitutes, and from the late 1750s the reputation of the gardens teetered towards the disreputable. Vauxhall survived until 1859 but the Turkish Pavilion was replaced by a ballroom in 1769.

In France the vogue for Turkish tents may have begun with a gift from the Ottoman Sultan to Louis xv of ornamental tents to be used for hunting, but instead they became a novelty for garden decoration. Louis xvi and Marie Antoinette also entertained in tents at Versailles and in 1789 one of the early demands of the revolutionaries was to examine the queen's garden tents, because it was rumoured they were of gold and silver cloth, although it transpired they were merely painted canvas and wood.[6] At Parc Monceau the Duc de Chartres had two Tartar tents, both striped. One was made of elaborately draped canvas, and an engraving by Carmontelle showed a turbaned servant nearby who offered camel rides. The other was of sheet metal

Canaletto, *Turkish Pavilion in Vauxhall Gardens*, painted in 1751. The blue oriental pavilion was built in 1741–2 for enjoying music and revels and was much patronized by Frederick, Prince of Wales.

251

Turkish Tent, Désert de Retz, 1777–82: the most permanent Turkish tent
created in France, being metal painted with swags and stripes.

painted in *trompe l'œil* to look like blue and gold striped canvas. These tents
were dated circa 1775 and therefore preceded the Turkish Tent at Désert de
Retz, which is the finest to survive. This Turkish Tent is rectangular with
a ridged roof painted in aquamarine and golden stripes, its metal sides
spreading outwards at the base like canvas. The design is simple but lovely.
Trompe l'œil golden drapes are drawn back from the entrance and golden
trompe l'œil tassels hang from the decorative valance pelmet. It stands with a
romantic air of neglect among tall trees, but originally it was the pavilion in
Baron de Monville's fencing ground.[7] Dated some time between 1777 and
1782, it is believed to have inspired the Swedish king Gustav III to create the
fabulous copper tents that still grace the parks of two summer palaces, Haga
and Drottningholm.

At Haga, north of Stockholm, the overall design of the royal park was
by the architect Frederick Magnus Pyper, who visited Painshill in 1779–80
and returned to Sweden with notes and sketches, including the Turkish Tent
with its spreading drapes. In 1784 King Gustav himself visited France, and
included the Désert de Retz in his itinerary. The Swedish version at Haga is
dated circa 1787–90, and could therefore be seen as an amalgam of the English
and French versions, as well as being on an altogether grander scale, since it
had a genuine military purpose, built to accommodate the palace guard. It
is dominated by a tall central tent that is circular with a high conical roof.

The rectangular wings spread either side like a veritable encampment. The court painter Louis Desprez was responsible for the illusionistic painting of the facades in vividly blue and gold vertical stripes, crossed by horizontal diamond patterns. There are tassels along the pelmets, golden drapes at entrances and pennants high above. The Turkish Tent at Drottningholm was also intended for the palace guard, made to a simpler rectangular design with a ridge roof, and therefore more akin to Désert de Retz, though the addition of side wings made it more extensive. The white and blue stripes of varying width and the golden 'trimmings' are subtler than at Haga, but neither quite matches the original appeal of Désert de Retz.[8]

There is one of these eighteenth-century garden tents still in existence that claimed to be Chinese rather than Turkish or Tartar, and well it might because inside there be dragons, bronzed and swirling against a golden ceiling, the arrow tips of their tails pointing upwards and their feathery wings spread out. There are twelve of them in the twelve panels inside the ceiling and another 24 in pairs, making arabesques of their tails in the frieze below. The tent has a wooden frame and panels covered in oilskin. Those at the side can be raised and lowered like awnings for shade or protection, and the whole tent is authentically collapsible to be moved as whim or the climate required. The roof is tent-like and has upward-curving gables with projections to hold twelve little wooden bells, and at the peak of the roof is one more dragon. It was made in 1745, in Knightsbridge, by 'Samuel Smith, tentmaker', and originally stood on the terrace of Montagu House in Whitehall. It can just be glimpsed in Canaletto's *View of the Thames from Richmond House*,

Turkish Tent, Drottningholm, Sweden, late 18th century.

painted in 1746, looking across the river towards St Paul's, a little summer gazebo then painted green.[9] John, second Duke of Montagu, who commissioned it, enjoyed unusual things, whether it was a plan to plant an avenue of elms all the way from London to his country seat at Boughton House in Northamptonshire or 'getting people into his gardens and wetting them with squirts . . . and twenty other pretty fancies'. The Chinese Tent was eventually moved to Boughton, painted black and housed safely indoors. A satirical ditty, written in 1774 as fashions changed, suggested there were plenty more of these tents, whereas now it is a unique treasure:

> The traveller with amazement sees
> A temple Gothic or Chinese
> With many a bell and tawdry rag on
> And crested with a sprawling dragon.

The tent-like structures morphed into open-sided gazebos, gilded and fretted *à la chinoise* and generally placed over water, a scene familiar from Chinese lacquered screens and furniture. One of the first may have been at Woburn, since an estate map of 1738 includes 'a Chinese Building on ye island' and a related invoice included stretched cloths painted with Chinese scenes, carved and gilded work and two dragons.[10] William Chambers's first Chinese Pavilion at Kew followed this model, standing in a circular pool in the centre of the menagerie, and the Pleasure Gardens at Ranelagh (in competition with Vauxhall) had an extensive openwork Chinese Pavilion in the canal that ran between the Great Walk and the Rotunda. At each of the four corners were conical roofs curved steeply upwards like tents, supported on columns between which the pavilion was open to the elements, with a low wall of diagonal fretwork to prevent the thronging pleasure seekers from falling into the canal; or, as the above ditty continued its description:

> A wooden arch is bent astride
> A ditch of water four feet wide
> With angles, curves and zig zag lines
> From Halfpenny's exact designs.[11]

The loveliest surviving chinoiserie pavilion in France also follows this concept, built on a very sturdy stone bridge over a lake in the Parc de Cassan, north of Pontoise in L'Isle-Adam. The pavilion was designed by the owner

Chinese Bridge Pavilion, Parc de Cassan, L'Isle-Adam, France, *c.* 1780. The pavilion is richly coloured and gilded, and was built over the water as garden pavilions often were in China.

himself, Pierre-Jacques Bergeret, circa 1780, and it has been suggested that the artist Fragonard, a friend of the family and frequent guest, took a hand in the design. The bridge is octagonal, like the pavilion itself, with three archways either side over the water, and the two land sides supporting steep stone steps. At the top of the steps Dogs of Fo guard the way as in a Chinese precinct, though whether they are dogs or lions remains undecided. The pavilion itself is golden with a double upturned roof of curving eaves, beautifully fretted windows and balustrades, and a lofty pinnacle. It is no ephemeral or movable tent, but the likeness is there. The sources of chinoiserie tents and gazebos were literary as well as visual. Marco Polo and Sir John Mandeville both described Mongol tents in the parks of Kubla Khan, and their adventures were rewritten through the centuries, stirring imaginations, until the tent even became Coleridge's 'stately pleasure-dome'. Marco Polo wrote of 'a sumptuous pleasure house which may be removed from place to place' supported by 'over 200 silken chords after the manner of tents', and some editions added 'handsome pillars gilt and varnished, [and] round each a dragon entwined its tail, while its head supported the projection of the roof'.[12]

However, the inspiration for the very first Chinese pavilion in Europe was not a tent but the porcelain pagoda of Nanjing (also known as the China Tower), which was illustrated in Jan Nieuhof's account of the Dutch embassy to China in 1655, published with over one hundred engravings in 1665. The Nanjing pagoda was entirely covered with glazed tiles, white for the walls and green for the ten roofs, which sparkled in the sunlight like nothing else. Since porcelain was also one of the most desirable commodities exported from China, this had a double fascination.[13] In 1670, when Louis XIV fancied having a porcelain folly at Versailles, no attempt was made to construct a pagoda. Instead the Trianon de Porcelaine consisted of three single-storey buildings grouped around a courtyard in fashionably Baroque style, with their walls and roofs covered in blue-and-white faience panels featuring cupids and birds. Louis' supreme confidence in French taste was not ill-founded, since in the Summer Palace in Beijing the Qianlong Emperor was soon asking his Jesuit visitors to devise pavilions for him in the French style. Although the Trianon de Porcelaine was too frail to survive many winters, it inspired the first German folly to embrace Chinese style (inside rather than out): a pale little Baroque building by a lake called the Pagodenburg, in the grounds of the Nymphenburg Palace in Munich, completed in 1719 for the sybaritic Elector of Bavaria. The chinoiserie consisted of blue-and-white Delft panels throughout the ground floor and, in the room above, silk screens covered in blossom alternating with dramatic black lacquerwork panels of garden scenes.[14]

The first surviving Chinese folly in England was the Tea House at Stowe, devised by the great impresario of architecture, William Kent, for Lord Cobham, and in existence by 1738, when it was anonymously described as 'this house built on piles after the manner of the Chinese . . . In the middle of an old pond'. Ten years later, when Jemima Grey of Wrest Park visited Stowe, 'The Chinese Room' was her favourite folly there: 'the prettiest I have seen and the only one like the prints of the houses, only the location is not ideal . . . it stands in a dirty little piece of water.'[15] So much for the Elysian Fields where it was placed at that time, although it was conforming to the idea that Chinese garden pavilions should overhang water. Or it may even have followed an early description of the European 'factories' at Canton, the only permitted trading posts, which until later in the eighteenth century were also built on piles driven into the waterfront. Through them flowed all the silks, porcelain, wallpaper, lacquerwork, tea and descriptions which inspired chinoiserie. In structure the Tea House at Stowe was still a little tent-like, with panels over a wooden frame, and it too has been moved to various places.

As a Tea House it was designed to be an appropriate setting for imbibing that most fashionable eighteenth-century drink, for which significant amounts of bullion were pouring into China, because they would accept nothing but silver in payment. For the Tea House, Kent's basic design was a simple rectangle, like the slightly later Chinese House at Shugborough. The roof projects widely but the gables are not upturned. As if in compensation, at either end of the roof ridge golden dolphins flick their tails and fins exuberantly. The innovative pleasure of the Tea House consists in the elaborately painted scenes all over it. The outside walls and latticed windows are green, with red, gold-framed panels where ladies fish, play music, dance and hold fans. Beneath them are floral sprays, and there are narrow calligraphic strips at the corners. Inside the Tea House there are more scenes of Chinese life, filling the walls with colour and action, including a mandarin riding a tiger.

Where Stowe led, other landscape gardens followed. In 1744 William Aislabie built the first Chinese folly in Yorkshire at Studley Royal. Its roof was red and conical with upturned eaves, and the decorations were gilded, but its most authentic aspect was its position above a steep gorge with the river below and a fine view across the valley. At Shugborough Admiral Anson had the distinction of being the first patron to have seen Chinese buildings before

Tea House, Stowe, built by William Kent in 1738, a theatrical departure from his usual style, rendered oriental with painted panels and latticed windows, and dedicated to the fashionable drinking of tea.

constructing one. In 1761 at Wrest Park a dainty Chinese House, double-roofed, with bells on the upturned gables and fretwork patterns painted on the wall panels, was placed near a serpentine canal. Some Chinese follies live only in illustrations, like Thomas Robins's delicious *Garden at Woodside, Berkshire*, done in the late 1750s. Some, like Alresford, Virginia Water and possibly Amesbury, were designed as fishing pavilions; Woburn had its Dairy; and many more were ephemeral, like the House of Confucius at Kew and the Chinese Pavilion at Stourhead. There were even one or two wooden structures like miniature pagodas: for instance, Lord Radnor's by the Thames at Twickenham, which so irritated his neighbour Horace Walpole that he became critical of the Chinese style, although he had espoused it enthusiastically at first.[16] By mid-century several further descriptions of Chinese gardens had consolidated the belief in their kinship to the landscape movement, and therefore seemed to justify including something as alien as chinoiserie in the English pastoral scene. In 1752 Joseph Spence popularized an abridged version of the Jesuit Father Jean Attiret's *Description of China*, including such key passages as:

> They go from one of the valleys to another, not by formal straight walks but by various turnings and windings, adorned at the sides with little pavilions and charming grottos; and each of these valleys is diversified from all the rest, both by the manner of laying out the ground and in the structure and disposition of the buildings, bright in their gilded woodwork and varnished tiles of many colours.[17]

The spirit of charmed emulation was not the whole story. William Chambers certainly made the most of it, and greatly encouraged it with his designs and publications, but of his most important royal commission he said, 'Kew is flat and commands no prospects,' so there was little chance of placing pavilions over gorges or beside fish-laden streams. What he achieved instead, with the pagoda he built at Kew, was a bold imperialist statement, commanding radiating tree-lined vistas, and visible far around (as Horace Walpole commented from Twickenham in 1761).[18] This was the first and tallest pagoda in Europe and it remained the archetype. In creating it William Chambers could claim the authority of having visited China, although the movements of foreigners were severely restricted to the approaches along the Pearl River and the Canton waterfront. Chambers's *Designs*, published in 1757, were more impressive than rival publications, and included a 'Pagoda near

William Marlow, *View of the Wilderness at Kew, showing the Alhambra, Pagoda and Mosque*, print from a watercolour of 1763, marking the time when the Pagoda reigned above several other oriental follies at Kew, now long gone.

Canton' of seven storeys. But the ten-storey pagoda at Kew was based on the old Nieuhof engraving of the glorious Nanjing Porcelain Pagoda. Chambers even copied an earlier mistake, because there were nine storeys in the original (nearly all pagodas have an odd number) and both Nieuhof and Chambers were wrong to make it ten. The Pagoda at Kew was undoubtedly built to last, with solid brickwork around a central spiral staircase (which made it a viewfinder too) rising over 50 metres (165 ft) and built very quickly between 1761 and 1762, aptly commissioned by Princess Augusta to herald the new reign of her son George III. Before it was even finished the Pagoda's sturdiness was put to the test. The Swedish botanist Daniel Solander wrote in 1761:

> All thought that a building so much out of proportion should have fallen down before it was finished, and no one believed it would stand the terrible thunderstorms and tempests which we experienced there a month ago and which were more severe than had ever been remembered. The Pagoda is now considered a masterpiece of art which in fact has stood the shocks so well.[19]

The Pagoda, which is octagonal, has a projecting ground-floor roof supported on columns and overall was painted green with white 'Chippendale Chinese' railings around each storey. On the gables of each roof were glittering dragons, eighty in all, 'covered with a thin glaze of various colours which produces a most dazzling reflection'. Equally striking were the roofs themselves, covered in multicoloured varnished iron plates. But here there were design faults: the iron tiles were dangerously heavy and the dragons were not aerodynamic. In 1784 the Kew accounts show payment for the roofing to be replaced by slates, and possibly the battered dragons were also removed then. Various repair projects finally achieved fulfilment in 2018: the dragons were reinvented in fibreglass and the original green colour of the Pagoda was restored, as was the magnificently gilded finial raising the rooftop an extra metre.

As additional proof that the Pagoda symbolized an intention to bring the East closer to Kew – just as Kew's botanists were poised to explore and appropriate the economic potential of oriental plant products – Chambers produced other oriental buildings. Flanking the Pagoda on one side was the 'moorish' Alhambra with highly painted verandas, and on the other side the Mosque with its three domes, crescent moon and slender minarets, for which Chambers 'endeavoured to collect the principal particularities of Turkish architecture'. Inside the Mosque the central dome was supported on eight green stucco palm trees. To some these seemed 'unmeaning falballas of Turkish and Chinese chequerwork', but Chambers knew the implications. When the *Plans, Elevations etc of the Buildings at Kew* was published in 1763, at George III's expense, he claimed that 'what was once a desert is now an Eden.' This was a matter of opinion; many, including Horace Walpole, were ready to deride Chambers and his follies at Kew, and Chambers in turn took issue with Capability Brown when he relandscaped the grounds at Kew, his efforts according to Chambers being 'no different from common fields'. In 1772, in his *Dissertation on Oriental Gardening*, Chambers reiterated the Chinese links, made earlier by Temple and Addison, between landscaping and scene-setting:

> They consider a plantation as painters do a picture . . . dividing scenery into pleasing, horrid and enchanted . . . nothing is more varied than the methods they use to create surprise, they lead you through caverns and gloomy avenues, which you leave to find views of a delightful landscape.

As for the all-important Chinese garden pavilions, 'architects take care like painters to create these little buildings serving a particular use, or inviting repose, or attracting the eye to a scene.' So powerful was Chambers's message in Europe that it had the unintended consequence of convincing them that the landscape movement was not originally English at all, and they called the result *jardins anglo-chinois*.

However, in the matter of pagodas Kew had only one serious rival in Europe. In 1770 the Duc de Choiseul, minister to Louis xv, was exiled from court to his estate at Chanteloup on the Loire. There he landscaped his hunting grounds with avenues centred on a large semicircular lake, and surrounded himself with a group of loyal friends, one of whom, the Abbé Bartholemy, described a sense of fun quite unlike life at court: 'All these people, all this shouting, noise, slamming doors, barking dogs, noisy conversations, voices, waving arms and gusts of laughter in the billiard room . . .'[20] The lakeside Pagoda at Chanteloup, completed in 1775, was said to be a gesture of thanks to these friends who had stood by him, and under the eaves of the ground floor were carved the Chinese characters for kindness, harmony, brotherhood, knowledge and understanding. If the pagoda at Kew proved to Choiseul and his architect Nicolas Le Camus de Mézières that such a structure could work,

The Pagoda, Chanteloup, Loire Valley, France, built in 1775, a sober but elegant, well-proportioned French version of chinoiserie, with the correct seven storeys.

they did not copy it. It is a more restrained and well-proportioned building and it consists of a correct seven storeys, reaching up to 44 metres (144 ft) high. It is supported on a round colonnade of sixteen Doric columns at the base, tapering in measured proportion into the sky like a spire and ending in a steep conical roof, topped with a golden ball – and when the reflection of the Pagoda is caught in the lake the illusion of height is doubled. It is of mellow tufa stone carved with key patterns and pineapple and acanthus cartouches, but not gaudily decorated. There are metalwork balconies circling four of the storeys like filigree, and the steep stairs mount to a panorama of the Forest of Amboise and the Loire Valley. The architect Le Camus de Mézières, true to his calling, was exploring form not orientalism, though obviously he was open to experiment:

> The arrangement of forms both individually and as part of the whole becomes the source of illusions. Our attempts to produce impressions with our architecture, and speak to the mind or move the soul, should be based on this principle.

In terms of authenticity, there is a pagoda in Munich, in the English Park, built in 1789, that comes closer to proportions that would be recognized in China. It is a wooden structure, five storeys high, plainly built with slightly undulating rooflines and fretwork railings on every floor. The reduction in scale between one storey and the next is harmonious in an oriental sense. It has no superfluous adornments; it is the brown of the wood it was built from; and although it has burnt down more than once, it now lives on undaunted and accessible in the midst of a beer garden. Well before this, the first chinoiserie in Germany was created by Frederick II, ruler of Prussia from 1740 to 1786, who was called the Great. He was a complex man, determined to bring his uncouth and borderline state into the forefront of German power-politics and culture. Stern militarism was the traditional answer, but deep in his heart Frederick yearned for a life of sybaritic ease, surrounded by beautiful young men, and he turned to the summer palace at Potsdam, called Sanssouci, for a few such moments. Among the elements of Chinese decorative art that appealed to Europeans were the ease and indolence of the little figures on porcelain bowls and lacquered screens who so enjoyed their garden pavilions and boating parties. So, as Frederick embellished the park with statues and fashionable buildings, affirming its light-hearted name Sanssouci, he included follies in the Chinese style.

The first of these was the green Chinese Tea House, which took from 1755 until 1764 to complete, the long delay being caused by the exigencies of the Seven Years War when, as the ally of England in a hostile Europe, Prussia was hard-pressed and impoverished until victory brought relief and work could resume. The Chinese Tea House was built in the shape of a trefoil and strongly recalled the theme of oriental tents, especially in the formulation of the roof, which ripples like green and gold silk and undulates at the roofline. Topping the pitch of the roof is a large, drum-shaped lantern with six oval windows, and above that on a shallow cupola a golden Chinese figure sits holding a golden umbrella. The unusual trefoil shape had been used earlier for a garden pavilion at Lunéville, the extravaganza created near Strasbourg for Stanislas, the exiled king of Poland. Around 1740 Stanislas had both a 'bâtiment à la turque' and a 'bâtiment chinois nommé le Trèfle'; they were both tent-like and Le Trèfle was green. Around the outer perimeter of this trefoil was a narrow sinuous gallery, also with an undulating roof, and the central salon had three chambers. Stanislas sent the published engravings of his follies to Frederick at Potsdam, and this was undoubtedly the chief inspiration for the Chinese Tea House at Sanssouci, although the latter is bigger than Le Trèfle was, and more sumptuous.[21] The three bays of the trefoil leave room for a wide veranda at the entrance, where the roof is supported by four gilded

Chinese Tea House, Sanssouci, Potsdam, created 1755–64 in the pleasure grounds of Frederick the Great of Prussia, once more emulating a tent and coloured green, which was considered authentically Chinese, with gilded figures and palm trees surrounding it.

Creaking Pavilion, Tsarskoe Selo, St Petersburg, built 1778–86 for Catherine the Great of Russia, approached by chinoiserie bridges and so called for the weathervane in the form of a Chinese banner, which creaked as it turned.

pillars like palm trees. These are surrounded at the base by life-size golden statues of Chinese figures in Rococo hats and masquerade clothes; some are musicians and the seated figures appear to be singing (Frederick loved music). More gilded figures seem to circle their way as if dancing around the outside of the pavilion, and above them on the gables are bells. Inside the Chinese Tea House light pours though the high windows, and above, in the *trompe l'œil* ceiling, oriental men stand behind a balustrade looking down into the room below. On the walls there is stucco-work *singerie* of monkeys playing music, and there are fine collections of Chinese and chinoiserie porcelain.

Later, in the early 1770s, Frederick built a modest pagoda of four floors which was called the Drachenhaus, on account of the sixteen dragons perched on the concave roofs of the first two storeys. It is an octagonal building and the walls are concave; the ground floor is enclosed and intended to be residential, and above are open arcades railed in to act as viewfinders. The Drachenhaus was built on the outskirts of Sanssouci among the vineyards of Klausberg, dear to Frederick because another of his passions was fruit and fruit-growing; indeed an unusual proportion of the grounds of Sanssouci was devoted to orchards of fruit trees, or else terraced for pots containing oranges, lemons, figs and pomegranates.

Frederick's greatest friend and rival in the eighteenth-century phenomenon known as Enlightened Despotism was Catherine the Great of Russia, who was herself Prussian by birth. She too was fascinated by orientalism, and in the late 1770s the Ekaterininsky Park at Tzarskoe Selo, south of St Petersburg, was relandscaped. Follies started to appear, partly inspired by Stowe, Painshill, Kew and the Désert de Retz. There were two Chinese Bridges, both exquisite. One was steep with a little Chinese kiosk perched in the middle and steps either side railed with gilded fretwork; the other had Chinese figures sitting cross-legged and holding lanterns. But the *pièce de résistance* was the Creaking Pavilion, built circa 1778–86. It owed its name to the weathervane in the form of a Chinese banner which creaks loudly as it turns in the wind. The pavilion is by a small lake, and from the waterside semicircular steps lead invitingly up to the door of the central hall. This is oval and topped by a series of roofs – one with dragons, one with upswept eaves supported on columns and one with a lantern supporting the weathervane/banner. Either side are square wings elongated by columned porches, and their roofs echo the design of the central roof, including two more banners. The original colouring may have been more sophisticated, the walls imitating marble and the roofs and pillars gilded, but now the paint is gaudy and in summer the Creaking Pavilion has a fairground aspect. But in the depths of a Russian winter, surrounded by the frozen lake and deep snow, with pale sunlight touching the trees, it evokes the cold of a Tolstoy sleigh ride, or the possibility that Baba Yaga might appear through the forest.[22]

One feature very typical of Chinese gardens but slow to reach Europe was a long, covered walkway, fretted and painted red and running alongside water. The first in England appeared with the Woburn Dairy around 1789, originally extending all the way from the house to the dairy and thus almost equalling in length the arcade in the Summer Palace in Beijing. The other, much shorter but even prettier, is in the Chinese Garden at Biddulph Grange. Despite all the talk of variation and scene-setting, there had so far been little attempt to surround Chinese pavilions with appropriate plantings – pines and bamboo for instance – or rocky escarpments; there was only a sense that they should be beside water. Then in 1840 James Bateman bought

Biddulph Grange in Staffordshire, and proceeded to divide the grounds into contrasting regions, including China.

The wealth that enabled Bateman to undertake this monumental project was inherited from industrial enterprise including coal mining, iron working and cotton mills, but at heart he was a plantsman and before turning his mind to marriage he made his name as a leading expert on tropical orchids. Then he married a wife who loved ferns and, together with their artist friend Edward Cooke, they transformed the grounds of Biddulph Grange, with theatrical flair, into geographical areas. There they collected rarities brought back by plant hunters, one of whom was Robert Fortune, who travelled in disguise through China, chiefly in search of tea bushes, but discovering much else besides and sending it back for English collectors.

To reach Bateman's version of China you start from the Italian terraces, descend via the rhododendrons to the Himalayan foothills, and by a circuitous route, passing a Great Wall of rocks covered in yews and pines, reach a massive stone doorway to China. Or you might walk the length of the terrace, past the dahlia beds, and arrive eventually via the Victorian stumpery. Either approach becomes dark and narrow until suddenly, opening into the light, a leafy view spreads over a little lake and a steep hillside, rising through maples, ferns and bamboos to a little joss house. Crossing the lake is an elaborate Chinese bridge – red, yellow and green – and presiding over the secret valley is the Chinese Temple and tea terrace, this being Bateman's name for the covered arcade with red pillars and a fretwork balustrade running alongside the lake. Setting aside the prevailing redness of the temple and arcade, the design is much like the blue-and-white willow-pattern motif, then at the height of its production in the local Staffordshire potteries. The open pavilion known as the Chinese Temple is very similar to that on the willow-pattern plate, with its double roof, upturned eaves and finial. The bridge is a replica of the bridge in the foreground of willow-pattern designs (and the willow tree itself hangs over the water nearby). On the roof of the Chinese Temple four gilded dragons with bells in their mouths writhe angrily over the gables and almost take flight. There is much vivid red and green patterning, and the arcade has a fine roof of zigzag tiling and whirligig red finials, and more bells. Among the surrounding rocks and trees an expert would spot historic survivors from the time of Robert Fortune's travels in China: a deciduous conifer, *Pseudolarix amabilis*, notable like the maples for its glowing autumn colours; *Spiraea japonica* 'Fortunei', which has pink flowers in summer and, when the temple was in a sorry state, succeeded in

Chinese Temple and Tea Terrace, Biddulph Grange, Staffordshire, built c. 1850 with a walkway painted red and in a garden of authentic plants, reminiscent of Woburn Dairy (see Chapter Five).

seeding itself in the crumbling mortar; and *Paulownia fortunei*, the foxglove tree, often planted in the precincts of Chinese temples.[23]

There is another equally dramatic temple precinct at Biddulph Grange, representing Egypt and set appropriately eastwards of the great Italianate terraces. It stands in a rectangular grass court enclosed in beech and yew trees, which frame a grand stone portal in the Egyptian style, with tapering sides surmounted by a cornice, on which is carved the winged disc of the sun. In Egyptian temples this sign represented the sun god Ra and guarded the entrance, which here is a dark rectangular hollow, inviting uncertainty. Flanking the approach are four sphinxes, in pairs, very fine ones with bodies of lions and heads of pharaohs, wearing the correct pharaonic headdress emblazoned with a rearing cobra, and gazing out not threateningly but with an air of total indifference, as sphinxes should. Much is owed, in this marvellously theatrical setting, to the clipping of the yews, creating the architectural green walls of the temple, the obelisks beside the path and the pyramid rising high above the portal itself. If they grow a little shaggy it is romantic, but without their significant shapes the architectural impact of the Egyptian folly would be lost.[24] Like the Chinese valley this is an example of Bateman and Cooke's skill in creating scenic settings through sophisticated horticulture. The

Egyptian Portal, Biddulph Grange, *c.* 1856, a fine copy of an Egyptian temple shrine in a theatrical garden setting, complete with a large topiary pyramid and sphinxes.

dark temple entrance leads through narrow tunnels and doorways towards a glowing red light, an effect derived from stained glass set in the roof, and squatting under the light is a shocking figure, neither ape nor human, with its hands on its knees, wearing a feathered cloak and an ugly grimace. It is identified as the Ape of Thoth, the baboon-headed Egyptian god of the Moon and wisdom, mathematics and time, inventor of hieroglyphics and possibly all science including botany. He is too crude to look capable of all this, and since Bateman and Cooke were both very disturbed by contemporary Darwinian ideas it may represent a half-humorous, half-appalled, rejection of man's relationship to apes.[25]

The Victorian fascination with Egypt was not a new phenomenon in Europe, but in previous generations obelisks, pyramids and sphinxes had been mediated through Roman culture. Obelisks were known to represent the sun's rays and also power; pyramids were known to be tombs, mainly from the examples along the Appian Way, the Roman avenue of the dead which, although not nearly as monumental as Egypt itself, were impressive, especially the tomb of Caius Cestius. Most curious was the widespread adoption of sphinxes into garden statuary, retaining the air of guardians and a certain enigmatic wisdom, but often decoratively endowed with bosoms and feminine hairstyles. In addition, the advent of Freemasonry with its mystic numerology, and its architectural fascination with civilizations of the ancient Near East, had brought these forms into prominence. Then Napoleon's invasion of Egypt caused a fresh surge of interest, and with it new fashions. The expedition started in 1798, and as well as soldiers Napoleon took artists, archaeologists, surveyors and scientists to record their findings. But since his main objective was to damage British interests, Nelson was sent to destroy the French fleet and after the Battle of the Nile the French expedition remained marooned in Egypt for three years, uncovering its wonders.[26]

One of the first architectural reactions to all this came in 1811–12, after William Bullock, an impresario from Liverpool, commissioned P. F. Robinson to add an Egyptian facade to his museum in London's Piccadilly.[27] It was based on the shrines at the heart of Egyptian temples, where the image of the god was kept, the same shape on which the hieroglyph for a shrine was based, sides tapering up to a curved cornice and a rectangular entrance. The entrance to Bullock's Museum passed between two Egyptian columns modelled (knowingly or otherwise) on bundles of papyrus reeds ending in capitals shaped like lotus buds. Above and far more arresting were the gigantic figures of Isis and Osiris with hardly any clothes. Winged sun discs were carved over the tapering windows of the museum, while cornices, friezes and mouldings framed the whole. Bullock's Museum became the talk of the town and people flocked to see the ethnographic curiosities within. When Bullock sold up with a lucrative auction in 1819 an Italian owner took over. His collection included the translucent alabaster sarcophagus of Seti I, which was later sold to Sir John Soane and can still be viewed in his Lincoln's Inn house. During Queen Victoria's reign the Egyptian House in Piccadilly became a music hall, but finally lost its facade, so that its location opposite Bond Street can now be distinguished only by its carved name over the doorway. However, its startling and incongruous appearance lives on in another Egyptian House in Penzance. Here the facade dates from circa 1835 (the heraldry of a royal coat of arms over the central window indicates it was completed before Victoria's accession in 1837). The overall design is credited either to P. F. Robinson himself or John Foulston of Plymouth, who was responsible for the Egyptian Library in Devonport. The colours that highlight the carvings of the facade rival expensive confectionery predominantly fudge browns framed in golden mouldings. White surrounds the tapering windows like icing sugar, highlighting the remarkable patterns of their glazing. By the door are two bulbous Egyptian columns, similar to those once in Piccadilly, painted brown, white, red and green. Above, instead

The Egyptian House, Penzance, c. 1835, a striking facade similar to the now vanished Egyptian Hall in Piccadilly, which advertised an ethnographic museum. This one displayed geological collections.

269

of Isis and Osiris are two female caryatids, looking startled, their bosoms suitably shawled, while their lower bodies form herms. Like the lotus columns, their details are picked out in bright colours, including red roses and green leaves.

This Egyptian facade in Cornwall was created for the dealer John Lavin who, in 1834, bought two adjoining properties in Chapel Street and turned them into a shop and museum for his mineral collection. Penzance was a target for geologists. The local beaches offered a wealth of interest among the pebbles, from quartz to chalcedony, and Cornish miners in different parts of the county unearthed rare specimens, like golden lumps of chalcopyrite. There were other private collections to be visited in Penzance, and Lavin's museum also contained fossils and body parts of strange creatures, which were starting to be identified as dinosaurs. So customers at the Egyptian House received an exciting taste of recent discoveries, and could also buy 'instructional cabinets with printed catalogue leaflets', enabling them to join the Victorian exploration of earth sciences and start their own collection. As in Piccadilly, the Egyptian style was a great attraction, providing valuable publicity for the entrepreneur. Other Egyptian facades fronted different Victorian purposes: a library at Devonport, a factory at Temple Mills in Leeds, the Freemasons Hall in Boston, Lincolnshire – but none of them really classifiable as a folly. The nearest almost-folly is in King Street, Canterbury, built in 1847 apparently by the Jewish community, but perhaps not as a synagogue. Its form again follows the hieroglyph for 'shrine', tapering up to a carved frieze, and the entrance is supported on columns with lotus capitals; this small building can be viewed from the gateway standing between two obelisks.[28]

The conundrum of defining a folly extends to the question of whether tombs could be follies, but for the pleasure of exploring Egyptian architecture in Europe it must be assumed they could. Setting aside Victorian cemeteries like Highgate and Kensal Green, there is a solitary tomb that follows the form of an Egyptian temple shrine, not merely as a facade but on all four sides. It was constructed by Francis 'Black Jack' Needham, Earl of Kilmorey, in 1854 and now stands enclosed by high walls in a wildlife garden where Twickenham and Isleworth meet. The design is very like a plate in the *Description de l'Egypte* published in 1809 by the French government following Napoleon's expedition. The proportions of the building are correct, as are the blocks of pink and grey granite which are used to form a contrast between the smooth (grey) and moulded (pink) areas of the shrine. Also accurate, according to an Egyptologist, are the stylized bundles of reeds bound

Kilmorey Mausoleum, Twickenham, Middlesex, built 1855 and placed in its present setting in 1868 as a tomb for Black Jack Needham and his mistress.

with spiralling cords and the winged sun disc with cobras, and 'the whole building impressive and beautiful in a romantic way, a first-rate example of the Egyptian revival style'.[29]

The story behind the tomb is sufficiently scandalous, sentimental and gothic to fill the pages of a fine Victorian novel. Black Jack Needham, a swarthily handsome adventurer of fine physique with 'fascinating manners, appreciative nature and ready wit', was prey to strong impulses, and 'these defects drew him into errors which society did not easily forgive.' The events of his youth included running away, joining Wellington's army in Spain to fight in the Peninsular War and becoming a member of the Hellfire Club. He married in 1814 and inherited the earldom in 1832 at the apparently respectable age of 45, but the real scandal was yet to come. In 1840 he abandoned his wife and absconded with his ward, Priscilla Hoste, the daughter of his old friend Captain William Hoste and Lady Harriet, a member of the Walpole clan. Priscilla was only five when her father died; however, she was twenty when she and Kilmorey disappeared together, pursued by her older brothers. No trace could be found until they returned to Twickenham in 1844, when Priscilla gave birth to their son Charles. Kilmorey was not free to marry, and ten years later Priscilla died of a lingering illness, said to be her heart. Her Mausoleum was first erected in Brompton Cemetery, but Kilmorey remained heartbroken, moving house repeatedly and electing to take the Mausoleum with him (at considerable expense). Finally in 1868 he settled at Gordon House in Twickenham and placed it on the edge of his estate. Installed on the back wall is a large marble relief made in Rome, showing Priscilla on her deathbed attended by Kilmorey and their son Charles. Placed either side are two coffins, hers inscribed 'The beloved of Francis Jack, Earl of Kilmorey', his empty until 1880. In the meantime it is said that a tunnel was built and his servants wheeled the earl, dressed in a white shroud, to lie in the Mausoleum with Priscilla. Whether this was a ritualistic communion with the dead or a wild rumour has never been revealed, but part of the tunnel was later unearthed.

Nearby at Mortlake, an even more restless and controversial Victorian adventurer lies in a mausoleum inspired by a Bedouin tent, the stone moulded into folds. Richard Burton died in 1890 and his adoring wife not only commissioned the tent (where she too was later buried) but burnt his correspondence and unpublished works in an effort to save his reputation. In his time Burton had been a great explorer and had certainly known the excitement of living in tents. As a brilliant linguist he had no problem mastering the languages and cultures of the places through which he passed. Starting his career in the East India Company army, he then explored East Africa under the auspices of the Royal Geographical Society. In 1853 he travelled disguised as a Muslim to Mecca, at a time when no infidel could enter the holy places and live. The following year he resumed his disguise to seek out Harar (now part of Ethiopia) and spent perilous weeks as the guest of the Emir. His great weakness was his uncircumcised state, which he had always to hide because it proved him to be no Muslim. In other ways it was his Victorian countrymen who found Burton unacceptable. His translations of the *Kama Sutra*, the *Perfumed Garden* and the unexpurgated *Arabian Nights* were too much. Also he fell into a notorious quarrel with Richard Speke, disputing who had discovered the source of the Nile on their joint expedition, which ended in Speke shooting himself. Now Burton lies at rest in a Catholic churchyard, the devout observances of his wife superseding his own atheism.[30] Around the back of their tent a little ladder allows a peep through a window at their two coffins. On the frieze around the valance the Muslim stars and crescents are incongruously surmounted by a crucifix.

Tombs in the form of pyramids also attracted eccentric occupants, or stories about them, either seated upright at a table with food and wine to keep them going until the Last Judgement, clutching playing cards to gamble with the Devil for their souls, or having glass strewn across the floor to hinder his approach. One of the earliest is the tomb of Dr Francis Douce in the churchyard of Nether Wallop in Hampshire, a 5-metre (16 ft) pyramid built in 1748 though not needed until 1760. Douce wrote a treatise on mummification methods and topped his pyramid with a flaming torch, so it can be assumed that he felt such extra measures increased whatever chances of immortality were gained as a Christian. A triangular granite pyramid, called the Knill monument, stands on Worvas Hill above St Ives in Cornwall, dated 1782 and acting as a landmark for shipping. It has inscribed on its sides *resurgam*, *nil desperandum* and 'I know that my Redeemer liveth,' suggesting that its perpetrator, John Knill, mayor of St Ives, customs official and bon viveur, meant to hedge his bets between Christianity and the old Cornish rites. These he instituted in perpetuity with payments and dinners. Every fifth summer ten little virgins in white, accompanied by two widows in black, a clergyman, a fiddler, the mayor and a customs officer, were to mount the hill and sing Psalm 100, 'All people that on earth do dwell'. Then the fiddler struck up the Floral Dance and they all circled round the monument line-dancing and singing local variants on the words. Knill died in 1811 and was buried in London, not in the vault under his pyramid, but hopefully this did not diminish the benefits of his preparations and ceremonies.

Naturally the largest of all pyramid tombs would belong to an aristocrat. In 1794 in the grounds of Blickling Hall in Norfolk, John Hobart, second Earl of Buckingham, was interred along with his two wives in a pyramid 15 metres (49 ft) high, made of Portland blocks by Joseph Bonomi. It stands in very English woodland, with the bull emblem of the Hobart family on one side and a massive entrance porch on the other, but no ghoulish tales or pagan rituals became attached. The best was yet to come.[31]

Mad Jack Fuller of Brightling in Sussex was a notable eccentric from a young age. Total self-indulgence was encouraged when he inherited his family fortune (which was based on iron foundries), followed by his uncle's estate at Brightling and his Jamaican sugar plantations. He grew enormously fat and was often drunk, not a desirable character; and when Mrs Thrale's daughter Susan refused to marry him he hired harlots to stalk her. But he was an enthusiastic patron of art with a special fondness for Turner (whom he invited to Sussex to paint landscapes); and also science – he was inspired by Faraday's electricity experiments to endow a professorship, and he built himself an observatory full of telescopes. Hilaire Belloc admired him:

Pyramid of Mad Jack Fuller, Brightling, Sussex, 1834, an imposing burial monument,
where legend claimed Fuller sat at table with a bottle of port and a roast chicken.

'he spent all his money in a roaring way and lived conscious of what was
worth man's while during his little passage through the daylight.' He sealed
his credentials as a man of the people when refusing a peerage with the words
'I was born Jack Fuller and Jack Fuller I'll stay.' And he could be generous
to the needy, or at least he set them to work, and was one of the landlords
whose follies were built to relieve unemployment, as were the miles of stone
wall around Brightling Park.

In return for another stone wall the rector of Brightling church granted
permission for Fuller's pyramid to be erected in the churchyard, and added
in the parish register on 15 November 1810: 'The wall is now finished and
John Fuller Esq has added hereto a couple of substantial stone pillars and an
iron gateway.' The church also received a peel of bells from Fuller, named
after Wellington's victories.[32] In Parliament his behaviour was less congenial;
William Wilberforce compared him to a mad bull and his general nickname was the Hippopotamus. In 1810 he was finally expelled for a drunken
denunciation of the government and for cursing the Speaker. Like other
extravagant characters of the time he was a gambler, and his best-known
folly (apart from the pyramid) is a cone nicknamed the Sugar Loaf (blocks
of sugar were in those days delivered to households as smooth cones), said
to have been built to win a wager. One evening at Rose Hill, which was the

old name of Brightling Park, Fuller boasted to the assembled company that from the dining room window one could see the spire of Dallington church. Since several guests knew perfectly well that the church lay hidden in a fold of the Downs, bets were laid. But by the time his guests came back in daylight to collect their money a cone-shaped spire lay in the view. It seems the Sugar Loaf was indeed erected in a great hurry from stones and mud, but it held together to provide a rare example of a folly built for a wager.

Mad Jack survived on his three bottles of port a day until 1834, when it was said his body was placed in his pyramid seated in an iron chair in full formal dress and top hat, behind a table with a roast chicken and a bottle of port. Perhaps he deserved this legend, but during later restoration work it proved to be unfounded. A similar tradition attached itself in Liverpool to William Mackenzie, a civil engineer responsible for the construction of railways and canals, who seems to have led a sober and very hard-working life. He died in 1851 and seventeen years later his brother had the pyramid built for him in the churchyard of St Andrew's Presbyterian church. Presumably this is why the stories began; not only was he said to be sitting there upright, ready to play cards with the Devil, but it was also claimed that he walked the churchyard as a phantom in top hat and cape. Perhaps the inhabitants of Liverpool were reacting to the pyramid in a manner they considered fitting.[33]

Freemasons also contributed to the idea that pyramids were full of secrets, and among architects Nicholas Hawksmoor especially acquired an aura of mystery. The pyramid he constructed in the churchyard of St Anne's, Limehouse, is not known to be a tomb – and none of his other pyramids is a tomb – so it may have been intended as a steeple to go on the church tower, like the pyramids of his other churches. It is 3 metres (10 ft) high and very slim, and is inscribed 'The wisdom of Solomon' in English and Hebrew – reminding us that for Freemasons the layout and measurements of Solomon's Temple contained a mystic geometry which they sought to divine and emulate. The St Anne's pyramid is divided into five horizontal segments, and the architect being Hawksmoor, one assumes this variation on the concept of a stepped pyramid has its own numerological significance. At Stowe Vanbrugh designed a tall, segmented pyramid for Lord Cobham, which was built just after Vanbrugh died, whereupon it was named as his memorial, because the two men were great friends and fellow Kit-Cat members. It was one of the most striking creations at Stowe, especially influencing those built later in Europe, but it started to crumble and was demolished in 1797. At Stowe it was echoed by other pyramids, by the two which originally topped Gibbs's

Boycott Pavilions and by Kent's significant little pyramid in the centre of the Temple of British Worthies. Kent also provided Masonic pyramids for other patrons, including at Rousham and Badminton.[34] Sir Charles Kemeys-Tynte had a small stepped pyramid at Halswell in Somerset, rather strangely placed over a well. Then there is the Cobham Mausoleum, which was never consecrated or used, raising the question whether it too was primarily Masonic. The third Lord Darnley, of Cobham Park in Kent, was inspired by going on the Grand Tour, and his idea for the Mausoleum was probably based on the tomb of Caius Cestius in the Appian Way, being a pyramid mounted on a cube. He may also have seen Poussin's painting *Sacrament of Ordination* in Rome, which lent the monument a Christian context. In his will Lord Darnley specified a square stone building with a 'prominent pyramid' and the fourth Earl commissioned the leading architect James Wyatt to design it, which he did and exhibited it at the Royal Academy in 1783, but the actual construction was supervised by George Dance. It is an impressive and solemn building, surrounded by Doric columns and rendered slightly concave by the projections at each corner, supported on extra columns and with sarcophagi on the four architraves. Above this the pyramid looms high. The walls are carved with medallions containing downturned torches, and over the entrance is the family crest. Inside it is lit through lunettes of amber-coloured glass and lined with shelves worthy of a catacomb, waiting for the coffins that never arrived. Instead, it stands empty, high on a wooded hill, which makes it more like a folly, and it is enriched with Dickensian and other ghoulish associations.[35]

Several European pyramids had a Masonic context. At Wilhelmsbad in Hanau, which became a spa in the 1770s, a great congress of Masons was held in 1782, which left the group known as the Illuminati in control, having purified their tenets of the accretions related to Templars and Jesuits. The celebratory pyramid, built in 1784, stands on a small island with a weeping willow. At Machern near Leipzig a pyramid built in 1792 also has a weeping willow, and an imposingly pedimented entrance with Doric columns and guarded by lion-headed sphinxes. Among the other follies in both gardens there is a ruined castle, as there was once alongside the pyramid at Parc Monceau, which was the folly garden of Philippe d'Orléans, Duc de Chartres, a Masonic Grand Master. At Désert de Retz, the Ruined Column was the most original of any Masonic building, and there the pyramid was made to double up as an ice house, but still maintained its mystique because the entrance is an arched doorway in a massive plinth, with steps leading up on either side in a hieratic zigzag to the pyramid itself. But the most stupendous pyramid

Claude-Louis Chatelet, *Mauperthuis Pyramid, c.* 1785, a monumental pyramid built in the 1760s as the grand entrance to the folly garden at Mauperthuis.

outside Egypt was built at Mauperthuis, east of Paris, early in the 1760s by the Marquis de Montesquiou-Fezensac. It marked the entrance to his newly landscaped *jardin anglais*, through a grotto-like tunnel beneath the pyramid. Its full glory is captured in a painting by Claude-Louis Châtelet circa 1785, where a golden light plays on the pyramid, and it is deliberately a little ruinous with greenery growing from its sides. There is a lake in front, and the roof beams of the tunnel entrance are upheld by four Tuscan columns. This entrance still remains, but the pyramid is now truly a ruin, sunk to the form of a jelly removed unsuccessfully from its mould. Another painting, by Hubert Robert done in 1780, shows the other side of the Mauperthuis pyramid, where the tunnel entrance was guarded by male and female caryatids, and beside the pyramid can be seen a single tall column and a huge sarcophagus on a plinth.[36]

As a pretty postscript to Egyptian influence on the European mind – as far as follies are concerned – Frederick Stibbert built a little temple shrine in his villa garden outside Florence. At the time, 1862–4, he was involved in the Italian Risorgimento, following in the military footsteps of his grandfather, a Governor of Bengal, and his father, who fought with Wellington in Spain.

Stibbert's Egyptian Temple, Florence, built in the 1860s as a waterside folly by the lake, in the shady garden attached to Stibbert's house and museum of exotic treasures.

Stibbert's mother was Florentine and there he chose to live, spending the family fortune on antiques (the most memorable room in his villa/museum is the Sala dei Cavalcanti, containing the mounted and caparisoned armies of Austria and Turkey). Stibbert's Egyptian Temple stands by the lake in his shady English garden, with steps leading down to the water between two pairs of sphinxes, one pair with pharaonic heads, the other with lions'. It is a creamy rectangular building modelled on an inner temple shrine, with painted flourishes, Isis and Osiris guarding the entrance and lotus columns either side of the building. There is an obelisk alongside and at the back of the temple is another avenue of more diminutive sphinxes.

Considering the importance of India to British interests it is surprising that Mughal or Hindu buildings did not exert more influence over folly architects until Brighton Pavilion burst upon the scene. There were some minor precedents, including the possibility that Vanbrugh was influenced in the flamboyance of his Baroque style by the monumental tombs of Surat. The vanished temples at Melchet Park in Hampshire (dedicated to the memory of Warren Hastings) and Great Stanmore in Middlesex (to house a collection of Indian gods) were modelled on Hindu shrines. There may have been more, judging by the scorn of James Malton, who wrote in 1798: 'The rude ornaments of Indostan supersede those of Greece and the returned Nabob heated in the pursuit of wealth imagines he imports the chaleur of the East with its riches.'[37] But in Europe there was less visual inspiration linked to Indian architecture compared to the chinoiserie delights so widespread and so widely copied. Even returning nabobs had to look at books of engravings for Indian inspiration and designs, most notably those of Thomas and William Daniell (uncle and nephew), who sailed east in 1785 and returned in 1793 to publish *Oriental Scenery* (in five parts with 144 plates) between 1795 and 1808. It was 'a rich and splendid display . . . one may almost feel the warmth of an Indian sky'.[38] Until this time George, Prince of Wales, had been in chinoiserie mode, ever since 1787, when Parliament had reluctantly agreed to pay his debts, after much angry debate, and on condition that he

278

reduced his extravagant lifestyle. He retreated to his modest Marine Pavilion at Brighton and decorated the interior *à la chinoise*. But in 1808, the same year that *Oriental Scenery* completed publication, the prince's massive stables at Brighton were also completed, in Indian Style, quite dwarfing the original pavilion. Some rethinking was necessary. In 1811 George became Prince Regent, and in a further bout of unpopular extravagance he turned to his favourite architect, John Nash, to create his Xanadu at Brighton, a stupendous series of domes, pinnacles, minarets, traceried arches and balconies – and even two tent-like roofs. It was built between 1815 and 1822, and in 1820 he became George IV. Meanwhile, thanks to its royal pavilion, Brighton grew into the leading fashionable seaside resort. In the eyes of the nation this stately pleasure dome was indeed the ultimate folly, and in relation to architecture the word was now used in England, echoing its earlier usage in France before the Revolution. In 1820 a satire entitled the 'FOLLY at Brighton' called it 'the queerest of all queer sights' and described the interior as 'all tea-things and dragons and bells', and the owner himself as 'an old fat MANDARIN . . . a patron of painters who copy designs, that grocers and tea-dealers hang up for signs'.³⁹ Its exotic unsuitability, and the money wasted, outweighed its beauty, and embarrassed Queen Victoria so much when she inherited it in 1837 that she sold it to the town.

Whether a palace or a residence should be defined as a folly is debatable, and the question shifts the scene to Sezincote, Gloucestershire, rebuilt contemporaneously from 1805 to 1820 for Sir Charles Cockerell, a nabob who had a prominent career in the East India Company, from his arrival in Bengal in 1776 until he returned home in 1801, retaining his banking interests in Calcutta and becoming an MP. The architect of Sezincote was his brother Samuel Pepys Cockerell, who had not been to India, so the brothers enlisted Thomas Daniell, Sir Charles's 'old India ally' for advice. The walls of Sezincote House are of Cotswold stone, but stained to the red sandstone colour typical of Mughal architecture. The onion domes are covered in copper and therefore green rather than the white marble of India. The line of graceful windows which extend in a crescent to include the orangery have pointed fan-lights to lend an Islamic touch. As at Brighton, minarets and pinnacles add the final effects. In the grounds there is a true folly, a little Indian shrine dedicated to the old Vedic sun god Surya, who sits inside with bulls guarding the threshold and a stepped pyramid above. In front, the picturesque round pool has a fountain which looks suspiciously like the lingam symbols of India. Now it is covered in moss, but when Thomas Daniell painted *Temple, Fountain*

Thomas Daniell, *Temple, Fountain and Cave in Sezincote Park*, 1819, a folly shrine in the grounds of Sezincote, Gloucestershire, built 1805–20 to bring the raj to the Cotswolds.

and Cave in Sezincote Park in 1819, he caused the waters of fertility to spurt and dazzle from it.

The loveliest offspring of Brighton and Sezincote is in Ireland, at Dromona in Co. Waterford, straddling a bridge over the river Finisk and named the Hindu Gatehouse. It is a fairy-tale pavilion, reflected in water like its greatest precursor the Taj Mahal, and likewise romantically linked with a marriage – that of Henry Villiers-Stuart and his Austrian bride Theresia. It was built to welcome them home from honeymoon in 1826. There is one copper dome over a central archway, side pavilions with ogee windows, eight finials and tracery balustrades around the roofs. As a small architectural ornament for a gentleman's grounds it was certainly a folly, although at first it was only meant to be temporary and had to be rebuilt in durable materials to stand the test of time. How temporary can a folly be? In 1814 there was a national jubilee to celebrate the centenary of the Hanoverian dynasty, and the Prince Regent commissioned John Nash to build a pagoda on the bridge over the lake in St James's Park. Turkish tents lined the banks on either side, and a grand fireworks display was launched from the pagoda. 'It appeared a blazing edifice of golden fire . . . the canopies of the roofs throwing up their bright wheels and stars . . . every rising tower of the pagoda pouring forth its fiery showers and rockets springing from its lofty top.' This lasted some time, but at midnight it became clear the pagoda was on fire; 'the fate of this erection was much regretted,' said the *Gentleman's Magazine*, 'as it was deservedly a favourite.'[40]

Despite his predeliction for expensive gilding and chinoiserie the Prince Regent also had a fondness for Turkish tents. Much time in his final years was spent on the island of Virginia Water, either in his Chinese fishing pavilion or dining *al fresco* in the nearby Turkish tents. During the nineteenth century the wheel came full circle, because many oriental garden pavilions were open constructions with an ephemeral air, more like their prototypes among the nomadic tribes of Asia. In China such pavilions were called *ting*, best translated as 'kiosks', meaning they had no walls, so the roof was supported only on thin columns, and being open on all sides they were intended for viewing lovely scenery, or the moon, or catching the scent of wild orchids growing

Indian Gateway, Dromona, Co. Waterford, Ireland, 1826, first built as a temporary structure to welcome returning honeymooners, and so admired that it was made permanent.

nearby. These kiosks appeared in many pattern books, and among those that remain some were installed in parks after first being used at an international exhibition. The Chinese Kiosk in London's Victoria Park was created for an exhibition in Philadelphia which was then brought to London in 1842. When the exhibition ended, its popularity caused it to be installed on Pagoda Island, with a Chinese bridge across the lake. The little Chinese pavilion at Cliveden in Berkshire first appeared in the Exposition Universelle in Paris in 1867, then moved to the Bagatelle Gardens, and was bought for Cliveden in the 1890s. At the same Paris exhibition, Mad Ludwig of Bavaria bought the Moorish Kiosk to add to his follies at Linderhof. One early nineteenth-century Russian kiosk expressed its orientalism with a delightful incongruity of mixed styles, very like those imaginary follies in Vanderbank's tapestries. It is in the Nikitsky Botanical Gardens near Yalta, founded in 1812, standing in the shade of an enormous Aleppo pine, with a straight avenue of cypresses beyond and yuccas and prickly pears at its feet. Its double roof is Indian, its one tall pinnacle and fretwork balustrade are Chinese, while the traceried arches supporting the roof look more Islamic, creating a blend like fine tea.

The enchantments of the Orient have not been altogether dispelled in folly architecture. Pyramids and upward-tilted gables still erupt occasionally, especially in France. For instance, in the mid-twentieth century at Château de Groussay, west of Paris, the *fabriques* of Charles de Beistegui, like the extravagant interior decors for which he was famed, gave rise to the term *goût Beistegui*. His lakeside pyramid at Château de Groussay, created in 1968, was based on the tomb of Caius Cestius in Rome, but it rests above a shell grotto dedicated to Venus. The walls of the pyramid are of mellow reddish brick, outlined with cubes of white stone – a striking contrast which is matched by the white stone portico. Also hovering over water, there is an octagonal *fabrique* like the tip of a pagoda, with grey slate roofs, golden gables and white fretwork. Third, Beistegui's Tartar Tent was inspired by the copper tents of Drottningholm, but lined inside with blue-and-white Delft tiles, a curious blend of styles previously used in the Munich Pagodenburg. As at Désert de Retz, this theatrical setting also called for an outdoor performance area, and here the grassy amphitheatre contains watchful statues.

Beistegui's architect was the Russian designer Alexandre Serebriakoff, who also created the follies at Château d'Agremont, which lies on the river Allier, a tributary of the Loire. At Apremont, in 1985, Serebriakoff designed a Chinese bridge and central archway, coloured with a brightness to rival the reds, greens and golds of the Chinese Temple at Biddulph Grange. The less flamboyant Turkish Pavilion is striped pale blue and white, a little octagon with a double roof and four ogee-arched doorways. These are outlined in gold ironwork, which is also used for the quatrefoils that decorate the walls and rooflines. It is a domed and delicate building, echoing the tent-like structures that first fascinated European eyes and were then woven into tapestries. It too rests over a lake, and is reached by stepping stones, to an interior of mirrored panels set alternately with paintings of Turkish ladies who evoke the *Thousand and One Nights*. The third folly at Apremont is a Neoclassical Belvedere (though topped with a gilded pineapple) and here the East beckons from inside, where eight panels of tile-work, painted by Serebriakoff, show masked characters from the commedia dell'arte on an exotic journey from Venice through Africa, India, China and Peru, until they arrive in raptures by the lake of Apremont.[41]

In England the spirit of the Indian raj has been recaptured on the Rushmore Estate in Wiltshire with a Mughal Gateway even higher than the Pagoda at Kew. It is set above a mile of tree-lined vista, along which, halfway up, a magnificent fountain spurts its jets and veils the distant folly in a mist of water droplets. The Mughal Gateway was completed in 2009 for William Gronow-Davis, whose forebear Lieutenant-General Augustus Henry Lane Fox Pitt-Rivers created Larmer Tree Pleasure Grounds at Tollard Royal. There the oriental follies were mostly reconstructed from items first displayed at the India exhibitions, which were popular in the late nineteenth century and generally held at Earl's Court in London. The Mughal Gateway at Rushmore was designed by Walshe Associates, with five copper domes spiked with golden ball finials – four to top the corners of the archway, with the fifth rising in the centre, Indian style – and the archway beneath is constructed of white limestone rendered with panels and patterns of dark orange ochre – authentic Mughal colours, though startling on their green English hilltop. The Gateway was initiated to house mobile-phone masts, but when the company pulled out it achieved its full status as a grand modern folly.[42]

Ruins of Leptis Magna, Virginia Water, Windsor Great Park,
assembled 1826 from Roman ruins imported from North Africa.

Eight

From Ruins to Gothic and Picturesque

Through long ages ruins have afforded a sinister pleasure to those who considered their implications. For Old Testament prophets they signified the destruction of enemy cities:

> The cormorant and bittern shall possess them; the owl also and the
> raven shall dwell therein; and He shall stretch out upon them the lines
> of confusion and the stones of emptiness . . . and thorns shall come
> up in their palaces and fortresses.

Classical writers accepted the wreck of time in a nobler spirit: Mycenae 'rich in gold, now more waste than any goat-pen . . . but he who looks on Troy whose walls I trampled shall know how mighty I was of old'.[1] In eleventh-century Persia, Omar Khayyám endowed ruins with romance: 'They say the lion and lizard keep/ The courts where Jamshid gloried and drank deep.' For Renaissance painters with the ruins of the Roman Empire all around them, crumbling walls provided a perspectival trick, to frame the Virgin and Child awaiting the arrival of wise men or shepherds through a distant landscape, which gave to ruins a Christian symbolism of redemption from the past. Early in the sixteenth century Vasari mentioned the first sham ruin, built in a park belonging to the Duke of Urbino at Pesaro, with a staircase copied from the Belvedere in Rome, 'a house which, representing a ruin, is very beautiful to see'.[2] This sentiment was endorsed in Francesco Colonna's influential *Polyphilus' Dream* when the two reunited lovers walked rhapsodizing through fallen columns and dilapidated temples, deciphering inscriptions and exploring subterranean passages. Small wonder that the Grand Tourists of England inherited the sense that a melancholy ruin would enhance their landscapes, as it did the paintings on their walls, and architects from William Kent to Robert Adam filled their minds and sketchbooks with the imagery of classical remains.

Surprisingly few of the sham ruins built in eighteenth-century England were classical: Painshill had its Mausoleum and Kew had its Ruined Arch, both enhanced by scattered bits of statuary and inscriptions, but they were far outshone by Frederick the Great's Ruinenberg at Sanssouci, also built in the mid-century. It began with a great water reservoir to supply the fountains of his formal gardens, which was excavated on the Hünenberg Hill (where there had been hunting grounds for pheasants and partridges). The reservoir was shielded with palatial ruins reached by stairways in the grassy hillside, rows of storeyed arches, the partial edifice of an amphitheatre and broken columns. Long after Frederick's time, when the pumping system he never achieved had at last been made to work, a medieval watchtower was added in 1846 to lend a further picturesque touch. In Poland the romantic landscape garden called Arkadia, created for Princess Radziwill at Lowicz circa 1780, has a large ruined aqueduct straddling the water, like an echo of the Pont du Gard near Nîmes, powerfully built of red brick but romantic in its tree-lined desolation, with a view of a classical temple through one of its arches. True to the garden's name, an island tomb in the lake is inscribed *ET IN ARCADIA EGO*. In France, as if impelled towards their own fate, the aristocracy on the eve of the Revolution built mock ruins in their folly gardens, among the most exceptional being the Ruined Column at Désert de Retz and the Temple of Philosophy at Ermenonville.[3]

In 1826, when such fashions were waning, some real Roman ruins plucked from the sands of Leptis Magna were erected near the lake at Virginia Water, in Windsor Great Park. They had arrived eight years earlier, organized by the British Consul, who requested them as a gift from the Bey of Tripoli. To be fair, the Consul realized how much the French had been appropriating for over a century, and how the locals rummaged the site for building materials and mill stones, and the Elgin Marbles had just been rescued from similar depredations allowed under Turkish rule in Greece. But when the ruins arrived at the British Museum they were abandoned in the forecourt until Sir Jeffry Wyatville was commissioned by George IV to erect them by Virginia Water, which was his favourite haunt by then. This Wyatville did with great flair: 'the work', wrote a contemporary, 'must have cost the architect as much intellect and labour as a finished building of similar proportions.' There were lovely columns, architraves, triumphal archways, inscriptions and fragments to be assembled into a coherent, if fake, archaeological site – which Wyatville built up, supplemented with stones from a recently demolished country house, even embellishing the nearby road bridge to resemble an arch in an ancient city wall. He called this whole creation the Temple of Augustus, although the emperor most associated with Leptis Magna was Septimius Severus, who came from North Africa and greatly enriched the city. Earlier, before the Romans descended, this region around Carthage had been powerful and prosperous, and the architecture retained an oriental delicacy and exuberance in its details. At Virginia Water the ruins are out of place and more embarrassing than a sham; their situation makes them a folly, but it also allows them more of their natural poetry than any museum would do, and a little of what Bernard Berenson felt when he viewed the originals *in situ* shines through: 'One suspects that ruins suggest sublimities that the completed building may not have attained. In their present state they are evocative and romantic to a degree that it would be hard to exaggerate.'[4] Three Medusa heads were also included in the shipment from Leptis Magna; curiously they were erected near the royal landing stage.

However great our admiration for the civilizations of the Mediterranean past, there were ruins of a different order at home, and during the eighteenth century the remains of medieval abbeys and castles grew closer to the nation's heart. Ever since the Tudors discouraged baronial castles and dissolved the monasteries many a battlement and gothic archway had been left to crumble in the countryside. Shakespeare, whose religious sympathies remain ambiguous, called them 'bare ruined choirs where late the sweet birds sang'. John Webster in *The Duchess of Malfi* endowed ruins with the same frightening qualities which later inspired gothic authors. Antonio, the doomed lover of the duchess, begins: 'I do love these ancient ruins, we never tread upon them but we set our foot upon some reverend history.' To which the echo, 'hollow and dismal', gives prophetic responses, concluding with 'a thing of sorrow'.[5] Vanbrugh is credited with the first architectural move towards gothic style, when in 1709 he suggested that the grounds of Blenheim Palace would be enhanced by turning the old manor of Woodstock into a feature, but the Duchess of Marlborough treated this idea with scorn. However, at Castle Howard Vanbrugh summoned the medieval past of the site in the magnificent ramparts and bastions he set around it, and the Belvedere Tower he built for himself at Claremont has a battlemented grimness. In 1721 at Cirencester Park Lord Bathurst built the first sham castle in a ruinous state and linked it with King Alfred. Back in Yorkshire the ruins of Fountains Abbey and Rievaulx were incorporated into the views from landscape gardens, and Thomas Wentworth vented his anger at failing to inherit Wentworth Woodhouse by building himself an ancestral folly of ruinous towers and encircling walls and calling it Stainborough Castle.

Batty Langley was the first architectural writer to describe how a ruin could be built to 'terminate a walk' (meaning to enhance a vista), rendering the concept more achievable by suggesting the folly ruin could be of bricks, plaster or even painted on canvas.[6] William Kent tended to use gothic facades at a distance to turn farm buildings into features, as Thomas Wright did later. Better still if one's folly incorporated real features plundered from a nearby medieval ruin. Lord Bathurst used parts of Sapperton Manor to extend Alfred's Hall; the Ruin at Mt Edgecombe, high over Plymouth Sound, has some genuine medieval recycling; Shenstone's ruined Priory at The Leasowes, and Hagley Tower nearby, contain parts of Halesowen Abbey; at Shugborough, the Ansons created their Ruin from fragments of earlier buildings including the Bishop of Lichfield's old palace; Kettlethorpe boat house has a facade from Wakefield chantry chapel; and at Raby Castle in Co. Durham, the long screen wall of the folly in the deer park incorporates the central barbican arch of the old Norman castle, once home of the Nevilles, where Cecily Neville, mother of the last Plantagenet kings, was born. Shobdon Arches in Herefordshire is a folly reconstructed entirely from church remnants.

When, in the 1750s, Lord Bateman rebuilt Shobdon church in gothic Rococo style, he at least had the grace to rescue the old Romanesque arches of the Norman church and place them up the hill as an eye-catcher – ostensibly where the old priory of Shobdon once stood. They form a five-fold screen, with the wide central archway looking like a stage set, supported at an angle by the side arches. All the arches have cable mouldings and chevrons crinkling their edges. There are three triangular gables, two crocketed pinnacles and a trefoil. But the carved figures on the tympana above the two side doorways have been badly worn, and the gyrating dragons struggling through the Romanesque coils on the pillars are weathering away. By contrast Scotney Castle in Kent is a composite ruin, preserved as a loving embodiment of ages past, in a manner worthy of the county that also inspired Virginia Woolf's *Orlando* – a book in which generations of the Sackville family were recreated in one flamboyant transgender personality. In 1836, when the new house at Scotney was built higher up the hill, the ancient fortified manor was turned into a picturesque eye-catcher. The rusty grey watchtower, the moat with its water lilies, the remains of the Elizabethan mansion with oak staircase and priest's hole, and the Inigo Jones wing rendered roofless and ruinous, were all combined under their cloak of creepers to become a most atmospheric folly. Around 1860 at Abingdon in Oxfordshire a reconstruction of the old abbey cloisters was undertaken by the ingenious Mr Trendall to enhance his own

Shobdon Arches, Herefordshire, rescued in the 1750s from the
remnants of the medieval church and set up as an eye-catcher.

garden in Abbey House, but accessible to all. It consists of genuine archways
and fragments assembled so convincingly that they arouse the indignation
of purists – also sometimes a sign of a folly.

The gothic style became politicized when the Whigs linked it to patriotism
– 'tending to excite free-thinkers to a sense of what is right'.[7] In this spirit
Lord Cobham at Stowe built his Temple of Liberty as a gothic folly halfway
between a cathedral and a fortress, and his brother-in-law Sir Thomas Lyttelton
followed suit soon after at Hagley, in Worcestershire, where Hagley Castle
became the archetypal sham ruin. Since it was built between 1747 and 1748
it was originally Sir Thomas's commission, for which Sanderson Miller the
leading creator of gothic ruins was summoned. But from the start this tour de
force was more associated with his son George, later Lord Lyttelton. George
Lyttelton inherited in 1751, having established his political career as Secretary

Sham Castle, Hagley, Worcestershire, 1747–8, an early and much admired example
of constructing one's own ancestral ruin, attributed to Sanderson Miller.

to Frederick, Prince of Wales, and, as one of Cobham's Cubs, in close league
with his cousins the Grenvilles and William Pitt. He rose to be Chancellor
of the Exchequer, although Horace Walpole sneered that he was 'strangely
bewildered with the figures'. However, Hagley Castle prompted unusually
generous enthusiasm in Walpole: 'There is a ruined castle built by Miller
that would get him the freedom even of Strawberry, it has the true rust of
the Barons Wars.' Lyttelton's neighbour and friend William Shenstone, in a
letter to Lady Luxborough, was less enthusiastic but more factual: 'It consists
of one entire tower and three stumps of towers with a ruined wall between
them. There is no great art or variety in the ruin but the situation gives it a
charming effect.' Shenstone was right that the ruin's position on its hillside
surrounded by trees and very quickly wreathed in ivy was important. 'The
mind naturally falls into reflections . . . what sieges it has sustained . . . what
blood has been spilt on its walls . . . in reality it is a modern structure, to give
a livelier consequence to the landscape, and for use.'[8] It was used by George

Lyttelton to entertain. In the one complete tower there are four storeys with an adjoining stair turret, and the top floor has large pointed windows and a domed ceiling with gothic plaster decoration. In 1749 Lyttelton was acquiring a 'proper table' and 'chairs of a gothic form'. All four towers of the ruin are round and form a rectangle enclosing a courtyard. As Shenstone said, three of them are just ruinous stumps, but concealed within they had sloping roofs and at some point housed livestock, while the main tower came to be used as an estate lodge. Although the towers set the scene, much of the ruin's harmony and sense of a past depends on the adjoining walls; one especially has a line of three tall windows (part ruined) and a door beneath. Far more can be imagined where there is a door, and it was his power to stir the imagination that sealed Sanderson Miller's reputation as the premier designer of sham ruins, so that even Dunstall Castle, the eye-catcher for Croome Court, was posthumously accredited to him. Miller has been considered less successful with the Ruin at Wimpole Hall, designed for Lord Hardwicke (who was a meaner and more successful Chancellor than Lyttelton), and perhaps the precision of Hardwicke's instructions to Miller cramped his style.

In fact it was Robert Adam who had to build Dunstall Castle, and Capability Brown completed the Ruin at Wimpole Hall. Similarly, Ralph Allen's Sham Castle in Bath was built in 1762 by the local architect Richard Jones (who also successfully created the Palladian Bridge in Prior Park for Allen). However, an initial design for the Bath Sham Castle has been traced to Sanderson Miller, who drew up plans in 1755, and there was also a friendship link, via George Lyttelton. In 1749 Henry Fielding dedicated *Tom Jones* jointly to George Lyttelton and Ralph Allen, the latter being widely identified as the model for Fielding's rich and benevolent Squire Allworthy.[9] Ralph Allen rose from humble origins by reforming the postal system, then reinvesting his wealth in the quarrying of Bath stone, at the time of Bath's growth as a fashionable Georgian town. Allen developed his own town property at Prior Park, a mansion from which he could 'see Bath and Bath could see him', together with a garden that was

Sham Ruin, Bathwick Hill, Bath, 1762, built as an eye-catcher to please and impress the inhabitants of Bath by Ralph Allen, who built Prior Park for himself.

Mow Cop, Cheshire, 1754. Situated high on a rugged outcrop, this is by far the most atmospheric of sham ruins, though it was built as a summer house.

landscaped with cascades, follies and a grotto. Among his philanthropic works he endowed Bath with its much-loved eye-catcher on Bathwick Hill, where it can be seen from afar by standing near Pulteney Bridge with one's back to the Abbey, although the view was better when there were fewer other buildings and trees. Strictly speaking it is not a sham ruin but a two-dimensional, straight screen wall, with two prominent round towers facing the city (which prove on inspection from behind to be semicircular). These towers flank a gothic arch and then extend into battlemented walls ending in two square towers, all with symmetrical blind windows and cruciform arrow slits. It is certainly theatrical, but has less of the 'true rust' that Hagley or Dunstall could claim, and that Wimpole, and Sanderson Miller's own Radway Tower at Edge Hill, may once have had.[10]

In 1754, while Sanderson Miller was stealing the show, Randle Wilbraham of Rode Hall, on the Cheshire/Staffordshire border, was building a far more rugged and atmospheric ruin on Mow Cop, a nearby hill on the moorland ridge with a steep and rocky approach. Built of harsh grey stone, it is best seen on a stormy day with racing clouds, when it lowers with a magnificent air of gloomy decline among the boulders. The round windows are like sightless eyes: the arched doorway appears open to the sky. Beside the broken tower the curtain wall slides downwards with the slope of the hillside. But Lord Wilbraham built it as a summer house! Presumably he intended to picnic there on fine days and enjoy the spreading views. Mow Cop was probably an Iron-Age hill fort and has been quarried for mill stones for ages past, and also used as a beacon. In 1807 and 1812 mass meetings of Methodists were held there, and it has become their place of pilgrimage, as well as a beauty spot for those with a taste for melancholy. It is one of the few follies to attract not only artists but multiple viewings of a ghost, who appears fleetingly at a window.

In the Scottish borders, near Kelso, lies Mellerstain, home of the Baillies, whose fortunes were in decline following the beheading of one of their number, until the heir befriended William of Orange, later William III. Secure in his inheritance, George Baillie commissioned William Adam, in 1724, to redesign his house and grounds. At this date vistas were still formal straight lines, and the finest at Mellerstain led up to the ridge crowned by Hundy Mundy Wood. Here there was an old tower, described in 1700 thus: 'They have ane old tower wt but one room off a floor about 5 storey high but it looks vert ruinous.'[11] This was one of many defensive towers built for protection against the reevers who for centuries made life wretched on both sides of the border. The old tower was dismantled to create William Adam's new gothic folly, one of the earliest in the century. It is not so much a ruin as a screen and certainly an eye-catcher, with a central archway and two four-storey towers, each topped by a pyramid. The total of nine empty windows, of varying size, all framing the sky, confirm the gothic bleakness of the two towers as they form their symmetrical and forbidding silhouette. The Baillies may once have held the secret of the name Hundy Mundy, by which both the wood and the tower are known. It is now said to be a corruption of Hundimundias, a Pictish princess who lived in the earlier tower, but that name has an eighteenth-century ring to it, and if the Picts had princesses they did not build towers. Perhaps it was a nursery tale told to the Baillie children, a version of Rapunzel, whose story would fit excellently with this witches' tower. Around it, Hundy Mundy Wood is now a graveyard for natural burials, marked with flat stones simply carved. It is not gothic in any dark sense, but recalls Oscar Wilde's poignant quotation: 'Death must be so beautiful. To be in the soft brown earth with the grasses waving above one's head and listen to the silence.' For dramatic scenery Scotland certainly holds the trumps. There are two breathtaking crags featuring round towers, both a little ruined and joined by broken walls

with pointed arches to add an ancient air. Kinnoull Tower overlooking the river Tay in Perthshire was built early in the nineteenth century by the Earl of Kinoull, who fondly remembered a youthful journey admiring the castles of the Rhine and (like Prince Albert) loved Scotland the more for its resemblance to Germany. In Fife, on the Colinsburgh estate, Balcarres Crag sports a ruined castle tower of grey-black granite with its arches, arrow slits and battlements outlined in startling contrast white. Yew trees and a ruined chapel serving as a mausoleum for the earls of Crawford and Balcarres add to the ancestral romance. The ruin was built in 1813 by the younger brother of the earl, returning from a career in India.

Alongside sham ruins and gaping turrets, another style of gothic developed early in the eighteenth century that was far prettier, making play with traceried windows, trefoils and vaulting and generating an air of lightness and fantasy. At Painshill, the Gothic Pavilion and the Ruined Abbey (when viewed from the lakeside) were in this tradition; and when placed by water other gothic edifices bathed their delicate reflections, like Fort Henry in Rutland, or the Orangery at Frampton Court in Gloucestershire, with its dainty octagons, ogee windows and castellations. The earliest manifestation of this more decorative gothic style, however, was probably the Gothic Temple at Shotover. Sometimes the structure of the early gothic follies was still based on classical proportions like the Gothic Temple at Bramham Park in Yorkshire. It dates from 1750 and is attributed to James Paine, but the design is from Batty Langley's *Gothic Architecture Improved* (1747) and it would seem that Langley lifted it from James Gibbs's *Book of Architecture* (1729), changing pilasters to buttresses, round arches to pointed and adding ogee gables with trefoils and finials. In 1738, at Studley Royal, William Aislabie (later a leading exponent of gothic and picturesque) converted his father's classical octagon tower into a gothic pavilion by adding a delightfully pinnacled belvedere. Quatrefoils were inserted in the eight upper facades and steps led up to an arched entrance in a gothic porch. Like many other gothic follies, it may have been a political statement, since William Aislabie was the author of the constitutional Whig *Essay upon Some Particulars of the Ancient and Modern Government from the Saxons until Edward I.*[12]

Sometimes medieval architecture was used for extravagant park lodges. At Milton Park near Peterborough (home of the Fitzwilliams and most notable

Hundy Mundy Tower, Mellerstain, Scotland, built 1724 by William Adam
and therefore one of the earliest gothic follies of the century.

Ruined Abbey, Painshill, 1772, a gothic folly with two distinct sides, light and ornamental
facing the lake, dark and rugged when approached down a bank of conifers.

for its castellated kennels) the design of the Gothic Lodge has been attributed variously to William Chambers, John Nash or Humphry Repton, who
all worked at Milton. It is a castellated stone octagon two storeys high with
slender pinnacled buttresses. The ground-floor windows are arched and the
main facade has an ecclesiastical air dominated by a rose window beneath
a triangular gable. This gable is outlined with a scallop frieze similar to that
in the Norman part of Peterborough Cathedral, and above the two ground-
floor arches there is an intricate quatrefoil frieze – all details that give the
lodge elegance and individuality. There is a far more eccentric Gothic Lodge
at Rendlesham in Suffolk, in the solitary flatlands where the kings of East
Anglia once reigned. The very rich Peter Isaac Thellusson had Rendlesham Hall
gothicized in the early 1800s by the architect Henry Hakewill. The scheme
was extended to the main entrance of his estate, the Woodbridge Lodge,
possibly to celebrate his elevation to Baron Rendlesham in 1806. Previously
it was a simple rectangular gatehouse, but subsequently hefty buttresses

crowded around it, lending extraneous support to the arched windows and intricately carved pinnacles. From the centre of this gothic pile rise five flying buttresses, curving and uniting to support a vastly ornate chimney 'like an insane chapter house for a madman's cathedral'.[13] It is satisfyingly bizarre by day and suitably eerie by night.

In Derbyshire there are two gothic follies with a certain affinity. The first was designed by Robert Adam (whose drawing survives) while he was working for Lord Curzon at Kedleston, from 1758 onwards. Now it lies outside the grounds in the village of Weston Underwood. It is beautifully complicated, and even has stylized leaf carvings on the capitals and above the windows, which is a rare luxury in a gothic folly, though widespread in medieval architecture. Like Adam's Fishing Pavilion at Kedleston, the front is tripartite: the three bays are divided by triple-shafted columns and each bay has a pointed window. Each window has three tall lights and above them three small lights, set into the tracery design in the pointed arch. Above each window the wall is moulded into an ogee arch which is trefoiled into three curves. The parapet at the roofline is carved with triangular motifs and the central bay has a taller parapet. Here the numerology shifts to four, with a cruciform arrow slit flanked by quatrefoils. There are four crocketed pinnacles, two at either corner of the roof and two on the central parapet. These ornate designs, complete with blank armorial shields, are replicated round the other sides of the building, and the interior of the building is decorated with stucco work. Trees close around it protectively, and for such an exquisite building it is surprisingly little known. On the other hand, the archway at Renishaw has been well loved and preserved, safe and purposeless, near the river and with a magnificent Italianate garden lying between it and Renishaw itself. The house was gothicized between 1793 and 1808 by Joseph Badger, in the time of Sir Sitwell Sitwell, who updated the dwelling – which had already belonged to his family for two hundred years, and still does. According to Osbert Sitwell, the gothic archway was designed by Sir Sitwell himself, who may well have known and admired the Gothic Temple at Kedleston, and he too followed a tripartite, though less ornate, style. Here the higher central bay contains the pointed archway, above which is a great painted crest and the Sitwell motto, *Ne cede malis* (Yield not to evil). The side pavilions have gothic windows and around the parapets are crenellations and pinnacles. One could imagine Edith Sitwell in her velvets, jewels and feathers declaiming her surreal poems here:

The air is like a jarring bell
That jangles words it cannot spell
And black as fate the iron trees
Stretch thirstily to catch the breeze.[14]

Alternatively, and in another mood, in 1942 John Piper painted Renishaw Arch bathed in an otherworldly golden light.

For gentle melancholy there is nothing to beat Clytha Castle in the Welsh borders near Raglan, built by William Jones around 1790 in memory of his wife Elizabeth, who died in 1787. A carved inscription on the wall reads, 'Undertaken for the purpose of relieving a mind sincerely afflicted by the loss of a most excellent wife'. It was also an eye-catcher overlooking Jones's house in Clytha Park, and in 1793 he confirmed its other function in a note: 'Now

John Piper, *The Gothic Arch at Renishaw*, 1942–3, capturing the allure, if not all the detail, in the artist's unique style of rendering architectural beauty.

Clytha Castle, near Raglan, Wales, *c.* 1790, built by William Jones in memory of his wife, unusually using a gothic retreat rather than an Egyptian folly to mark a bereavement.

building a castle, a gothic summerhouse, which will be a memorial to my wife.'[15] It is an L-shaped building consisting of three towers two storeys high joined by two curtain walls. The first tower is a hollow oval whose function is to balance the building; the middle tower is a sturdy square containing living rooms, plus a circular stair turret; the third is round and habitable on the ground floor. All have arched windows and battlements, but what makes the building sing is the curtain wall that curves upwards to a central peak with a little flourishing turret to round off its castellations, which is a unique feature. Quatrefoils, cruciform slits and friezes provide decoration, but it is restrained.

Small wonder that this fine building has been attributed to a premier architect, and a payment of £10 to John Nash 'for his plan' was made in 1790. By this time Nash had moved to Carmarthen, which would make this an early example of the 'vigorous picturesque asymmetry that characterised his houses from this time'. However, many more payments starting in 1789 were made to John Davenport, a Shropshire architect who had designed a mildly gothic orangery for Warren Hastings at Daylesford – which tips the scales in Davenport's favour without entirely ruling out a touch of Nash's stardust. All William Jones's detailed accounting is preserved, enabling further credit to be allocated to those who brought the Bath stone across the Bristol Channel, up the river Usk, then by waggon for the difficult final haul up the steep hill; and also the builders and carpenters: Thomas Jones for five dozen scaffolding hurdles, Thomas Waters for his 'cart and two horses hauling water'. As if to accentuate the domestic aspects of a happy marriage, which the folly celebrated as well as mourned, from 1791 Jones's accounts record payments for furnishing the 'lodging rooms' including silks, French chintz, paintings for the chimney pieces, gothic-style furniture and Wedgwood china. Soon after all this was completed, Archdeacon William Coxe, author of *An Historical Tour of Monmouthshire*, stayed with William Jones for a few happy days at Clytha and described the view from Clytha Castle over 'the southern extremity of the Vale of Usk', where the bewitching scenery 'gradually expanded into hills and mountains, among them the Skyridd, the Sugar Loaf and the Blorenge are most conspicuous and contrasted'. Had the Archdeacon stayed in bluebell time he could also have described the enchantments of the woods above Clytha Castle.

Even though the folly at Clytha had the name and attributes of a castle, it belonged in the category which came to be known as 'Strawberry Hill Gothic' after Horace Walpole's home at Twickenham – graceful and decorative rather than ruined, rugged or military. On the other hand, it was Walpole who endowed gothic irretrievably with its spooky aspects, though he was not alone, and Thomas Robins's black-bordered illustrations of Painswick, dated 1744–8, showed the pinnacled pavilions of Pan's folkloric territory in a state of dangerous enchantment.[16] Robins's paintings coincided with the date when Walpole was embarking on his project and setting himself against the taste for classicism, which still prevailed when it came to residences. In 1747 Walpole acquired a riverside cottage from the owner of a London toy and trinket shop, and this provenance was also woven into the spirit of the house when Walpole called it his 'little plaything', 'gingerbread house', 'the prettiest bauble you ever saw'. According to one architectural historian, 'It is certainly not a folly, it is a proper serious building designed to influence and educate people about style and design'[17] (which admirers of follies would consider a passable definition of one).

Walpole was a collector, and his 'summer villa' was designed like a treasure chest to incorporate quantities of medieval stained glass, and to recreate fireplaces and *trompe l'œil* wallpaper based on various designs of medieval tombs. There was a fan-vaulted ceiling in the gallery made of papier mâché; in the library the bookshelves of 'pierced work' were like the choir of old St Pauls; and the grand staircase was based on the library of Rouen Cathedral.

Strawberry Hill was also a cabinet of curiosities housing items like John Dee's black mirror, Cardinal Wolsey's scarlet cardinal's hat and Anne Boleyn's clock. Another collection, Walpole's armoury, was carefully sited on a dark half-landing to suggest medieval ancestry, 'items that might be supposed to be taken by Sir Terence Robsart in the holy wars' (including the slightly anachronistic parade armour attributed to Francis I of France, a Persian shield and a Chinese bow).

The outside of the villa was another joyous pastiche of light-hearted gothicism. Walpole acknowledged this, because when he wrote his *Description of the Villa* in 1744 he hoped to 'recall the good humour of those who might be disposed to condemn the fantastic fabric'. The centrepiece is the round and turreted Beauclerk Tower, though this was not added until 1776, and the rambling asymmetry of the building is its greatest charm: quatrefoils here, pinnacles there, and various types of ogee and lancet windows everywhere, also castellations. Walpole had

The Chapel, Strawberry Hill, Twickenham, 1771. The house at Strawberry Hill may or may not be called a folly, but the unconsecrated chapel, dedicated to meditation, certainly is.

it limewashed and now it is once again icing-sugar white.[18] Another problem with the folly definition of Strawberry Hill is Walpole's vituperative criticism of the Gothic Pavilion at Painshill: 'an unmeaning edifice, the Goths never built summerhouses and temples in a garden.' Though he was undoubtedly an arbiter of taste Walpole was a spiteful and inconsistent man. All that can be said for him in this particular instance is that his own small garden folly was not a temple or pavilion, but took the form of a lovely little chapel (unconsecrated of course). It was built in 1771 in the woodland walk which ran along the roadside boundary, partly to accommodate Walpole's ever-growing collection of stained glass. The setting of the chapel among dark conifers and yews is ideal; the convincingly medieval facade is dominated by a large traceried window, and beneath it a monastic wooden door is guarded by a niche for a saint. Inside, the hushed atmosphere associated with the glow from the glass exactly fits the lines from Walpole's beloved Milton:

And storied windows richly dight
Casting a dim religious light.

The words are from 'Il Penseroso', a poem in which a soul dedicated to meditation and learning would be happiest in the 'studious cloister', in contrast to its companion piece, 'L'Allegro', a poem about the light-hearted pleasure seeker. Milton's juxtaposition appealed greatly to Walpole, who 'played many parts and overacted them all'. He was a worldly creature who loved the artefacts and sensations of the historic past, and when this involved Catholicism a 'frisson of the forbidden' was added, since Catholic worship still incurred suspicion and restrictions, and Walpole did not intend his chapel for religious observance. But it perfectly expressed 'gloomth', a word Walpole had coined to signify the softly coloured glow from stained glass, combined with an atmosphere that summoned the supernatural, preferably in a titillatingly sinister form. Also, Walpole's capacity for humour must not be underestimated; it could be delightful, as when he wrote that he had just seen Alexander Pope's ghost 'skimming under my window by a most poetic moonlight'.[19]

In 1764 Walpole published his gothic novel *The Castle of Otranto* (anonymously at first), characteristically pretending that the author had discovered the story in 'the library of an ancient Catholic family in the north of England'. Otranto itself is in the southern tip of Italy, and probably Walpole knew of its castle from a print, but of all his Italian experiences it was crossing the Alps that provided the most gothic sensations of his Grand Tour: 'Precipices, mountains, torrents, wolves, rumblings, Salvator Rosa!' This was for him the supreme moment when awesome beauty combined with genuine fear to create a sense of the sublime. His allusion to Salvator Rosa included artistic expression as part of this sensation, because Rosa was a much-admired seventeenth-century artist who specialized in painting fear. Of course exploring dark matters has always challenged and attracted the human mind, but the eighteenth century felt a new urge to rationalize this further. In 1757 Edmund Burke wrote his *Philosophical Enquiry into the Origin of Our Ideas of the Sublime and Beautiful*, his theme being that 'whatever is fitted in any sort to excite the ideas of pain and danger . . . whatever is in any sort terrible . . . is a source of the sublime' – one of his examples was infinity, or as he put it 'things multiplied without end'. Fortified with this concept of the Sublime, the thrills of horror could be unleashed. Meanwhile, the Italian artist Piranesi portrayed the ruins of ancient Rome as if the dead were rotting among the stones, followed between 1745 and 1761 by a series called *Carceri* (Prisons), which de Quincy later assumed were opiate visions:

> Vast gothic halls on the floor of which stood instruments of torture, war and power. Then a staircase forever mounting in fresh flights until the unfinished stairs and the hopeless Piranesi are lost in the upper gloom of the hall.[20]

That Walpole relished Piranesi's work was evident when, in 1771, in *Anecdotes of Painting*, he wrote: 'the sublime dream of Piranesi, who conceived visions of Rome savage as Salvator Rosa, scenes that would startle geometry . . . piles palaces on palaces, bridges and temples on palaces, scales heaven with mountains of edifices'.

In *The Castle of Otranto* Walpole's levity mitigates both the sense of the sublime and any architectural extremes, but he would surely have liked Piranesi to illustrate the secret passage down which Isabella fled in terror from the Castle to the convent:

> The lower part of the castle was hollowed into several intricate cloisters, an awful silence reigned . . . except now and then some blasts of wind shook the doors she had passed . . . and re-echoed through the long labyrinth of darkness.

In Walpole's novel, a more direct borrowing from Piranesi was the mighty plumed helmet that heralded Manfred's fate, because two Piranesi images included such a helmet, one of which hung threateningly over a small figure beneath. But it was Walpole's own beautiful grey staircase at Strawberry Hill which was the main *mise-en-scène* for his novel. The suit of armour waited in the gloomth of the half-landing to give a thrill of recognition to anyone who had read *Otranto*, or who knew the dream derivation Walpole gave it in a letter of 1765:

> An ancient castle (a very natural dream for a head filled like mine with Gothic story) and on the uppermost bannister of a great staircase I saw a gigantic hand in armour. In the evening I sat down to write without knowing in the least what I meant to say or relate.[21]

Thus Walpole spawned a melodramatic new genre and endowed gothic buildings with a literature of the supernatural. His successors included Mrs Radcliffe, whose prolonged adventures of maidens in distress popularized the genre; Jane Austen, who, in *Northanger Abbey*, simultaneously used and mocked it; 'Monk' Lewis, whose eponymous book made gothicism far more illicit, like the Marquis de Sade; Mary Shelley, whose *Frankenstein* carried it into science fiction; and Edgar Allan Poe, who came closer to the sublime than any other. Painting too was infected and in 1781 Henry Fuseli summed it all up with *The Nightmare*, a swooning white-clad damsel with a hobgoblin seated on her chest and the mare with streaming mane and fearsome eyes staring at her through the black bed curtains.

Only William Beckford followed Horace Walpole, both with a gothic novel and also a penchant for architecture. Unlike Walpole, whose homosexuality seems to have been sublimated, Beckford was a more tortured soul – 'some people drink to forget their unhappiness, I do not drink, I build.'[22] Son of Alderman Beckford of Fonthill in Wiltshire, who died when he was nine, William was immensely rich, sensitive and intelligent, but dangerously spoilt. He said he wrote *Vathek* after two exotic parties at Fonthill, for his coming of age and for Christmas. Both the parties (and the book) were strongly influenced by *The Arabian Nights* and lasted for days, 'an orgy of acting, music and lovemaking'. They provoked scandalous comment, but the scandal that embittered the rest of Beckford's life broke in 1783, after his marriage to the sweetly complaisant Lady Margaret Gordon, when his passion for William (Kitty) Courtenay was made public. The Beckfords fled abroad and from then on William travelled restlessly but not fruitlessly – socializing, collecting and writing – because he was not a pariah abroad as he was in England. *Vathek* was belatedly published in 1786 (the year Margaret died in childbirth) and claimed to be based on the discovery of an oriental text. It featured a magnificent caliph, Vathek, whose ruthless search for forbidden pleasures was modelled on himself, but whose death-dealing stare probably owed more to memories of his father the Alderman. The evil mother, Carathis, was in part Beckford's own (whose overbearing ambition contributed to this emotional whirlwind). Before being married she was Maria Hamilton (cousin of Charles Hamilton of Painshill). Among the cast of oriental characters in *Vathek*, the voluptuous Nouronihar and her effeminate brother Gulchenrouz may both have been summoned from erotic memories of Kitty. The gothic elements existed in spells, skulls, stairways and subterranean passages and, like Walpole, Beckford acknowledged his inspirational debt to Piranesi. Characteristically,

Beckford reacted ghoulishly to a gondola ride under the Bridge of Sighs in Venice: 'Horrors and dismal prospects haunted my fancy . . . on my return I drew chasms and subterranean hollows, the domain of fear and torture . . . chains, racks, wheels in the style of Piranesi'; and crossing the mountains in Germany, 'vast and wild prospects which I mounted on the chimeras of my imagination and built castles in the style of Piranesi upon most of their pinnacles . . . the magnificence and variety of my aerial towers hindered my thinking on the way.'[23] Vathek himself with the help of a Genii built a tower, 'from the insolent curiosity of penetrating the secrets of heaven', and having mounted its 1,500 stairs for the first time he 'beheld men not larger than pismires [ants], mountains than shells and cities than bee hives'. This tower was linked by a subterranean passage to his palace and, until his final departure to seek the talismans that rule the world, Vathek used it for necromancy and astrology, for impressing his subjects and for 'supping gaily' by starlight.

Beckford's first real tower was built at Fonthill, where he commissioned James Wyatt in 1796 to design him a gothic fantasy based on monastic buildings and to be called Fonthill Abbey, with a central tower nearly 100 metres (328 ft) high, reminiscent of a cathedral spire. On his European travels Beckford learnt to love the trappings of Catholicism, and seemed to yearn for redemption while believing only in damnation. The building proceeded sporadically, becoming notorious, and finally turning Beckford's fortune into a debt. The Alderman's Fonthill Splendens was demolished to provide stone. Nelson and Emma Hamilton visited Fonthill Abbey in 1800, by which time there was fan vaulting in the great gallery, but many parts were unfinished and sealed off, remaining invisible in the torchlight by which Nelson saw it. In 1807 Beckford moved in to live there but found it melancholy and full of foreboding – 'oh what a fatal abode' – the great gothic tower moved and groaned in the wind, not to mention more humdrum ills like smoking chimneys, icy draughts and rheumatism. Beckford sold up in 1822 and Fonthill tower collapsed in 1825. His move to Bath at the age of 63 was initially desolate, but he found peace there, living in Lansdown Crescent amid his collections of books, paintings and exquisite *objets de vertu*. For grounds he bought a mile of land rising behind the Crescent up Lansdown Hill and at the summit he built a tower of lasting value. There he would ride every day with his retinue of servants, dogs and a dwarf, along the meandering track named Beckford's Ride, which was lined by the gardens he created and plantations of the latest exotic trees.

Beckford's Tower, Bath, 1825–7, built on Lansdown Hill and eclectically combining Greek and Italianate elements, though it still retains the gothic atmosphere with which Beckford associated himself.

Beckford's (or Lansdown) Tower is not exactly gothic, although an initial drawing showed a sturdy Saxon tower; then came a variation on an Italian campanile, which proved to be a stage towards the final result, a combination of Italianate and classical elements, concocted by Beckford himself and a long-suffering Bath architect and friend called Henry Goodridge.[24] It was built between 1825 and 1827 (as Fonthill Tower collapsed). The main shaft is a tall square tower with narrow windows, comprising about 30 of the total 50 metres/ 164 ft (half the height of Fonthill Tower). Above this a jutting cornice hints at the proportions of a medieval Italian watchtower, while the elaborate carvings visible on the underside are Greek key-fret decoration. The next section is the belvedere: on each side there are three arched and recessed windows set between square piers, and each has a carved balustrade, creating shadow and pattern to please the eye. Upwards again the decorative elements intensify, more friezes, balustrades, orbs and urns, a polygonal plinth and a gilded octagonal lantern. The lantern is Greek Revival, as introduced at West Wycombe and Shugborough, but here combining elements from both the Tower of the Winds and the Choragic Monument of Lysicrates. The tower may be termed Neoclassical but it is a unique blend – it is amazing that the balance works, since the story goes that as it was built Beckford still cried 'higher, higher'.

Inside the tower a stone spiral staircase with elegant banisters mounts up to the belvedere, where the view stretches on all sides framed by those arched windows (and in Beckford's time heavy golden curtains). The tower was also there to be viewed, and Beckford in deprecating mode once called it 'a famous landmark for drunken farmers on the way home from market'. At night, if the lights were on in the belvedere, shining dimly through the recessed windows, then the tower did appear gothic. At the base of the tower is a two-storey block resembling an Italian villa, with a loggia and a balustraded roofline adorned with a small triumphal arch. It was built to house more of Beckford's collections, with plush drawing rooms coloured red and purple, lined with mirrors, paintings and ornate display cabinets. A long narrow room called the oratory was completely devoted to religious paintings, part of his lifelong fascination with a religion he could not believe, or, as he explained, 'one must become half-Catholic to enter fully into the glories of Italian art.' Like Horace Walpole, Beckford was an avid collector, especially adept at buying bargains discarded as the French aristocracy was liquidated, and his Tower, like Vathek's, had 'immense treasures lavished upon it'.[25] After Beckford's death the collections were dispersed and the area around the Tower became a beer garden, which Beckford would not have liked, but then it was converted into a graveyard, where he himself was brought back to rest in a raised sarcophagus of pink granite. As the elaborate Victorian monuments to the dead accrued among the trees, and the bats took up residence, the Tower was finally endowed with enough of the macabre to ensure its gothic spirit.

The word 'gothic', despite its eighteenth-century links with Whig enlightenment, English patriotism and the literary output of Walpole and Beckford, despite its supremely lovely architecture, could still also be taken to mean wild, barbarous and crude. In this it overlapped with ideas of the 'Picturesque', a word possibly first used by Pope in 1712, which signified a landscape that resembled a fine picture, but in accordance with contemporary taste it too became associated with wildness and ruins. There was also the paradoxical concept of the sublime being beauty mixed with terror. In 1834 an admiring review of Beckford's published travel writings declared: 'His rapture amidst the sublime scenery of mountains and forests . . . is that of a spirit cast originally in one of nature's finest moulds . . . he fixes it in a language simple, massive, nervous . . . the perfection of art.'[26] Architecturally Beckford's Tower also belonged within this concept of the picturesque, since it combined various styles in harmony, just as the disparate elements of a natural landscape are part of its appeal. The derivation of the word 'picturesque' is important because in Italian *pittoresco* meant an approach to composition that was asymmetrical and bold, in order to stimulate the imagination. Similarly the word 'romantic', originating from tales of chivalric adventure in romance languages, meant arousing the imagination through allusions to the heroic past. On the other hand, the word 'horrid' has shifted much further from its scenic hinterland, since the Italian *orrido* simply meant a ravine.[27]

Owning a wild river valley was a gift to anyone wishing to create a picturesque landscape garden, and William Aislabie, who inherited Studley Royal from his father in 1742, owned one at Hackfall, 7 miles away, where steep wooded hillsides tumbled down to a narrow valley around the river Ure. It had been bought in 1731 for timber and stone quarrying, but William Aislabie saw its picturesque potential. Its many subsequent visitors spoke rapturously of trees, cascades and views and – in acres of prose – used the prerequisite labels: 'Hackfall is romantic beyond description, it has every beauty nature could bestow'; 'a great and commanding situation adorned with rocks and woods . . . sublimity is the reigning idea'.[28] The youthful William Beckford, touring Yorkshire in 1779, in romantic distress after starting his affair with Kitty Courtenay, described 'A deep rocky valley rapt up in groves and thickets. The solitary air and unexpected wildness of the prospect inspired a sentimental serenity and freedom.' He lay on a bed of moss watching dappled sunlight through the trees and 'cliffs with ruins on their craggy summits and a river rolling beneath precipices on every side'.

The Rev. Richard Warner picked up on the importance of sound in the making of a picturesque landscape – 'a limpid brook feasting the air with its agreeable murmur as it rolls over its pebbly bed' – and he emphasized how completely fashion had moved towards naturalism: 'it instantly flashed upon my mind the superiority of these wild and artless features over elaborate and formal decoration.' Nevertheless there was plenty of artful manipulation at Hackfall, most notably in the follies which created focal points among the trees. Turner needed these when he painted Hackfall in 1816 and included Fisher's Hall in the middle distance and Mowbray Castle high above the rim of the gorge.[29] The romance of Hackfall was much enhanced by hints at its history. The Mowbrays were Norman knights, crusaders and sometimes rebels and their name resonated for centuries not only in Yorkshire. In 1626 Chief Justice Sir Randolf Crewe, in a lawsuit about the Earldom of Oxford, made a speech that was still quoted in the twentieth century: 'For where is Bohun? Where is Mowbray? Where is Mortimer? Nay which is more and most of all, where is Plantagenet? They are entombed in the urns and sepulchres of mortality.' The ruin called Mowbray Castle stands on land they once held, masquerading as a genuine remnant, a battlemented tower with arched doorways and many arrow slits, built of rugged sandstone so that its different facades and details catch sunlight, moonlight and shadow to best advantage. It was always a hollow shell, used only as an eye-catcher and a destination for walks and rides, its importance resting in its commanding position and its name.

Robert Adam, 'Design for a Capriccio of a Roman Ruin', c. 1757,
which inspired The Ruin at Hackfall, Yorkshire, built c. 1765.

The other ruin at Hackfall is generally called 'The Ruin', but was also known as the Banqueting House since it functioned for entertainment, and other times it was confusingly called Mowbray Point, after the spot where it was built overlooking the gorge.[30] The facade seen by visitors approaching from the track across the fields is classical but not remarkable, nor is the view. It merely provides an entrance and the surprise is yet to come, hidden on the other side, where suddenly the gorge of Hackfall plunges down, and beyond it the Vale of Mowbray stretches towards York for mile upon mile. It was a view that Gilpin praised unreservedly, and to the right Mowbray Castle could be seen on another promontory above the trees of the valley. This ruin is in Roman style, its roof consisting of rough-hewn rounded arches that are both arresting and incongruous. The largest arch is in the centre with smaller ones either side, each rising above an arched and recessed wall containing a doorway into three separate small rooms. It is unique and the design has been traced to a drawing by Robert Adam labelled 'Design for a Capriccio of a Roman Ruin', painted either during his visit to Rome in 1755–7 or just after.[31] The three arches owe most to the Baths of Diocletian, and the 'Design for a Capriccio . . .' was found in a folio created for Kedleston, where Adam started work in 1758, and for which he did devise follies that were never built. But there is a degree of mystery surrounding its realization in Hackfall a few years later. While in Rome, Adam had written home in 1756 about the imprudence of publishing his architectural designs until 'I should have the fortune to execute a dozen temples . . . then is the time to publish, dedicating each plate to the proprietor of the different plates.' However, despite his wariness of plagiarism, Adam is known to have carried a portfolio of drawings such as this to show prospective clients. Adam's first visit to Studley was in 1758, and he was next in Yorkshire at Newby Hall in 1766; on either of these occasions William Aislabie might have seen this unusual drawing. There is some evidence in Aislabie's accounts, which show increased costs for Hackfall between 1765 and 1766 (later than the other follies, which were built in the 1750s). The expenditure related to levelling, plastering, roofing and locksmiths, which suggests that The Ruin was built then. But was Adam involved, or had Aislabie, like the proverbial canny Yorkshireman, committed the design to mind? The latter scenario would be in line with the other follies at Hackfall, which were constructed according to patterns devised or copied by Aislabie and his stonemasons. Either way all turned out well, since Robert Adam worked on Aislabie's London house in the 1770s and had little need to feel cheated. By then Hackfall was receiving high praise, and The Ruin itself was included among the elite follies depicted in Catherine the Great's Frog dinner service, created for her by Wedgwood in 1773–4.

By comparison, the follies below The Ruin in the valley of Hackfall were disappointing. Gilpin especially found them trivial and superfluous, and they have not stood the test of time. A temple and a grotto are now reduced to heaps of stones, but Fisher's Hall, which was the first folly to be built, in 1750, still has the air of a gothic hermitage. It is octagonal, now missing its thatched roof, but still with its pointed doorway and lancet windows. Dorothy Richardson called it 'The Hermitage, Fisher's Hall, built entirely of petrification [tufa] on the side of one of the hills in the centre of three valleys', and Beckford found it 'a venerable cell mantled with ivy, probably the abode of an anchorite . . . I suppose he shunned me and sought the depths of the thickets.' Fisher was the name of Aislabie's chief gardener at Studley Royal, who died in 1743, so, unless he was regarded as a friendly ghost, his presence in a hermitage dedicated to him would have been, as Beckford found, elusive. Or possibly the name included a reference to fishing, which would have been an ideal pastime among the streams that flowed through the valley.

In Shropshire there was another fortunate owner of a picturesque ravine ripe for development. Isaac Hawkins Browne, who inherited wealth derived from coalfields, and later became owner of the largest ironworks in Shropshire, went on the Grand Tour from 1775 until 1776, which confirmed his antiquarian tastes. Between 1784 and 1812 he was MP for Bridgnorth, earnestly representing the industrial interests of the region. This worthy and hardworking man lived at Badger Hall, and in 1779 he called in James Wyatt, who was then a youthful architectural prodigy and not yet the dilatory and eclectic prima donna who maddened his patrons with delays. From 1779 to 1783 Wyatt was busy with Badger Hall itself, and probably the lovely little folly overlooking the ravine was designed towards the end of this time.[32] Meanwhile William Emes, who had been head gardener at Kedleston Hall from the 1750s (and knew both Wyatt and Robert Adam), set to work on perfecting the landscape of the nearby Badger Dingle, where the Snowden Brook (a tributary of the Worfe) flowed between steep wooded banks. Later Isaac Hawkins Browne bought up more land to extend his pathways around both sides of the dingle, and the Snowden Brook was dammed to form three long and very picturesque pools.

High above this landscape and set into the precipitous hillside, Wyatt built a temple in Greek Revival style, using the local red sandstone in picturesque contrast against the massed green of the trees. It is entered at the back through the basement, above which is an elegant room. This opens onto a curved viewing platform supporting a semicircular balcony, which looks steeply down over the Upper Pool. As at Hackfall Ruin the view comes as a surprise, the trees enclose the ravine on either side and the birds sing and fly at eye level. This is probably why the temple came to be known as the Bird House – which is the name appearing on the estate map of 1837 – or perhaps it was especially due to the occasional jewelled flash of a kingfisher, skimming over the water far below. The all-important semicircular platform supports a colonnade of four slender Doric columns topped by a shallow domed roof. On either side the walls are rectangular, but with shallow arched niches moulded into them. Wyatt's design seems simple, but perfectly apt, containing the grace he displayed in his other classical follies, including the Panorama Tower at Croome Park. However, only here did Wyatt match classical harmony with a scene that exemplified the picturesque mode.

Shropshire boasted another and more public example of the picturesque folly garden at Hawkstone Park, where development began circa 1750 and was continued by successive members of the Hill family into Victorian times.[33] The craggy landscape was ideal for sublime experiences, provided the visitor avoided a fatal fall and did not find his poetic solitude marred by too many other sightseers. The summits and ledges were adorned with a series of follies and tunnels, steps, bridges and handrails. In 1784 William Emes was called in to create a lake in the surrounding park. By 1800 the Hawkstone Inn was welcoming many tourists to this fashionable spot, and they could also find refreshment at the Gingerbread House along the arduous way.

This proto-theme park is now restored, and contains one or two iconic follies, of which one may not be a folly at all, but the ruin of a medieval border castle, built in the thirteenth century and named the Red Castle because of its sandstone colour. If genuine, it rose out of the solid rock to watch the Welsh Marches, although it is not an ideal defensive position. Another is the Gothic Arch, the rudiments of a sham ruin, but so high up on the cliff edge that it is bound to be impressive. Below are the grotto tunnels, still long, but now denuded of the stained glass and geological encrustations that would have enhanced their appeal. There is also an insignificant tower whose main folly characteristic is its name, the White Tower, although it too is red sandstone; here an obelisk turns out to be the column for a statue, with a spiral stair-case for anyone who has not climbed enough or seen sufficient views. The Hermitage is a small stone hovel with a thatched roof where a real hermit may first have been employed (and talking of employment, a good deal was provided locally to carve out Hawkstone and its follies, making it another in the category of unemployment relief). Later a waxwork hermit was sub-stituted, with rolling eyes and a movable mouth, through whom the guide would address his group having nipped inside the Hermitage and assumed a different voice. In 1851 the hermit also made a surprise appearance at Lord Hill's birthday party, confirming his importance as a family joke. By then Hawkstone had a Windmill, a Chinese Pavilion and an Egyptian Tent, a Swiss Scene, an Indian Rock and displays of ethnographia. It had come a long way since Dr Johnson's visit with Mrs Thrale in 1774, when the spirit of the place had caught him full on: 'The ideas which it forces upon the mind are the sublime, the dreadful and the vast. Above is inaccessible altitude, below is horrible profundity' (he was of course demonstrating the correct use of the words 'dreadful' and 'horrible').

There was a triumvirate of writers who brought concepts of the pictur-esque to the forefront of the late eighteenth-century mind. Best known and loved was William Gilpin (1724–1804), a schoolmaster, cleric, author and artist, who by the time he became famous had settled down as vicar of Boldre in the New Forest. One of his early publications, in 1748, was *A Dialogue upon Stowe*, for which he created two fictional characters, Callophilus (who appreciated harmony and symmetry and quoted the classics in relation to every statue and folly) and Polypthon (who found this artificial, and related everything to natural scenery, music and gastronomy, referring to follies as 'very beautiful little garnished dishes'). Both disliked formal gardens and political follies, both considered a ruin at the head of a lake added greatly to its beauty. They then puzzled together how a neglected building could be more beautiful than an industrial one, having to admit that 'in a moral view the industrious mechanic is a more pleasing object than the loitering peasant, but in a picturesque light it is otherwise.' During the 1760s and '70s Gilpin spent his summer holidays visiting the remote and rugged parts of Britain, notably the Wye Valley, Wales, the Lake District and Scotland. In the 1780s he began publishing his *Tours* with his own illustrations of beauty spots, rendered as lovely gloomy mezzotints. With travel in Europe restricted after the French Revolution, and with the improvement of road communications at home, domestic travel for pleasure (and for sketching scenery) became increasingly fashionable, as Jane Austen's characters regularly testified, most memorably in *Pride and Prejudice*.[34]

Two Herefordshire landowners, Uvedale Price and Richard Payne Knight, augmented the writing and campaigning of Gilpin with their own. Both had densely wooded estates; the former had a tower and the latter had tunnels leading to a ruined 'Roman' bath; all three joined forces to criticize Capability Brown's methods of taming the landscape. Even Humphry Repton was a friend, until 1794, when they turned the controversy on each other. Price wrote *An Essay on the Picturesque*, Knight wrote a verse treatise called *The Landscape*, while Repton, hurt by their personal attacks, defended the need for practical considerations. Debate raged for several years, adding greatly to the general interest; small wonder that they became subjects for satire. It was Gilpin who lent himself best to caricature, emerging in 1812 as Dr Syntax, a spindly white-haired figure in clerical black, mounted on a lean mare called Grizzle and encountering every possible ludicrous adventure in search of the picturesque. The author was William Combe, who followed his success with sequels, while the illustrations by Thomas Rowlandson ensured that the series was much reproduced in prints and on pottery. The best scenes included Dr Syntax chased by a bull; Dr Syntax losing his way across a lonely moor by a misdirected signpost; and Dr Syntax falling in a lake trying to get the best angle on a tumbledown castle.

While this was going on, Thomas Love Peacock wrote *Headlong Hall* (1816), the first in a series of satirical novels, based on disparate characters assembled for a house party, eating, drinking and discussing topical matters. Headlong Hall is in the picturesque wilds of Snowdonia; Marmaduke

Thomas Rowlandson, *Dr Syntax Drawing a Castle and Falling in the Water*,
c. 1812, a popular skit on Gilpin's well-known devotion to the picturesque.

Milestone arrives to improve the grounds and, faced with the rocks of
Llanberis, he suggests the capabilities for improvement thus: 'Blow up the
rocks, cut down the trees, the wilderness and all its goats shall vanish like
mist.' After much debate over the picturesque, with the ladies eulogizing
the sounds of the wind in the pines and the melody of miniature cascades,
in Chapter Eight Squire Headlong, on the advice of Mr Milestone, sets out
to blow up the rocks near his tower, prior to covering everything with turf.
Since the Squire thinks 'with many others that a copious supply of provi-
sions is a very necessary ingredient of all rural amusements', he takes half a
dozen servants and labourers with pickaxes, gunpowder and a poker, together
with a basket of cold meat and several bottles of Madeira. At the moment
when Mr Milestone ignites the gunpowder, Mr Cranium and Mr Panscope,
two ardent advocates of the picturesque, appear at the top of the tower with
their telescopes, 'having ascended unseeing and unseen on the opposite side'.

Great European gardens often included areas of 'wilderness' around the
formal gardens – Versailles had its *bosquets* – but few adopted the romantic
possibilities of letting a rugged landscape dictate the layout. The excep-
tion was Sanspareil, which was developed by the Margravine Wilhelmina
of Bayreuth, sister of Frederick the Great, to whom she wrote that 'Nature
herself was the architect.' Brother and sister were both redeveloping old
hunting grounds, and the creation of Sanspareil was contemporary with
Ruinenberg at Sanssouci, in the mid-eighteenth century. Sanspareil was

blessed with amazing clefts and overhangs among the Jurassic boulders, the entrance lay through two towering rocks which had clashed together overhead, rough steps were carved through gullies and natural grottos were given classical names. The weathering, moss and lichen that beautified the rock faces were left undisturbed and the beech trees grew over and among them, the route being dictated and designated by their presence. But Sanspareil also led its visitors through a world of associations – the Grotto of Calypso, Vulcan's Cave, the Temple of Aeolus, Pan's Seat, Sibyl's Grotto – all of which referred to the journey of Telemachus in search of his father, Ulysses. In 1699 and 1717 François Fenelon, Archbishop of Cambrai and tutor to Louis xiv's grandson, published *The Adventures of Telemachus*, an influential book of the Enlightenment. In it Fenelon denounced luxury, war and autocracy, and also the exploitive elements of capitalism, although he remained in favour of a benevolent hierarchy lording it over a primarily agrarian society.[35] Inspired by Fenelon, Sanspareil did not leave the picturesque sensations aroused by its rock formations to the imagination, but loaded them with classical allusion and Enlightenment theories. There were follies, belvederes, hermitages, broken columns and a temple of classical proportions rusticated with tufa called Morgenlandischer Bau (Building of the Morning Lands); but finest of all was the Ruined Theatre, another proof that this primitive landscape was regarded as primarily cultural. The auditorium of the theatre lay inside a natural grotto while the orchestra pit, the backdrop arches and the back wall were constructed from quarry stones, assembled in all their roughness, so that the spectator in the grotto viewed the action through a series of receding arches in an apparently ruinous state. It was a powerful reminder that grottos, drama, music and dance were originally used to summon the gods. 'Behind this miraculous arch you can see the theatre emerging from rocks and embellished and corrected by the hand of art, the whole makes a powerful and indescribable impression.'[36] Although its itinerary was classical, Sanspareil proved to be an early manifestation of the Romantic movement in Europe, and led the way for an upsurge in ruined castles like those at Machern and Wilhelmsbad, followed at the turn of the nineteenth century by the paintings of Caspar David Friedrich, setting dark and ruinous churches in cold and misty landscapes, into which a skeletal knight might ride, as if gothic itself were returning to its heartlands.

Dinton Castle, Buckinghamshire, 1769, a little mock castle built to house
a fossil collection and with large ammonites embedded in the walls.

Nine

Hermitages and Tree Houses

Hermitages have a venerable history, traceable to angry Old Testament prophets and the early saints like Jerome and Anthony who retired into the wilderness to expiate their sins and temptations. Every eighteenth-century art connoisseur would have seen paintings of St Jerome with his lion, St Anthony with his pig or St Francis receiving the stigmata, nearly always outside a cave-like dwelling. Closer to home there was the Warkworth hermit of Northumberland, a story based on a cave hewn from the sandstone cliff, with dwelling chambers and gothic vaulting over a chantry chapel, dating from the late fourteenth century, which is accessible only across a river. Since this was on land owned by the Percy family, earls of Northumberland, the Warkworth Hermitage did not sink into obscurity. In Tudor times, according to estate records, the 'hermit' was a land agent for the earl, granted pasturage for cattle and his horse, plus fishing rights and an allowance of firewood (was he perhaps a priest in disguise?). At some point the Hermitage was built up with steps and a stone facade, so that it might qualify as a rustic folly with a vista back to Warkworth Castle. Finally, in 1771, when hermitages had become the height of fashion, a ballad appeared relating back to Hotspur, the most romantic member of the Percy family. Sir Bertram, who had been Hotspur's ally against the Scots, had become the Hermit of Warkworth in expiation of a romance and a murder, and in the course of a long and entirely fictitious ballad he recited these lines, which sum up the eighteenth-century view of a hermit's purpose in life:

No more the slave of human pride,
Vain hope and sordid care;
I meekly vowed to spend my life
In penitence and prayer . . .

Oft the great Earl from toils of state,
And cumbrous pomp and power,

Would gladly seek my little cell
To spend the tranquil hour.[1]

There was, of course, the dramatic possibility that the hermit was an escaped criminal or an evil magician, an option which Edmund Spenser explored in *The Faerie Queene*, where Archimago lured the Red Cross Knight and Lady Una into his cell for no friendly purpose. More often during the seventeenth century the hermit was a Royalist retreating from the Civil War or its outcome. This would surely have been in the forefront of Milton's mind when he wrote 'Il Penseroso' in the 1640s. His hermit sounds more like a Cavalier than a Roundhead; despite Milton's own loyalty to Cromwell, his vision is a very traditional and romantic one of studious cloisters, antique pillars, stained-glass windows, twilight groves of pine and oak and the murmuring waters of a brook. At much the same time John Evelyn in *Elysium Britannicum* (composed mainly in the 1650s) was describing a hermit's grotto:

> We once observed a dry grott, artificially made with the extravagant and vast roots of trees, fastened with wires and ironwork and so covered with ivy that we never beheld a more delightful spectacle . . . most fit for retirement and profound contemplation, for so the hermits lived in times of persecution.[2]

A real-life exponent of this lifestyle was Thomas Bushell, who in 1621 was charged with corruption in government office and retired to a cabin on the Calf of Man 'to make a perfect experiment upon myself for the obtaining of a long and healthy life' (as well as for repentance) 'by a parsimonious diet of herbs, oil, mustard and honey with water sufficient . . . which I most strictly observed as if obliged by a religious vow'. This was only the start. On returning to worldly life at Enstone in Oxfordshire he created a retreat in a hillside cave above a stream. According to John Aubrey's description in *Brief Lives*, the cave had stalactites 'pendant like icicles as at Wokey Hole, which was the occasion of making that delicate grotto and those fine walks'. Aubrey also claimed that Bushell could make an artificial rainbow across the grotto by turning a cock, 'and in a small pool he had a statue of Neptune aiming his trident at a duck, which perpetually turned round with him'.[3] Charles I and his queen both visited him there in the 1630s, but when the Civil War broke out Bushell fled to Lundy Island in the Bristol Channel, which he defended for the Royalist cause. Around 1648 he returned secretly and lived

William Richardson, *The Dinton Hermit*, 1787, a shabby but imposing figure representing the mysterious regicide reputed to haunt Dinton Castle.

in Lambeth Marshes, 'being obnoxious to Parliament'. Here he adorned his long gallery with black drapes painted with skeletons and morbid mottos, such as Aubrey reckoned had previously adorned his Oxfordshire hermitage. By 1650 his skills as a mining engineer earned his pardon, and he lived on into healthy old age, dying £120,000 in debt – financial embarrassment being another possible motive for taking up a hermit's way of life.

The Parliamentarian side in the Civil War had an even more exciting hermit, who it was said haunted Dinton Castle in Buckinghamshire (which has recently been 'restored' as a dwelling). Dinton Castle was an exquisite little ruinous folly, an octagonal miniature castle built in the grounds of Dinton Hall by Sir John Vanhatten in 1769 in order to house his fossil collection, and also embedding several giant ammonites in the rugged walls of the castle. There are two circular towers in the east and west walls, one for the chimney, the other for a winding stair to the upper floor. The Dinton Hermit, who may have haunted the folly, existed a century earlier and lived in a cave on the estate. He was depicted in 1688 with a long white beard, dressed in a patched leather cloak with a curious horned hood, holding a round leather bottle in his hand and with two more hanging from his belt. His shoes are preserved, one at Dinton Hall, the other in the Ashmolean Museum in Oxford, made of many leather patches nailed over one another, covering the original worn-out shoe. His name was John Bigg, and he died in 1696. He was clerk to Simon Mayne, who was a magistrate, MP for Aylesbury, friend of Oliver Cromwell, a judge at the trial of Charles I and the fortieth signatory of the king's death warrant. At the Restoration Simon Mayne was imprisoned in the Tower as a regicide, dying there in 1661, after which he was brought back to be buried at Dinton Church. But the ghost of Dinton Castle is not Simon Mayne, it is the ghost of his clerk John Bigg, who seems to have been the ultimate regicide, because he was reputedly the secret masked and hooded executioner of Charles I. Whether he became the Hermit of Dinton to escape retribution or from remorse cannot be known.[4]

During the eighteenth century, caves continued to be possible dwellings for hermits. At The Leasowes, the first of William Shenstone's several hermitages, built in 1740 at the outset of his building programme, was like an excavated cave, just below a gothic alcove known as the Hermit's Seat. At Carden Park in Cheshire a large cave was occupied by the hermit John Harris for over twenty years from the 1740s, after which he moved on to other caves and allegedly lived to be over a hundred. In Worcestershire there were caves at Blackstone Rock opposite Ribbesford, Redstone Rock near Stourport and Radstone's Ferry at Astley, all with tunnels, cells or chapels and all near water, which offered views conducive to meditation, and alternatively provided hiding places with a means of hasty escape by boat. At Downton Castle in Herefordshire Richard Payne Knight, leader of the Picturesque movement, had a hermit's cave approached by a scary tunnel leading along the cliffside which overhung the river, and ending in the ruins of a 'Roman' bath. Since Payne Knight was the author of a treatise on Priapus, which brought him more notoriety than his views on landscape, he might be linked with other possible uses for a hermitage. Also suggestive was a rhyme inscribed in the hermitage at Hagley, written by a minor poet called Joseph Giles, from the circle of William Shenstone:

May I while health and strength remains
And blood flows warm within my veins
Find out some virgin soft and kind
Who is to social joy inclined.[5]

Dr Johnson weighed in with *Rasselas, the Adventures of an Abyssinian Prince*, who travels with his friends in search of the meaning of life. The Hermit of Egypt, whom they encounter 'in a cavern in the side of a mountain overshadowed with palm trees', says he has lived fifteen years in solitude and has no desire that his example should gain imitators. He is fed up with studying plants, his fancy 'riots in scenes of folly' and he assures them, 'the life of a solitary man will certainly be miserable but not certainly devout.' He ends up accompanying them back to the city which, as he approaches, 'he gaze[s] at with rapture'. Erotic possibilities have also been attached to Stancombe Park in the Cotswolds, where nineteenth-century tunnels were excavated beside the lake, at the furthest point from the house. The tunnels fork between archways and Egyptian portals and are said to have been the rendezvous of the vicar of Nibley and a Gypsy.

For the eighteenth century the idea of a hermit contemplating in his cave was brought up to date by Alexander Pope in his grotto beside the Thames. William Kent drew him several times, seated there at his desk, with a gentle touch of wizardry emanating from his glitter ball and the geological encrustations on the walls. Everyone knew Pope was a great scholar, poet and social commentator, but at the same time ill health and Catholicism kept him somewhat retired from the world as 'The Hermit of Twickenham'. Since he was a good friend of both William Kent and Lord Cobham he must have participated in the schemes to build the first hermitages that were also eighteenth-century architectural follies, at Stowe and Kew; since they are very similar it is academic to worry about which came first.

At Stowe the Hermitage was built in 1731, at the same time and in the same area of the grounds as the Temple of Venus (away towards the boundary beyond the lake). They mark the beginning of Kent's involvement at Stowe and are built of the same tawny limestone along Palladian lines, with a central pediment. But the Hermitage is a tiny building, the stones are heavily rusticated, and of the two little corner turrets one is a bell tower and the other is deliberately ruinous (one of the earliest examples of designing a ruin). On the pediment is a carving of Pan's pipes surrounded by a wreath, combining the classical and bucolic moods, while the heavy evergreens planted

William Kent, *Alexander Pope in His Grotto*, a lively sketch of uncertain date between 1720 and 1740, showing Pope as 'the hermit of Twickenham'.

behind the hermitage lent it the necessary air of melancholy. Here too there were links with Edmund Spenser's *Faerie Queene* because, when Kent published his illustrated version, the Stowe Hermitage appeared as the villainous Archimago's cell. In the Temple of Venus, other episodes from Spenser were originally painted on the walls, telling of the aged Malbeco's marriage to the youthful Hellinore, in the course of which she took her pleasures elsewhere – including all across the walls of the Temple of Venus. In disgust Malbeco became a hermit. Since Lord Cobham married a worthy heiress of his own age the parallels are not obvious, but if he retreated to the Temple of Venus for titillation, he may well have sought out the Hermitage when in contemplative mood. From inside, the view across the ripples of the lake is very conducive to 'a green thought in a green shade', and possibly this was Pope's favourite spot when he came to visit Stowe and composed the lines which begin: 'Consult the genius of the place in all . . .'[6]

The Hermitage that Kent built for Queen Caroline in the royal garden at Richmond/Kew in 1731 was larger than Stowe. The central part with its arched entrance, pediment and bell tower was the same design, but there was an extra bay either side and two more arched entrances under an overall roof that rose up behind the pediment. The whole building backed onto a hillock covered in rocks and conifers, which gave it the required ruinous and cavernous look, 'Very gothic, being a heap of stones thrown into very artful disorder and curiously embellished with moss and shrubs to represent rude nature'.[7] In choosing a garden folly in a style recognized as gothic, Queen Caroline was cleverly linking her own Germanic origins with a fashion soon to be seen as authentically English rather than European – like the Hanoverian dynasty. Inside she emphasized the message, filling the Hermitage with busts of Isaac Newton, Robert Boyle and John Locke along with other English thinkers, presumably standing in for hermits. They were much visited and there was so much flattery in the press that Pope grew mocking: 'Every man and boy is writing verses on the Royal Hermitage.' Some verses were less than admiring:

> And here is built a clumsy heap,
> Thought beautiful in ruin,
> Three holes there are through which you peep,
> Three seats to set your arse on.

In 1735 Queen Caroline and William Kent followed up their success with Merlin's Cave, not a cave except by allusion to past hermits, but a thatched, rustic, gothic extravaganza dedicated to ancient Britain's favourite wizard. There was a central pavilion and two octagonal wings, all three with conical thatched roofs startlingly like a row of beehives. The entrance was a large arch flanked by buttresses; inside large wooden pillars supported the ceiling and the side walls were lined with gothic bookcases. The central apse had pointed niches containing six life-size waxwork figures – Merlin sat at his desk opposite his secretary with a globe and other mathematical and magical instruments. The other figures were female and there is no clear account of their identity, which also puzzled contemporaries, although another link with Edmund Spenser was probable. There was a figure in a ruff like Queen Elizabeth I, Spenser's *Faerie Queene* herself, and a lady in armour who was most likely Britomart, Spenser's warrior princess and legendary ancestress of the British race, while the others seem to be their attendants. Since Spenser's verse is meandering and obscure, but known to be admirable and patriotic, his characters tended to be plucked out to give allegorical support to eighteenth-century causes, including the Hanoverian dynasty, Whig politics and the Kit-Cat Club. *Fog's Weekly Journal* in December 1735 surmised astutely that the figures were 'Emblematical, Typical and Symbolical conveying lessons of Policy to Princes and Ministers of State'. But along with the confusion came ridicule: Horace Walpole was typical in calling it an unintelligible puppet show, and when Queen Caroline asked George II to do something about these insults he replied, 'I am very glad of it . . . you deserve to be abused for such silly childish stuff.' Both Caroline's hermitages were swept away when Capability Brown relandscaped Kew Gardens circa 1770, provoking the lines 'untutored Brown . . . Has rudely rushed and levelled Merlin's Cave,/ Knocked down the waxen wizard, seized his wand/ Transformed to lawn what late was fairy-land.'[8]

In 1742 Royston Cave in Hertfordshire was discovered to contain quasi-religious carvings which have baffled interpretation, but among the leading theorists was William Stukeley, an antiquarian, member of the Royal Society and Society of Antiquaries, Trustee of the British Museum and Foundling Hospital, and a Freemason. He was a man of authority and winning charm, although his historical theories and wild surmises did arouse scepticism – his lasting legacy was his enthusiasm for Stonehenge and the Avebury Stone Rings, which he associated with Celtic druids. Stukeley reckoned Royston Cave was the hermitage of Lady Rohese de Vere, a powerful twelfth-century aristocrat who ended her days at Chicksands Priory in Bedfordshire, which she founded. At the time of the discovery Stukeley had his own hermitage in his garden at Stamford, where he retired from London life and became vicar of All Saints in 1729 (returning to London in 1747). During his time in Lincolnshire he founded a local society called the Brazen Nose, which discussed a range of topics from astronomy to wasps' nests and medieval seals. Stukeley's hermitage was built of rough stone, assembled haphazardly to resemble the traditional cave, but incorporating a gothic window rescued from a medieval church and an arch crowned with a Masonic symbol. Surrounding it were a grove of trees, a spring and a herb garden. Inside was a portrait of Sir Isaac Newton, who was a friend, and who also had a tendency to esoteric ideas despite his scientific genius. Stukeley built his hermitage by 1738, putting him among the first as well as the most profoundly eccentric of the eighteenth-century intellectuals who posed as hermits, joining Pope, Shenstone and Thomas Wright.

Shenstone started creating The Leasowes in the 1740s and, although it was primarily a *ferme ornée*, it had so many attributes of a scholarly retreat that it called to mind a hermit's life. First came the original hermit's cave and seat, later there were root houses and meditative inscriptions, then Shenstone painted himself in monkish garb by the Ruined Priory, looking every inch the hermit. To confirm the matter, in 1779 Richard Graves modelled his novel *Columella; or, The Distressed Anchorite* on Shenstone.[9] Graves was vicar of Claverton near Bath and a satirical writer who had been a friend of Shenstone since their Oxford days. His Columella dismissed an applicant to the post of hermit because he was himself a hermit and lived in his own wood addicted to his melancholy. The portrait was exaggerated and posthumous – indeed, it was belied by the fact that Shenstone was a gentleman farmer, a poet and very sociable – but Graves believed passionately that if a person,

William Shenstone, *The Ruined Priory at The Leasowes*, c. 1745, possibly representing Shenstone himself as a hermit-like figure in his garden.

qualified by his education to follow a profession, failed to do so he was bound to be unhappy, and in their discussions and correspondence Graves had received confidences about Shenstone's solitary side which he later poured into *Columella*. In moments of exasperation Shenstone had written: 'their conversations give me no more pleasure than the canking of a goose,' or 'I had rather live entirely alone than be entertained with such idle company.' With the onset of winter Shenstone had described being delivered up to silence and reflection after the gaiety of summer, which Graves rendered bitter as Columella's words: 'I can support my solitude with tolerable cheerfulness in summertime and fine weather, but will you leave me for a whole winter to the horror of my own thoughts.' Graves also satirized the Picturesque movement, root houses and shaded walks; and to be fair he even mocked himself in *Columella*, as the Rector, 'a poor hectic miserable-looking creature' whose sermons lacked conviction. At least when it came to building follies Shenstone had an understanding neighbour in George Lyttelton at Hagley, where there was a Hermitage Wood which Horace Walpole visited in 1753 and declared, 'I wore out my eyes with gazing, my feet with climbing and my tongue with commending.'[10] It contained not only the Hermitage, enlivened with inscriptions from Milton and Joseph Giles, but also a root house and one or two *sedes contemplationis*, all made from tree trunks and roots with moss filling the cracks. Contemporary accounts emphasized how the quietude was full of birdsong, and it is certain that Shenstone and Lyttelton encouraged one another and often visited their respective hermits' groves.

The fashion spread through society, and one of the few hermitages still to be seen (in replica) was built by Matthew Boulton at Soho House in Birmingham. Boulton would have been quite beyond the touch of Richard Graves's satire on idle hermits: he was a prominent industrialist associated with everything from the design of James Watt's steam engines to buttons. Boulton was a vital member of the intellectual Lunar Society, to whose house the members came for discussions when the moon was full, and he was also a leading philanthropist who endowed the first allotments for the health of his factory workers. Boulton's hermitage was designed for him by James Wyatt circa 1790. It was circular with two gothic windows and rusticated with a facade of bark and a roof thatched with heather. Boulton called it his 'building adapted for contemplation'. It was hidden among the trees overlooking the lake, far from the house, much as Lord Cobham's hermitage had been sixty years earlier.[11]

Gilbert White was the most endearing of all the eighteenth-century characters who built themselves a hermitage. He lived as a humble curate at Selborne in Hampshire, avoiding the preferment that would have taken him away from his home and garden at the Wakes. Above all he was an outstanding naturalist who showed that true science is based not on having a theory to prove but on minute and honest observation. He had a self-deprecating sense of humour and a sophisticated circle of friends (Pope sent him a dedicated copy of his translation of the *Iliad*). John Mulso, later Canon of Winchester, wrote before a visit to Selborne in 1744: 'I look for Arcady with you, and I expect some kind whispers from the unseen genius of the woods.' These woods were the spectacular beech forests of Selborne Hanger, lying beyond the lawns and meadows of Gilbert White's own garden, up which he and his brothers created a steep zigzag path, embellished with obelisks and a series of retreats in which to sit. The first arbour was made in 1750 and John

S. H. Grimm, *The Hermitage at The Wakes, Selborne*, 1776,
showing Gilbert White's brother Harry dressed up to act as the Hermit.

Mulso teasingly called it *nidus acherontiae* (anchorite's nest), thus simultaneously alluding to White's observations of bird behaviour.[12] The Hermitage itself
was a circular straw-clad cell, mainly constructed by Gilbert's younger brother
Harry, and described in a letter as a 'grotesque building contrived by a young
gentleman who used to appear on occasion in the character of a hermit'. This
was an enduring entertainment enjoyed by family and guests. In the summer
of 1763 Miss Catherine Battie and her sisters were staying at the nearby vicarage
and she breathlessly recorded the parties in her diary. On 24 June,

> at 2 we ascended the zigzag up to that enchanting spot where we
> dined. After dinner we went to the tent. Here we sat till 6 when we
> went back to the Hermitage for tea. In the middle of tea we had a
> visit from the Old Hermit, his appearance made me start. After tea
> we went into the woods, returned to the Hermitage to see it by
> lamplight, it looked sweetly indeed.

A month later Gilbert White himself described a tea party at the Hermitage
which included John Mulso and family as well at the Misses Battie. Everyone
dressed as shepherds and shepherdesses, and entertained each other by singing, 'a most elegant evening . . . the Hermit appeared to great advantage.'
But when the parties of that magical summer had ended Gilbert and Harry

White were left in their bachelor state, and Gilbert dedicated to the ladies *A Winter Piece* (full of genuine melancholy, reflecting the feelings expressed by William Shenstone and exaggerated in *Columella*):

> Amidst this savage landscape bleak and bare
> Hangs the chill hermitage in middle air
> Its haunts forsaken, and its feasts forgot
> A leaf-strewn, lonely, desolated cot!
> Is this the scene that late with rapture rang
> Where Delphy danced and gentle Anna sang . . .

In 1776 the Selborne garden and its views were recorded in a series of watercolours by the fashionable artist Simon Hieronymous Grimm, who was commissioned by White's other brothers, Thomas, a Fellow of the Royal Society, and Benjamin, a publisher and bookseller, together with William Curtis, founder of the *Botanical Magazine*.[13] Grimm depicted Harry as the Hermit, dressed up in hood, cloak and garters, with a crook and crucifix, in front of the Hermitage, which looks much like a haystack with a large straw crucifix plaited on top. In the background is a rustic seat, in the foreground the zigzag path drops away and an extensive view spreads beyond the tops of the beech trees. Another of Grimm's views was done from the hillside of the Lythes, looking across at Selbourne church, the Wakes and the Hanger with its zigzag path and the hermitages – a second hermitage was built in 1776 just before Grimm painted the scene. Here the edge of the tent mentioned by Catherine Battie in 1763 can also be seen, blue and white with drapes reminiscent of Painshill, although it was probably a temporary structure put up for summer entertainments.

The idea of adding to the fun of a hermitage by dressing up in character was never more charmingly embodied than it was by Harry White, but it took various forms elsewhere. In the folly garden of Enville near Hagley, the hermitage was occupied by the keeper of the pheasants, who may have filled the role of hermit when called upon. At Kew, Queen Caroline hired a minor poet called Stephen Duck as librarian at Merlin's Cave, while his wife had care of the Hermitage. Much satire was directed at Duck's versifying and he may have been expected to enact the role of poetic hermit for visitors. In Ireland John Boyle, Earl of Orrery and Cork, friend of Pope and Swift and relative of Lord Burlington, built a hermitage on his estate at Caledon in Co. Tyrone in 1746: 'we have built at the expense of five pounds a root house or hermitage, to which on Sunday the country people resort.'[14] Mary Delany (who built her own root house, called the Beggar's Hut, at Delville) visited Caledon in 1748 and described a winding walk through trees to reach the hermit's cell. The inside was equipped with a table on which lay a manuscript, spectacles and a leather bottle. Disposed around the walls were an hourglass, several mathematical instruments, bookshelves and bowls for the hermit's food. Sometimes visitors had to imagine the recluse had recently gone out or hidden, but if they were lucky the hermit was Lord Orrery himself. At Stourhead, in 1771, when Henry Colt Hoare added a zigzag path and a rustic hermitage above the classical circuit, he joked about 'being myself the hermit'. His hermitage was lined inside and out with 'old gouty knobbly oaks with the bark on', and a drawing entitled 'Druid's Cell' shows that some at least had their roots turned upwards to look stranger still. The association with druids testified to Colt Hoare's antiquarian leanings, which he shared with William Stukeley and many others.

By mid-century there were a number of pattern books with rustic designs for hermitages, testifying to their increasing popularity and the amusement it gave to guests staying in country houses to mull over them. In 1742 Batty Langley led the way with *Gothic Architecture Improved*, then William Halfpenny (with his son John) produced innovative and popular patterns, with practical information for builders and advice to 'gentlemen draughtsmen' on how to design follies for themselves. His best-known publication, on Chinese taste, published in 1750, was followed in 1752 by *Rural Architecture in the Gothick Taste*, which included hermitages. In 1767 William Wrighte's *Grotesque Architecture; or, Rural Amusement* offered various hermitages: a root house; a cell complete with skull over the doorway; an Augustinian hermitage with a classical pediment supported on tree trunks and a library inside; a winter hermitage 'lined with wool or other warm substance mixed with moss'; and an oriental hermitage with a conical 'Chinese' thatched roof through which a living tree sprouted and spread its branches overhead.[15] (Little was then known of the venerable Chinese tradition of the scholar retreating from public life, in retirement or disgrace, to contemplate nature and philosophy in harmony together, while living in a humble abode, but it would have been much appreciated.)

The hermitage designs which have won the most acclaim were by Thomas Wright, who in 1755 published Book I of *Universal Architecture*, containing six designs for arbours or hermitages. This was towards the end of the period he spent at Badminton, from 1748 to 1756, under the patronage of the Duke of

The Hermitage at Badminton, c. 1750, created by Thomas Wright in the style made famous in his publications, and used by himself during his stay at Badminton 1748–56.

Beaufort, designing castellated farm buildings as well as his masterpiece, the Hermitage or Root House. It is a sturdy rectangle under a sweeping thatched roof. Knotty trunks form the corner posts and the roof pediments, the forked branches of a huge tree frame the entrance, and at the rear a similar inverted fork hangs over a rustic seat with inviting inscriptions. Between the timbers the walls are made up of a mass of branches, planks, roots and gnarled woody fragments, while inside the walls and ceiling are still lined with ancient moss. Each side wall has a curved bay with a gothic window, and the inside recesses are arched over with more hefty trunks. Ribs of wood run across the ceiling, and roundels set into the roof pediments are made from hollow trunks which may once have held stained glass. Everywhere is riddled with worm holes and the furniture is gone except for a hollow stump of elm which once supported a central table. Though the Hermitage still stands, the woodland that once surrounded it is reduced to a few ancient trees. It was a place of enchantment rather than a mere hermitage, and according to an inscription, 'Here Urganda in woods dark and perplexed inchantments mutters with her magic voice.' This referred to a play that was a popular part of the repertoire of the Haymarket Theatre, in which Urganda was a benign fertility spirit:

> Let sage Urganda wave the circling wand
> On barren mountains, or a waste of sand

The desert smiles, the woods begin to grow
The birds to warble and the springs to flow.[16]

On the other hand, an oral tradition suggests that Thomas Wright himself bore the character of hermit within the Beaufort household, either knowingly performing the part at times or as a family joke. While his scientific and mathematical attainments were appreciated, and professionally he acted as tutor to the children, there was magical entertainment in the Hermitage, where the floor had mathematical figures that seem to have represented Urganda's spells. Thomas Wright, in his dual role as tutor and hermit, was part of the inspiration for Tom Stoppard's play *Arcadia*, written in 1993, in which the tutor Septimus Hodge proves towards the end to have been the hermit at Sidley Park – a 'mathematical lunatic', tragically working for twenty years on the iterated equations and chaos theory that his pupil Thomasina was discovering before she died. The Regency setting at Sidley Park was a green Arcadia which the garden designer Mr Noakes was transforming into a picturesque 'eruption of gloomy forest and towering crags', complete with a hermitage. Lord Byron was an unseen visitor to Sidley Park, adding greatly to the complications facing the garden historians in the contemporary part of the play, who are trying to prove their rival theories about the identity of the hermit. They are armed with Mr Noakes's plan of the hermitage, on which Thomasina sketched her tutor with his tortoise. (Although historically speaking it was Gilbert White who had the tortoise.)

The elusive qualities of Tom Stoppard's hermit and Thomas Wright were well matched, especially when it came to Wright's time in Ireland. He was there during the 1740s, before he went to Badminton, and his main patron was James Hamilton, Lord Limerick, who later became Earl of Clanbrassil. His estate at Tollymore in Co. Down is near the Mountains of Mourne, and the Shimna River creates gorges, waterfalls and pools as it courses through the woods of Tollymore. Wright was certainly there, and the follies in this entirely picturesque setting follow his style, but the Hermitage has a plaque claiming it was erected in 1770 by the second earl in memory of his friend Lord Monthermer.[17] However, in an estate map of 1777 it is designated The Old Hermitage, so possibly the earl was reclaiming a building initiated by Thomas Wright. Approached either along steep footpaths or across bridges, or viewed from the water below, the hermitage seems to be watching from two hollow eyes – an effect produced by the twin archways in a simple rock-work cell with a conical dome. A short battlemented wall forms a bridge to

The Hermitage at Painshill. Built in 1752 as a distant retreat in the woods,
this was the first folly at Painshill, and may once have been occupied by a hermit.

a turret that is pierced by another, smaller arch. The whole edifice seems to
hang over the water, clothed in moss and ferns, and, although no tale of a
hermit attaches to it, the style and setting are the pinnacle of picturesque.

In the village of Berkeley in Gloucestershire, about 15 miles from
Badminton, a rustic hut named the Temple of Vaccinia stands in its original
wood. The fame of Thomas Wright (not to mention any hermit there may
once have been) is completely overshadowed by that of Edward Jenner. Not
that Jenner lived in this tiny place, but here he experimented with the first
vaccinations against smallpox. In 1796 he scraped the pus from the cowpox
blisters on the hands of a milkmaid, who had caught the relatively mild dis-
ease from a cow named Blossom. With this Jenner vaccinated the gardener's
son, rendering him, and then others, so vaccinated, immune to the far dead-
lier smallpox. (Earlier immunization with pus from smallpox blisters was
a far riskier matter.) Jenner continued to use this hut, tucked away in the
woods, to vaccinate the poor free of charge, and although it was more com-
monly known as Jenner's Hut he endowed it with the loftier title of Temple
of Vaccinia. It still stands as his memorial, built of brick and rubblestone
within a rustic frame of gnarled tree trunks and a dome of thatch. It is a little
reminiscent of the grander and more eccentric hermitage at Badminton.[18]

One of the best-known eighteenth-century hermitages was at Painshill.
It was the first folly that Charles Hamilton created, in 1752, in the furthest

and wildest part of the grounds, emulating Lord Cobham's sense that a retreat should be distant and encircled by heavy trees, and also heralding the Picturesque movement by placing the hermitage above a steep drop down to the river. Visitors testified to the surrounding gloom. In 1763 John Parnell wrote:

> You strike into a wood of different firs . . . and serpentising through
> it arrive at an hermitage formed to the front with trunks of fir trees,
> their branches making natural gothic windows, from it you command
> a pretty view of the country.[19]

And, as the taste for the picturesque intensified, so did the narrowness of the path and the overhanging gloom of the conifers. Gilpin certainly approved, and visited twice in 1765 and 1772. His sketch showed the hermitage from the conventional side appearing as a timber-framed octagon with gothic windows and a conical thatched roof topped with a belfry. On the other side it was far more unusual since it rested on a platform raised on gnarled and bending tree trunks – a tree house in fact. This is how Friedrich Ludwig von Sckell depicted it in the 1770s, rising as if from a prehistoric swamp of mortified trees, with a hermit in profile at the window.

Pitchford Tree House, Shropshire, first recorded in 1692, much altered since but still supported in the original lime tree, with much extra propping.

Tree houses were not entirely new, although they were rare and not previously regarded as hermitages. The oldest in existence is the Pitchford Tree House in Shropshire, mentioned for the first time in 1692, when it was built among the branches of a lime tree, and rendered to look like a little stone house. Pitchford Hall itself is a Tudor half-timbered building, and the Tree House has been altered to match its timbered appearance; it is therefore in mock-Tudor style rather than rustic/picturesque – though it has gothic ogee windows. The inside was decorated with plasterwork in the 1760s, with a radiant sun in the middle of the ceiling and blind gothic arches tied with bows around the cornice. In 1832 the young Princess Victoria visited and remarked on 'the little house in a tree', from which she watched a fox hunt. In the twentieth century the tree house finally acquired its hermit, Lady Sibyl Grant, who was allegedly afraid of ghosts when she stayed in Pitchford Hall, so she moved into the Tree House, where James Lees-Milne met her in 1944, a waddling figure in a long blue cloak and trailing an orange scarf. A drawing done in 1854 by W. Cowan shows the tree house at its best, tiny amid the spreading branches of the lime tree, with no mock-Tudor beams or artificial supports. Inevitably now the vast age of the lime tree (possibly nine hundred years) means that metal frames, struts and wires surround the

Robert Peake, *Princess Elizabeth*, 1603, showing the daughter of James I.
See the detail of an arbour trained as a tree house in the background.

tree and its folly. The Pitchford Tree House has been described by some as Jacobean, which would date it to the beginning rather than the end of the seventeenth century.[20]

At this time, both in England and Europe, it was fashionable to train arbours with 'carpentry work', as Francis Bacon called it, transforming shaded walkways into quasi-architectural features with green pillars supporting domes and topiary finials. The largest examples formed compartments with seats for *al fresco* dining, like little green banqueting houses. Such features can be seen in both Italian and Netherlandish paintings, and sometimes the branches of a tree would be trained into such an arbour, reached by stairs.[21] The original germ of this idea may be in Francesco Colonna's *Polyphilus' Dream*, where his imaginary journey took in an arbour of intertwining branches of fruit trees, so artfully twisted together that Polyphilus could ascend by them and not be seen. In the sixteenth-century Medici gardens of Castello and Pratolino there were *al fresco* banqueting houses raised on platforms set into oak trees and reached by spiral stairs. In 1629 John Parkinson described a large lime tree at Cobham Hall which had its branches trained to form three arbours, one above the other, where many people could sit. This sounds like a fantasy, but it comes to life in a portrait dated 1603 by Robert Peake, court artist to James I, where his daughter Princess Elizabeth (later queen of Bohemia) is shown as a girl in a stiff white dress and ruff. Behind her in a green landscape is a stream or moat crossed by a bridge to a zigzag path. This leads up a mound to an arbour tiered like a wedding cake, formed from trees. The upper branches of the central tree are arched into a dome to give the overall shape of a classical rotunda, with a circle of smaller trees forming greenery pillars and trained into a series of archways, including an arched central entrance. In the centre, around the trunk of the main tree, is a circular bench on which two ladies can be glimpsed exchanging confidences. Perhaps it was an imaginary playhouse for a princess, but at least the idea had been formed into a visual reality.

Apart from being virtually a tree house, the Painshill Hermitage was also remarkable in setting the trend for hiring an ornamental hermit, required to act the part and entertain guests with ironic witticisms, in the manner of Shakespeare's world-weary Jacques in the Forest of Arden: 'I can suck melancholy out of a song as a weasel sucks eggs.'[22] The Painshill hermit may have been illusory, although the room with its sparse furniture was equipped as a bedroom and part of the atmosphere certainly derived from a supposed inhabitant. Joseph Spence, describing the Painshill Hermitage in 1752, wrote

Hubert Robert, *The Hermit in the Garden*, 1790, the ultimate expression,
by a French artist, of an ornamental hermit pursuing his meditations in a rustic setting.

of sitting for a while 'in the poor hermit's bedchamber', but this was the only
contemporary reference that hinted at a real hermit. A later and probably
apocryphal account – oft repeated – set out Hamilton's conditions of employment: to wear a camlet robe and leave the hair and nails uncut; to walk free
in the grounds but not leave them; to be given food, a Bible, spectacles and
an hourglass, a mat and hassock, and 700 guineas after seven years' service.

The best detail is that after a mere three weeks the hermit was found drunk under the table of the nearest inn. Newspaper advertisements for ornamental hermits have been quoted, setting out the proverbial seven years' service, and in one instance at least the situation was reversed when, in 1760, Robert Drummond of Drummonds Bank in Charing Cross bought Cadland Manor on the Solent as a retreat. He received an anonymous letter with a rough drawing of a hermitage and an offer to construct and live in it,

> near your honers house in a wood with a high wall round it . . .
> 7 years without seeing any human creture to see what nature
> woud turn to in that time. I mean not to cut my hair nor beard
> nor nails in that time. I shoud wish to have all neseres of life
> brought to me in a privat plase without seeing anybody etc.
> God Bless your honer.[23]

By far the most ornamental such hermit was painted in an imaginary scene by the French court artist Hubert Robert, sitting in dappled sunlight at his desk under a rose arbour, with his tiny thatched hermitage nearby, the door standing invitingly open onto a potager. Above the wall in the background of the painting runs the balustrade of a terrace in the park beyond, where some girls are leaning and looking down at him. This departure from the earlier idea of being, oneself, the hermit in search of solitude, or getting family or friends to enact the part for fun, became prevalent enough to be mocked. In 1780 Horace Walpole declared a hermitage 'the ornament whose merit soonest fades. It is almost comic to set aside a quarter of one's garden to be melancholic in,' although his own chapel at Strawberry Hill would have made an excellent hermitage.[24] Richard Graves in *Columella* described an encounter with a fraudulent hermit with two sticks for a crucifix and a string of peas for a rosary, who claimed to have left his previous employment when told to keep his hermitage clean, but who was in fact sacked when found in possession of beer, tobacco and a dairy maid. In 1754 a hermitage was set up in Vauxhall Pleasure Gardens. At first the hermit was a painted figure reading a book, then picturesque scenery was added, 'weird and awful mountains and precipices', and sometimes a real hermit was installed to act as a fortune teller: 'the old man with a white beard and staff comes up from the mysterious depths of a pasteboard ravine.'[25] In Thackeray's *Vanity Fair* (1848) poor faithful Captain Dobbin leaves the party at Vauxhall:

'I should be de trop,' said the Captain looking at them rather wistfully, 'I'd best go and talk to the hermit.' And so he strolled off into the dark walk at the very end of which lived that well-known paste-board solitary.

This popular and sometimes real figure was the subject of cartoons and ditties:

Turn gentle hermit of Vauxhall
And let me know the way
In which within that cavern small
You pass your time away
There's nothing but a little lamp
A pitcher and a cat
The place must be extremely damp
Why don't you wear a hat.

The sense of the ridiculous also attached to the hermit of Hawkstone Park in Shropshire, who alternated over the years between a real Father Francis, a stuffed dummy and a waxwork.

In Scotland, hermitages attracted higher literary aspirations. Two were associated with Robert Burns and the composition of his poems. First is the Hermitage at Craigieburn, near the spa town of Moffat, a tiny cell with a gothic door, up on the bank above the burn, linked to a love poem that begins 'Sweet fa's the eve on Craigieburn' and includes the line 'I hear the wild birds singing.' Second is the Friars Carse Hermitage at Ellisland, which was modelled on a medieval anchorite's cell and has the air of a wayside chapel, with a little architectural flourish provided by crow step gables. Burns was given a key to come and write here by his friend Robert Riddell, with whom he also enjoyed drinking sessions in the Hermitage, and probably stayed overnight, although the friendship ended abruptly in 1793.

At Dunkeld the fictitious bard Ossian had both a cave and a hall dedicated to him. Dunkeld was the seat of the Dukes of Atholl, where a forest of spectacular trees included the tallest Douglas firs and stately cedars, spread overall with the scent of pines. The works of Ossian embodied a great deal of Gaelic heritage, gathered and invented by the poet James Macpherson, but based on oral traditions and cleverly marketed in the 1760s as the work of an ancient blind bard. Dr Johnson recognized it for 'as gross an imposition as ever the world was troubled with', but many believed Ossian existed and the controversy only fuelled the popularity of his epic poems. All over Europe artists pictured Ossian with flowing white hair, beard and harp, or illustrated his tales in melodramatic scenes of love and loss. Ossian's Cave in the folly garden at Dunkeld is a simple stone cell, but Ossian's Hall is a picturesque viewfinder beside the Black Linn Falls. Inside was rendered ornate with a circular hall of mirrors creating views of the Falls cascading down every wall, and the curvature also amplified the sound. Since the entrance to Ossian's Hall hid the Falls from sight this came as a shock – a very picturesque kind of horrid. The Wordsworths visited in 1803 and Dorothy wrote of 'a room dizzy and alive with waterfalls that tumbled in all directions, the cascade being reflected in innumerable mirrors on walls and ceilings'. But William called this device 'baubles of theatric taste'. Another visitor described windows of red glass 'through which you see the river falling from a surprising height into the horrid gulf beneath, with a most terrifying noise – it appears to be sheets of liquid fire rolling down the rock like the lava of Mount Etna.'[26] The stunned visitor was able to proceed from the sound and visual effects of Ossian's Hall onto a balcony, to view the Falls in reality and restore a calmer sense of the poetic scene.

For those European monarchs, or popes, who had greatness thrust upon them, or who had grown weary of its challenges and trappings, the idea of a retreat from worldly affairs was especially attractive. Charles V of Spain, sixteenth-century ruler of half Europe and most of the New World, abdicated to end his days in monkish calm, not exactly in a hermit's cell but in a miniature palace, set in an orchard of orange trees near the monastery of Yuste. Various rulers of Spain and France, and of Italian and German principalities, created similar retreats (without abdicating) and the word 'hermitage', then came into play. Some had a religious element, more were palatial complexes, often with separate 'hermitages' for favoured courtiers. Finally, Catherine the Great of Russia exploded the concept by using the name Hermitage for one of her gilded palaces in St Petersburg. Also lost during this process was the whimsical and experimental aspect that could turn a hermitage into a folly. However, in France a combination of Rousseau's ideas and the fashion for *jardins anglo-chinois* did cause some aristocrats to name one of their small garden buildings a hermitage. At Ermenonville the Marquis de Girardin built a simple cabin for Rousseau himself, where he died in 1778, not necessarily due to the rigours imposed by this dwelling. More light-heartedly the Comte d'Artois included a hermitage among his many follies at the Bagatelle Gardens and 'the hermit who lived in this charming place was depicted in wax in one corner of the room.'

The Magdalenenklause, Nymphenburg Park, Munich, 1725–8, a hermitage with
a religious aspect, its baroque style mellowed by Byzantine and ruinous touches.

In less secular mode was the Magdalenenklause, a hermitage built for
the Elector of Bavaria in the grounds of the Nymphenburg Summer Palace
outside Munich. Early in the eighteenth century the park and gardens, which
were formal in the French style, were updated with Baroque follies. Beside
one lake the Pagodenburg was built with its oriental interior, and for the
adjoining deer park there was a pink and white hunting lodge called the
Amalienburg. Later, when the Elector Maximilian Emanuel felt the need
to retreat, the hermitage was created between 1725 and 1728, and finished
by his son Karl Albrecht. It is an exquisite and original building, not overly
Baroque, mildly ruinous, subtly blending medieval, classical and even Eastern
elements. The mellow brickwork is patterned with curves suggesting blind
arches, then stuccoed with extra niches and diamond patterns to create the
effect of a place of worship in a romantic state of deterioration. The windows are gothic, some pointed, some ogee, and glazed with circular patterns
radiating like wheels. The entrance to the chapel rears up into an elaborate
broken pediment, which is reminiscent of a Roman ruin and adds elegance to
the dimensions, while a series of round corner turrets and larger semicircular
apses give the hermitage chapel a faintly Byzantine air. The rest of the building
is rectangular and comprises the Elector's apartments: quiet panelled rooms
including a refectory. The extravaganza is yet to come, because the interior

of the chapel is like a grotto: walls and recesses, pillars and arches, all intricately patterned with pebbles, shells and stucco, except for the ceiling, which is frescoed with the golden clouds of a heavenly scene, in bright contrast to the grey geometrics beneath. The chapel is dedicated to Mary Magdalene, who in European folklore developed into a repentant hermit living out her life in a cave, where she grew her hair long to cover her ragged nakedness, and lamented her sins in a torrent of tears. A large recess to the side of the altar sanctuary, with cruder rock work, represents her cave, in which is placed her statue staring at a crucifix. It is in striking contrast to any British hermitage; whether it is any more numinous is probably a matter of taste. When completed in 1728 the Magdalenenklause became a place of annual pilgrimage, taking place every 22 July on the Magdalene's saint's day, and augmented when a nearby spring was endowed with healing properties. At the end of the eighteenth century the grounds of the Nymphenburg Palace were redesigned by Friedrich Ludwig von Sckell (who had visited England in the 1770s to study landscaping and sketch follies). He reduced the formality and integrated the parkland more harmoniously with the gardens, a movement towards Romanticism taking place all over Europe.

Sigurtà, an Italian garden of the Veneto, received similar landscaping treatment in the 1790s, and the outcome included a hermitage as sophisticated and eccentric as any recluse from the cradle of European architecture could have wished. It is approached theatrically up wide, shallow steps that rise steeply between long, clipped hedges. The slender building is framed asymmetrically by cypresses 'pointed and dark, more solemn than the pyramids, more enigmatic than obelisks'.[27] Its tallness is accentuated by a pedimented roof and very narrow gothic windows, dark slits in the elegant cream-coloured facade. The hermitage acted as a study rather than a religious sanctuary and retains an air of secret assignations and conspiracy. There is another, discreet path to

Sigurtà Hermitage, Sigurtà Garden, Veneto, Italy. Built in the 1790s, it stands elegant and romantic above a long flight of steps lined with clipped evergreens.

the hermitage among the trees. The lower room is reached by a narrow side passage, the upper room by an outside staircase. On the walls are classical fragments, shields and frescoed coats of arms. There is a bell tower and two *torchères*. High in the upper room is a round stained-glass window. Looking across the grounds of Sigurtà is a vista to a medieval castle that once belonged to the della Scala family of Verona, who sheltered Dante in his exile. He was grateful but nevertheless wrote a bitter pun on his predicament and on their name, which means 'stairs': '*Com'e duro calle ho scendere e'salir per l'altrui scale*' – 'How hard is the way up and down another's stairs.' Just as the best English hermitages summoned to mind quotations from Milton, and in Scotland Robert Burns, this one evokes Dante.[28]

There is a fine latter-day hermitage at Highgrove in Gloucestershire, built for Prince Charles and named the Sanctuary. It is an endearing mixture of styles, with sturdy columns supporting the rustic tiled roof of the porch and a steeply pitched gothic roof framing a round window which peers down from above like one eye. The building has little wings with tiny windows and a chimney like a small tower to one side. Its walls are painted a cheerful primrose yellow to give it a playful air amid the dark surrounding trees. There is also a tree house at Highgrove, set into a holly tree with thatched roof and shingled walls. The front door is like a holly leaf and touches of red represent the berries. Whether for children or adults, tree houses have thrived in modern times, and some are original and beautiful enough to be considered follies. There are those that perch in their trees like birds' nests. On the shore of Long Island in New York the Lake Nest Tree House is in fact two nests, one above the other such as herons might achieve, with a naturalistic untidiness of twisted branches obtained from salvaged lumber. They are reached by ladders and consist of viewing platforms where children can play and adults can drink cocktails as the sun sets. In winter when the trees are bare the nests make poetic silhouettes by the waterside; in summer they are almost hidden among the leaves. In the far north of Sweden at Harads, there is the Treehotel complex consisting of many sorts of tree house from shingle cabins to metal boxes. Here, set into a ring of tall slender conifers, is the Bird's Nest, which is perfectly round but decorated with so many protruding twigs that it seems to be the creation of some gigantic mythical bird, like the roc of *The Arabian Nights*, or a phoenix adapted to northern climes. Inside, the circular space is ultra-modern with no trace of bird life; the walls are clad in pale smooth plywood, the windows are portholes and modern conveniences are neatly fitted in.[29]

The Mirrorcube at the Treehotel, Harads, Sweden, 2010,
placed in grounds full of varied tree houses in startlingly modern styles.

Also at Harads Treehotel is a most successful modernistic tree house. The Mirrorcube is a 4-metre (13 ft) cube of lightweight aluminium lined inside with plywood and outside with mirrors, so that it reflects the surrounding sky and pine forest to magical effect. It is reached by a stepped ramp and a metal balcony, but even so it almost disappears into its forest environment. Only at twilight and night, if a glow of artificial light is shining from its windows, does it become apparent what is mirror and what is glass, and the chequered effect is even more otherworldly.[30] Less impressive but great fun is the Goji Berry in Brook House Woods, Herefordshire, a round red tent dangling from ash and oak trees. The Berry is manufactured from synthetic canvas on a round framework of aluminium, with plywood interiors, and it sways in response to wind or movement within. Beside it are wooden steps and decking, which detract a little from its fruity presence. But the woodland setting, especially at bluebell time, and the view towards the Malvern Hills, are all that could be desired for this modern version of the exotic canvas tents of the eighteenth century. Goji berries, *Lycium barbarum*, are akin to tomatoes but sweeter, and in this context more evocative since, like the tents, they are of Eastern origin. They have been cultivated in China for centuries, as medicinal plants, and were introduced into Britain in the 1730s (the heyday of follies), gaining the nickname 'the Duke of Argyll's tea plant'. Argyll was a Campbell, also known by the title Lord Ilay, a prominent member of Walpole's government. His garden at Whitton contained a collection of exotic plants and was described by his friend Alexander Pope as a paradise 'with all its plants but the forbidden tree'. Argyll's greenhouse was designed by James Gibbs and his folly was a triangular, castellated tower. Some of his finest trees were later replanted in Kew Gardens, but his tea plant took to the wild and is still to be found in the hedgerows of East Anglia.

Most tree houses, naturally, are made of wood. Some are spheres so light they too can be suspended from trees and seem to float on high; many more rise in stages among the branches joined together by ladders and walkways, looking either deliberately rustic or smoothly modern. One of the largest is part of Alnwick Castle garden in Northumberland, a complex of multi-layered wooden rooms arranged around the trunks of many trees and veiled in their leaves. These are lime trees, a pleasing link with the earliest tree houses in England at Cobham and Pitchford. It is raised on struts with interlinking wooden balconies and haphazard windows, shingle roofs and a conical turret at the highest point. The wooden effects are varied, using cedar, redwood and pine and with different styles of planking and shingling. Some of the most attractive wooden tree houses use a vernacular style, echoing the spirit of past generations and blending into the surrounding woodland in a way that is both historical and ecological. The Solace Tree House, perched in an American plane or buttonwood tree in New Jersey, is constructed from traditional clapboard, with its upper rooms attached asymmetrically to fit inside the enclosing branches. There is a turned-wood balustrade serving for a veranda and the large windows are subdivided by wooden glazing bars, all in the style of America's pioneering farmsteads. The interior is equally wooden, with the buttonwood trunk rising through the centre. The floor and walls are planked, the furniture is bentwood, there is a woodburning stove and newspapers cover the walls as insulation. The maker, Daniel Mack, described it as 'hobo style', to foster the impression that its charm lies in being constructed ad hoc from found materials, added to which hobos have a wandering folklore in America, with traditional sayings and railroad adventures all their own.

For a different take on ethnicity, another American architect, David Greenberg, was inspired by tree houses he saw in Hawaii, which are built to

The Tree House, Alnwick Castle, Northumberland. Built in 2004 of varied woods and in a series of levels, walkways and rooms, to be used for functions in the quirky spirit traditional with follies.

blend in with tropical heat and foliage – seeming to consist mainly of flimsy wooden balconies and a suspension bridge far above *terra firma*. He transported the concept as far as Hainan Island in the South China Sea for the Big Beach in the Sky Tree House. The walls look like bamboo blinds and to catch the breezes there are as many openings as walls. The trunks and branches of the host tamarind tree weave in and out all through the fabric of the building, making house and tree feel as one. Still higher and more ventilated is the Canopy Tree House in the Amazon rainforest of Peru's Inkaterra Reserve. This little nest is wedged into the fork of a tree trunk 27 metres (89 ft) above the ground and fanned by palm leaves. It is hardly more substantial than a large veranda, criss-crossed with timber supports and covered in a leaf-thatched roof. It is breathtakingly high in the forest canopy and reached only by a slatted rope ladder dangling down to earth like the tail of some primitive creature.[31]

An alternative kind of primitive – stark, pure and ageless – exists in Japanese tradition and is manifested in Terunobu Fujimori's tree houses.[32] The idea is that a tea master designs his own tea house as an act of dedication and in a simple style of his own. So even though Fujimori is a renowned architect, for him too it is the ultimate personal expression in architecture. His Teahouse Tetsu is set amid the cherry trees whose pink spring blossom is an object of pilgrimage for the Japanese. Only in Japan could an oddly shaped rhomboid be perched like a bird table on the stump of a cypress tree and look so perfectly right. The walls are roughly plastered in mud; the roof is steeply pitched with grey shingles and overlaps one wall more than the others, while from it rises a thin tapering chimney. Inside is very plain, with tea bowls on the floor and tatami mats. There are two little side windows, and a large one whose view replaces the traditional picture scroll that is changed according to the seasons. There could be no mistaking that this space is suitable for meditation, and it belongs in the same tradition as Zen gravel gardens, pared down haiku poems and ikebana with one perfect flower.

Fujimori's best-known tea house is his own, built on family property overlooking the town of Chino where he grew up and known either as the Chino Tea House or *taka sugi-an*, meaning 'tea house built too high'. It rests on two spindly chestnut trunks, looking both more precarious and daintier than the Tea House Tetsu, which it strongly resembles, only its rectangular chimney

The Chino Tea House, built by the Japanese architect Terunobu Fujimori for himself in 2004. He gave it the Japanese name 'teahouse built too high'.

346

pokes straight up from the centre of the roof. A taller ladder is needed to reach it, and midway up there is a platform for removing shoes. The largest viewing window has a bamboo lattice which can be drawn at night so that moonlight casts shadows onto the tea room walls, it being another strong Japanese tradition to have a pavilion associated with viewing the moon.

A third tree house by Fujimori, the Irisentei Tea Nest in Taiwan, looks more flimsy and tribal, standing as it does on the banks of a fast-flowing river in the midst of lush tropical foliage. It is raised over 7 metres (23 ft) high on five thick bamboo poles, which sway off-centre as they reach into the floor of the tree house, and indeed all Fujimori's tea houses do sway, which makes them less resistant and therefore stronger in storms and earthquakes. The Irisentei Tea Nest is dark and coffin-shaped, walled with charred plywood and with eaves jutting out like thatching twigs. Carbonizing wooden boards in this way is a technique called *yaki sugi*, which helps to preserve them in humidity and also deters rats and termites. Fujimori chars the planks himself according to the old methods (which can be seen in Japanese prints of people at work, including Hokusai's 34th view of Mount Fuji from the mountains of Totomi). The Irisentei Tea Nest is entered through a curious cage-like tube, a safety device set over the ladder, and looking so like an oversize fish-trap that the riverine scenery and the little folly floating above it all flow into one timeless entity. Fujimori's architecture, despite its references to earlier and more natural lives, is nevertheless regarded as cutting-edge modern; his fellow architect Kengo Kuma said it 'packs a punch of a kind no one else has achieved in modernism'. His insistence on using local materials places Fujimori in the vanguard of ecological practice, and his reinterpretation of the Japanese past is individualistic and humorous to a degree no one has matched. Recognizing this quality, in 2010 the Victoria and Albert Museum in London invited Fujimori to exhibit a 'space of refuge and retreat', which he created from charred cypress planks, raised high on four stilts and named the Beetles House.

The Well, Quinta da Regaleira, Sintra, Portugal, *c.* 1900, an inverted tower, plunging down to exit tunnels, but no water. The descent is by steps spiralling down the walls.

Ten

Into the Future

In modern times follies have become increasingly surreal, various and international; and although they stretch the usual definitions, certain folly characteristics survive, especially eccentricity and experimentation. More than ever, modern follies provide artistic expressions of contemporary thinking and styles, and even when they stick out like sore thumbs their creators have been reacting strongly to their environment. Towers feature as much as ever, and around 1900, as the modern era struggled into being, there was a fine manifestation of alternative thinking when Quinta da Regaleira in Portugal sported not only a tower that went upwards but one that went downwards, hollowing out a well that is not a well. António Carvalho Monteiro, heir to a fortune made with Brazilian coffee and gemstones, commissioned Luigi Manini, an Italian architect who also designed sets for La Scala, to create for him an allegorical villa and folly garden at Sintra, on a property he purchased in 1896 from the Regaleira family.[1] There are elements drawn from classical, gothic and Masonic sources, and much elaborate ornamentation characteristic of the Manuelian period of Portuguese architecture – spirals, plant motifs, twisted rope work, curlicues. Above all, the obsessive references to the Knights Templar, in the house, chapel and follies, seem retrospective, but the unashamed level of fantasy and innovation heralds the age of Surrealism.

The park at Quinta da Regaleira is steep and densely covered in trees, with myriad footpaths above ground and forking tunnels beneath. The approaches are marked by the Promenade of the Gods – here again are Venus, Hermes, Pan, Ceres and Bacchus – and the first of many water features, the Egyptian House of Thoth enclosing a spring. Thoth, the god of wisdom, was represented at Biddulph Grange by a grotesque baboon; here his entirely different shrine encloses an alcove of blue mosaic inlaid with sacred white ibis stalking among white lilies, surely signifying purification. The spring gurgles into a font that curves in wave patterns, the windows either side are gothic, framed by a Greek key pattern, and along the roof are urns. Further on is the Portal of the Guardians, a curving wall that supports the Celestial Terrace, which has a panoramic view. There are small towers at either end in the style of a medieval Portuguese watchtower, and in the centre between them is a domed and balustraded rotunda, elongated to create a third tower, which looks slightly Indian. Below the rotunda another spring flows through the wall into a fountain bowl and beside it is an entrance to the tunnels and grottos which lead, sooner or later, to The Well. This inverted tower plunges down 20 metres into the rock with a grey stone stairway spiralling around its walls, which are galleried all the way down by columned arches. Numerology attaches significance to each set of fifteen steps, interspersed with a landing, descending down nine levels. Eerie touches are added by the moss that coats the walls, making them feel soft to the descending hand, and by colonies of bats. This uniquely beautiful excavation claims to be designed for a Templar initiation ceremony and although it is called The Well the bottom holds no water; instead it is marked with a Templar cross inside an eight-pointed star, and from here there is a way back into the tunnels. The Well is the *coup de théâtre* of the gardens, and the climax it achieves is faintly echoed, in reverse, at the Regaleira Tower, where another staircase circles, this time outside the gothic walls to the Moorish castellations. From here the view opens out to the mountains and the other palaces of Sintra. There is a further echo at the Unfinished Well, where the steps down are straight but connected by a series of ring-shaped floors against the walls, and the element of water continues throughout the gardens with its cascades, fountains, grottos and two lakes.

Water is also a dominant feature at La Scarzuola in Umbria, which is named after a marsh reed, *scarza*, and here too the past hangs heavy. The Franciscan convent in the grounds was founded when St Francis himself built a hermit's hut from the reeds and caused a spring to gush forth. Around the remnants of the holy place, acquired in 1956, Tomaso Buzzi, a Milanese architect, built the semblance of a city, a puzzling dreamlike place of temptation and initiation, where the paths and stairways lead in multiple directions and the buildings are often unbalanced or broken.[2] There is an echo here of Bomarzo, especially at the Gate of Jonah, a gaping monster mouth with a fat curving fish-tail rising above it, carved within a ruinous broken pediment. This is a way through to the old Franciscan convent and, like Jonah's whale, being swallowed by the monster's mouth might be redemptive rather than dangerous. Beyond it the path leads straight between square pillars, along the base of a grassy slope, to a building in the form of a Broken Column, a smaller version of Désert de Retz, at which point the path turns steeply up between more square pillars. Tomaso Buzzi spoke of the difficulty of human

La Scarzuola, Umbria, Italy. Built from 1956, the Acropolis is piled with classical and medieval replicas, and everywhere symbols exude a mysterious significance.

existence, struggling through the profanities of worldly life in search of spirituality, and he called La Scarzuola 'my folly great or small, to which I have anchored my present and my future'.

Possibly he intended it all to fall into picturesque ruins, which would have added the final romantic touch to the Acropolis which towers over La Scarzuola.[3] Here sections of classical replicas are piled together, the Parthenon and the Pantheon, the Colosseum and a triumphal arch, the Temple of Vesta and the Temple of the Winds, and towering even higher above them all is a medieval watchtower. The tawny stones, bricks and roof tiles from which the replicas are built make them look like sandcastles in the air, with stairways leading nowhere – no eighteenth-century *capriccio* painting was ever brought so vividly to life. Beside the Colosseum and balancing the watchtower is a tall crystal spire with a spiky golden star on top, catching the light. A large weathervane of a floating airborne creature, its toes splayed like another star and playing a pipe, balances the golden star. More stars of beaten metal decorate the walls of other follies and adorn enigmatic figures bearing scrolls and inscriptions. There are stone balls wearing crowns, wings and bees are attached to certain doorways, and below the Acropolis a life-size skeleton dances behind prison bars. In the middle of the garden, among its formal pools, is a series of seven theatre platforms, all grouped around a central, stepped amphitheatre with a grassy labyrinth for a stage. Raised up by a wall behind this, like a terrace, another stage has a labyrinthine floor pattern of black and white tiles and its backdrop is cypress trees and a wide view over the Umbrian countryside. Below this terrace/stage, facing across the central amphitheatre, is a podium with a huge Masonic eye carved to stand out in relief, and the eyeball that gazes across the grass reflects green. Between the semicircular steps around the amphitheatre are two more podiums form-ing little circular stages. The floor tiles of one stage are inset with a radiant sun, those of the other with a crescent moon, giving them an astronomical air, as if there might have been an ancient observatory here. Between these two circular podiums is another monster mouth. Elsewhere in the garden is the Theatre of the Bees, entered through a small triumphal arch; and there is also a *naumachia*, a rectangular pool reminiscent of Hadrian's Villa and the eighteenth-century version in Parc Monceau. Stranger even than all this, but summing up La Scarzuola, is a stairway of intricately latticed stone called the Tower of Babel, a theme which over and over again still resonates in modern architecture.

During the twentieth century the use of new materials enabled architects to experiment with unprecedented shapes and techniques for buildings large or small. An early stage was marked by the inventiveness of Antoni Gaudí. Not that covering a surface with ceramics was anything new in the Mediterranean and Islamic world but the way he did it was. However, the only construc-tion by Gaudí that was officially named a folly was the Sunflower Villa or El Capricho, a youthful project built in 1883 near Comillas in Cantabria for Máximo Quijano. As a general rule a residence is not a folly – a caveat also attached to Strawberry Hill, the Brighton Pavilion and (later) the Glass House – therefore with El Capricho it is best to concentrate on the tower, which is covered with a chequerboard design of alternating green and sunflower tiles. It looks a little Moorish, especially in certain details like the foliar capitals of the four pillars that support the tower, and the stepped window arches and cornices of the balconies. In Spain these Islamic elements are known as the Mudéjar heritage, and in its gracefulness the tower resembles a minaret. The two balconies which surround its base and summit are of finely wrought iron,

Antoni Gaudí, El Capricho, Cantabria, Spain, 1883. An exuberant early work:
a villa where the Moorish tower covered in sunflower tiles could qualify as a folly.

curving into foliar outlines like fantastic garlands of leaves. Like many modernists, Gaudí espoused organic motifs with the maxim 'there are no straight lines or sharp corners in nature. Therefore buildings must have no straight lines or sharp corners.'

No folly could look more organic than some of Niki de Saint Phalle's structures in her Tarot Garden; several have rooms inside them and are too magnificently large to be called sculptures.[4] Instead they could be regarded as the most surreal of follies. Inspired by Gaudí, many are covered in brightly patterned ceramics; and with the sacred grove of Bomarzo as another inspiration they have a mysterious narrative sequence. Niki de Saint Phalle found this dreamscape in the Maremma, the coastal area of southern Tuscany, where her friend Marella Agnelli (wife of the Fiat magnate) had her family home. Marella's brothers Nicola and Carlo Caracciolo ran the family estate of Garavicchio near Capalbio while also (as men of letters) leading the environmental movement in Italy. Originally Maremma was a malarial marshland but, now that it is drained, fields of wheat and sunflowers and olive groves roll down towards the coast. In 1978, in the hillside above Garavicchio, Niki chose a natural amphitheatre looking across this view. It was the site of an old stone quarry where an Etruscan burial ground had been uncovered, enclosed by oak trees, juniper and broom, rocky and a little forbidding as enchantment has to be. Niki de Saint Phalle was already famous, especially for her Nanas, monumental female figures begun in the 1960s, originally as a feminist protest but then as joyous dancing creatures painted in bright colours. Her most famous partner, artistic and marital, was Jean Tinguely ('we are in competition', she once said, 'to amaze one another'); he sculpted in metal and in 1983 they collaborated to adorn the Stravinsky fountain near

Niki de Saint Phalle, The Tower, Tarot Garden, Garavicchio, Tuscany, 1984,
a folly taking its significance from the tarot card of a ruined tower,
with a bike instead of lightning crashing at the top.

the Beaubourg in Paris. Their Tarot Garden contains all 22 figures from the major arcana, which are known as trumps, from the Italian *trionfi*, meaning 'triumphs'. Many esoteric and prophetic meanings have been attached to the tarot cards and the sense of an initiatory journey is present in them as well. The sculptures were worked on for over twenty years, and for those that are as high as 15 metres (49 ft), and could be called follies, Tinguely's skill was essential, to construct and weld the steel frames and reinforcements on which the layers of cement, tar and ceramics were laid. For this Saint Phalle worked with and trained large teams, meaning that she belonged in the tradition where folly buildings provided much local employment – they were, as one said, 'as if transported from a countryside village to another planet'. Among her professional collaborators was the architect Mario Botta, who built the wall surrounding the Tarot Garden with its vaginal entrance.

As the most architectural card from the tarot pack, the Tower in Niki de Saint Phalle's garden is a luminous white beacon in the Garavicchio landscape, covered as it is in shining monochrome tiles and split by arched and circular windows, no two the same but uniformly dark. Inside are rooms where some of her assistants have lived and, as the eye moves upwards, the drama erupts at the top, which is torn back, windows and all, and left to hang sideways as if about to break off. According to the tarot this is the Tower of Destruction – the image on the card shows it being struck by lightning and figures falling from the battlements, obviously an omen of disaster, or sometimes in the hands of fortune tellers signifying a life-changing event. Here on the ruined roof, instead of falling figures, is Tinguely's motorbike forever driving over the edge. Niki feared that his contribution might bode ill for him, and the following year he nearly died of a heart attack. But there has never been agreement about whether Tinguely's sculpture is the lightning bolt or the falling man. Or whether the Tower is a prison from which escape is only possible when the top is blown off – in which case it could even be meant as a beacon of enlightenment, the central force in the garden, as indeed it appears to be. It is linked by a colonnade of 22 columns (the number of the trumps) to a contorted castle, which stands for the Emperor card. This is topped by a golden minaret and is covered like the whole colonnade in a breathtaking encrustation of ceramic tiles. These were created on site in workshops and kilns supervised by Venera Finocchiaro, resulting in a multitude of colours, shapes and patterns, some protruding in globes and spirals, others decorated with stars, skulls, numbers and snakes, while shards of glass and fragments of mirror glimmer among the colours and reflect them.

As compelling as the complex comprising the Emperor and the Tower is the figure of the Empress, inside whose vast bosoms Niki de Saint Phalle had her living rooms for many years, where she would entertain at a long table in the Empress's belly. The face of the Empress is black, her veil is heavenly blue patterned with stars and planets, her crown is red, and viewed from behind she is discovered to be a vast sphinx, which would help to explain the hypnotic power of her staring eyes. Other traditions more ancient than the tarot are referenced in the garden. There are many ceramic serpents: writhing around a tree of life where the Hanged Man dangles upside down; circling the globe of The World on which a Nana dances; and out of a pool where Tinguely has welded the Wheel of Life rises the largest serpent of all, stretching alongside steps up to a monster mouth, which is the entrance to another large folly/ statue representing the High Priestess (also known in the tarot cards as the Female Pope). Thus archaic symbols form startling combinations with contemporary ideas and materials – and yet in all sorts of different ways this has been a recurring element in the creation of follies.

Ceramics are also the touchstone for Grayson Perry and FAT Architects' tribute to the county of his birth, a folly called A House for Essex, built as a shrine to the fictitious Julie Cope, an Essex everywoman who died in a collision with a delivery man on a moped. A House for Essex overlooks the grey river Stour towards the cranes of Harwich docks, which at night look like fairyland. It is reached down a rutted track amid the scrawny fields and hedges of the East Anglian countryside, where beyond lie the mudflats and behind are suburban houses. The village is called Wrabness; the Norse suffix -*ness* means promontory and one can imagine the Vikings landing bleakly long ago. The architecture of A House for Essex echoes the wooden stave churches of medieval Norway with their steeply pitched roofs layered and set at angles to one another. This inspiration may be the work of ancestral forces winning through, because early sketches showed more curvaceous rooflines, twisting upwards and showing the initial influence of small south Asian shrines. There was another oriental strand, because on a holiday of a lifetime in India, with her second husband, Julie told him she had never been so happy and he promised if she should die that he would build a Taj Mahal for her. Luckily orientalism was superseded by a more vernacular fantasy, but Perry is fascinated by shrines, and for an inauguration ceremony in 2015 he led a pilgrimage from Canvey Island, where Julie was born, to Wrabness, with seven women from Essex named Julie riding bicycles. On another Essex estuary, the tiny Saxon church of St Peter on the Wall at Bradwell is still a

Grayson Perry and FAT Architects, A House for Essex, Wrabness,
inaugurated 2015, glittering with ceramic tiles, commemorating a fictitious
life and death, in the sense of a shrine to everyday people.

pilgrimage destination, and the extraordinary appearance of A House for
Essex is tempered by this sense of reverence for an ordinary life, fictional but
representing everyone, mundane and tragic.[5]

The exterior of A House for Essex shows five divisions, layered in size
from the front porch to the largest section in the centre and diminishing
again to the back. The golden roofs are steeply pitched, stacked into one
another, inset with arched dormer windows which grace the roofline with
curves. On the apex of the gables are strange finials, acting like the crucifixes
and gargoyles fixed above Norwegian stave churches or the protective prows
and shields on Viking ships. One is a silver image of Julie; another looks like
an egg chequered in green and white like the tiles on the walls below. These
tiles are the glory of A House for Essex. There are nearly 2,000 of them, and
they stretched terracotta manufacturing techniques to the limits. The larger
green tiles feature Julie as a primitive fertility goddess, with rounded breasts
and belly and tiny arms and legs spread wide. In attitude she is like a crude
Sheela-na-gig on a medieval church, but her bouffant hair sets her in Essex.

During manufacture every nipple had to be attached by hand, having defied the moulding process. On each tile Julie's image is set into a little arch over twisted columns like an idol in a niche. The smaller tiles are triangular, alternating white and green, running in strips round the walls and gables and making the building sing out underneath its golden roofs. Seen up close, these tiles have relief designs of safety pins, hearts and cassettes. Behind the red doors and window frames the interior is equally amazing: a red 'chapel' where a large ceramic Julie is set aloft, this time manifesting as an entirely yellow blonde, opening her arms towards the moped that killed her, which hangs from the ceiling like a saint's symbol of martyrdom. Brilliantly coloured tapestries tell Julie's story, both in the 'chapel' and in the two bedrooms, setting her back into the context of a lifetime where, as the tale unfolds, she did her best against the odds.

At Xilitla, in the mountainous northern province of Mexico, English eccentricity took on a more exotic form after Edward James, hunting for orchids in the rainforest, stumbled upon a series of pools fed by waterfalls and, plunging into the cool green water, was surrounded by iridescent butterflies. The enchantment never ended; he bought the whole area, which was an abandoned coffee plantation, and named it Las Posas, meaning 'the pools' – that was in 1945.[6] Previously James had used his wealth as a patron of art, music and ballet, notably Stravinsky and the Surrealists; Magritte painted his portrait from behind, staring in a mirror which also showed the back of his head;[7] for him Dalí made the lobster telephone and the sofa like Mae West's lips. Dalí paid James this tribute – 'he is crazier than all the Surrealists put together, they act it but he is the real thing.' Praise indeed, but they did not admire his own art, and his wife Tilly Losch, a ballet dancer, enjoyed his wealth and then divorced him. In Mexico he found a substitute family with Plutarco Gastelum, his Mexican guide, who moved his family to Xilitla and organized the construction of James's follies. A large local workforce including carpenters and masons was assembled and trained, leaving an abiding memory of James's generosity and strange ideas, guarding his memory and artefacts ever since his death in 1984. Construction work started in 1962 and James still travelled widely. He would send his ideas on postcards to Plutarco, architectural inspirations sparked by gothic windows or Italian arcades, and these Plutarco would explain to his workers until they were transformed into concrete follies in the jungle.

This is a landscape of seeming ruins, which may grow more ruinous as the jungle encroaches, but for now achieves a miraculous balance between

Edward James, Las Posas, Xilitla, Mexico, created from 1962. Wonderful cement
follies in the jungle evoking vegetable forms and used for poetic retreat.

real foliage and fantasy, because primarily the forms are organic, shaped like monstrous flowers, leaves, stems and tendrils. Columns like the trunks of trees rise up many metres forming canopies, arcades and filigree walls. Floors and stairways end abruptly in the sky. They have no function other than to rejoice at the jungle around them, but they do have names, although in the confusion of the steep and twisting paths one might lose one's way and mis-name them: The House with Wings; The House with a Back Like a Whale; The House on Three Floors, or Five or Four or Six; The Bamboo Palace; The Stairway to Heaven. The pavilions with their uncertain staircases have inde-terminate levels, and once seen they give castles in the air an extra meaning and a fully surreal dimension. Many of the columns are modelled on bamboo, slender and intersected, providing a favourite motif, while lotus and lilies best lend their shapes to the cement flowers.[8] Among them real creepers dangle their tropical blooms, butterflies spread their glittering wings and birds and crickets raise a cacophony that is both beautiful and raucous. In his own weird way Edward James spent his fortune on protecting the natural envi-ronment. Once, when asked his purpose, he replied 'pure megalomania', but a poem he wrote towards the end of his life belied that dismissive answer:

> I have seen such beauty as one man has seldom seen,
> And the sound, the sound of green.[9]

In a very different dry and grassy landscape in the South of France, the German artist Anselm Kiefer also used concrete to create his landscape of seemingly ruinous towers.[10] They rise up, tottering above underground tun-nels and caverns, and glass pavilions dedicated to art installations. La Ribaute at Barjac was once a silk factory, set among the hills of the Cévennes, and from 1993 to 2008 Kiefer built and excavated until the whole site was a mon-ument to his ideas of destruction and regeneration, resounding with names like Palmsonntag and Sternenfall, while the towers were named after Babel and Jericho. (Whether Kiefer would care to see them classed as follies, how-ever respectfully, is another matter.) Since Kiefer is haunted by the German past, sometimes the towers become the watchtowers in concentration camps, and reappear in his paintings of German forests among ash and snow accom-panied by runic inscriptions and quotations. At other times Kiefer claims his first inspiration was a cityscape of skyscrapers, the symbols of modern aspi-ration and vanity, and linked to a biblical-sounding phrase, 'Over your cities grass will grow.'[11] Also in Old Testament vein (though apocryphal), Kiefer has linked the towers to Lilith, the first wife of Adam, who refused to join him in Eden and turned into a siren who haunted ruins. She became a great and destructive temptress, threatening civilization: 'I thought', Kiefer wrote, 'of the end of the city, its dispersal into ashes.' But despite these ancient cultural associations the towers are most like the ruins of an industrial age, instilling a sense of melancholy closer to ourselves than classical ruins and literary allusions. They are made from the concrete casts of empty containers, precariously and asymmetrically stacked (by crane) and balanced on layers of lead, a material which Kiefer also uses to create massive sculptures of burnt books. The steel rods and cables, which hold the concrete containers together, often protrude, adding to the ruinous appearance, as if the towers were eroding, though in fact the steel binds with the cement and reinforces the structure, and the towers are certainly more carefully balanced than they seem.

The towers were begun as an experiment with materials and ideas, which is often the way that Kiefer works, as if in play, and later the installations are charged with layer upon layer of meaning, which can then be turned upside down thus: 'I don't at all regard these ruins as ominous, on the contrary they mark the beginning of a new cycle' (an augury that could be straight from a positive tarot reading of the Tower of Destruction). In London in 2006 two of Kiefer's towers were exhibited under the name Jericho (in the Old Testament the trumpets of Israel caused the towers and walls of Jericho to collapse). But in Milan seven towers of different heights were exhibited as Seven Heavenly Palaces, signifying an ascent through levels of spirituality.[12] The duality is an echo of the original Tower of Babel: to the Jews it was a symbol of human vanity offending God, but to the people of Babylon a ziggurat was intended as a stairway to their gods and an observatory to seek guidance from the heavens.

Gesamtkunstwerk has no English equivalent, since it expresses in one long word the totality of a work of art in relation to its environment, which is exactly how any satisfactory folly should relate to the landscape around it. Anselm Kiefer is among those artists who dislike seeing their work taken out of context and crammed into an all-purpose exhibition space. Another German artist/architect went beyond the Atlas Mountains into the desert of southern Morocco to find his perfect space. In the endless open landscape of the Plaine de Marha, broken only by thorny bushes where goats and camels browse, Hannsjörg Voth built three follies related to the stars.[13] He employed local craftsmen and traditional construction techniques to mould stones, sand and clay into towers and spirals and each of the three buildings protects a

Hannsjörg Voth, City of Orion, Morocco, 1998–2003, 22 clay towers with linking walls that represent the stars of the constellation Orion. They act as observatories.

freshly dug well, in accordance with both necessity and local mythology. First came the Stairway to Heaven, constructed between 1985 and 1987, a geometric wedge rising out of the sand 16 metres high and 23 metres long (52 × 75 ft), with 52 steps along the hypotenuse to a platform. By day one could glimpse the Atlas Mountains on the horizon, and at night all the panoply of stars. From this platform two living rooms could be accessed, one above the other, and a sculpture of metal feathers spreads out to symbolize human dreams of flight. Next came the Golden Spiral, built between 1992 and 1997, a low wall whirling into the sand towards the centre of the spiral and a hundred steps beside it leading down to the living quarters and the well on which a golden ark floats. The main material used was lava rock from the surrounding area, and the spiral was constructed as nine quarter circles, whose radii increase outwards in accordance with the Fibonacci sequence.[14]

Voth's third building was the City of Orion, made between 1998 and 2003, tracing the image of Orion's constellation in the sand. The teams, totalling about fifty local Moroccans, built 22 clay towers and their connecting walls, the tallest tower being 16 metres (52 ft) high, and each representing a star in the constellation. Three towers mark the middle line, known as Orion's belt, and the central one has the well beneath it. The constellation of Orion is visible worldwide, and it is the first known to have been traced and recorded, on a piece of prehistoric mammoth ivory found in Germany. Most civilizations interpreted it as a striding or dancing figure, and in ancient Babylon it was the Good Shepherd or Messenger of the Gods, but to the Greeks it was The Hunter, named Orion, with a sword hanging from his belt, his left arm raising a club and his right outstretched with a shield. The towers that Voth set around the outline of Orion act as observatories, and their steps lead up to seats, angled to view the sky through strategic slits in the walls.

The Swiss landscape artist Not Vital has also used the sandy clay of Africa for some of his most beautiful follies. Starting in 2005 at the oasis settlement of Aladab in Niger, using mud, straw and dung in a traditional mixture and following traditional building styles, his aim is to suit the vernacular but also to create just enough surprise and tension between the installation and its environment to cast both in a new light. Altogether in Niger Vital has constructed three follies: a House against Heat and Sandstorms, which is a cone with wooden poles protruding from the walls for reinforcement in the traditional way; a House to Watch the Night Skies, a tall stepped wall; and a House to Watch the Sunset. The last is one in a series of towers intended for different parts of the world, using the same dimensions but different local materials. Steep flights of steps lead up on three sides to different heights, reaching doors in the walls of the tower. At Tarasp in Switzerland, among the mountain conifers, The House for Watching the Sunset is a white tower made of cement mixed with local sand from the river Inn. In the Amazon jungle the material used to achieve the same design was Brazilian hardwood. In Indonesia the formula varied, because here it was a House to Watch Three Volcanoes, or to be precise one volcano called Kelimutu which has three crater lakes, where the colours of the water vary dramatically between blue, green and red according to the interaction of volcanic gases and minerals (or the indigenous spirits). This is on the remote island of Flores, which is accessible only via Bali. In this House the steps to the viewing platform are black against the white of an almost triangular edifice that matches the slant of the steps. Jutting beneath it a white rectangular block provides a meditative space lined inside with bamboo and thatch. The House to Watch Three Volcanoes is hard to find, a feature common to each of these far-flung follies (indeed to many wayside follies), and can be reached only with the guidance and transport provided by local people. For Vital this process of negotiation and discovery is part of his own philosophy, and he leads a nomadic life delving for a while into all aspects of the areas where he works.

This intense commitment was born of Vital's devotion to the mountain landscape and sagas of his own Swiss homeland. His Fundaziun is at Sent, a mountain village in the Engadine where the original Romansh language is preserved – Vital speaks it himself and names all the follies built there in Romansh.[15] Life is harsh, with long winters, and the nomadic tradition which originated in the search for shelter and pastures remains strong. Vital says the people of Sent 'are always homesick even when they are at home in Sent'. The previous owner of the land where Vital created the Fundazion made his money in Italy and terraced the wild hillside to plant exotic trees. Vital played there as a child, making dens, and bought it in 1998, determined to harness the magic he had always found there into his adult installations. The Chamonna sull'aua is a wooden structure built around two trees to hang over the torrent that races through the valley. In the floor is a window to look down at the foaming water and hear nothing but its rushing sound. Elsewhere is the Punt, an 'invisible' bridge enclosed in stainless steel, so reflective that it melts into the surrounding green, and a person crossing it disappears and goes nowhere, because the bridge does not cross the water to reach the other side.[16] Here too was Vital's first installation for watching the sunset, though it was called Tuor da Silenzia, an eyrie in the crown of a fir tree. But Vital's most extraordinary tower at Sent is covered in artificial hair and named Tuor per ir pella bos-cha (roughly translated as 'crazy tower'). It is built into a steep slope of the valley, where a covered walkway runs into the top of the tower, meeting it at right angles and forming a platform with windows. The artificial hair is dark reddish-brown, matching the trunks of the surrounding conifers, but its shifting texture makes the whole edifice appear to float in the wind. Clinging to another slope among the dark trees is a small 'chapel' of shining white glass, the work of a Venetian glass blower, as pure as a block of ice and designed to feel like the inside of a glacier. Its Romansh name Chamonna da Glatsch resonates with this connection between language, dream, folly and landscape.

New ways of using building materials, especially glass but also cement and steel, revolutionized twentieth-century architecture. One direction taken was utilitarian and often ugly, the other was experimental and occasionally beautiful. The potential of these materials for folly building was recognized by Hermann Finsterlin, whose architectural sketches evolved from his background in natural sciences into skeletal forms and visceral curves and tubes, fantasies too organic to be realized. His descriptions involved words like 'mutation', 'hybridization' and 'fluidity', and he imagined using colour and glass in his constructs. One multicoloured drawing dated 1920 was labelled 'Trauma aus Glas' (Dream in Glass). Other leading architects who wished to breathe new soul into their work, such as Erich Mendelsohn and Walter Gropius, joined with Finsterlin in a published correspondence called *The Glass Chain*, exploring shapes unprecedented in architecture.[17] Mendelsohn's main achievements were with concrete, and his fantasy sketches known as Pleasure Pavilions were like shells and spinning tops. In 1924 his experimental Einstein Tower, an astrophysical laboratory, was built in Potsdam. It had concave and convex walls and angled windows, which were inspirational but caused continuous practical problems. Later in the century, when advances in technology and digital design made such innovations more viable, the influence of these original ideas was acknowledged.

It was Philip Johnson, whose lifetime virtually spanned the twentieth century, who gave tangible form to the glass ideal when he built the iconic Glass House on his estate in Connecticut in 1948–9, and rapidly became notorious as the Man in the Glass House. It is a long rectangular glass box with one glass door on each side and streamlined furniture creating the separate living spaces. Its proportions are classical and its spell lies entirely in the transparency and layered reflections of its glass walls. Johnson claimed it is the only house in the world where you can see the sunset and moonrise at the same time while staying in the same place. As a space for living in, it provokes fascination rather than emulation; in fact Johnson later took up residence in the nearby Brick House and used the Glass House for entertaining, which made it a latter-day banqueting house. A green and pleasant landscape stretches all around, matching Johnson's concept of eighteenth-century England – smooth lawns, slender well-spaced trees and, because the Glass House stands on a hilltop, panoramic views. For some time Johnson had searched his estate for a perfect site before deciding on this 'little knoll' and a particular oak tree, in which he saw a potential resemblance to a Poussin landscape.[18] However, most observers ignore previous centuries and react to its stylish Modernism, with delight in the delicacy of this cuboid bubble, through which its green surroundings seem to float; which is as it should be because Johnson wished to use innovation and glass to create a seamless integration with the natural surroundings. Since he had a flair for publicity, and many contacts in the world of art and architecture, his example probably did more than anyone's to make Modernism fashionable in America. He also suffered from much trespassing.

Over the fifty years that he lived on the Glass House estate (a period he called his fifty-year diary) Johnson designed thirteen buildings in various styles, which he called his follies. These included an underground art gallery with an entrance modelled on Menelaus' tomb, a Ghost House built out of chain-link fencing with lilies planted inside and, best of all, the gatehouse which he called Da Monsta, possibly alluding to the monsters of mythology that guarded entrances and treasure. Da Monsta was built in 1995 with curving lines and sharp angles and was formed into two distinct sections, the larger red and the smaller black. When seen facing towards the entrance the two sections almost resemble spread wings, but from all other viewpoints Da Monsta is totally asymmetrical. There are no right angles, even in the doorway and windows, and the light-filled spaces inside are like the smoothed-down walls of white caverns. The exterior consists of rhomboids, semicircles and creased angles, which were constructed on torqued frameworks covered with gunite, a concrete solution sprayed on at force. From every angle the shapes assume a different character – the monster is either looming, crouching or taking flight. The various surfaces, being either heavily shadowed or catching the light, seem to make slight movements like breathing, in which case they are the dreams of Finsterlin and the members of his Glass Chain coming to life.

Philip Johnson, Da Monsta, Connecticut, 1951. Famous as the architect who lived in the Glass House, Johnson also built himself follies and Da Monsta was placed like the gatehouse to the property.

Dan Graham, the American conceptual artist, has been creating pavilions of glass and steel since the 1980s. His spaces are enclosed by mirrors and curves, where those who enter find themselves amid huge panes of glass or mirrors, or half-mirrored glass, which are both reflective and transparent and where the light is distorted. This means that they explore their own images in curiously reflecting and abnormal surroundings, disorienting and liberating in equal measure. In the rooftop park in West 22nd Street in New York, the Two-Way Mirror Cylinder creates an intense visual effect with the sky; in Minneapolis glass cubes enclosed by hedges make a Two-Way Mirror Labyrinth; in Berlin the Glass Pavilion forms an S-shaped curve and in Stuttgart it is triangular. In the Art Park at Verzegnis in Italy a Two-Way Mirror Triangle, at the foot of a mountain slope, echoes the alpine landscape but also causes it to float and disappear like a mirage. In the Ekebergparken in Oslo, Graham's Glass Pavilion occupies the site of a derelict dance hall, where now visitors may dance with their own reflections or catch fleeting mirrored views over Oslo Bay. For added resonance the park was once the site of Stone and Iron Age cults and burials, and it is said to lie in the background of Munch's *Scream*.[19]

For Olafur Eliasson, not only landscapes and space but also keen environmental concerns are the inspiration behind his work, and like Dan Graham he uses his materials above all to provoke new ways of looking. His architectural installations are often co-operative ventures and, although he is Icelandic-Danish, in 1995 he established his studio in Berlin. Known as the Institut fur Raumexperimente, it has become a laboratory to harness the thoughts of both artists and scientists for publicizing environmental and spatial research. Among his leading collaborators are the author Svend Åge Madsen, whose writings challenge existing concepts of space and time; Einar Thorsteinn, an architect famous for his geometric expertise, who could work a mathematical entity like a toroid into architectural form;[20] and Kjetil Trædal Thorsen, who uses his status as an award-winning architect to give pre-eminence to environmental concerns and sustainability. Olafur Eliasson's Blind Pavilion, which first appeared at the Venice Biennale in 2003 and has since travelled to Iceland, Berlin and Beijing, consists of two concentric steel frameworks glazed with alternate panels of clear glass and opaque black glass. These partially reflect but also obscure what can be seen from a wooden walkway that leads through the pavilion, giving glimpses of the scenery outside which is also reflected inside. At the centre of the Blind Pavilion the panels of black glass line up exactly so that all vision is lost, hence the name. For those seeking explanations it is an exercise in orienteering, investigating how responses are heightened when the normal uses of sight and memory are disturbed, and a book named after the Pavilion offers contributions from scientists, poets and artists exploring these themes. Your Invisible House (2005) in the sculpture park of Zealand in Denmark is also based on two steel structures, one within the other, this time glazed with mirrors which reflect the surrounding pine trees, so that the whole pavilion shimmers as if it might dematerialize. The geometric shapes and angles of the glass panes create multiple perspectives, and once inside the Pavilion the illusions intensify, since the trees and heathland appear and disappear and reflect like a melting landscape. And yet the reaction is to 'really feel the force of nature, the landscape is so powerful'– which makes it another exercise in disturbing perception in order to heighten it. Much like walking into a kaleidoscope and oneself dissolving into many green pieces.

In 2007 Eliasson created the annual Serpentine Pavilion in London's Kensington Gardens, this time experimenting with an upward-winding ramp that completed two circuits to the top, at which point the park could be viewed through twisted cord louvres, which enclosed the ramp and distorted the view. The Pavilion was timber-clad and shaped like a spinning top;

Olafur Eliasson, Blind Pavilion, built in 2003, here seen in Iceland. So called for the black panes of glass which disorient those within, it has travelled to Berlin and Beijing.

SelgasCano Pavilion, 2015, first built for the Serpentine Gallery, London, and now in Los Angeles. Its iridescent tunnels are made from sustainable plastic in nineteen colour shades.

daylight entered the interior (where the Serpentine Pavilion always contains a café) through an oculus at the summit of the pavilion. From here, where the circling ramp ended, the interior could be viewed as well as the park. This kind of temporary pavilion enables experimentation, including trying out new materials that might not be durable enough for a permanent structure. In some ways this situation is ideal for a folly, although it is questionable whether ephemera should be classified as follies, just as the movable Turkish Tents made of canvas in the eighteenth century, however fanciful, could not compare with those designed to last. However, the Serpentine Pavilions are intended to be sold on for use elsewhere, and several have been too ground-breaking to ignore. The 2015 Serpentine Pavilion was designed by the Madrid architects José Selgas and Lucía Cano, famous for their colourful work with synthetic materials, and it is called the SelgasCano Pavilion. To convey its unique beauty it ought to be called the rainbow pavilion, and to identify its unique substance it should be called the plastic pavilion, but instead its nick-names have included psychedelic wormholes, iridescent polytunnels and at night the glow-worm. It is definitely organic and like a creeping thing, far stronger than its fragile appearance would suggest, because it has resistance to corrosion and is adaptable to extremes of temperature. In 2019 it was re-erected in Los Angeles.[21] The plastic skin is double-layered, wrapped over a series of polygonal metal arches, and the plastic itself is a substance called ethylenetetrafluoroethylene, a fluorine-based polymer, ETFE for short, which can absorb subtle and translucent colours – in all there are nineteen shades in the SelgasCano Pavilion. The structure is reinforced by coloured plastic webbing, woven through and looking like ribbons. For added colour, as with stained glass, the light pouring through the plastic also casts pools of colour onto the floor of the pavilion. There are four corridors, sometimes referred to as tentacles, leading inwards to the central space where, as always, refreshments and events take place. Among the architectural inspirations for Selgas and Cano was the Mexican architect Luis Barragán, who painted individual walls in the villas he designed with startling pinks, yellows, reds and purples which harmonized in the bright sunshine with the same grace as flowers do. Another starting point was the London Underground, which Selgas described as many-layered and chaotic and yet structured to organize the flow of people moving through London. Above all the Pavilion achieved a new sense of something as fragile as we are, and in that sense the organic element was realized as never before. In Spain Selgas and Cano teach a design course on Nature and Climatology and have laid out their credentials as 'we need to go back to nature and see the world with new eyes.'

In 2013 the Serpentine Pavilion was designed by a young Japanese architect, now increasingly famous, Sou Fujimoto. His Pavilion was nicknamed The Cloud, because its irregular shape and white openwork structure made it soft-edged and seeming to float and blur against the park and the sky. It was constructed from a lattice of white steel poles rising like delicate scaffolding, with glass steps forming terraces to climb and sit, and circular perspex discs up above to create shelter. In that way the pavilion preserved its transparency while providing a space to explore or sit and relax, and as ever it contained at its centre a café and events area. Although it was playfully greeted as a climbing frame by adults and children alike, as a futuristic pavilion it inspired comparison to digital designs and grid systems. The naturalism of its shape-shifting steel frame was of course an illusion, but a necessary one because Fujimoto is also exploring 'how architecture could be part of nature, or how they could be merged, what are the boundaries between nature and artificial things'. In Japan there are a series of inland islands which have become Art Islands, the largest of which is Naoshima.[22] In 2016, by the waterside where the ferries dock, Sou Fujimoto created a pavilion as an introduction to an area where all the structures are surprising. It is an irregular polyhedron, made up of many triangular surfaces of different shapes and sizes, like a cut crystal. Lit up at night, reflecting in the black water of the harbour, and with the dark wharf in the background, it becomes a diamond. It is raised on a wide plinth with one ramped entrance and seating inside, so that, although lacking conventional walls, it is still a space to be inside, like his Serpentine Pavilion, and it too is irresistible for children to climb. The steel mesh casts shadows like nets, and on the inside it has the effect of blurring the sight, although at the same time the sense of hearing is intensified, so that the pavilion plays with the senses like other modern follies.

Naoshima Island has another architectural folly, created by Hiroshi Sugimoto, who in 2002 converted a traditional Japanese Shinto shrine into the modern vernacular. The original Go-oh Shrine dated from the Muromachi period (1336–1578) and its recreation was mainly a work of imagination, but it was based on a natural force field provided by a gigantic slab of flat rock, which is separated and sanctified by the wide borders of pebbles set all around it. On this flat rock the Main Sanctuary stands, a plain wooden structure, just a roof supported at the four corners over open walls, uniquely Japanese in its simplicity and sense of harmony. The Worship Hall is smaller and higher, a little primitive shrine supported on stilts on a high pedestal of rough-hewn stones. It is made of wooden slats, arranged horizontally for the walls and vertically for the roof, which is overlapping and high-peaked. The only way to move from the Main Sanctuary to the Worship Hall is up a glass staircase, with large slabs of optical lens which give each step a disturbingly ethereal quality. A second optical glass staircase leads underground to a rock chamber and a concrete walled passage to a portal with a view over the sea. If one believes in the spirits of nature, which is what the Shinto faith is based on, they are surely here. The modern name of the Go-oh shrine is Appropriate Proportion, and that reliance on perfect balance is also part of Shinto tradition. In 2018 Sugimoto brought a Glass Tea House to Versailles, where it was erected in the formal water of the Trianon Garden, with a causeway of stone slabs to reach it. Previously it had been exhibited at the Venice Biennale of 2014. Within this pure glass cube the full Japanese Tea Ceremony was performed. The European name given to the Glass Tea House was Mondrian, perhaps to emphasize its kinship to the abstract and structural lines of his paintings, but also because his name, broken into Japanese syllables and characters, means a simple pavilion where you can hear the birds singing.

Hiroshi Sugimoto, Go-oh Shrine, Art Island, Naoshima, Japan, 2002, a recreation of
an ancient shrine but with modern surprises, like steps made from disorienting optical glass.

What Hiroshi Sugimoto has done in transforming the Japanese vernacular
into modern follies, the Chinese-American architect I. M. Pei has paralleled
for China. Although most of his eminent career was spent in America, and
his best-known European structure is the glass pyramid fronting the Louvre
(opened in 1988 amid challenging controversy), in 2002 he was commissioned to build a new annexe to the Museum in Suzhou, the ancestral home
of his family and the favourite remembered place of his childhood. Suzhou
is the city (inland from Shanghai) of magical Chinese gardens with names
like the Garden of the Master of the Nets, full of traditional features like
moon gates, and pavilions whose balconies dream over lotus pools. It is also
a city of canals lined by black and white houses with steeply pitched roofs.
All these elements were ingeniously reflected in Pei's ultra-modern design for
the new museum, built on the site of the Loyal Prince's House and blending with the nearby Garden of the Humble Administrator. The architectural
correspondences between the old and new were emphasized by traditional

planting, ornamental rocks and a formal pool. Beside this pool Pei designed a glass and steel pavilion for a reception and performance area, not in itself a folly. But by the time it was unveiled, in 2006, Pei had also created (in 2003) an almost identical glass and steel pavilion in a garden in Wiltshire belonging to Henry and Tessa Keswick. The Keswick family, whose ancestral lands are in the Scottish borders, are old China hands, *tai-pan* (rich foreign merchants) based in Hong Kong and trading with China through Jardine Matheson. Henry's cousin Maggie Keswick wrote the definitive book describing Chinese gardens and explaining the traditions behind them. Their fathers knew Pei's father, who was also a banker.

The Keswick property in Wiltshire is called Oare House, a Georgian mansion whose smooth lawns and tree-lined vistas lead into the undulating Wiltshire landscape. The pavilion sits in the main axis of this vista from the house and is called Oare Pavilion.[23] It was first presented to the Keswicks as an exquisite little model in a box, to be completed with every modern comfort, including an openwork statue by Antony Gormley. Both the Suzhou Pavilion and Oare Pavilion are octagonal in the sense that the sloping glass and steel panels of the lower roof number eight, alternating triangles and squares to angle their inward slant. Raised up above this, a smaller glass

I. M. Pei, Oare Pavilion, Wiltshire, 2003, a garden eye-catcher made from glass and steel, recalling his glass pyramid at the Louvre and also hinting at a Chinese pagoda.

roof consists of four triangular panels that tilt outwards over the roof below. Thus the air of a mini pagoda is created and a jaunty finial confirms it. The Oare Pavilion has glassed-in walls below the larger roof, repeating the octagon, and it stands on a cruciform concrete base containing the entrance and stairs (the Suzhou Pavilion has open sides and an octagonal base). Under this spreading glass canopy pale oak dominates the interior of Oare Pavilion, the view spreads in all directions, glass doors slide at the touch of a button, sophisticated shades control sunlight and heat levels, and all is laid ready to entertain. The Keswicks asked Pei – it was the last commission of his grand old age – 'to combine architecture and nature in a mutually supportive way'. The Georgian Group offered their architectural award for providing 'an eyecatcher . . . bravely contemporary in its design but also entirely harmonious in its setting'. All true, but the chinoiserie element captured for the first time in glass is the most exciting aspect of all.

The landscape architect Charles Jencks was married to Maggie Keswick, Henry's cousin, and at their Scottish home near Dumfries they designed the Garden of Cosmic Speculation in the 1990s.[24] This combined Jencks's scientific ideas on the nature of the universe with Keswick's knowledge of *feng shui*, the Chinese concept of harmonizing humanity with the forces that control the natural landscape. At the heart of the garden are two crescent pools encircled by terraces of grass that twist sinuously up to green peaks. These serene earthworks of wave-like formations can be enjoyed without any theorizing, but they are typical of Jencks's landscapes, and they contain fractals, the irregular curves produced by repeated subdivisions in mathematics. Jencks was fascinated by the fact that waves and spirals are basic patterns of existence, found in the wave function of atoms, in the double helix of DNA, in sound waves and brain waves and in the unpredictable activities of economics, populations, climate and the cosmos itself. Given the discovery that the universe is not a precise mechanism but a process that advances by jumps – which could be called emergencies because they are sudden and cause a new order to emerge – in 1995 Jencks wrote *The Architecture of the Jumping Universe*, arguing that modern architecture must aim to express this process and its complexity. In nature it is constant and sometimes familiar, like the seasons and the metamorphosis of insects, and now it can be observed in the cosmos itself, which is also fluctuating and evolving, a process Jencks called cosmogenesis.

Among the historic architectural examples that Jencks gave to illustrate systems pushed out of continuity were the sham ruin and the broken column;

and up at the edge of the Garden of Cosmic Speculation, among the trees, there is a little folly to prove his point that 'the single pavilion is a generative form.'[25] Geometric black grids hold and frame rectangular white walls and panels of glass. Their diverse sizes and angles offer mathematical puzzles and proportions. They are not enclosed but stand open like screens around the stairs up to the roof-top viewing platform. A vertical red tube marks the height between floor and ceiling, and red and blue horizontal tubes lie along one side of the roof, measuring its width; however, being curved, they are also part of Jencks's stipulation that, in order to echo the activities of the universe, modern architecture must contain variation and surprise – folds, twists and curves – as natural systems do.

Charles Jencks, Pavilion, Garden of Cosmic Speculation, Dumfries. The garden was started in the 1990s, designed to reflect the mathematical principles that govern the universe and nature.

Among the other natural forms that Jencks saw as ripe for architectural experiment were clouds, crystals and fractured planes. On the roof is an angled glass plane in a grid, serving no other purpose than to express this theory and to reflect clouds and the branches of trees. Branches and twigs exemplify another cosmic code, self-similarity, a growth system that allows for great diversity and adaptability within a cohesive system, also known as a fractal code of bifurcation. The stairs at the centre of the folly are no ordinary steps; they too offer unpredictability and surprise, because each step is halved to mount alternately, creating a zigzag of movement, and this pattern of upward progress is repeated in the square grids that frame the stairs like a bannister. According to Jencks, 'architecture is built meaning', and here we have a model to illustrate 'the discontinuities of emergent structures'.[26]

While Charles Jencks proposed that the universe and everything in it is most creative when it reaches a stage poised between order and chaos, the leading twentieth-century philosopher Jacques Derrida espoused a system of analysis called Deconstruction which also values the unpredictable. 'Not the mixture but the tension . . . something absolutely new and a break.' His ideas exasperated more traditional philosophers, who found them 'lacking in

Bernard Tschumi, Parc de la Villette, Paris, one of 25 red steel follies created from
the 1980s as an exercise in deconstruction, hollowing out traditional designs.

clarity and rigour',[27] but for others they were inspirational: 'You may search
just for the sake of searching, and try for the sake of trying. So there is a possibility of what I would call playing.' His challenge to the assumptions of
Western culture, and his enigmatic sayings that sought to undermine them,
were labelled Deconstructionism, and the follies that are its best architectural expression are in Parc de la Villette in Paris. The French-Swiss architect
Bernard Tschumi discussed their design with Jacques Derrida and Peter
Eisenman, and controversially won the commission in the 1980s.

Parc de la Villette, to the northeast of Paris, had housed the slaughter-
houses and meat market of Paris and, when those were moved (by 1974), a
space was left bare for redevelopment; only the Grande Halle de la Villette,
which was once the old cast-iron abattoir, was retained to hold fairs and
festivals. The Canal de l'Ourcq crosses the centre of the park like a back-
bone, linking with other waterways. Derrida and Tschumi were certainly
Postmodern, but for their starting point they turned back to Plato's definition

of *khora*, meaning 'space' – as something through which everything passes but nothing is retained – whose entity could be expressed by physical objects like a sieve, a mirror or a musical instrument. To them parkland was another expression of *khora*, and given the bare spaces of Parc de la Villette they set out to revise conventional ideas, challenging such normal activities as gently drifting past traditional landmarks, or taking short cuts through green places. Instead they created an exercise in orienteering through a rigid urban environment.

Parc de la Villette has cultural venues that look like industrial buildings, mitigated by themed gardens where plants compete with sculptural forms. Tschumi organized the park into a grid of points, lines and surfaces, the last being expanses of grass, gardens or gravel, the lines being pathways or shaded avenues and the points being constructions. Twenty-six of the constructions were his red metal follies, set like way-markers and each with a name and a grid code. They look both magnificent and startling against the green of grass and trees, or lining the Canal de l'Ourcq. Some are in use as cafés, performance areas or children's playgrounds, the best remain purely as follies (Tschumi named them so) and all have become iconic. Like the park itself they are intended as a Deconstructionist vacuum, a cut-out or hollow created by some former function. However, they are interrelated, because they are all cleverly based on the deconstruction and rearrangement of a 10-metre (33 ft) cube. Folie de l'Écluse stands beside a lock and includes a large skeletal water wheel and pulley within its uneven grid of walls. Folie Horloge showcases the monumental clock previously installed at the slaughterhouse in 1877. Folie des Vents et des Dunes is a children's playground. For all the denials of conventional norms, perhaps even because of them, these deconstructed follies with their open walls, grids and tubular curves, their Brutalist metal forms and blood-red colour, do suggest the actual history of the site, together with a more general sense of regenerating industrial wasteland. Tschumi aimed for a place where the natural and artificial are forced together into a state of constant discovery, not in the old romantic ways but in startling new forms. Evidently he intended it all to be seen as a palimpsest of past, present and future full of hidden meanings. For instance, the most iconic of all, the Folie Belvédère, is a viewfinder beside the Canal, with spiral steps curving ornamentally up its harsh metal side, platforms up aloft and a ramp reaching out from its innards, inviting entry and enjoyment – just as a good folly always has.

If modern follies are more astonishing than their predecessors, even rating concepts above ornament, it could be argued that follies always reflect their age, both aesthetically and politically, and the theories behind them have always been part of their story. Such adaptability is a reassuring sign that folly-building may live on, for architects to experiment and others to relish and puzzle over. Mathematical calculation and proportion, being an essential part of architecture, are now less a matter of seeking harmony and more like a series of questions. Religious and political protest as motives for building follies have been replaced by environmental angst; and appreciating nature for the vistas and settings it provides has become the more urgent matter of rethinking our whole relationship to our planet. In the eighteenth-century heyday of follies the past was a primary source of inspiration; now it is something to challenge and escape. And the curious pleasure derived from exploring and exploiting other cultures has given way to a multiculturalism that sees follies springing up in every continent. Long may that continue and increase. It would be a very healthy sign.

References

Introduction: A Taste of Follies

1 Edmund Spenser, *The Ruines of Time*, from lines 85–96. Written in 1591 and addressed to Mary Sidney as a lament for the death of her brother Sir Philip Sidney. The lines quoted describe the ruins of Rome, but have been extracted from the prevailing gloom.

2 The Chateau is now a property belonging to the Landmark Trust, which rescues important follies and restores them as holiday lets. In addition the Trust produces detailed *History Albums* which can be viewed online. The Chateau's *History Album* is the major source of information and subsequent quotations; see also Gwyn Headley and Wim Meulenkamp, *Follies, Grottoes and Garden Buildings* (London, 1986 and 1999), a marvellous folly gazetteer, p. 335.

3 Belton House, ibid., p. 329.

4 Gervase Jackson-Stops, George Mott and Sally Sample Aall, *Follies and Pleasure Pavilions* (London, 1989), p. 77; Edward Pearce, *Robert Walpole: Scoundrel and Genius* (London, 2008), is the source of the quoted description.

5 The drawing of the Water House which references the Earl of Pembroke is in the Metropolitan Museum, New York. As earl he was involved in architectural improvements to his own estate at Wilton including the Palladian Bridge.

6 Jack the Treacle Eater is in almost every folly book, starting with Barbara Jones, *Follies and Grottoes* (London, 1953 and 1989), pp. 227–30. Jones was the earliest folly authority, and she exploded the idea that it was built by the Messiters for famine relief, because she was shown the family portraits in Barwick Park of John and Grace Newman, a childless couple from whom their nephew Thomas Messiter inherited.

7 Hermes inherited the powers of Priapus, a more primitive garden god whom the Greeks erected as an idol with an exaggerated penis. Over time the herm lost its visible attributes and became a head on a rectangular column. The goddess Venus was a female equivalent, whose image also became smoothed over time, but still associated with gardens and fertility. See Chapter Three.

8 Castletown: Jones, *Follies*, p. 121; Speaker Connolly became the wealthiest man in Ireland, having supported William III during the Glorious Revolution of 1688, and a great landowner after the confiscations of Catholic property. He led the Protestant political group the Undertakers. Hence the resentment of Irish poets such as Michael Hartnett – the poem was first published in *Collected Poems* (Dublin, 1985 and 1987).

9 Lord Macartney's Embassy to China took place in 1792–4. Coleridge wrote his poem 'Kubla Khan' in 1797, though it was not published until 1816. For the links between Coleridge and Culbone see J. Mays, 'King Kubla's Folly', *TLS* (1 August 2008); for Lord Macartney's comparisons to Stowe see Patrick Conner, *Oriental Architecture in the West* (London, 1979), quoting J. L. Cranmer-Byng, ed., *An Embassy to China* (London, 1962), p. 127.

10 Alexander Pope, *An Epistle to the Right Honourable Richard Earl of Burlington*, 1731–2, lines 35–48. For descriptions of Stowe see Chapter Four.

11 Gilbert West, 'Stowe, the Gardens of the Right Honourable Richard Lord Viscount Cobham. Address'd to Mr. Pope', 1732. For more quotations on ruins see Chapter Eight.

12 Clavell Tower, Landmark Trust, *History Album*, available at http://landmarktrust.org.uk – this includes the contemporary descriptions and an account of its rescue and restoration from the crumbling clifftop. This is the most notable example of the Trust's dedication and brilliance in rescuing historic buildings. Funding and permission were finally gained in 2006 and among the supporters was the author P. D. James, whose novel *The Dark Tower* used Clavell as the scene of a murder.

13 Horton Tower: Headley and Meulenkamp, *Follies*, pp. 205–6, including the evidence of Edward Gibbon.

The tower is now in use for mobile phone masts, which hopefully ensures some preservation.

14 Charborough Tower: Headley and Meulenkamp, *Follies*, pp. 208–9. The quoted descriptions are from Hardy, *Two on a Tower* (London, 1882), Chapter 1.

15 Laughton Tower, Landmark Trust *History Album*, available at http://landmarktrust.org.uk – includes the quotations from Virginia Woolf's *Diaries*.

16 Headley and Meulenkamp, *Follies*: Solomon's Temple, p. 176; the Pepperbox, also known as Eyre's folly, p. 537; Farringdon and Sway Towers, pp. 254 and 263; Wainhouse Tower, pp. 552–3 – note that the origin of the tower as a chimney coincided with the Smoke Abatement Act of 1870.

17 Headley and Meulenkamp, *Follies*: Hadlow Tower, pp. 297–8; Racton Tower, p. 512 (together with many online accounts of spooky experiences). Lord Halifax's other follies include Horton Menagerie, see Chapter Five, and Hampton Grotto, see Chapter Six.

18 For more follies built to commemorate victories see Chapter Four.

19 Quex Tower: Jones, *Follies*, p. 207, quoting J. A. Parnell, *The Gothic Traveller* (London, 1819), who described the opening ceremony and the tower in admiring detail. The spire was planned from the start though not finished in time for the inauguration in August 1819.

20 The 'briny fluid' gives a good sense of the grey chill of the sea along the north Kent coast.

21 Information mainly online, including the verses in honour of the departing vicar of Bollington, 1856, which testify to its whiteness at that time, and images showing various attempts to paint it.

One **Seeking Out the Origins**

1 For Henry v's folly see Howard Colvin et al., *The History of the King's Works*, II (London, 1963), p. 685. Henry VIII's is cited in Roy Strong, *The Renaissance Garden in England* (London, 1979 and 1998), p. 131.

2 Several early banqueting houses are described in Gervase Jackson-Stops, G. Mott and S. S. Aall, *Follies and Pleasure Pavilions* (London, 1989), p. 10.

3 Adam Nicolson, *Sissinghurst* (London, 2008), p. 183. For glimpses of Tudor and Stuart banqueting houses in the background of portraits see Roy Strong, *The Artist and the Garden* (London and New Haven, CT, 2000), especially Holbein's portrait of Sir Thomas More and his family, reproduced in detail on p. 29, which shows his pavilion by the Thames at Chelsea.

4 The pageantry at Kenilworth was described by a contemporary witness, Robert Laneham, in *A Letter* (Leiden, 1983); Elisabeth Woodhouse, 'Kenilworth: The Earl of Leicester's Pleasure Grounds following Robert Laneham's Letter', *Garden History*, XXVII/1 (1999), p. 127, and 'The Symbolic Garden Created for the Earl of Leicester at Kenilworth', *Garden History*, XXXVI/1 (2008), p. 94.

5 Francis Bacon's essay 'Of Gardens', 1625, available in numerous editions. See also Paula Henderson, 'Sir Francis Bacon's Essay "Of Gardens" in Context', *Garden History*, XXXVI/1 (2008), p. 59.

6 Lyveden New Bield, National Trust Guidebook (n.d.); Celia Fisher, 'The Lost Gardens of Lyveden New Bield', *Hortus*, 21 (Autumn 2007), p. 75; Andrew Eburne, 'Sir Thomas Tresham and Lyveden', *Garden History*, XXXVI/1 (2008), p. 114.

7 Robert Lyminge's design for Blickling Banqueting House is owned by the National Trust and reproduced in Jackson-Stops et al., *Follies*, p. 8.

8 Strong, *The Artist and the Garden*, p. 114, describes and illustrates the sets of Inigo Jones, and quotes 'Curious arbours'.

9 The Chipping Campden Banqueting Houses are described in the Landmark Trust *History Album*, available at http://landmarktrust.org.uk. See also Paul Everson, 'The Gardens of Campden House', *Garden History*, XVII/2 (1989); Timothy Mowl, *Historic Gardens of Gloucestershire* (Stroud, 2002); Gerard Noel, *The Noels of Chipping Campden and Exton*, Campden and District Historical Society (2004).

10 Cornelius Johnson, *Arthur Capel and His Family*, c. 1641, National Portrait Gallery; described and illustrated in Strong, *The Artist and the Garden*, pp. 17 and 53; Celia Fisher, 'Lord Capel's Garden', *Ulemhas Review* (2007), p. 10.

11 Swarkestone Pavilion, Landmark Trust *History Album*, available at http://landmarktrust.org.uk.

12 Swarkestone: Lucinda Lambton, *Beastly Buildings* (London, 1985), p. 49.

13 Freston Tower, Landmark Trust *History Album*, available at http://landmarktrust.org.uk.

14 Luttrell's Tower, Landmark Trust *History Album*, available at http://landmarktrust.org.uk, the source of the subsequent quotations.

15 Rudyard Kipling, 'A Smuggler's Song', first published in *Puck of Pook's Hill* (London, 1906).

16 William Gilpin, *Forest Scenery* (London, 1792), quoted in Luttrell's Tower, Landmark Trust *History Album*.

17 Anthony Clayton, *London's Coffee Houses* (London, 2003), p. 18.

18 The Music Room, Lancaster is described in the Landmark Trust *History Album*, available at http://landmarktrust.org.uk.

19 Richard Bradley, *Survey of Ancient Husbandry and Gardening* (London, 1725); see Stephen Bending, 'Horace Walpole and Eighteenth-Century Garden History', *Journal of Warburg and Courtauld Institutes* (1994), p. 209.

20 John Rea, *Flora seu de Florum Cultura*, 1665, quoted in Anna Pavord, *The Tulip* (London, 1999), p. 119.

21 John Harris, 'The Summer House at the Vyne', *Apollo* (April 2002), p. 32.

22 Ben Jonson, *B. Jon: His Part of King James his Royall and Magnificent Entertainment* (Edward Blount, 1604), p. 14 (B2-3).

23 Rose Macaulay, *Pleasure of Ruins* (London, 1953 and 1984), p. 208.

24 Mussenden Temple: Jackson-Stops et al., *Follies*, p. 52; Caroline Holmes, *Follies of Europe* (London, 2008), pp. 126–7.

25 Garrick's Villa and Temple to Shakespeare: *Local History Notes*, Richmond upon Thames Libraries, pp. 1–7, available at www.richmond.gov.uk. Shakespeare's statue is now in the British Museum with a replica in the temple. The two paintings by Zoffany: Garrick Club, London.

26 Halswell Temple: Timothy Mowl, *Historic Gardens of Somerset* (London, 2010).

27 *The Rievaulx Terrace*: National Trust Guide, 1999; Giles Worsley, 'Duncombe Park, Yorkshire', *Country Life* (24 May 1990), p. 116, and *Country Life* (31 May 1990), p. 138.

28 Oval Pavilion: Jackson-Stops et al., *Follies*, p. 58.

29 Macaulay, *Ruins*, pp. 204–5.

30 See Chapter Three for more on William Kent and Rousham; for his classical influences see John Dixon Hunt, *William Kent* (London, 1987).

31 For Pope's observations on landscape gardening and paintings see Douglas Chambers, *The Planters of the English Landscape Garden* (London and New Haven, CT, 1993), p. 160; Addison, *The Spectator* (June 1712).

32 Poussin's two landscape companion pieces, *The Funeral of Phocion* and *The Widow with His Ashes* were completed in 1648; the former is in the Louvre, the latter in the Walker Art Gallery, Liverpool. Poussin's *Orpheus and Eurydice*, c. 1650, is also in the Louvre. Claude's influential *Landscape with Aeneas at Delos*, 1672, is in the National Gallery, London. Canaletto's finest *Capriccio of Ruins*, c. 1751, is in the Museo Poldi Pezzoli, Milan.

Two **Some Names to Conjure With**

1 Robert Tavernor, *Palladio and Palladianism* (London and New York, 1991).

2 Patrizia Granziera, 'Freemasonic Symbolism and Georgian Gardens', *Journal of Esoteric Studies*, V (2003); James Stevens Curl, *The Art and Architecture of Freemasonry* (London, 1991).

3 C. Ridgeway and R. Williams, *Sir John Vanbrugh and Landscape Architecture in Baroque England* (London, 2000); see also its review in *Garden History*, XXVIII/2 (2000), p. 288.

4 Vanbrugh's sketch of the British cemetery in Surat is in the Bodleian Library.

5 Ophelia Field, *The Kit-Cat Club* (London, 2008); the Wikipedia entry is excellent.

6 Kneller, Kit-Cat portrait of Newcastle and Lincoln, is in the National Portrait Gallery, London, among the series of Kit-Cat portraits.

7 Vaughan Hart, *Nicholas Hawksmoor* (London, 2002); Fischer von Erlach, the leading architect of the Habsburg court in Vienna and a Freemason, published *Entwurff einer historischen Architectur* in 1721. It was influential throughout Europe and contained fine prints, not only of his own Baroque creations. He also attempted to reconstruct the wonders of the ancient world, most notably the tomb of Mausolus at Halicarnassus (now Bodrum). Pliny the Elder had described it as a high rectangular structure of great beauty. The upper section is surrounded by a colonnade roofed with a pyramid and adorned with statues and carved friezes.

8 The 1715 rebellion was when the Old Pretender, son of James II, tried to regain the throne from George I. Being a Stuart, his insurrection was regarded as Scottish, hence the lion of England fighting the unicorn of Scotland. The popular verse went 'The lion and the unicorn/ Were fighting for the crown/ The lion beat the unicorn/ All around the town.' William Hogarth's print *Gin Lane*, 1751, coincided with the Gin Act, designed to mitigate the evils of gin drinking.

9 For details of Queen Anne's Summerhouse (the folly related to the footstool incident), and Archer's Grand Pavilion at Wrest Park, see Chapter Four.

10 The first European edition of the *Thousand and One Nights* was the French translation by Antoine Galland in 1704. In English the *Arabian Nights Entertainments* first appeared in instalments in a Grub Street edition between 1706 and 1721, making it contemporary with Archer's pavilion.

11 *Orleans House: A History*, Richmond Borough Collections (2007), pp. 12–21 and 37.

12 John Harris, 'Castle Howard and Chiswick', *Garden History*, XXXII/1 (2004), p. 132; Jane Clark, 'The Mysterious Mr Buck', *Apollo*, CXXIX (1989), p. 319; Cinzia Maria Sicca, 'Lord Burlington at Chiswick', *Garden History*, X/1 (1982), p. 43.

13 Alexander Pope, *Epistle to Burlington*, 1731–2, lines 23–6.

14 Jonathon Richardson, *Lord Burlington with the Bagnio in the Grounds of Chiswick House*, c. 1717, National Portrait Gallery, London. The view of the goose foot by Rigaud, dated 1734, is in the Chatsworth Collection. For Pope's reference to music in the grounds see Letter to Martha Blount, 1716, in *Correspondence of Alexander Pope*, ed. George Sherburn (London, 1956), vol. I, p. 338. For quotations from Colen Campbell see *Vitruvius Britannicus*, vol. III, 1725.

15 Ricky Pound, 'Chiswick House – a Masonic Temple?', *Brentford and Chiswick Local History Journal*, 16 (2007), which quotes the Masonic verse in full.

16 Arthur Devis, *Lady Burlington in the Grounds of Chiswick House*, Historic England Photo Library, ref. K050051, reproduced in Roy Strong, *The Artist and the Garden* (London and New Haven, CT, 2000), p. 69. Other images of the orange-tree garden include Kent's sketch (in the Chatsworth collection) showing Lady Burlington by the Temple and a gardener with a barrow at work – reproduced in John Dixon Hunt, *William Kent* (London, 1987), p. 132. The temple has a leafy portico but no dome so it is considered as a *capriccio* rather than a study. Best of all is Peter Andreas Rysbrack, *View of the Orange Tree Garden and Ionic Temple*, c. 1728–32, also in the Chatsworth Collection, which includes a collection of exotic birds – reproduced in Strong, *Artist*, p. 207.

17 For Flitcroft's work at Stourhead see Chapter Three, and at Wentworth Woodhouse see Chapter Four.

18 Walpole's Excise Bill of 1733, seen as damaging tax for trade, caused a number of resignations; Lord Cobham retired to Stowe and Burlington to Chiswick, where both concentrated on developing their grounds – examples of how folly-building was entwined with politics, as described in Chapter Four.

19 Dixon Hunt, *Kent*, p. 97.

20 Letter to Carlisle, MS held at Castle Howard, quoted by Dixon Hunt, ibid., p. 46.

21 Kent's drawings are catalogued and illustrated by Dixon Hunt, ibid., pp. 110–71.

22 John Milton, *Paradise Lost*, Book 4, first published 1667. The quotations are short phrases selected from a magnificent but lengthy description of paradise.

23 Horace Walpole, *History of Modern Gardening*, is part of his *Anecdotes of Painting*, vol. IV (London, 1770), p. 264.

24 Quoted by John Dixon Hunt, *The Genius of the Place* (London, 1975), p. 54. For descriptions of *fermes ornées* see Chapter Five.

25 Letter from William Mason to Humphry Repton, published in *Sketches and Hints* (London, 1795).

26 John Milton, the 'Mermaid's Song', from *Comus, a Masque*, 1637, Act III, lines 1–3. For the history, architecture and bibliography of Croome Park see National Trust Guide, 2008.

27 For Chatelherault see Chapter Five.

28 John Fleming, *Robert Adam and His Circle* (London, 1962); for the ruins of Diocletian's Palace see Rose Macaulay, *The Pleasure of Ruins* (London, 1953), pp. 411–13.

29 Mrs Delany, *Autobiography and Letters*, ed. Lady Llanover, 1861–2; Walpole, *History*; William Chambers's criticisms of Capability Brown were published in *Dissertation on Oriental Gardening* (London, 1772).

30 Chambers's classical-style follies feature in Gervase Jackson-Stops, G. Mott and S. S. Aall, *Follies and Pleasure Grounds* (London, 1989): the Casino at Marino, p. 81; Osterley, Temple of Pan, p. 91; Wilton House Casino, p. 120. For Chambers's work at Kew see Chapters Five and Seven; for Amesbury see Margaret Fisher, *Tales of People Connected with Amesbury Abbey* (London, 1982); Patrick Conner, *Oriental Architecture in the West* (London, 1979), p. 83.

31 Judy Preston, 'Thomas Wright', *Garden History*, XXXVIII/2 (2010), p. 159.

32 Ibid.

33 Roy Bolton, *Thomas Wright of Durham at Halswell*, at http://halswellpark.wordpress.com, April 2016, fully illustrated; see also Gervase Jackson-Stops, 'The Bathstone Bridge at Halswell', *Country Life* (February 1989); Timothy Mowl, *The Historic Gardens of Somerset* (London, 2010). Hogarth, *Sir Charles Kemeys-Tynte*, 1753, is in the National Portrait Gallery, London. Wright's sketch entitled *Breakwater* is in the Avery Architectural Library, Columbia University.

34 Eileen Harris, 'Batty Langley: A Tutor to Freemasons', *Burlington Magazine*, CXIX (May 1977), p. 327.

35 Croome Park, National Trust Guide, p. 21.

36 Jennifer Meir, 'Sanderson Miller and Lancelot Brown', *Garden History*, XXX/1 (2002), p. 26.

37 For Hagley and Wimpole Towers see Chapter Eight.

Three **Telling a Story**

1 Francesco Colonna, *Poliphilus' Dream*, 1499, published with original illustrations by Thames and Hudson (London and New York, 2003).

2 Contemporary descriptions and inscriptions from Luke Morgan, *The Monster in the Garden* (Philadelphia, PA, 2016); see also Caroline Holmes, *Follies of Europe* (London, 2008), pp. 22–7.

3 There are remains of Etruscan tombs in the area around Bomarzo, and Orsini created another in the Sacro Bosco.

4 The Italian inscription beneath the other sphinx reads, in translation: 'Whoever walks in the garden without raising their eyebrows and remains tight-lipped would never even admire the seven wonders of the world.'

5 Virgil, *Aeneid*, Book VI, trans. W. F. Jackson Knight (London, 1956) pp. 148–51.

6 Dante, *Inferno*, Canto III.

7 There are other monster mouths at Bomarzo, including the so-called Mask of Madness with the emblems of Orsini on its head (a globe topped by a castle). The Giant wrestling has been variously interpreted as Ariosto's Orlando Furioso, or Hercules, although the nearby inscription refers to the Colossus of Rhodes. Originally the statue of Victory or Fame on a tortoise held a trumpet, probably intended as a satire on the slowness of good fortune to arrive, or it may be akin to the motto *Festina lente* (Hasten slowly).

8 For the walls, bastions and triumphal gateways of Castle Howard see Barbara Jones, *Follies and Grottoes* (London, 1953 and 1989), pp. 26–9.

9 For the geometry and layout of Castle Howard see Caroline Dalton, *Sir John Vanbrugh and the Vitruvian Landscape* (London, 2012).

10 Lady Irwin's verse quoted by J. Dixon Hunt, *The Genius of the Place* (London, 1975), p. 229.

11 For Hawksmoor's involvement in Castle Howard see Vaughan Hart, *Nicholas Hawksmoor* (London, 2002).

12 In Virgil's fifth *Eclogue*, a description of the funeral of Daphnis in Arcadia includes the words *Daphnis ego in silvis*, which is said to have inspired the seventeenth-century Pope Clement IX to coin the phrase *Et in Arcadia ego*, associated with death.

13 John Dixon Hunt, *William Kent* (London, 1987), p. 83. See also pp. 79–89 for an overall description of Rousham.

14 Death in Arcadia could be violent, as in the Rousham statues, or in a Poussin painting; see *Landscape with a Man Killed by a Snake*, 1648, National Gallery, London.

15 Hunt, *Kent*; see the catalogue of Kent's sketches, p. 103, cat. no. 105.

16 Daniel Mytens, *Thomas Howard Earl of Arundel*, 1618, National Portrait Gallery, London.

17 David Coffin, 'Venus in the Eighteenth-Century English Garden', *Garden History*, XXVIII/2 (2000), p. 173.

18 Gervase Jackson-Stops, G. Mott and S. S Aall, *Follies and Pleasure Pavilions* (London, 1989), p. 70.

19 For details and sources relating to Stowe and its follies see Chapter Four.

20 Francis Coventry, in *The World*, 1753, quoted Jackson-Stops, Mott and Aall, *Follies*, p. 18.

21 Hubert Robert, *The Bathing Pool*, Metropolitan Museum, New York. Commissioned by the Comte d'Artois, 1777, for the bathing room at Château de Bagatelle; see also Chapter Four.

22 Dashwood's original statue was the *Medici Venus*; it is now replaced with a replica of the armless *Venus de Milo*.

23 Michael Symes, 'West Wycombe Park', *Garden History*, XXXIII/1 (2005), p. 1; Jones, *Follies*, pp. 100–107.

24 West Wycombe was painted in the 1750s by William Hannan, with works subsequently engraved by William Woolett, and in the 1780s by Thomas Daniell. These and the final portrait of Francis Dashwood in oriental dress are owned by his descendant Edward Dashwood and the National Trust.

25 Both Poussin's *Triumph of Pan* and *Revels of Bacchus* are in the National Gallery, London.

26 Timothy Mowl, 'In the Realm of the Great God Pan', *Country Life* (17 October 1996). The paintings by Thomas Robins are privately owned; for reproductions see Roy Strong, *The Artist and the Garden* (London and New Haven, CT, 2000), p. 247.

27 Michael Symes, *Mr Hamilton's Elysium: The Gardens of Painshill* (London, 2010); Tim Richardson, 'Painshill, Surrey', *Country Life* (December 2000).

28 Hamilton worked for Frederick, Prince of Wales, as Clerk of the Household from 1738 to 1746, while his sister Lady Archibald was Frederick's mistress. At this time Frederick was part of the Whig opposition and much involved with Lord Cobham at Stowe and the Grenvilles and Lytteltons, all creators of folly gardens. Frederick himself was developing the gardens at Carlton House and Kew. For more on politics see Chapter Four.

29 Opening lines of Alexander Pope, 'Prologue to Mr Addison's Cato', 1713.

30 Ray Desmond, *The History of the Royal Botanic Gardens, Kew* (London, 1995), pp. 54–5.

31 Johann Nieuhof, *An Embassy from the East India Company of the United Provinces to China*, first published in Dutch in 1665 and in English in 1669.

32 Kenneth Woodbridge, 'Henry Hoare's Paradise', *Art Bulletin*, XLVII/1 (1965), p. 83; Malcolm Kelsall, 'Iconography of Stourhead', *Journal of the Warburg and Courtauld Institutes*, 46 (1983), p. 133; Oliver Cox, 'Stourhead', *Garden History*, XL/1 (2012), p. 98.

Quotations from Virgil, *Aeneid*, Books III and VI, trans. W. F. Jackson Knight (London, 1956).

33 Addison in *The Spectator* (June 1712).

34 William Chambers's Temple of the Sun at Kew, which he modelled on the prototype at Baalbek, is long gone, having been crushed by a falling cedar tree in 1916.

35 Daniel Defoe, *A Tour thro' the Whole Island of Great Britain* (London, 1724–7).

36 Gwyn Headley and Wim Meulenkamp, *Follies, Grottoes and Garden Buildings* (London, 1999), pp. 468–72; for the reference to Sir Percy Brett's drawing of Canton see David Beevers, ed., *Chinese Whispers* (London, 2008), p. 59, and Headley and Meulenkamp, *Follies*, p. 464.

37 William Gilpin, *Observations Relative to the Picturesque* (London, 1772).

38 The name given to the building in Athens since the Middle Ages may have been a confusion between Demosthenes and Diogenes. The latter was an eccentric philosopher who went looking with a lantern in daylight to try and find a virtuous man. Demosthenes, the democrat and orator, would have appealed more to eighteenth-century ideology. As a folly the choragic monument reappeared at Tatton Park and Alton Towers. In Paris Napoleon recreated it, but it was destroyed in 1870.

39 Walpole, *Correspondence*, ed. W. S. Lewis, 48 vols (London, 1937–83) – letters from Paris written in the 1770s: Letter XXVIII, publ. 1955, p. 222, and Letter XXXV, pub. 1973, p. 137, quoted by John Harris, 'L'Idole du Temple', *Garden History*, XXIX/1 (2001), p. 36.

40 John Dixon Hunt, *The Picturesque Garden in Europe* (London, 2002), pp. 54–8 and p. 123; Holmes, *Follies of Europe*, pp. 120–23; Michel Saudan and Sylvia Saudan-Skira, *From Folly to Follies* (Geneva, 1987; Cologne, 1997).

Four **Concepts of Freedom and Victory**

1 Barbara Jones, *Follies and Grottoes* (London, 1953 and 1989), p. 1.

2 Mark Girouard, *Rushton Triangular Lodge*, English Heritage Guidebook, 2004.

3 Oliver Garnett, *Westbury Court Garden*, National Trust Guidebook, 2007.

4 Alexander Dumas, *The Black Tulip* (Paris, 1850), Chapter 5.

5 Stephen Bending, 'Horace Walpole and Eighteenth-Century Garden History', *Journal of the Warburg and Courtauld Institutes* (1994), p. 209; K. Halpern, 'Wrest Park and Dutch Influence', *Garden History*, XXX/2 (2002), p. 173.

6 Daniel Defoe, *A Tour thro' the Whole Island of Great Britain* (London, 1724–7); Stephen Switzer, *Ichnographia rustica* (London, 1721); Horace Walpole, *History of Modern Gardening*, in *Anecdotes of Painting*, vol. IV (London, 1770).

7 Malcolm Balen, *A Very English Deceit: The Secret History of the South Sea Bubble* (London, 2003); Queen Anne's Summerhouse, Landmark Trust *History Album*, available at http://landmarktrust.org.uk.

8 Carole Fry, 'Neo-Palladianism Spanning the Political Divide', *Garden History*, XXXI/2 (2003), p. 181.

9 Stowe Landscape Gardens, National Trust Guide, 1997/2005 – a comprehensive account of every folly plus bibliography (Congreve quotation, p. 38); Celia Fisher, 'The Creation of Stowe as a Landscape Garden', *Hortus*, LXXX (Winter 2006), p. 59.

10 Stowe National Trust Guide, ibid., p. 5, with a suggestion that the concept for the Elysian Fields with its three temples came from Addison in *The Tatler* of January 1710, describing a dream with very similar iconography. For the Gothic Temple at Stowe see Landmark Trust *History Album*, available at http://landmarktrust.org.uk.

11 John Wilkes, sometime friend of Francis Dashwood and member of the Hellfire Club, MP and journalist, was a consistent troublemaker but also seen as a champion of freedom.

12 For Lyttelton's own property at Hagley and its follies see Chapters Five and Eight.

13 Gwyn Headley and Wim Meulenkamp, *Follies, Grottoes and Garden Buildings* (London, 1999), p. 239, for the quotations and a comprehensive description of Cirencester Park.

14 Chris Brooks, *The Gothic Revival* (London, 1999), p. 51.

15 Marcus Binney, 'Wentworth Woodhouse, Yorks', *Country Life* (January 1991), p. 59; Headley and Meulenkamp, *Follies*, pp. 564–8; Caroline Holmes, *Follies of Europe* (London, 2008), pp. 80–83.

16 Binney, 'Wentworth Woodhouse', p. 61 – the prototype at St Rémy appeared in a painting at Rokeby House in Yorkshire which Carr would have known; it also appeared in Francis Harding's *Sacrifice of Iphigeneia* at Stourhead.

17 Culloden Tower, Landmark Trust *History Album*, available at http://landmarktrust.org.uk.

18 Gibside Banqueting House, Landmark Trust *History Album*, available at http://landmarktrust.org.uk.

19 Reynolds, *Sir William James*, National Maritime Museum, Greenwich.

20 The quotation, originally from Seeley's 1762 *Guidebook to Stowe*, is repeated in Stowe Landscape Gardens, National Trust Guide, p. 49.

21 See Chapter Two for Kemeys-Tynte's portrait and Thomas Wright's folly.

22 Robin Hood's Hut with the history of Halswell and Kemeys-Tynte's political career is detailed in the Landmark Trust *History Album*, available at http://landmarktrust.org.uk.

23 Headley and Meulenkamp, *Follies*, pp. 83–4.

24 The Library, Landmark Trust *History Album*, available at http://landmarktrust.org.uk.

25 Bernard Bailyn, *Voyages to the West* (London, 1987); John Lingston Lowes, *The Road to Xanadu* (London, 1927 and 1978). Denys Rolle's pamphlet *Account of East Florida* is in the British Library.

26 The Pineapple, Landmark Trust *History Album*, available at http://landmarktrust.org.uk.

27 Originally Blaikie was a botanical plant hunter travelling in Europe; then he became a sought-after gardener in Paris, tending exotics and *jardins anglo-chinois*. John Harris, 'I'Idole du Temple', *Garden History*, XXIX/I (2001), p. 36.

28 Carmontelle, *Parc Monceau*, 1779, Musée Carnavalet, Paris. Carmontelle also published a folio of views of the park. John Harris, *L'Idole*; John Dixon Hunt, *The Picturesque Garden in Europe* (London, 2002).

29 Dixon Hunt, ibid., p. 109; Tom Turner, *European Gardens* (London and New York, 2011), p. 262.

30 Gabrielle d'Estrées, the legendary mistress of Henri IV, the most romantic of French kings.

31 Dixon Hunt, *The Picturesque Garden in Europe*, p. 159; Michael Symes, *The English Landscape Garden in Europe* (London, 2016).

Five **Hunting and Husbandry**

1 Susan Lasdun, *The English Park* (London, 1991), pp. 21–50. For an example of tapestries showing hunting scenes and elaborate medieval dress see Linda Woolley, *The Devonshire Hunting Tapestries* (London, 2002). The tapestries are in the V&A Museum, London.

2 Stella Margetson, *Leisure and Pleasure in the Eighteenth Century* (London, 1970), pp. 156–9.

3 Balthasar Nebot, *View of Dogmersfield Park Hampshire*, mid-eighteenth century. Private collection.

4 Gwyn Headley and Wim Meulenkamp, *Follies, Grottoes and Garden Buildings* (London, 1999), p. 261, and p. 255 for the related Farley Mount Pyramid.

5 Katie Fretwell, 'A Rare Surviving Deer Course', *Garden History*, XXIII/2 (1995), p. 133; Lucinda Lambton, 'The Grandest Grandstand', *The Oldie* (March 2020), p. 94.

6 William Gilpin, *Observations Relative to Picturesque Beauty Made in Scotland* (London, 1776).

7 Lucinda Lambton, *Beastly Buildings* (London, 1985), p. 22.

8 Shakespeare, *Much Ado about Nothing*, Benedick's description of Claudio, Act II, Scene i; The Warren House, Landmark Trust *History Album*, available at http://landmarktrust.org.uk; Tom Williamson, *The Archaeology of Rabbit Warrens* (London, 2006).

9 Lasdun, *Park*, pp. 52–70.

10 Alexander Pope, 'Satires, Epistles and Odes of Horace Imitated', line 137, from *Complete Poetical Works* (London, 1733).

11 Lord Shaftesbury, *Characteristics of Men, Manners, Opinions, Times*, vol. II (London, 1709), p. 255, quoted by Lasdun, *Park*, p. 77.

12 Addison in *The Spectator* (June 1712 and August 1714).

13 Pope, *Epistle to Burlington*, 1732, lines 185–6.

14 John Dixon Hunt, *William Kent* (London, 1987), quoting Macclary, p. 83.

15 For the reference to Dr Pococke describing the poultry house in the form of a temple see Gervase Jackson-Stops, G. Mott and S. S. Aall, *Follies and Pleasure Pavilions* (London, 1989), p. 22; the other contemporary quotations appear in Douglas Chambers, *Planters of the English Landscape Garden* (London and New Haven, CT, 1993), pp. 156–63, which also includes the lines 'Wooburn for me superior charms can boast/ Where Nature's still improved but never lost,' probably written by Lady Irwin, the versifying daughter of the Earl of Carlisle.

16 Shenstone's publisher was his friend Robert Dodsley, who compiled three volumes of his work published between 1764 and 1769: vol. I included the poems, vol. II Dodsley's own description of The Leasowes and vol. III the letters. See also Chambers, *Planters*, pp. 177–84; and Christopher Gallagher, 'The Leasowes', *Garden History*, XXIV/2 (1996), p. 201.

17 See Chapter Nine for Shenstone posing as his own hermit.

18 John Dixon Hunt, *The Genius of the Place* (London, 1975 and 1988), p. 246.

19 Quoted by Gallagher, *The Leasowes*, p. 203.

20 Quoted by John Phibbs, 'The Persistence of Older Traditions in Eighteenth-Century Gardening', *Garden History*, XXXVII/2 (2009), p. 178.

21 In *History of Modern Gardening*, from *Anecdotes of Painting*, vol. IV (London, 1770), p. 279, Horace Walpole

wrote: 'The flocks and herds that now are admitted into our cultivated plains are ready before the painter's eyes, and group themselves to animate his picture.' On occasion Walpole's own cows came to the terrace to be milked for syllabubs.

22 There are two companion pieces by Edward Haytley: *The Brockman Family at Beachborough Manor*, 1744–6, National Gallery of Victoria, Melbourne, and illustrated in Roy Strong, *The Artist and the Garden* (London and New Haven, CT, 2000), pp. 78–9.

23 Moulin Joli: John Dixon Hunt, *The Picturesque Garden in Europe* (London, 2002).

24 Le Hameau: ibid., p. 129.

25 Ray Desmond, *History of the Royal Botanic Gardens Kew* (London, 1995), pp. 54–5.

26 Pompeo Batoni, *Thomas Coke, Later 1st Earl of Leicester*, 1774, Holkham Hall Collection; for the follies see Gwyn Headley and Wim Meulenkamp, *Follies and Grottoes* (London, 1999), p. 369.

27 Cobham Dairy, Landmark Trust *History Album*, available at http://landmarktrust.org.uk.

28 Gunnersbury Dairy, Gunnersbury Park Museum leaflet (n.d.).

29 Soane's pattern for a dairy, Lambton, *Beastly Buildings*, p. 106.

30 Belvoir dairy, ibid., p. 118.

31 Woburn dairy, ibid., p. 111; and Lucinda Lambton, 'Chinese Whispers in Bedfordshire', *The Oldie* (February 2020), p. 90; Patrick Conner, *Oriental Architecture in the West* (London, 1979), p. 30.

32 For the grotto in the dairy at Rambouillet by Hubert Robert see Tim Richardson, ed., *The Garden Book* (London and New York, 2000), p. 383.

33 Méréville: Michel Saudan and Sylvia Saudan-Skira, *From Folly to Follies* (Geneva, 1987; Cologne, 1997), p. 195.

34 Conical barns: Barbara Jones, *Follies and Grottoes* (London, 1953/89), pp. 220 and 432.

35 Badminton: Lambton, *Beastly Buildings*, p. 120.

36 Lucinda Lambton, 'The Coo Palace, Borgue, Dumfries', *The Oldie* (Summer 2015), p. 62.

37 The Pigsty, Robin Hood's Bay, Landmark Trust *History Album*, available at http://landmarktrust.org.uk.

38 John Warren Barry, *Studies in Corsica* (London, 1893).

39 Knole Bird House: Lambton, *Beastly Buildings*, pp. 154–5.

40 Jones, *Follies*, p. 140.

41 Jackson-Stops, Mott and Aall, *Follies and Pleasure Pavilions*, p. 75, which gives the quotations from Horace Walpole. It was Jackson-Stops who rescued Horton Menagerie from dereliction and made it his home.

42 The Sheep's Barn, aka Colin's Barn, is hard to find, but clues are given online. See also Caroline Holmes, *Follies of Europe* (London, 2008), pp. 222–5.

Six **Waterside Follies and Grottos**

1 Philip Sidney, *Arcadia*, in *Complete Works* (London, 1939), p. 17.

2 Walton was a Royalist and during the Civil War he came and went between Staffordshire and London, at one point being entrusted with a royal jewel after the Battle of Worcester which he delivered to London to be taken to Charles II in exile. Also during the Civil War he bought a farm near Shallowford with the river Meece at its boundary for fishing.

3 Eileen Harris, 'The Fishing Room at Kedleston, Derbyshire', *Apollo* (1 April 2006), p. 27.

4 Jacob Knyf, *Corney House from the River Thames*, c. 1670, Museum of London.

5 Gervase Jackson-Stops, G. Mott and S. S. Aall, *Follies and Pleasure Pavilions* (London, 1989), p. 107.

6 Monkey Island is now part of a luxury hotel at Bray; Gwyn Headley and Wim Meulenkamp, *Follies, Grottoes and Garden Buildings* (London, 1999), p. 122.

7 Patrick Conner in David Beevers, ed., *Chinese Whispers* (London, 2008), pp. 57–69. The quotation from Mrs Philip Lybbe Powys (dated August 1766) is in her *Diaries* (edn London, 1899), p. 114.

8 In Beevers, ed., *Chinese Whispers*, the Mandarin Yacht is illustrated on p. 58, William Daniell's painting of the Fishing Temple is on p. 69 and further images are catalogued on pp. 133–4.

9 Ibid., p. 69.

10 John Constable, *Alresford Fishing Pavilion*, 1816, National Gallery of Art, Victoria, Melbourne. Quotation from his *Correspondence*, vol. II, Suffolk Records Society (Ipswich, 1964), p. 196. See also Jackson-Stops, Mott and Aall, *Follies*, p. 27; Patrick Conner, *Oriental Architecture in the West* (London, 1979).

11 Tendring Hall: Jackson-Stops, Mott and Aall, *Follies*, p. 109; Lucinda Lambton, *Beastly Buildings* (London, 1985), p. 54.

12 Netherby Fish House: Lambton, *Beastly Buildings*, p. 58; 'Young Lochinvar' is part of Sir Walter Scott's epic poem *Marmion*.

13 Harris, 'Fishing Room', p. 27.

14 In 1754 Arthur Devis produced at least one portrait of the Curzon family, so he was known to them as his patrons.

15 See Walton Bath House, Landmark Trust *History Album*, available at http://landmarktrust.org.uk, for all quotes – John Flyer, *An Enquiry into the Right Use and*

Abuses of the Hot, Cold and Temperate Baths (London, 1698), recommended quick immersion; Dr Oliver, *Practical Dissertation on the Bath Waters* (London, 1707), recommended the social aspect; the *History Album* also gives quotations from Lord Dacre and Mrs Delany.

16 Capability Brown's bath houses at Corsham and Burghley are described in Jackson-Stops, Mott and Aall, *Follies*, pp. 49 and 42; Headley and Meulenkamp, *Follies*, pp. 528 and 339.

17 Gunnersbury Park Museum, 'Princess Amelia's Bathhouse', information leaflet produced for London Open House (September 2002).

18 Kate Felus, 'Boats and Boating in the Designed Landscape, 1720–1820', *Garden History*, xxiv/1 (2006), p. 22, covering Enville, Wrest Park, West Wycombe, Newstead Abbey and Lord Bute.

19 Exton: Headley and Meulenkamp, *Follies*, pp. 327–8; Jackson-Stops et al., *Follies*, p. 57.

20 Michel Saudan and Sylvia Saudan-Skira, *From Folly to Follies* (Geneva, 1987; Cologne, 1997), pp. 48–51.

21 Felus, 'Boats and Boating', p. 28.

22 Homer, *Odyssey*, Book 13 (Odysseus lands in Ithaca), trans. E. V. Rieu (London, 1946), p. 204.

23 Egeria's Grotto is off the Appian Way in Rome.

24 In France the loveliest early example of an indoor grotto was at La Bastie d'Urfé, near Lyon; in 1553 Claude d'Urfé returned from Italy and created his *salle de fraicheur* with pebble mosaics, herms, statues and water jets – see Saudan and Saudan-Skira, *From Folly to Follies*, p. 52. In England the first grottos were also indoors; Lord Burghley had one at Theobalds in the 1580s – a great chamber with rocks, minerals and statues. There were others at Woburn, Chatsworth, Beddington and Skipton Castle.

25 Bernard Palissey described the similar grotto he created earlier at Écouen in *Architecture et ordonnance de la grotte rustique*, quoted in Ernest de Ganay, *Les Jardins de France et leur décor* (Paris, 1949).

26 John Evelyn, *Diary* for May 1645, quoted in Mercedes Aguirre and Richard Buxton, *Cyclops: The Myth and Its Cultural History* (London, 2020), p. 280.

27 Saudan and Saudan-Skira, *From Folly to Follies*, pp. 50–59; in recent times Wideville belonged to the couturier Valentino.

28 Leonard Knyff, *Topographical View of Wilton*, c. 1700, Wilton House Collection, shows the facades of both grottos and their waterworks, reproduced in Roy Strong, *The Artist and the Garden* (London and New Haven, ct, 2000), p. 191. John Aubrey, *Natural History of Wiltshire* (written 1656–91, reissued London, 2006), Part 2,

Chapter 2, refers to the Loggia at the end of the 'great walk' as a portico of stone, with alcoves for figures of white marble 1.5 m (5 ft) high, and either side steps with sea monsters 'casting water to one another'. The tank holding water for the fountains was on top of the loggia.

29 The water mills were vital to the Evelyn family fortune, which was founded on manufacturing gunpowder. Now Wotton is a hotel near Dorking and the grotto is preserved in the grounds. Evelyn's own sketches of the garden, with one showing the grotto, are in the British Library. Roy Strong, *Artist*, p. 127, shows the view from the terrace above the grotto.

30 Dr Johnson, *Works* (edn London, 1825), vol. iv, p. 199.

31 For Kent's three sketches of Pope's grotto see John Dixon Hunt, *William Kent* (London, 1987), catalogue pp. 114, 115, 145.

32 To have this rare experience one must be in the right place at the right time, sometimes under the arch of a river bridge. It can be seen at its most magical in the Moorish Gardens of Alfabia in Majorca. At Virginia Water, it is possible to discern the effect of such reflections in the lost grotto, because at certain times the light plays on the rocks in the spot where it was swept away by a flood.

33 Anthony Beckles Willson, 'Pope's Grotto at Twickenham', *Garden History*, xxvi/1 (1998), p. 31; information leaflet, Pope's Grotto Preservation Trust (2019).

34 Information leaflet, ibid. – Pope's stalactites were said to come from Wookey Hole.

35 Stowe Landscape Gardens, National Trust Guide, 1997/2005, p. 31; this gives Seeley's description of the grotto in 1744, the engraving from the Bickham guidebook of 1750 and the description by an anonymous visitor in 1738.

36 The quotation reads *Intus aquae dulces vivoque sedila saxo nympharum domus* (Inside are sweet waters and seats of rock where nymphs have their dwelling), a quotation from Virgil's *Aeneid*, Book 1. (Milton was referencing this myth in his lines about Sabrina in *Comus* – see Chapter Two for her statue in the grotto at Croome Park.) The Stourhead grotto was made of brick covered in stone and tufa, under Flitcroft's direction, by a local mason, William Privett of Chilmark, c. 1751.

37 Timothy Mowl, 'Fonthill and the Lanes', *Garden History*, xxx/1 (2002), p. 102. There was also a boat house at Fonthill, which has now been restored, described by Pevsner in *Wiltshire* (London, 1975), p. 249, 'like a crypt with nave and aisles, only flooded'. It had a three-arched opening onto the north end of the lake, and a circular pool inside, which made it also a bath house.

38 Michael Symes, *Mr Hamilton's Elysium: The Gardens of Painshill* (London, 2010), pp. 96–102. Symes points out that the tufa is strictly speaking English porous limestone, and the kind used at Painshill has been sourced to Gloucestershire and possibly Bristol (p. 97). Concerning the chinoiserie inspiration for the grotto's rock formations, Symes quotes Pyper, who visited in 1779 and wrote 'this species of stone resembles that used by the Chinese for their gardens' (quoted p. 68).

39 Ibid., Symes quoting Pyper, p. 100.

40 Barbara Jones, *Follies and Grottoes* (London, 1953 and 1989), pp. 145–66, describes Ascot, Oatlands, Wardour and Bowood.

41 R. Savage, 'Goldney Grotto', *Garden History*, XVII/1 (1989), p. 31. The Dutch grotto was in Utrecht, in the grounds of the silk mill of David van Moollon. See Savage for all biographical, shell and mineral details, and quotations. Savage also suggests the lion's den at Goldney, a unique feature, may have been inspired by Aladdin's Cave in the newly translated *Thousand and One Nights* (see Chapter Two, note 10). Savage is the source of subsequent descriptions and quotations relating to Goldney Grotto.

42 Mrs Delany's grottos: see Savage, ibid.; Jones, *Follies*, p. 148. For Walton Bath House, see its Landmark Trust *History Album*.

43 Irish grottos: see Jones, *Follies*, pp. 166–7.

44 Goodwood Grotto: ibid., pp. 154–5.

45 Henry Fox, friend and patron of Charles Hamilton, was regarded as a potential prime minister. A man of great influence and friend of George II and the Duke of Cumberland, his rivalries with the Duke of Newcastle and the Elder Pitt prevented this, as did his reputation for corruption. Among his leading accusers was Alderman Beckford as Lord Mayor of London, who in 1769 called him 'the public defaulter of unaccounted millions'. His son was the equally notorious Whig politician Charles James Fox, whose rivalry with the Younger Pitt echoed that of their fathers.

46 For the possible link between Margate Grotto and the Fox estate, see Headley and Meulenkamp, *Follies*, pp. 301–2.

47 For the local memory of the builders of the Margate grotto, see Jones, *Follies*, p. 173.

48 Hampton Court House is now a school; see their information leaflet, *A Brief History of Hampton Court House, Shell Grotto and Gardens* (n.d.).

49 Caroline Holmes, *Follies of Europe* (London, 2008), pp. 238–41.

Seven The Lure of the East

1 Vanderbank tapestries can be seen in the following collections: The Vyne, Hampshire; Belton House, Lincolnshire; Russborough House, Co. Wicklow; V&A Museum, London; Metropolitan Museum, New York. See also David Beevers, ed., *Chinese Whispers* (London, 2008), catalogue, p. 119.

2 Temple was Ambassador to the Hague in 1668; his description was published in 1690 in *Upon the Gardens of Epicurus*, and reprinted in 1757 at the height of the chinoiserie fashion. For all the collected *sharawadgi* references see Ciaran Murray, *Sharawadgi: The Romantic Return to Nature* (London, 1999); also Ciaran Murray, 'Sharawadgi: The Romantic Return to Nature', *Garden History*, XXIX/1 (2001), p. 106. It was Murray who traced the word to Japan, and Temple would have picked it up from the Dutch, who were the only Europeans allowed to trade in Japan. The Addison quotation is from *The Spectator* (June 1712). Walpole in 1750: 'I am almost as fond of the Sharawaggi or Chinese want of symmetry in buildings as in grounds or gardens' – though he later changed his mind, and his *History of Modern Gardening* set out to explode the myth that the English were borrowing from Chinese taste; David Porter, 'From Chinese to Goth', in *Eighteenth-Century Life*, vol. XXIII (London, 1999), p. 50; see also John Dixon Hunt, *The Picturesque Garden in Europe* (London, 2002).

3 William Hannan, *View of the Lake at West Wycombe*, 1752, West Wycombe Collection, illustrated in Roy Strong, *The Artist and the Garden* (London, 2000), p. 256; William Tomkins, *The Elysian Fields at Audley End*, 1788, Audley End Collection, illustrated Strong, ibid., p. 269. Gilbert White's tent appears in S. H. Grimm, *View of Selborne Hanger*, 1776, watercolour and engraving. For Mrs Philip Lybbe Powys's description of the Turkish Tent at Stourhead see Barbara Jones, *Follies and Grottoes* (London, 1953 and 1989), p. 48. In 1769 Sir John Parnell described it in his journal as 'a Turkish tent taken from Mr Hamilton's, very elegant but rather inferior to his'.

4 Thomas Whateley, *Observations on Modern Gardening* (London, 1771), p. 84.

5 Henry Fielding's *Amelia* appeared in 1752; the quotations are given in David Coke and Alan Borg, *Vauxhall Gardens* (London, 2011), p. 64. See also Sarah Downing, *The English Pleasure Garden* (London, 2009). Canaletto, *View of the Grand Walk at Vauxhall*, 1751, Compton Verney Collection.

6 Michel Saudan and Sylvia Saudan-Skira, *From Folly to Follies* (Geneva, 1987; Cologne, 1997), p. 135.

7 For the Désert de Retz see Chapter Three.

8 Haga and Drottningholm: John Dixon Hunt, *The Picturesque Garden in Europe* (London, 2002), p. 144.

9 Canaletto, *The Thames and City of London from Richmond House*, 1746, Goodwood House Collection.

10 Patrick Conner in David Beevers, ed., *Chinese Whispers* (London, 2008), p. 56. William Chambers's Chinese Pavilion in the Menagerie at Kew and the Chinese Pavilion at Ranelagh Pleasure Garden are known only from prints.

11 The ditty appeared in Robert Lloyd, 'The Cit's Country Box', *The Connoisseur* (August 1756). William Halfpenny produced popular chinoiserie pattern books, starting in 1750 with *New Designs for Chinese Temples*.

12 Saudan and Saudan-Skira, *From Folly to Follies*, p. 134; Marco Polo, *Travels*, ed. N. M. Penzer (London, 1929), p. 60, and Mandeville are both quoted in Patrick Conner, *Oriental Architecture in the West* (London, 1979), pp. 153–5.

13 Johann Nieuhof, *An Embassy from the East India Company of the United Provinces to China* (first published in Dutch in 1665 and in English in 1669), gave Europe the image of the Porcelain Pagoda, which was also referred to in English as the China Tower. The nineteenth-century Landmark Trust folly of that name in Devon was originally painted white, and may have got its name because it caught the light like porcelain; it is unlikely to have housed a collection of china for which it was not well designed.

14 For the porcelain pavilion at Versailles see Saudan and Saudan-Skira, *From Folly to Follies*, p. 104, and for the Pagodenburg, ibid., p. 104; see also Conner, *Oriental Architecture*.

15 Stowe Landscape Gardens, National Trust Guide, 1997/2005, p. 45; *Chinese Whispers*, pp. 55–6, and p. 60 for the link to Canton waterfront; Conner, *Oriental Architecture*, for contemporary comments; the Tea House was first moved to join Grenville's Turkish Tent at Wootton Underwood, then taken to Ireland, and now it is restored to Stowe but on dry land. For William Kent's other Chinese designs (not realized) see John Dixon Hunt, *William Kent* (London, 1987), p. 159.

16 For Walpole's attitude to chinoiserie see Conner, *Oriental Architecture*, p. 57; For the Chinese follies at Shugborough, Alresford, Amesbury, Virginia Water and Woburn see previous chapters. Wrest Park Chinese House survives. Thomas Robins, *The Chinese Kiosk, Woodside*, c. 1770, Private Collection, reproduced in Roy Strong, *The Artist and the Garden* (London and New Haven, CT, 2000), p. 267.

17 Jean Attiret, *A Particular Account of the Emperor of China's Garden near Pekin*, trans. Joseph Spence (London, 1752), p.7.

18 Horace Walpole to Lord Strafford, July 1761, *Correspondence*, ed. W. S. Lewis, 48 vols (London, 1937–83).

19 Solander's account of the storm in a letter to Linnaeus, quoted in Ray Desmond, *History of Kew Gardens* (London, 1995), p. 49. During the Second World War bombs fell near the Pagoda without harming it, and it was used to experiment with the design of smoke bombs. For an account of the 2018 restoration and related research, see Lee Prosser, *The Restoration of the Pagoda at Kew* (publication hopefully forthcoming).

20 Saudan, *From Folly*, pp. 133–4.

21 Only the plans of Lunéville, made by the architect Emmanuel Héré, remain. On the death of Stanislas in 1766 the estate reverted to Louis XV, who did not care for the follies, which housed Stanislas's mistresses. For descriptions of Lunéville and Sanssouci see: Conner, *Oriental Architecture*; Dixon Hunt, *Picturesque Garden in Europe*; Caroline Holmes, *Follies of Europe* (London, 2008), pp. 100–105.

22 Tsarskoe Selo: Dixon Hunt, *Picturesque Garden in Europe*, ibid.

23 Biddulph Grange, National Trust Guidebook (1992), pp. 42–7.

24 Ibid., pp. 37–9. The greenery was lost during the twentieth century when it was cut away, but has now been magnificently restored by the National Trust, even down to the authentic planting of golden yew for the plinths at the base of the obelisks, which themselves are ordinary yew.

25 The statue of Thoth was probably made by Waterstone Hawkins, who was also responsible for the dinosaurs at Crystal Palace. However, Edward Cooke must have been involved in its design. In 1872 he published *Grotesque Animals*, illustrated with the bizarre creatures of his imagination.

26 Among the artefacts confiscated by the English was the Rosetta stone. In 1801 Napoleon's expedition returned to France, and in 1802 the French artist and archaeologist Vivant Denon published *Journey into Upper and Lower Egypt*, 2 volumes, with engravings of temples, columns, carvings, symbols and deities. He was appointed Director of the Louvre and in 1809 the French government published its official *Description de l'Égypte*.

27 Robinson was a pupil of the leading architect Henry Holland, who also trained John Soane. Robinson had been involved with the Prince Regent's decors including

Brighton Pavilion. For the Egyptian House in Penzance and John Lanvin's geological museum, see the Landmark Trust *History Album*, available at http://landmarktrust.org.uk.

28 Among these buildings that are perhaps not follies, but endowed with Egyptian facades, is the pumping station on the Isle of Dogs, designed by John Outram, completed in 1988 and called the Temple of Storms.

29 A.C.B. Urwin, *Guidebook to the Kilmorey Mausoleum* (Twickenham, 1997).

30 Burton's tent is at the back of St Mary Magdalen's Church, North Worple Way, Mortlake.

31 For pyramid tombs see Gwyn Headley and Wim Meulenkamp, *Follies, Grottoes and Garden Buildings* (London, 1999): Nether Wallop, p. 260, Knill Monument, pp. 161–2, Blickling, p. 365.

32 Headley and Meulenkamp, *Follies*, pp. 501–5, Jones, *Follies*, p. 232.

33 At Pentwillie in Cornwall there really is the petrified figure of a man, Sir James Tillie, sitting awaiting the Last Judgement, and possibly he originally had his roast and his port. His mausoleum was erected in 1712 but it is a tower not a pyramid.

34 Among Kent's other pyramids, the roofs of the deer houses at Chiswick originally had pyramids, and he proposed pyramids for Holkham and Chatsworth, for which drawings survive: Dixon Hunt, *Kent*, p. 138 and p. 118 respectively.

35 There were paintings by Poussin in the Darnley Collection at Cobham, but the *Sacrament of Ordination*, 1644–8, remained in Rome until 1798, when it was bought by the Duke of Bridgewater. It is now in the National Gallery of Scotland, Edinburgh, and the tomb is prominent in the background of the painting. The failure to use the Cobham Mausoleum for burial may have been due to the difficulty in getting the Bishop of Rochester to consecrate the site. The ghoulish associations at Cobham include the early scenes in Charles Dickens's *Great Expectations* and the nearby spot where Richard Dadd murdered his father – see Headley and Meulenkamp, *Follies*, p. 291, for further details.

36 Claude Louis Châtelet, *Pyramid at Mauperthuis*, c. 1785, sold Christie's New York, May 2000; Hubert Robert, *Pyramid at Mauperthuis*, 1780, Alte Pinakothek, Munich. For Stibbert's Egyptian Temple in Florence see Charles Quest-Ritson, *Gardens of Europe* (London, 2001), pp. 104–5.

37 James Malton, *Essay on Gothic Architecture* (London, 1798), quoted in Conner, *Oriental Architecture*, p. 120. For Melchett Park and Great Stanmore see Conner,

ibid., p. 117. A rather tenuous association with India extends to cone-shaped buildings including: Castletown and Rathfarnham in Ireland, the grain stores and dovecotes; Brightling Sugar Cone; The Cone at Barwick Park in Somerset; the Sorrel Sykes follies near Aysgarth, North Yorkshire; and the three Sugar Loaves at Warrington Park near Launceston in Cornwall.

38 William Hone, 'The Joss and His Folly', 1820, quoted in Headley and Meulenkamp, *Follies*, p. 505.

39 Thomas Daniell's painting, *Temple Fountain and Cave in Sezincote Park*, 1819, Yale Center for British Art; for Sezincote see Conner, *Oriental Architecture*.

40 The fate of St James's Pagoda was described in *The Gentleman's Magazine*, quoted by Conner, *Oriental Architecture*.

41 Both Château de Groussay and Château d'Apremont are described in Caroline Holmes, *Follies of Europe* (London, 2008).

42 Peter Ashley, *Preposterous Erections: A Book of English Towers* (London, 2012).

Eight From Ruins to Gothic and Picturesque

1 For the quotations from Isaiah, Pompeius – and many more – see Rose Macaulay, *The Pleasure of Ruins* (London, 1953), pp. 2–6.

2 Vasari, *Lives of the Painters, Sculptors and Architects*, 1550, quoted ibid., p. 16.

3 For the Ruinenberg see John Dixon Hunt, *The Picturesque Garden in Europe* (London, 2002); it was painted by J. F. Nagel in 1788. For Arkadia see the Phaidon *Garden Book*, ed. John Richardson (London and New York, 2000), p. 375. In France the aristocracy built many mock ruins in their folly gardens. The most exceptional was the Ruined Column at Désert de Retz (see Chapter Three); the most aspirational was the Temple of Philosophy at Girardin's Ermenonville, dedicated to thinkers of the Enlightenment (see Chapter Four).

4 Macaulay, *Ruins*, pp. 134–6; Berenson at Leptis Magna is quoted in Mary Berenson, *A Vicarious Trip to the Barbary Coast* (London, 1938), quoted in Macaulay, *Ruins*, p. 135.

5 Shakespeare, Sonnet 73; Webster, *The Duchess of Malfi*, Act V, Scene iii.

6 Batty Langley was the first to mention placing ruins in garden vistas, in *New Principles of Gardening* (London, 1728). There may have been various ephemeral examples painted on canvas, such as Gilbert White created at the Wakes in Selborne, which were recreated in the restoration of the garden; see Celia Fisher, 'The

Restoration of Gilbert White's Garden at Selborne', *Hortus*, 56 (Winter 2000), p. 83.

7 A ditty summed it up, quoted by Macaulay, *Ruins*, p. 336, from William Woty, 'Church Laryton', 1770: 'Gothic the style, and tending to excite / Free thinkers to a sense of what is right . . .'. For a survey of gothic ruins and follies see Michael Symes, *The Picturesque and the Later Georgian Garden* (London, 2012).

8 Michael Cousins, 'Hagley Park', *Garden History Supplement*, 1 (2007), pp. 1–152; there was a contemporary account by Joseph Heeley, *The Beauties of Hagley and the Leasowes* (London, 1777); Shenstone's remarks were made in his correspondence with Lady Luxborough; for Horace Walpole's 'true rust' description, made in 1753, see *Correspondence of Horace Walpole*, ed. W. S. Lewis, 48 vols (London, 1937–83), vol. XXXV, p. 148. This remark was historically resonant because the Barons' War (1263–7) was a rebellion led by Simon de Montfort against Henry III, amid disagreement about the status of Parliament in government; the Lytteltons could trace their ancestry back that far, and all Whigs were obsessed by parliamentary and constitutional matters.

9 Cousins, 'Hagley Park', for links between Ralph Allen, Lyttelton and Fielding.

10 The eye-catcher at Wroxton Abbey in Oxfordshire, built around 1750, may also be by Sanderson Miller. He lived nearby and did other designs for the Earl of Guilford, although no designs survive for the eye-catcher. It is symmetrical: just a pointed arch between slender towers.

11 Kitty Cruft, *The Buildings of Scotland: Borders* (London and New Haven, CT, 2006), p. 529; The Oscar Wilde quotation is from 'The Canterville Ghost'.

12 For more details of the above follies and the links between gothic and politics see Chapter Four. The gothic flavour of Shotover Pavilion, as it faced the house across the water, is captured in a print by George Bickham, *Shotover House and Garden*, 1750, British Museum.

13 Rendlesham: Gwyn Headley and Wim Meulenkamp, *Follies, Grottoes and Garden Buildings* (London, 1999), p. 380.

14 Edith Sitwell, 'Pedagogues', from *The Canticle of the Rose: Selected Poems, 1920–1947* (London, 1949), p. 26.

15 Clytha Castle, Landmark Trust *History Album*, available at http://landmarktrust.org.uk. This is the source of subsequent quotations relating to Clytha Castle.

16 For Painswick and Thomas Robins see Chapter Three.

17 Michael Snodin, *Horace Walpole's Strawberry Hill* (London, 2010).

18 Walpole described Painshill Pavilion as 'an unmeaning edifice' in his *Journal*, pp. 36–7, originally published by the Strawberry Hill Press; see also S. Lewis Wilmarth, *Rescuing Horace Walpole* (New Haven, CT, and London, 1978). The Beauclerk Tower was linked to Walpole's friend Lady Diana Beauclerk, and the Beauclerk Closet was the final room Walpole created, shown only to a few intimate friends and containing the text of his verse tragedy *The Mysterious Mother*, a tale of incest. It was illustrated by Lady Beauclerk, whose 'seven incomparable drawings' hung around the wall.

19 Among Walpole's other gothic quotes, 'gloomth' came in *Correspondence*, vol. XX, p. 372; the Alps and Salvator Rosa are in *Correspondence*, vol. XXXV, p. 148.

20 De Quincey, *Confessions of an English Opium Eater*, described how he and Coleridge were looking at *The Antiquities of Rome* and spoke together of Piranesi's 'Dreams' that 'represented vast Gothic halls'; Walpole referenced Piranesi in *Anecdotes of Painting*. For the influence of Piranesi see Mario Praz, 'Introductory Essay', *Three Gothic Novels* (London, 1968 and 1986), p. 19, which also cites the quotation from Edmund Burke, p. 16.

21 Praz, ibid., p. 17, cites Walpole's letter of 9 March 1765.

22 James Lees-Milne, *William Beckford* (London, 1976) (surely the perfect biography at 142 pages).

23 Praz, *Gothic Novels*, p. 18, quoting Beckford's *Dreams, Walking Thoughts and Incidents* (London, 1783), p. 18.

24 Beckford Tower, Landmark Trust *History Album*, available at http://landmarktrust.org.uk.

25 Among Beckford's treasures, known as *objets de vertu*, jewelled and gilded pots, bowls and chalices abounded, some with stories attached. A Hungarian topaz vase, ringed with gold and diamonds, was allegedly made for the marriage of Caterina Cornaro to the king of Cyprus, and surely recalled for Beckford his Venetian romance when he seduced a youth of the Cornaro family while the two Cornaro sisters fancied him in vain. Or a gothic reliquary, modelled on the Sainte Chapelle, and not unlike that in Rogier van der Weyden's *The Exhumation of Saint Hubert*, which Beckford also owned – it is among a number of paintings from his collection that are now in the National Gallery, London.

26 Lees-Milne, *Beckford*, p. 124.

27 Michael Symes, *The Picturesque and the Later Georgian Garden* (London, 2012), gives the derivation of 'horrid'.

28 The Hackfall quotations, in order, are from *The Journal of Dorothy Richardson*, 1771; William Gilpin, *Observations Relative Chiefly to Picturesque Beauty*, 1772; William Beckford, *Fragments of an English Tour*,

Bodleian Library, Oxford, MS Beckford d.3.1779; Rev. Richard Warner, *Tour through the Northern Counties of England*, vol. 1 (London, 1802).

29 J.M.W Turner, *Hackfall*, 1816, Wallace Collection, London; his sketches of Hackfall are in the Tate Gallery Collection.

30 The Ruin, Hackfall, Landmark Trust *History Album*, available at http://landmarktrust.org.uk.

31 Robert Adam's *capriccio* related to The Ruin, entitled *Proposed Ruin To Be Built at Kedelston*, is in the Soane Museum Collection, reproduced in Susan Lasdun, *The English Park* (London, 1991), p. 113.

32 Wyatt's folly at Badger Dingle, now called The Bird House: see Landmark Trust *History Album*, available at http://landmarktrust.org.uk.

33 Sir Rowland Hill began making the area accessible in 1750–80. His sons Richard and John continued, and the work was completed by his grandson Sir Rowland Hill, best known for inventing the postage stamp. Dr Johnson's remark was quoted in [James] Boswell, *Life of Dr Johnson*, ed. Hill and Powell (London, 1950), vol. v, p. 434.

34 Francesca Orestano, 'William Gilpin and the Picturesque', *Garden History*, xxxi/2 (2003), p. 164, gives extensive quotations from Gilpin's writing, including *A Dialogue upon Stowe*. In Jane Austen's *Pride and Prejudice* Elizabeth Bennett goes on a fashionable scenic tour of the Peak District with her aunt and uncle, which is when she ends up at Pemberley, Mr Darcy's home. Earlier in the book Gilpin is referenced when Mr Darcy is walking with Mr Bingley's two sisters, leaving Elizabeth to walk behind them. She jokes that three is picturesque but four would spoil the scene, a witty allusion to Gilpin's opinions about cows in a landscape.

35 Fenelon's philosophizing format of teacher and pupil inspired the subsequent works of Voltaire's *Candide* (1759) and Rousseau's *Émile* (1762).

36 Sanspareil was described in *A Travelogue*, dated 1812; see Michel Saudan and Sylvia Saudan-Skira, *From Folly to Follies* (Geneva, 1987; Cologne, 1997), p. 101; Dixon Hunt, *Picturesque Garden*.

Nine **Hermitages and Tree Houses**

1 The Warkworth Hermit ballad is available online; for the architectural details of his cave see Michael Symes, *The Picturesque and the Later Georgian Garden* (London, 2012).

2 Symes, ibid.; Gordon Campbell, *The Hermit in the Garden* (London, 2013), who quotes John Evelyn.

3 William Stukeley's hermitage is described in Campbell, *Hermit*, p. 25, Stukeley's biography is well summarized by Wikipedia, and for Thomas Bushell see John Aubrey's *Brief Lives*, ed. O. Lawson Dick (London, 1949), p. 202.

4 James Caulfield, *Portraits, Memoirs and Characters of Remarkable Persons* (London, 1794–5), p. 9. The best engraving of the Dinton hermit was by William Richardson, 1787. Until recently Dinton Castle was ruinous but romantic, and beautiful enough to merit a painting by John Piper, until a modern architect was allowed to turn it into a modernized dwelling, which he rapidly offered for resale.

5 For the caves in Worcestershire see Michael Symes, *The Picturesque*; for Hagley, and the ditty in the hermitage, see Campbell, *Hermit*; for Dr Johnson's Hermit of Egypt see Johnson, *The History of Rasselas, Prince of Abissinia*, 1759, Chapter xxi; for Stancombe Park see Gwyn Headley and Wim Meulenkamp, *Follies, Grottoes and Garden Buildings* (London, 1999), p. 247.

6 Quotations: 'a green thought' is from Andrew Marvell, 'The Garden'; 'Consult the Genius of the place', from Alexander Pope, *Epistle to Burlington*. William Kent's drawings of Pope in his grotto are reproduced in John Dixon Hunt, *William Kent* (London, 1987), pp. 114–15, and Kent's illustration of Spenser's *Faerie Queene* with the hermitage in the background, p. 150. For the significance of Spenser to supporters of the Hanoverian dynasty see Hazel Wilkinson, *Edmund Spenser and the Eighteenth-Century Book* (London, 2017).

7 Ray Desmond, *History of Kew Gardens* (London, 1995), pp. 13–18; the quotation 'very artful disorder' is from *The Craftsman*, 480 (September 1735). The quotation 'here is built a clumsy heap' is from *The Gentleman's Magazine* (1733), quoted by Campbell, *Hermit*.

8 Desmond, *History*; Barbara Jones, *Follies and Grottoes* (London, 1953 and 1989), p. 178, gives the quotation 'transformed to lawn what once was fairyland' from William Mason, *An Heroic Epistle to William Chambers*, 1773. The Kew Hermitage was situated a little to the north of the present vista between the Palm House and Syon House, nearer the Palm House, and Merlin's Cave was also in that area but nearer the river. At the time this was in the Richmond Garden, which ran along the riverbank, while the Kew Garden was a much smaller area, at the Kew end.

9 For references to Columella and quotations from Shenstone's letters see Charles J. Hill, 'Shenstone and Richard Graves' Columella', *PMLA*, xlix (1934), p. 566; and Nigel Temple, 'A Hermit for Cadland', *Follies Journal*, 3 (2003).

10 Walpole, *Correspondence of Horace Walpole*, ed. W. S. Lewis, 48 vols (London, 1937–83), vol. xxxv, p. 148.

11 Boulton's hermitage was originally far from the house in his once extensive grounds, a view known only from old prints; the replica is now placed on the lawn behind the house. Sarah Couch, 'Review of *A Lost Landscape: Matthew Boulton's Gardens at Soho* by Phillada Ballard, Val Loggie and Shena Mason', xxxviii/1 (2010), p. 150.

12 On Gilbert White, his circle of friends and his follies, see Celia Fisher, 'The Restoration of Gilbert White's Garden at Selborne', *Hortus*, 56 (Winter 2000), p. 83.

13 S. H. Grimm's watercolours were engraved, and used to illustrate White's *Natural History and Antiquities of Selborne* (London, 1789), often reproduced.

14 Lord Orrery at Caledon: Campbell, *Hermit*.

15 William Wrighte, *Grotesque Architecture, or Rural Amusement*, first edn 1767 and various subsequent editions with charming plates; it is now available in paperback.

16 Thomas Wright at Badminton: Campbell, *Hermit*. There is a drawing by Thomas Robins in the V&A Collection. The sorceress Urganda was as well-known as a pantomime figure; for instance, she was described as the wife of Don Belianis of Greece in Laurence Sterne, *Tristram Shandy*, Book 2, Chapter 19.

17 Tollymore hermitage: Campbell, *Hermit*, p. 166; Jones, *Follies*, pp. 91–3. Lord Monthermer was John Montagu, whose portrait by Pompeo Batoni hangs in the ancestral home at Boughton in Northamptonshire.

18 Temple of Vaccinia, Headley and Meulenkamp, *Follies*, p. 235.

19 John Parnell's 1763 description of Painshill tree house is quoted by Campbell, *Hermit*; Thomas Whately, *Observations on Modern Gardening*, 1770, quoted in Michael Symes, *Mr Hamilton's Elysium: The Gardens of Painshill* (London, 2010), p. 94; Gilpin's 1772 sketch is reproduced in Symes, p. 143, and also a sketch attributed to S. H. Grimm after von Sckell (who visited in the 1770s) is reproduced, p. 94.

20 Lucinda Lambton, 'Pitchford Treehouse', *The Oldie* (May 2019), which quotes James Lees-Milne's *Prophesying Peace: Diaries, 1944–1945* (London, 2003) and reproduces the sketch from W. Cowan dated 1854; G. Jackson-Stops, G. Mott and S. S. Aall, *Follies and Pleasure Pavilions* (London, 1989), p. 92.

21 John Parkinson, *Paradisi in sole* (London, 1629), p. 610; for early Florentine examples see Hans Bol, *Spring*, and Utens, *Medici Villa, Pratolino*, both reproduced in Roy Strong, *The Artist and the Garden* (London and New Haven, ct, 2000), p. 43. Robert Peake, *Portrait of Princess Elizabeth*, National Maritime Museum, Greenwich, is reproduced in Strong, *Artist*, p. 42. The tree house at Cobham Hall in Kent was made for William Brook, Lord Cobham, who entertained Queen Elizabeth there in 1559. It was described as 'a banqueting house with a goodly gallery thereto composed each side of a fair row of hawthorn trees, which nature seemed to have planted of purpose in summer to welcome her Majesty' (Sir John Thynne in *Holinshed's Chronicle*).

22 Shakespeare, *As You Like It*, Act ii, Scene v.

23 Joseph Spence, *Observations, Anecdotes and Characters of Books and Men*, ed. J. M. Osborn (London, 1966), vol. i, p. 417, quoted by Symes, *Elysium*, p. 94 (Symes does not think there was a hermit at Painshill). For the accounts of hired hermits see Temple, 'Hermit for Cadland'. These colourful accounts appeared in Edith Sitwell, *English Eccentrics* (London, 1933), p. 34, who quoted John Timbs, ditto 1875, who was quoting 'Notes and Queries' in *Hermits Ornamental and Experimental* (London, 1852) – after which the trail goes cold. The quotation from Horace Walpole, mocking the idea of setting aside one's garden to be melancholy, comes from John Dixon Hunt, ed., *History of Modern Taste in Gardening* (London, 1995), p. 5.

24 Hubert Robert, *Hermit in a Garden*, 1790, Speed Art Museum, Louisville. Robert did several paintings of hermits, always watched by or watching women, seemingly designed to titillate – for instance, *A Hermit in a Hermitage Belltower* watching women wading in a river, 1796, Barber Institute, Birmingham, and several paintings of a hermit praying amid the ruins of Rome, with onlookers.

25 Vauxhall and its hermit are described in Campbell, *Hermit*, including the ditty and a contemporary cartoon.

26 Campbell, ibid., p. 182, describes the visitors to Ossian's Hall; the description of the red windows was by Mary Ann Hanway.

27 Gabriel d'Annunzio, *Pleasure*, 1889, trans. L. G. Raffaelli (London, 2013), p. 141.

28 Dante, *Paradise*, xvii, line 58.

29 Philip Jodidio, *Tree Houses: Fairy Tale Castles in the Air* (Cologne, 2017): New York Lake Nest Tree House, p. 314; Harads Hotel, Bird's Nest, p. 94.

30 Ibid., Mirror Cube, p. 358.

31 Ibid., Solace Tree House, p. 444, Big Beach in the Sky tree house, p. 86, Canopy Tree House, p. 124.

32 Ibid., Fujimori's Teahouse Tetsu, p. 472, Chino teahouse, p. 464, Irisenti tea nest, p. 272; Fujimori's Beetles House can be found on the V&A website.

Ten **Into the Future**

In this chapter, more than any of the previous ones, information and images found online proved not only valuable but sometimes essential for research.

1 Caroline Holmes, *Follies of Europe* (London, 2008), pp. 174–7.
2 Ibid., pp. 206–13.
3 Buzzi died in 1981 and La Scarzuola has been rescued by his nephew Marco Solari, who opens the site to the public.
4 Jill Johnston, *Niki de Saint Phalle and the Tarot Garden* (Bern, 2010).
5 Grayson Perry's House for Essex is now managed by Living Architecture as a holiday let.
6 Silvia Langen, *Outdoor Art* (Munich, London and New York, 2015), pp. 50–57.
7 Magritte's portrait of Edward James, called *Not to Be Reproduced* (1937), is in the Boijmans Museum, Rotterdam.
8 Cement has a limited lifetime, especially in wet tropical conditions amid encroaching forest, but Las Posas is now managed by the Fondo Xilitla and Cemex, the cement works of Mexico. In 2010 it was included in Watch and the World Monuments Fund.
9 Langen, *Outdoor Art*, p. 54, Edward James poem quoted.
10 Ibid., pp. 116–20.
11 Sophie Fiennes's film about Anselm Kiefer at Barjac, made in 2010, is called *Over Your Cities Grass Will Grow*, which references Psalm 103, 'The days of man are but as grass.'
12 The number of planets known to the classical and medieval world was seven, the number that inspired the stages of mystic journeys such as Mohammed's and Dante's. The Old Testament story of the fall of Jericho is in Joshua, Chapter 6. Anselm Kiefer upholds the folly tradition of creating layers of meaning and cultural allusion.
13 For Hannsjörg Voth see Langen, *Outdoor Art*, p. 29.
14 These follies are also referential – for instance, the winged sculpture and the flight of Icarus; the Fibonacci sequence: a mathematical pattern seen frequently in nature, where each number is the sum of the two preceding numbers, for example 1, 1, 2, 3, 5, 8 . . . Orion's belt is significant worldwide, and in ancient Germany it was carved on a piece of mammoth ivory, discovered in 1979, thought to be over 30,000 years old. The Old Testament has the enigmatic reference 'Can you loosen Orion's belt' in Job, Chapter 38.

15 For the Fundaziun Not Vital at Sent see Langen, *Outdoor Art*, pp. 43–9; his follies outside Europe are online.
16 Stainless steel has also been used for another of Not Vital's 'Houses to Watch the Sunset', exhibited in Denmark and intended for Mongolia. It would not seem to be a very environmental or organic substance, but its reflectivity makes it tempting for modern tree houses and for other artists, including Dan Graham and Olafur Eliasson.
17 From 1919 until 1920 the *Glass Chain* letters and drawings centred around designing glass pavilions in fluid and organic forms. The movement was initiated by Bruno Taut, who in 1914 had created a concrete and glass pavilion in Cologne, to exploit the reflective and prismatic qualities of glass. See Iain Boyd Whyte, ed., *Crystal Chain Letters; Architectural Fantasies by Bruno Taut and His Circle* (Cambridge, MA, 1985).
18 Philip Johnson, *Diary of an Eccentric Architect* (New York, 1997). Johnson was a curator at the Museum of Modern Art in New York but he too referenced the past, not only in seeking a spot for the Glass House reminiscent of an eighteenth-century landscape painting, but in placing a version of Poussin's *Funeral of Phocion* inside the Glass House.
19 For Dan Graham's pavilion in the Ekebergparken, see Langen, *Outdoor Art*, p. 84.
20 A toroid is a surface revolution with a hollow centre, at its simplest like a tyre, but not necessarily circular – found in galaxies, seashells, coils of DNA – and expressed mathematically by equations. For examples of Eliasson's pavilions see Langen, *Outdoor Art*, pp. 14, 166 and 184.
21 The SelgasCano Pavilion was set up in La Brea Tar Pits in Los Angeles for an organization called Second Home in partnership with Natural History Museums of Los Angeles.
22 The Benesco Art Site is spread over three Japanese islands – the Seto islands – as a setting for contemporary art of all kinds amid nature. It too has been described as *Gesamtkunstwerk* and its indigenous setting is not easy to reach. See Langen, *Outdoor Art*, pp. 87–93.
23 Oare Pavilion: Caroline Holmes, *Follies of Europe* (London, 2008), pp. 242–3.
24 Charles Jencks, *The Architecture of the Jumping Universe* (London, 1995) and *The Garden of Cosmic Speculation* (London, 2003); Langen, *Outdoor Art*, pp. 64–71.
25 Jencks, *Jumping Universe*, p. 68.
26 Ibid., p. 12.
27 These were the words used in 1992 by those who opposed Derrida being awarded an honorary degree at Cambridge.

Further Reading

Campbell, Gordon, *The Hermit in the Garden* (London, 2013)

Chambers, Douglas, *The Planters of the English Landscape Garden* (London and New Haven, CT, 1993)

Conner, Patrick, *Oriental Architecture in the West* (London, 1979)

Dixon Hunt, John, *William Kent: Landscape Garden Designer* (London, 1987)

—, *The Picturesque Garden in Europe* (London, 2004)

Garden History, Journal of the Garden History Society

Headley, Gwyn, and Wim Meulenkamp, *Follies, Grottoes and Garden Buildings* (London, 1999)

Holmes, Caroline, *Follies of Europe* (London, 2008)

Jackson-Stops, Gervase, George Mott and Sally Sample Aall, *Follies and Pleasure Pavilions* (London, 1989)

Jones, Barbara, *Follies and Grottoes* (London, 1953 and 1989)

Lambton, Lucinda, *Beastly Buildings* (London, 1985)

Landmark Trust, *History Albums*, at http://landmarktrust.org.uk

Lasdun, Susan, *The English Park* (London, 1991)

Macaulay, Rose, *The Pleasure of Ruins* (London, 1953)

Morgan, Luke, *The Monster in the Garden: The Grotesque and the Gigantic in Renaissance Landscape Design* (Philadelphia, PA, 2015)

Richardson, Tim, ed., *The Garden Book* (London and New York, 2000)

Saudan, Michel, and Sylvia Saudan-Skira, *From Folly to Follies* (Geneva, 1987, Cologne, 1997)

Strong, Roy, *The Artist and the Garden* (London and New Haven, CT, 2000)

Symes, Michael, *Mr Hamilton's Elysium: The Gardens of Painshill* (London, 2010)

—, *The Picturesque and the Later Georgian Garden* (London, 2012)

Acknowledgements

Various parts of this book are a homage to the Landmark Trust, which has rescued so many of the finest follies and made them available to stay in. I would like to express my gratitude to my publisher, Michael Leaman, for encouraging me to develop my fascination with follies in book form; to the librarians in the Herbarium Library at the Royal Botanic Gardens, Kew, especially Anne Marshall, for their help and for allowing me to browse among the garden history books; to Jonathan Holt of the Folly Fellowship for his patience and expertise in checking my text; and to my husband Robert Fisher for all those inspirational trips to seek out follies.

Photo Acknowledgements

The author and publishers wish to thank the organizations and individuals listed below for authorizing reproduction of their work.

Alamy: pp. 12 (1webbtravel), 28 (Angelo Hornak), 39 (UK City Images), 167 (David Thompson), 192 (Pictorial Press Ltd), 212 (John Keates), 220–21 (Design Pics Inc), 239 (SWNS), 244 (Ian Bottle), 290 (Bildarchiv Monheim GmbH), 294 (David Kilpatrick), 372 (Jayne Lloyd); Bridgeman Images: p. 181; British Library, London: p. 11; © The Trustees of the British Museum, London: pp. 46, 148, 150, 209, 232; Christie's: p. 87 (© The Piper Estate/DACS 2022); Celia Fisher: pp. 33, 37, 63, 82, 113, 116, 134, 140, 152, 157, 172, 193, 195, 240, 249, 250, 257, 278, 306, 314, 322, 325, 327, 334 (left and right), 336, 341, 368; Robert Fisher: pp. 84, 95, 284, 281, 291, 316, 373, 375; Flickr: pp. 14 (John Fielding), 18 (Ilja Klutman), 66 (Michael Day), 74 (Marilyn Peddle), 124 and 296 (Mark Wordy), 126 (Cattan2011), 137 (Canis Major (Steve)), 138 and 155 (Glen Bowman), 154 (Steve Hodgson), 161 (Mark Longair), 199 (Simon Watt), 236 (tpholland), 243 (Alastair Campbell), 245 (Gordon/plant), 289 (Amanda Slater), 299 (Steve Brown), 346 (Nicolás Boullosa), 369 (Iwan Baan); Gallerie dell'Accademia, Venice: p. 57; Geograph: pp. 112 (© Copyright Des Blenkinsopp/The Temple of Music/CC BY-SA 2.0), 127 (© Copyright Jeff Buck/The Ruin at Shugborough Hall/CC BY-SA 2.0), 179 (© Copyright Des Blenkinsopp/The Warren House, Kimbolton/CC BY-SA 2.0), 215 (© Copyright Des Blenkinsopp/The Bath House/CC BY-SA 2.0), 216 (© Copyright Richard Humphrey/Burghley Bath House/CC BY-SA 2.0), 223 (© Copyright Alan Murray-Rust/Fort Henry, Exton Park/CC BY-SA 2.0); Jonathan Holt: pp. 21, 56, 71, 75, 128, 357; Insall Associates: p 67; iStockphoto: pp. 91 (FotoMonkee), 234 (Tom Meaker); Metropolitan Museum of Art, New York: pp. 228, 248, 259; David Jeffrey Morgan: p. 22; National Gallery of Victoria: pp. 186, 211; National Portrait Gallery, London: pp. 38, 64, 70, 86; © The Piper Estate/DACS 2022: p. 298; public domain: pp. 17 (Sotheby's), 34, 72, 105, 183, 189, 208, 251, 277; Shutterstock: pp. 16 (murbansky), 58 (Thomas Fabian), 102 (Steve Allen), 115 (A C Manley), 158 (Charles Bowman), 253 (Joyce Nelson), 255 (Pack-shot), 263 (LoCrew), 264 (Yulia_B), 267 (Jacqueline Glynn), 292 (johnpcarr), 333 (Brian Bould/ANL), 340 (inavanhateren), 343 (Kedardome), 345 (Gail Johnson), 351 (javarman), 354 (Marti Bug Catcher), 362 (marketa1982), 376 (Tommy Larey); Städel Museum, Frankfurt: p. 32; Tate Britain: p. 77; Victoria and Albert Museum, London: pp. 219, 309; Kent Wang: p. 50; Wellcome Collection: p. 319; Wikimedia Commons: pp. 11 (Kognos/CC BY-SA 4.0 International), 25 (Daderot/CC0 1.0 Universal Public Domain Dedication), 27 (Ckings6056/CC BY-SA 4.0 International), 30 (j.e.mcgowan/CC 2.0), 42 (Jsc83/Public Domain), 44 (Geni/CC BY-SA 3.0 Unported), 48, 54 (August Schwerdfeger/CC0 1.0 Universal Public Domain Dedication), 55 (Nicholas Jackson/CC BY-SA 3.0 Unported), 65 (Tony Hisgett/CC BY 2.0), 80 (Photograph by Mike Peel (www.mikepeel.net)/CC BY-SA 4.0 International), 81 (Karen Roe/CC BY 2.0), 89 (Gavin Lynn/CC 2.0), 97 (Ben Skála/CC BY-SA 3.0 Unported, 2.5 Generic, 2.0 Generic, 1.0 Generic), 100 (Peter Astbury/Public Domain), 106, 109 (NH53/CC 2.0), 120–21 (Hamburg103a/CC BY-SA 4.0 International), 130 (Elring/CC BY-SA 3.0 Unported), 142, 145 and 146 (All: Daderot/CC0

Index

Page numbers in *italics* indicate illustrations

Adam, Robert 79–82, *81*, 90, 118, 156, 177–8, 180, 203, 212, *212*, 297, 309, *309*, 310
Adam, William 80–81, 177–8, *178*, 293, *294*
Addison, Joseph 55, 56, 61, 77, 122, 182, 248
Aislabie, John 71, 141–3, 257
Aislabie, William 295, 308–10
Alberti, Leon Battista 31, 34, 59
Alfred, King 73–4, *74*, 125, 145, 147–8, *148*, 156
Alnwick treehouse 344, *345*
Alresford fishing pavilion 210, *211*
Althorpe Falconry 180–81, *181*
America 146, 153, 162–7, 342, 344, 365
Amesbury Abbey 84, *84*
Apollo (statues and temples) 15, 107, *111*, 112, 122–4, *124*, 225–6, *225*
Archer, Thomas 65–7, *66*, 138
Aske Temple 155
Aubrey, John 230, 318–19
Audley End 81–2, *81*, 156, 248
Austen, Jane 20, 304, 313
aviaries and birdhouses 49, 199–203

Baalbek Temple 60, 117, 123, 159
Babel Tower *6*, 8, 26–7, 60, 132, 352, 360–61
Bath sham ruin 291, *291*
bathhouses 213–18, *212*, *215*, *216*
Beckford, Alderman 235, 304
Beckford, William 27, 237, 304–8, 310
Beckford's Tower 305–7, *306*
Bellmount Tower 12–13, *12*
Belvoir Dairy 191–2, *192*
Biddulph Grange 255–68, *267*, *268*
Bird House, Badger 310–11

Blaise Castle 20
Blind Pavilion 367, *368*
boat houses *212*, 213, 218–22, *219*, *220–21*
boats (as follies) 45, *46*, 208, *209*, 219, 222
Bomarzo 94–8, *95*, *97*, 131, 353
bowling 33, 39–40, 89, 230
Bramham Gothic Temple 88, *89*
Bridgeman, Charles 62, 77, 143, 212
Brightling pyramid 273–5, *274*
Brighton Pavilion 279
Broadway Tower 82
Brown, Lancelot 'Capability' 78–83, 90, 156, 185, 203, 216, *216*, 235, 249, 266, 324
Burley Bath House *216*, 217
Burlington, Lord 67, 68–76, *70*, 109, 144, 182
Burns, Robert 338

Campbell, Colen 15, 69–73, *71*, 108, 119, 142, *142*, 230
Canaletto 57, *57*, 250, *251*, 253
Carr, James 154
Cascade House, Chatsworth 66, *66*
Casino Marino, Ireland 83
Cassiobury 37, *38*
Castle Ashby menagerie 202
Castle Howard 62, 98–103, *100*, *102*, 153
Castle of Otranto 302–3
Castletown, Ireland 17, *18*, 196
Catherine the Great 117, 265, 310, 339
cattle 183–98, *189*
Chambers, William 78, 83, *84*, 117, 123, 158, *158*, 187, 191, 201, 258–60, *259*
Chanteloup Pagoda 261, *261*
Charborough Tower 24
Chateau, The 10–12, *11*
Chatsworth Tower 40

China and chinoiserie 18–19, 83, *84*, 118–19, 125–6, *126*, 132, 192, *193*, 201, 208–10, *208*, *209*, 247, 253–67, *255*, *257*, *259*, *261*, *263*, *264*, *267*, 345, 372–4, *373*

Chipping Campden Banqueting Houses 36, *37*

Chiswick House 67, 69–72, *70*, *72*, 75–6, 109, 182

Civil War 36–7, 40, 90, 136, 175, 181, 231, 318–9

Claremont Belvedere 62–4, *63*, 77

Clavell Tower 20, *21*

Clifton Tower 41

Clytha Castle 298–9, *299*

Cobham, Kent 189, 275

Cobham, Lord 62, 67, 108, 111, 143–7, 159, 185, 249, 256, 275, 289, 321–2, 326, 333

Coleridge, Samuel Taylor 247, 255

Colonna, Francesco 93, 229, 285, 335

Compton Pike 28

cones 15, 16, 29, 111, 196, 204, 274–5, 363

Coo Palace *197*, 198

Corinthian columns 49–51, 53, 65, 99, 123, 129, 168, 188, 226

Corsham Bath House 216

Croome Park 79–83, *79*, *82*, 90, *91*, 235

Cruikshank, George 46, *46*

Culloden 28, 40, 73, 152, 154–5, *154*, 208

dairies 188–95, 189, 192, 193

Daniel, Thomas and William 111 *208*, 278–80, *280*

Dante 97

Dashwood, Sir Francis 109–12, *109*, *112*

de Caus, Isaac and Solomon 49, 230

deer 13, 34, 36, 38, 40, 64, 75, 101, 175–7, 176, 177, 181–3, 188, 195, 203, 218, 288, 340

Defoe, Daniel 124, 139

Delany, Mrs Mary 52, 83, 148, 215, 240–41, 329

Denmark 368

Derrida, Jacques 375, *376*

Désert de Retz 130–32, *130*, 251, *251*, 276, 350

Dilettanti, Society of 54, 112, 128, 159

Dinton Castle *316*, 319–20, *319*

Doric style 14, 51, 53, 83, 118

dovecotes 196

Dromona Gatehouse, Ireland 280, *281*

Duncombe Estate 53

Dunstall Castle 90–99, *91*

Dutch style 78, 136–9, *137*, *138*, 170, *172*, 174, 182, 239, 335

Egyptian House, Penzance 269–70, *269*

Egyptian style 267–78, *268*, *271*, *278*, 321, 349

see also obelisks; pyramids

Eliasson, Olafur 367, *368*

Endsleigh 193–4

Enville 219, 328

Ermenonville 169–71, *170*, 187, 339

Evelyn, John 49, 65, 107, 181, 231, 318

Exton Park 195–6, *195*, 223–4, *223*

fabrique 9, 131, 169, 282

famine relief (and employment) 13, 16–17, 274, 355, 358

Farley Mount pyramid 174–5

Farnborough Oval Pavilion 54, 55

Farringdon Tower 26

ferme ornée 184–7, 203

Fielding, Henry 173, 250, 291

Finsterlein, Hermann 364–5

fishing 52, 84, *84*, 205–13, *206*, *208*, *211*, *212*

Flitcroft, Henry 73–4, *74*, 123, 153, 234–5, *234*

Fonthill 26, 235, 304–5

Fort Putnam 166, *170*

Fortuna Primigenia, Temple (and related follies) 55, 107

Fortuna Virilis, Temple (and related follies) 53–4, *54*, 118

fossils 233, 239–40, *316*, 319–20

France 9, 56, 129, 132, 167, 171, *169*, *170*, 182, 187, 194–5, *194*, 224, 226, 229, 251, *252*, 254, *255*, 261, *261*, 276–7, *277*, 282–3, 286, 339, 376, *376*

Freemasonry 60–61, 65, 69–72, 85–8, 131, 151, 153, 168, 237, 275–6, 324, 349–50, 352

Frederick, Prince of Wales 115, 145, 147, 219, 233, 250, 290

Freston Tower 41, *42*

Frederick the Great of Prussia 159, 262–5, *263*, 286, 314

Fujimori Teronobu 345–7, *346*

gambling 151–2, 274–5

Garrett, Daniel 154–6, *154*, *155*

Garrick's Temple 51–2, *52*

Gaudí, Antoni 352, *353*

Germany 171, 226–7, 256, 262, *263*, 276, 314–15, 340, *340*, 360, 364

Gibbs, James 67, *67*, 69–71, 146–7, *146*, 344

Gibside Banqueting House 155–6, *155*

Gilpin, William 45, 127, 177, 309, 312, *314*, 333

Glass House, The 365–6, *366*

Goji Berry, The 343

Goldney Grotto 238, *239*

Goodwood House 241, *240*

Gothic Pavilion, Painshill 115–16, *115*, 295, 301

Gothic Pavilion, Shotover 149, *150*

Gothic Temple, Stowe *146*, 147–50

Graham, Dan 367

Grand Tour 9, 49, 55, 65, 68, 81, 82, 105, 310

Greek architectural influence 51, 53, 60, 65, 103, 111, *112*, 118, 127, 128, 129, 144, 159, 188, 198, *199*, 306, 311, 351, 376–7

Grimsthorpe Castle 62

grottoes 217, 225–46, *225*, *227*, *232*, *234*, *236*, *239*, *240*, *246*

Gunnersbury Park 191, 217

Hackfall 308–10, *309*

Hadlow Tower 26–7

Hagley Castle 91, 109, 184, 289–91, *290*, 320–21, 326

Hall Barn 71, *71*, 108

Halswell Estate 53, 85–7, *86*, *87*, 160–62, *161*, 276

Hamilton, Charles 114–19, 237, 304, 332, 336

see also Painshill

Hampton House grotto 244

Hardy, Thomas 20–24

Hawksmoor, Nicholas 64–5, *65*, 99–103, *100*, *102*, 108, 275

Hercules (temples and statues) 51, *120*, 123, 141

Hermes/Mercury (statues) 15, *16*, 106, 144, 349

hermitages 310, 312, 317–33, *316*, *322*, *325*, *327*, *330*, *332*, *333*, 335–42, *336*

Highgrove 342

Hogarth, William 52, 65, 86, *86*, 129, 250

Horton menagerie 202

Horton Tower 23–4, *22*

Houghton Water House 13–15, *14*

Hundy Mundy Tower 293, *294*

hunting 39–45, 76, 83, 173–82, 334

see also deer; rabbits

Iceland 367

Indian influence 61, 156, 162, 197, 247, 278–83, *280*, *281*, 356

Indonesia 363

Ionic style 51, *52*, 53, *54*, 72–3, *72*, 81–2, *81*, 89, 110, 144, 198, *199*

Ireland 17–18, *18*, 50–51, *50*, 196, 220–21, 222, 280–81, *281*, 328, 331

Islamic style 201, 203, 248, *259*, 260, 272, 282, 350, 352, *353*

Italy 47, *58*, 59, 228–9, *228*, 278, *278*, 335, 341, *341*, 350–56, *354*

Jack the Treacle Eater 15–17, *16*, *17*

James, Edward 358–60, *359*

Japan 248, 345–7, *346*, 370–72, *372*

Jencks, Charles 374, *375*

Jenner's Hut 332

Johnson, Philip 365–6, *366*

Johnson, Dr Samuel 52, 108, 185, 231, 312, 321, 338

Jones, Inigo 36, 37, 48, 69, 73–4, 175–6, 230

Kedleston 212–13, *212*, 297

Kenilworth 31–2, 91

Kent, William 55–6, *56*, 62, 74–6, *75*, 104–8, *105*, *106*, 143–5, *145*, 147, 149, 183, 188, 219, 222, 231–4, *232*, 256, *257*, 276, 288, 321

Kenwood 189, *189*

Kettlethorpe boathouse 218–19, *219*

Kew 23, 44, 77, 83, 84, 117, 123, 158–9, *158*, 183, 187–8, 201, 254, 258–60, *259*, 323, 328, 344

Kiefer, Anselm 350

Kilmorey Mausoleum 270–72, *271*

King John's Hunting Lodge 173–4, *172*

Kinnoull Tower 295

Kit-Cat Club 61–6, 68, 98, 143, 180, 324

Knight, Richard Payne 313, 320

Knole Bird House 201–2

La Scarzuola 350, *351*

Lane, Joseph and Josiah 235–8, *236*

Langley, Batty 88–9, *89*, 116, 288, 295, 329

Larchill Fort, Ireland *220*, 222
Las Posas, Mexico 358–60, *359*
Laughton Tower 25–6, *25*
Leasowes, The 170, 184–5, 320, 325, *325*
Leicester Monument, Holkham 188
Leonardo da Vinci 59, 93
Leptis Magna, Virginia Water 286–7, *284*
Library, The 163–4, *163*
Lodge Park, Sherborne 175–6, *175*
Lorrain Claude 56–7, 77, 119
Luttrells Tower 43–4, *44*
Lyminge, Robert 35–6, *35*
Lyttleton, Lord 109, 128, 144, 147, 184, 185,
    214, 289–91, 326
Lyveden New Bield 33–5, *33*, 133–5, *134*

Maison Carre, Nîmes 53, 118
Mandarin Yacht 209, *209*
Margate Grotto 242–4, *243*
Mausoleum of Halicarnassus 65, 103
mausoleums 101, *102*, 117, *116*, 153–4,
    270–72, *271*, 275
Melford Hall 32
Mendelsohn, Erich 365
Mercury *see* Hermes
Mereville Dairy 194–5, *194*
Mexico 358–60, *359*, 370
Miller, Sanderson 55, 90–92, *91*, 214–16,
    219, 289–92
Milton, John 76–7, 79, 145, 182, 301–2, 318,
    326
Milton Park 178–9, 295
Monceau, Parc 168–9, *169*, 224, *224*, 251,
    276
Monkey Island 207
Montacute 32
Morocco 361–2, *362*
Mount Edgecombe 288
Mow Cop 292–3, *292*
Music Room, The 46–7
Mussenden Temple, Ireland 50–51, *50*

Nash, John 279, 299
naumachia 168, 219–25, *223*, *224*, 352
Needle's Eye 151–2, *152*
Nelson, Horatio 162, 163, 305
Netherby salmon coop 212
Niger 363
Norway 356–7

Oare Pavilion 373, *373*
obelisks 16, 17, 28, 32, 49, 60, 65, 72–3, *72*,
    99, 180, 203, 268
observatories 21, *21*, 23–4, *22*, 361, *361*
octagonal buildings 29, 32, 41, 47, 48, 67–8,
    67, 88–9, *89*, 143, 191, 193, 194, 196,
    207, 214, 259, 295–6, 310
Orleans House Octagon *67*, 68
Ossian's Hall and Cave 338

pagodas 247, 256, 258–64, *259*, *261*, 281
Paine, James 89–90
Painshill 114–19, *115*, *116*, 124, 236, 237, 249,
    249, 252, 295, *296*, 332, *332*, 335
Painswick 113–14, *113*, 300
Palladian style 14–15, 48, 67–78, 75, *75*, 80,
    81, *100*, 101, 104, 108, 141, *142*, 177–80,
    178, *179*, 202, 211
Palladio 34, 47, *58*, 59, 70, 226
Pan 15, 80, 83, 106, 112–14, *113*, 132, 229,
    315, 349
Pantheon (and imitations) 51, *52*, *58*, 60, 67,
    69, *70*, 73, 82, 114, *120*, 122, 351
patterns and designs 35–6, *35*, 43, 59–60, 71,
    84, 85, 88, 92, 203, 245, 254, 258–60,
    282, 309–10, *309*, 329
Paxton's Tower, Wales 162
Pei, I. M. 372–4, *373*
Pepperbox, Salisbury 26
Perry, Grayson, and FAT Architects 356–7,
    357
Picturesque 307–15, 325, 333
Pigsty, The 198–9, *199*
Pineapple, The 164–6, *165*
Piper, John *87*, *298*
Piranesi, Giovanni *228*, 229, 302–4
Pitchford Treehouse *333*, 334
Platt, John 11
Poland 286
Pope, Alexander 19, 56, 61, 69, 71, 76–7,
    116, 145, 174, 182, 302, 344
Pope's Grotto, Twickenham 231–3, *232*, 321,
    322
Port Meirion Bath House 218
portraits (with follies) 16, *17*, 37, *38*, 62, 70,
    70, 73, *77*, 86, *86*, 325, *325*, 334, 335
Portugal 349
Poultry House, Leighton 200–201, *200*
Poussin, Nicolas 56–7, 103–4, 112, 276
Praeneste, Rousham 55, *56*, 106–7

Price, Uvedale 313
pyramids 28, 32, 60, 61, 65, 67, 99–100, 109,
    131, 143, *145*, 151–2, *152*, 168, 174, 268,
    272–7, *274*, *277*

Queen Anne's Summerhouse 139–40, *140*
Quex Tower 28–9, *28*
Quinta de la Regaleira *348*, 349

rabbits (linked to follies) 36, 135, 139, 155,
    179–80, *179*
Raby Castle 288
Racton Tower 27–8, *27*
Radway Tower 90–91
Rambouillet Dairy 194
Ranelagh Gardens 254
Rendlesham Lodge 296–7
Renishaw 297, *298*
Repton, Humphrey 189–90, 201, 296, 313
Revett, Nicholas 111–12, 128–9
Rievaulx Terrace 54, *54*
Robert, Hubert 170, 187, 194, 277, *336*, 337
Robin Hood's Hut 160–62, *161*
rotundas 49–50, 53, *55*, 61, *71*, 79, 80, 108,
    142, 143, 159
Rousham 55, *56*, 104–7, *105*, *106*, 276
Rousseau, Jean Jacques 170–71, 184, 187,
    339
Royston Cave 324
ruins 19, 49, 53–5, *57*, 81, 87, 90–92, *90*, 117,
    126–7, *127*, 131, *130*, 143, 144, 148, *148*,
    168, *169*, 185, 187, 216, 277, *277*, *284*,
    285–315, 358, 361
Rushton Triangular Lodge 133, *134*, 180
Russia 264, 265, 282

Saint Phalle, Niki de 353–6, *354*
Sandby, Thomas and Paul 44, 73
Sanspareil 314–15
Sanssouci 262–4, *263*, 286, 314
Scotland 80, 164–6, *165*, 177–8, *178*, *197*,
    198, 293–5, *294*, 338, 374
Scotney Castle 288
SelgasCano Pavilion 369, *369*
Seven Years War 81, 125, 129, 153, 156, 158–9,
    158, 162, 164, 170, 263
Severndroog Castle 156–7, *157*
Sezincote 279–80, *280*
Shakespeare, William 8, 51–2, 145, 179, 287,
    335

sheep 182–8, *183*, 204
shellwork 215, 218, 229–33, *231*, 235–7, 239,
    239, 240
Shenstone, William 170, 184–7, 214, 290,
    320, 325, *325*
Shobdon Arches *287*, 288
Shotover Park 149, *150*
Shugborough 125–9, *126*, *127*, *128*, 257
singerie 126, 207, 264
Sissinghurst 25, 32, 40
slave trade (and sugar) 20, 61, 235
smuggling 22, 44–5
Smythson, John 40
Soane, Sir John 61, 191, 203, 211, 269
Solomon's Temple 60, 65
Solomon's Temple, Buxton 26
South Sea Bubble 119, 139, 142, 144
Spenser, Edmund 318, 322, 323
Stainborough Castle 151
Stibbert's Egyptian Temple 278, *278*
Stourhead 74, *74*, 119–25, *120*, *124*, 234–5,
    234, 249, 329
Stowe 19, 61, 67, 78, 108, 111, 118, 128, 143–7,
    145, *146*, 159–60, *183*, 185, 219, 227,
    233–4, 256–7, *257*, 275, 321
Strawberry Hill 185, 300–304, *301*
Stuart, James 111, 127–9, *128*
Studley Royal 71, 141–3, *142*, 257, 295
Stukeley, William 324, 329
Summer House, The Vyne 48, *48*
Swarkestone Pavilion 38, *39*
Sway Tower 26
Sweden 252–3, *253*, 342, *342*
Switzer, Stephen 78, 139
Switzerland 363–4
Syon Fishing Pavilion 206–7, *206*

tapestries 173, 247–8, *248*, 358
tarot cards 95–6, 354–6, *354*
tea houses 81–2, *81*, 256, *257*, 263–4, *263*,
    267
Temple of British Worthies 144, *145*, 276
Temple of the Four Winds *100*, *101*
terraces (with follies) 31–8, 53–5, 93, *101*,
    104, 141, 190, 266, 337, 352, 374
Thames, River 31, 45, *46*, 51–3, *52*, 67,
    68–70, 76, 107, 158, 182, 184, 185, 206,
    206, 231, 232, 253, 258, 321
Thousand and One Nights 67, 240, 250, 283,
    304, 342

Tories 67, 77, 136, 139, 140, 147–8, 174
Tree Hotel, Harads 342, *343*
Tresham, Sir Thomas 33–5, *33*, 133, *134*
triangular follies 20, *22*, 23, 27, 73, *74*, 82,
    124, 147, 153, 156, *157*, 273, 344
Tschumi, Bernard 376, *376*
Turkish (or Tartar) tents 117, 118, 125, 132,
    248–53, *248*, *249*, *250*, *251*, *252*, *253*, 263,
    263, 281–3
Turner, William 210, 244, 273, 308

Uppark 162–3

Vanbrugh, Sir John 53, 61–4, 99–103, *100*,
    102, 108, 143, 180, 275, 287
Vanderbank 247–8, *248*
Vathek 304–5
Vauxhall Gardens 250, *251*, 337
Venus 9, 15, 23, 71, *71*, 101, *105*, 106, 107–10,
    109, 213, 226, 227, 229, 234, 237, 245,
    282, 322, 349
Versailles 187, *225*, 226, 251, 256, 314
Vesta, Temple of (and imitations) 49–50, *50*,
    53–4, 81, 82, *82*, 111, *112*, 144, 168, 170,
    170, 357
Villa d'Este, Tivoli 94, 105, 225
Villa Rotonda, Vicenza *58*, 60, 101
Villette, Parc de la 376–7, *376*
Virgil 49, 55, 93, 96, 103, 104, 114, 122ff,
    185, 214
Virginia Water 73, 153, 208–10, *208*, *209*,
    284, 286–7
Vital, Not 363–4
Voth, Hannsjorg 361, *362*

Wainhouse Tower 26–7
Wales 162, 200–201, *200*, 218, 298–300, *299*,
    313–14
Walpole, Horace 43, 52, 61, 67, 76, 78, 83,
    101, 112, 114, 116, 117, 123, 129, 139, 151,
    168, 185–7, 202, 227, 248, 258, 260,
    290, 300–304, *301*, 324, 326, 337

Walpole, Robert 13–15, *14*, 144–6, 173
Walton Bath House 214–16, *215*
Warkworth hermitage 317
Warren House, The *179*, 180
water pageants *see naumachia*
Waterloo memorials 28–30, *28*, *30*, 238
Wedgwood, Josiah 117, 129, 190–91, 194,
    300, 310
Wentworth Woodhouse 73, 149–53, *152*
West Wycombe 109–12, *109*, *112*, 128, 222,
    248
Westbury Court 136–7, *137*
Westonbury Bottle Grotto 245–6, *246*
Whigs 60–68, 77, 111, 136–72, 188, 289, 295,
    324
White, Gilbert 248, 326–8, *327*
White Nancy 29–30, *30*
Whitton 343
Wilton House 230
Wimpole Hall 13, 91
Woburn 192–3, *193*, 201, 254, 265
Wooburn Farm 184
Woolf, Virginia 24–5, 288
Worlitz 108, 171
Wotton Underwood 249, *250*
Wren, Sir Christopher 60–61, 64
Wrest Park 137–9, *138*, 218, 222, 258
Wright, Thomas 85–7, *86*, *87*, 127, *196*, 197,
    202, *244*, 245, 329–31, *330*
Wrighte, William 92, 245, 329
Wyatt, James 82, *82*, 190, 191, *192*, 207, 276,
    305, 311, 326
Wyatt (Wyattville), Jeffry 193, 209, *284*,
    286–7

Zoffany, Johann 52, *52*